California
Government Today

Politics of Reform?

California Government Today

♦

Politics of Reform?

Charles G. Bell

Department of Political Science
California State University, Fullerton

Charles M. Price

Department of Political Science
California State University, Chico

1988   Third Edition

The Dorsey Press
Chicago, Illinois 60604

Acquisitions editor: Leo Wiegman
Project editor: Mary Lou Murphy
Production manager: Charles J. Hess
Compositor: Compset, Inc.
Typeface: 10/12 Times Roman
Printer: Malloy Lithographing, Inc.

ISBN 0-256-06075-4
Library of Congress Catalog Card No. 87–50772
Printed in the United States of America

1 2 3 4 5 6 7 8 9 0ML 5 4 3 2 1 0 9 8

Preface

In preparing this new edition we faced the inevitable challenge: updating the constantly changing California political landscape. Describing the key actors and background of the ongoing California political drama requires a substantial rewriting chore. The one constant in California politics is change.

Much has happened in California politics since our second edition was published in 1984: (1) the state supreme court has swung dramatically from a proliberal majority to a staunchly conservative majority (five–two) because of the confirmation defeats of Rose Bird, Joseph Grodin, and Cruz Reynoso in 1986 and their replacement by three new Deukmejian nominees Marcus Kaufman, David Eagleson, and John Arguelles (see Chapter 11); (2) federal courts have ruled that political parties may endorse in partisan primaries which may strengthen the hand of parties, but, at the same time, the U.S. Supreme Court has ruled that parties may allow independents to vote in their primaries and this may further weaken political parties (see Chapter 6); (3) the Moriarity scandal, involving a fireworks tycoon convicted of buying influence in state and local government, and the conviction of former assemblyman-lobbyist Bruce Young and possibly others may provide the impetus for new campaign reform laws (see Chapter 5); (4) the continued growth of initiative politics—six statewide initiatives were on the ballot in 1986 (see Chapter 4); (5) state voters overcame a spending blitz by California horsetracks to adopt a new state lottery whose campaign was heavily financed by the out-of-state Scientific Games Corporation (see Chapter 4); (6) a new U.S. Supreme Court ruling declares partisan gerrymandering unconstitutional—how this will affect the California reapportioning of 1991 will be interesting to watch (see Chapter 7); (7) state government has gone from a sizable state debt of $1.5 billion to a substantial surplus in 1984–85 to a constricted, Gann budget with limited spending in 1987–88 (see Chapter 10); (8) local governments have grown increasingly dependent upon state government for financial bailouts because of court rulings, the end of revenue sharing, and the Jarvis-Gann Proposition 13 property tax relief initiative (see Chapter 12) and, (9) three Californians who had an enormous impact on state politics over the last several decades have died: state treasurer Jess Unruh, petition sponsor Howard Jarvis, and Congressman Phil Burton. These, and other new developments, will be discussed in the chapters that follow. What is clear is that reform issues remain at the center of California politics. Dominating this agenda in the 1990s are possible reforms in reapportionment, political parties, selection and election of judges, the determinate sentence, the initiative process, and campaign finance. Chapter 1 presents an overview of the California reform model. It has been thoroughly rewritten from the previous edition. In truth, we have become increasingly pessimistic about whether California government in the latter 1980s can still claim to be a reform model.

Finally, the authors would like to thank our anonymous reviewers; also, Elisabeth Kersten, director of the Senate Office of Research, for her thoughtful suggestions on the budget chapter; Tom Hoeber, publisher of the *California Journal* and Peter Detwiler, consultant to Senate Local Government, for their incisive comments on the local government chapter; and Dorsey Press for its superb editorial assistance. We would also like to thank the many writers and researchers at the Institute of Governmental Studies in Berkeley, the Field Institute in San Francisco, Institute of Governmental Affairs in Davis, and the various capitol reporters writing for publications such as the *Sacramento Bee, Los Angeles Times,* and *California Journal* for their insights into the state political process which have strongly influenced this volume. Finally, we want to thank our teaching colleagues and students who have challenged and stimulated our thoughts.

This book is dedicated to our wives, Claudia and Marge, and families for their continued encouragement and support. Lastly, Claudia Bell merits separate recognition. While Charles G. was recovering from a serious medical crisis, Claudia provided helpful editing and research assistance for this project. As is customary, any mistakes found in the following chapters are the fault of—others. All right, all right, we grudgingly accept full responsibility for any errors of omission or commission.

Charles G. Bell, University of California, Davis
Charles M. Price, California State University, Chico

Contents

1

California—Critical State

California is, without question, one of the most important states in the nation. California's significance is based on a number of factors including size, location, resources, people, climate, and economy.

THE DUALITY OF CALIFORNIA'S "GOOD LIFE"

California, the proverbial "Land of Plenty," represents what many Americans see as the "good life"—sprawling ranch-style homes, color TVs, personal home computers, swimming pools, shopping centers, fast-food restaurants, backyard patios, outdoor living, and, above all, affluence. Paradoxically, California is also the harbinger of the technological society run amok: smog, water pollution, toxic wastes, threatened redwoods, bulldozed orchards, prime soil and farmlands lost to shopping centers and apartment complexes, crowded and violent freeways, unemployment, expensive housing, urban crime, and assembly-line food in plastic, franchise restaurants. This duality of promise and peril is part of the California enigma.

This paradox notwithstanding, Mervin Field in a 1985 survey found that most Californians (78 percent) continue to rate California as "one of the best" places to live, while only a few (2 percent) thought it a "rather poor" place to live.

Ed Salzman (May 1977) was probably right when he stated:

> Given a choice, most of us who live in San Diego, Los Angeles, San Francisco, and Sacramento would not trade places with fellow Americans

in New York, Washington, Philadelphia, and Chicago, and that's probably the best test of the quality of life in California today.[1]

George Leonard (1962:31) in describing California noted:

Here is the most fertile soil for new ideas in the U.S. The migrating millions who vote with their wheels for California are responding not only to the lure of sunny skies, but to the lure of opportunity. Already, this state shows the way with a revolutionary master plan of higher education for practically everybody; with an increasingly egalitarian society; with unprecedented opportunities for personal pleasure and fulfillment. Most important of all, California presents the promise and the challenge contained at the very heart of the original American dream; here, probably more than at any other place or time, the shackles of the past are broken. In helping to create the society of the future, a man is limited only by the strength of his ambition, the dimension of his concern, and the depth of his courage to face the dangers of his own creation.

While Leonard's comments about California are admittedly overblown, California is still viewed by its own citizens and others as a "relatively" good place to live. As previously noted, most Californians like life in the Golden State. In fact, Californians in the mid-1980s have become more optimistic about their financial situation and future than they were in the previous two decades (Field Institute, November 1985). In contrast, journalists and economists have recently warned that in the near future California may develop a two-tiered economic class society, suffer from a decline in real wages, and experience growth in racial-ethnic divisions (Walters, 1986).

GEOGRAPHY

California is the third largest state in the nation covering some 160,000 square miles. A trip from San Diego at the southwest end of the state along the coast to Crescent City near the Oregon border is an 876 mile drive. This is greater than the distance between New York and Chicago! On the eastern side of California, the Sierra Nevada stretches some 400 miles. The mountains (many with peaks rising more than 13,000 feet above sea level) presented a formidable barrier to explorers and early settlers attempting to enter this state. The Sierra Nevada along with the Cascade and Klamath Ranges, the Coastal Range on the west, and the Tehachapis in the south enclose one of the world's most fertile agricultural regions—the Central Valley. These mountains trap

[1]However, whether Californians living in the Marysville-Yuba City urban area would like to trade with their fellow Americans in Pittsburg, Pennsylvania is debatable. This, in spite of the fact that Rand McNally in their 1985 rankings of the quality of life in American Urban communities, placed Pittsburg first and Marysville-Yuba City dead last. These rankings were compiled *prior* to the disastrous floods that hit Marysville-Yuba City in the spring of 1986.

much of the snow and rain that come in from the northwest Pacific area. Thus, northern and central California have ample water, sometimes floods, while southern California has to import water. Use of state water, its allocation for agriculture, and its transport to the southern parts of the state has been one of the most consistently controversial regional issues dividing northern and southern Californians. Finally, as a western Pacific rim state California usually leads or is one of the leaders among the states in a rather dubious category—number of significant (above 3.0 on the Richter Scale) earthquakes per year.

CLIMATE

For many Californians, the state climate is its most admirable feature. While there are widely varying temperature extremes—the harsh cold and deep snows of the High Sierras and the blistering heat of Death Valley—it is the mild weather of the coastal regions that has lured millions to California. Dry, moderate warmth in the summer contrasts markedly with the muggy heat of the southern and central states and much of the Atlantic seaboard. The warm, sunny days of winter in the southern part of the state contrast dramatically with much of the rest of the country. Many easterners and midwesterners shivering in the cold must rue their fate as they sit watching on television the swimsuit-clad beauties cavorting under sunny skies at the Rose Bowl Parade in Pasadena on New Year's Day.

POPULATION

According to population projections of the state Department of Finance, by 1990 California will have a population of approximately 28 million. While California's natural increase (births over deaths) has stabilized at about a 200,000 gain each year, a much more significant factor in population increase is migration to the state. Between 1970 and 1980, California gained more than 3.5 million people! The population gain in California of 3.6 million in the 1970s alone is almost equal to the total population of the twenty-third most populous state in the nation—Kentucky (3,661,433). Although the number of people moving to the state has fluctuated widely over the last several decades, one fact stands out: In the 1970s and 1980s, approximately 25 percent of all documented nonrefugee immigrants settled in California, and about one-third of all recent southeast Asian refugees have come to this state. Moreover, Mexico's troubled economy and exploding birthrate, political instability in Central America, and continued turbulence in much of Asia suggest that additional waves of immigrants will be seeking the "California dream" in the years ahead.

What is California's carrying capacity? How many more people can be accommodated before the dream of the "good life" becomes a

1-1 *In search of the golden dream. By covered wagon or Dust Bowl auto, California has historically offered another chance to those who needed it.*

Photo courtesy California State Library

Photo courtesy United Press International

myth? Have we already reached that point? Obviously, rapid population growth impinges on the supply of energy, water resources, maintenance of prime agricultural land, use of wild and scenic rivers, use of urban parks and recreation facilities, and school and highway construction, to name but a few areas. But population concerns are seldom referred to by state political leaders—the subject is too sensitive.[2]

Finally (as we shall discuss in Chapter 2), California has sizable black, Asian, and Hispanic minorities in its overall population. Some experts have predicted that by the year 2000, the white-Anglo portion of the state's population will be a minority.

Urban–Suburban

California is an urban state. In fact, with 91 percent of its population living in various urban concentrations it is the most urbanized state in the nation. But this urban pattern is substantially different from most other large, industrial states. Due to relatively low land costs (historically at least), the desire for room, an extensive freeway system, and the willingness to commute long distances to work, Californians have spread across the state. One national columnist once referred to Los Angeles as "seven suburbs in search of a soul." (Today, it's 107 suburbs in search of a soul.) More than half of all Californians live in suburbs.

In the 1950s and 60s, California's suburban growth was massive—whole counties seemed to mushroom overnight. Orange County, south of Los Angeles, grew by 99 percent in the 1960s, while Santa Clara, south of San Francisco, grew by 63 percent (San Francisco was actually losing population during this period). Orange and Santa Clara counties accounted for over two-thirds of the state's population growth between 1960 and 1970.

In the 1970s and 1980s this suburbanization pattern has changed. Instead of rapid growth taking place in areas close by major cities, the most significant gains in population have been in rural areas away from the major cities. In particular, some rural counties in the Sierra foothills and in other bucolic northern areas witnessed prodigious gains in the 1970s—Alpine, 127 percent; Mono, 114 percent; El Dorado and Nevada each 96 percent; Lake, 86 percent; and Mariposa, 85 percent. Lake and Nevada counties will nearly double in population between 1980 and 1990.

Here and there, pleasant, quiet, semirural towns suddenly attracted thousands of new settlers fleeing the urban or suburban "rat race." Redding, Santa Rosa, and Napa in northern California; and Camarillo,

---

[2]Former Governor Jerry Brown's resources secretary, Huey Johnson, raised the issue of population growth and its impact on state resources during Brown's second term. Johnson was bitterly criticized from many quarters for his comments and Governor Brown came under intense pressure to fire Johnson.

1-2 *Passengers waiting for a BART (Bay Area Rapid Transit) train at the Embarcadero station. BART serves the San Francisco Bay Area and is California's only mass public rapid transit system.*

Photo courtesy of BART

San Juan Capistrano, and Oceanside in southern California are good examples of this changing pattern. In southern California, while San Diego has continued to grow steadily, thousands have moved out from the Los Angeles-Orange County complex looking for affordable housing in San Bernardino, Riverside, and Ventura Counties. In northern California, thousands have fled the San Francisco Bay basin, moving over the hills to Contra Costa county, down the peninsula to Santa Clara county, or over the Golden Gate Bridge into the Marin-Santa Rosa areas.

OVERVIEW

Let us now turn our attention to the major factors contributing to California's overall economic, social, and political importance nationwide.

ECONOMIC SIGNIFICANCE

Perhaps the most unique feature of the California economy is its diversity. California grows more crops, produces more food, builds more airplanes, and manufactures more computers and space/military hardware than any other state in the nation. Unlike many of the major industrial states of the eastern seaboard, California has an exceedingly important and varied agricultural sector. And, distinct from the major industrial states of the Midwest, which do have an important agricultural base, the California economy includes other diverse activities, such as mining, communications, finance, lumber, and petroleum.

Overall, when we consider the major factors shaping the state's economy—rapid population growth, climate, a broad range of industrial activity (with emphasis on communications, electronics, and space/defense), percentage of work force in defense-related jobs, importance of tourism, and number of retirees, California's economy most resembles a few of the southern or southwestern states, such as Florida, Texas, or Arizona. However, it should be emphasized that the *diversity* of California agriculture; the affluence of its petroleum industry; the importance of the motion picture, record, and television industries headquartered in the state; and trade/exporting help make the state unique economically.[3]

California business leaders and politicians have long boasted that the Golden State by itself surpasses most countries of the world in gross national product (GNP). According to Wells Fargo Bank economic projections, by the year 2000 California will rank fifth in GNP among nations of the world. Only the United States, the Soviet Union, Japan, and West Germany will have larger GNPs. One-fifth of this nation's fastest growing companies are located in California.

Land Ownership and Use

As with most of the other western states, a large percentage of California land is federally owned (45.2 percent). When state and county land is added to the federal total, over half of California is government-owned (50.2 percent). Table 1–1 shows that in addition to a large percentage of California land being government-owned, a few major corporations control vast tracts of California's privately owned land. Interestingly, the great majority of Californians lives on only 2½ percent of the land.

However, there has been a persisting trend in California for prime agricultural land to be gobbled up by new shopping centers, housing developments, and freeways. California is currently losing about 50,000 acres of prime agricultural land and another 100,000 acres of

[3]According to *California Business* (May, 1982), the top 10 California corporations in terms of net worth and net income in 1981 were: (1) Standard Oil, (2) Atlantic Richfield, (3) Safeway, (4) Bank of America, (5) Occidental Petroleum, (6) Getty Oil, (7) Union Oil, (8) Pacific Telephone and Telegraph, (9) Lucky Stores, and (10) Pacific Gas and Electric.

TABLE 1-1
California Land Use and Ownership

Class of Land	Number of Acres	Percent of State's Area
Total	100,185,000	100.0
Forest land	42,416,000	42.3
Agricultural	35,722,000	35.7
Urban and suburban land	2,200,000	2.2
Other land	19,847,000	19.8
Government Owned	**Number of Acres**	**Percent of Area**
Total	50,335,946	50.2
Federal	45,251,036	45.2
State	2,437,809	2.4
Cities	865,895	.86
Counties	691,827	.69
Special districts	461,868	.46
Indian land	540,471	.54
School districts	80,025	.08
Junior college districts	7,012	.01
Privately Owned		
Total	49,847,735	49.8
Southern Pacific	2,411,000	2.4
Newhall Land Co.	1,590,000	1.6
Shasta Forest Co.	479,196	.4
Tenneco Inc.	362,843	.4
Tejon Ranch Co.	348,000	.3
Standard Oil of California	306,000	.3
Boise Cascade	303,000	.3
Georgia Pacific	278,000	.3
Pacific Gas and Electric Co.	250,000	.2
Occidental Petroleum	200,000	.2
Sunkist Corporation	192,000	.2
Other "smaller holdings"	43,127,714	43.0

Source: California Land Use Task Force. Department of Finance. *California Statistical Abstract,* and Ralph Nader's *Who Owns California?* (Washington, D.C., Center for Study of Responsive Law).

nonprime land a year to development. While some experts claim this is no problem, since there are hundreds of thousands of acres of potential farm land that could be converted into agricultural use if needed or if water were available, environmentalists are concerned that it is the most productive lands that are being lost to residential and commercial development.

Agriculture

Agriculture, or perhaps more accurately, agribusiness, is an important pillar in the state's economic structure. Although the state has relatively few farms and only a small percentage of its population lives in rural areas, it is the nation's leading farm state (Iowa ranks second) based on overall value ($15.6 billion in 1985) of agricultural crops and livestock. A recent U.S. Agriculture report notes that the Pacific Rim states (California, Oregon, and Washington) had the largest percentage (22.9) of all big farms ($500,000-plus annual sales volume) in the nation. Key features of California farming include: large acreages, mechanization, extensive use of pesticides, a growing percentage of prime agricultural land owned by foreign conglomerates, increasing unionization of poorly paid farm workers organized by the United Farm Workers Union, extensive use of temporary legal green-card workers and illegal aliens, and futuristic farming techniques (cloning, genetic engineering, and computerization). Earlier efforts by the Department of the Interior to limit federal water deliveries in reclamation districts to farms of less than 160 acres ran into considerable opposition from a wide spectrum of California politicians and growers and no longer applies.

With just 3 percent of the nation's farm land, California produces 10 percent of national gross farm receipts. California ranks first among the states in fifty-three different crop and livestock commodities, and more are being added to the list each year. For example, kiwifruit is just beginning to be grown in California (seedlings were imported several years ago from New Zealand); in time, this fruit may become yet another major cash crop for California farmers. Additionally, eight California counties rank among the top ten in the entire country in terms of the total value of their agricultural production.[4] California leads the

---

[4]According to a 1986 report of the state Food and Agricultural Export Department, California leads all other states in the following crops and live stock commodities:

Alfalfa seed	Dates	Nectarines	Prunes
Almonds	Eggs	Nursery products	Rabbits
Apricots	Figs	Olives	Safflower
Artichokes	Garlic	Onions	Spinach
Avocados	Green lima beans	Oriental	Strawberries
Broccoli	Grapes	vegetables	Sudan Grass
Brussels sprouts	Honey	Peaches	Sugar beets
Cantaloupes	Honeydew melons	Pears	Tomatoes,
Carrots	Kiwifruit	Persian melons	processing
Casaba melons	Ladino clover	Persimmons	Vegetable and
Cauliflower	seed	Pigeons & Squabs	flower seeds
Celery	Lemons	Pistachios	Walnuts
Chinchillas	Lettuce	Plums	Worms
Cranshaw melons	Mushrooms, fresh	Pomegranates	
Cut flowers	market	Potted plants	

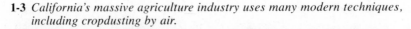

1-3 *California's massive agriculture industry uses many modern techniques, including cropdusting by air.*

Photo courtesy Sacramento Bee

other states in cash receipts from crop marketings, and is one of the leaders in cash receipts from livestock marketings. More than half of California's cotton, rice, wheat, and almond crops are exported to other nations. California farm exports brought in $2.7 billion in 1985. (Foreign competition, high production costs, and a rise in the value of the dollar between 1980–1985 brought about a one-third decline in California exports during this period.)

Compounding the problems for California farmers in the future are such imponderables as the availability of cheap water, pesticide regulations, overmortgaged land, and an adequate labor supply. While agribusiness will continue to be an important part of the state economy, farmers in this state and across the nation will face considerable instability in the years ahead. And farm problems have a direct impact on the state economy. The 1985–86 disastrous farm economy so damaged California's prestigious Bank of America that it became the object of a major takeover attempt by another much smaller bank!

Of course, uncounted in the lush agricultural California bounty is probably the single most important cash crop in the state—illegally grown marijuana. State and federal drug agents report that marijuana is grown in at least forty-three of California's fifty-eight counties. A single female plant can net a grower $6,000. The total yearly California harvest is estimated to be worth more than $1 billion! In terms of cash value, no other crop grown surpasses marijuana in California.

Postindustrial Economics

In addition to its agricultural base, California is also a leading industrial state. Construction, one of the key components of the California economy, produces billions of dollars annually for the state. Particularly interesting, when considering California employment patterns, is the proportion of the nonagricultural labor force working in white-collar rather than blue-collar jobs. Today, approximately 70 percent of all California jobs are service-related. While some two million Californians belong to a labor union—about 18 percent of the labor force—most other industrial states have a higher percentage of their work force in unions. Through most of the 1960s and 1970s, the state's unemployment rate was consistently higher than the national level. However, since mid-1979 it has been close to the national average. More people are employed in trade—grocery, clothing, or music sales, for example—than in any other activity, while the percentage employed in manufacturing has been declining steadily. Dan Walters (1986) notes that "the new industrial jobs that have been created, especially those in high-tech and services, are overwhelmingly non-union with non-professional wage scales in the sub-$10-per-hour range." According to California Economic Development Department of Finance statistics, the state's employment breakdown in 1986 was as follows:

Services	23%
Trade	22
Manufacturing	18
Government	16
Finance, insurance, and real estate	7
Transportation and utilities	4
Construction	4
Agriculture	3

If present trends continue, manufacturing will drop to fourth place in a few years.

One expert, Ted Bradshaw (1976:1–6), contends that California is the world's most advanced industrial society because of its high-technology industry, heavy concentration of workers in service-sector industries, considerable interdependence, rapid change, and innovation. In this same vein, Todd La Porte and C. J. Abrams (1976:101) argue that California is one of the world's best examples of a postindustrial society. These authors note that the state's innovations in petrochemicals, agriculture, transport, aerospace, electronics, nuclear energy, medicine, education, and biology are examples of the sophisticated nature of the California economy.

Silicon Valley

Much of the world's research in microelectronics is conducted in Santa Clara County's "Silicon Valley," one of fourteen high-tech regions in the state. As Michael West, Bristol (England) Economic Development Office observed: "Silicon Valley will always have an esteemed place in economic history for the sheer number of products and industries founded here in a brief period." (USA TODAY, November 19, 1986). Not surprisingly, California leads in the number of personal computers—over 20 percent of the nation's total.

International Trade

California's international trade grew from $2.6 billion in 1960 to $67.3 billion in 1983 which puts it first among the fifty states. The Golden State's geographic location makes it the prime headquarters for the nation's growing Pacific basin trade—with Japan heading the list. Other nations listed in order of total trade dollars with California are Canada, Taiwan, South Korea, Hong Kong, Singapore, Australia, Malaysia, and Mexico. These Pacific basin nations accounted for 77 percent of California's international trade in 1983. Only one nation outside the Pacific basin, West Germany, makes the state's "top ten" list.

Aerospace/Defense

California's aerospace/defense industry has always been heavily dependent upon the federal government for health and vitality. If California were an independent nation, it would rank among the top ten military powers of the world. Approximately one-fourth of federal defense dollars go to California. Nearly one-third of the nation's aerospace companies, one-fifth of aircraft manufacturing, and three-fifths of missile and space equipment are located in California, and there are more engineers here than in any other state.

In 1985, California was awarded $29.1 billion in prime defense contracts, first among the states. Texas ranked second with $10.6 billion for that year. California ranks first among states in net gain from defense spending—about $18 billion yearly. With 10.6 percent of the nation's population, California received 12.4 cents of every federal tax dollar in 1985. An estimated 750,000 Californians are employed in defense related industries—7 percent of the state's work force. Without federal spending, California's economy would be far less prosperous.

Tourism

In addition to agriculture, industry, construction, and high-tech, another critical component of California's economic picture is tourism.

According to the state Department of Economic and Business Development, 1985 tourism generated nearly $20 billion for the state. Supplementing the international attractions of Disneyland and San Francisco, other major tourist attractions include Knott's Berry Farm, Hollywood movie studios, Napa Valley premium wineries, San Diego's zoo and Sea World, California's south coast beaches, Tahoe, and the Mendocino coast.

Aside from a few economic trouble spots, the state's overall financial health improved markedly in the early 1980s. As a result, a 1986 survey of state residents revealed that a clear majority (52 percent) believed they were better off financially than the year before. Four years earlier (1982), less than a third (32 percent) felt they were better off compared to 42 percent of the sample who felt they were worse off.

SOCIAL SIGNIFICANCE

Two prominent features of the California social potpourri deserve comment: (1) it has been the haven and at times birthplace for a variety of exotic religious cults, offbeat political movements, and extremist groups; and (2) it has been a major contributor to American "pop" culture and social patterns. While the endless discussions of the zany California social milieu have been overdone by writers—after all, a large, diverse, populous state is sure to have a certain number of eccentric types—nevertheless, much of this nation's sociopolitical exotica either started in California or found particularly fertile soil here from the 1960s through the 80s.

Diversity and Extremes

1970s extremist groups such as the Black Panthers and the Symbionese Liberation Army got their start in California. The John Birch Society, the now defunct Weathermen, and the American Nazi party, while not launched in California, successfully recruited many members from the state. Perhaps the most controversial contemporary political fringe group is the Lyndon La Rouche organization. Among some of the zanier views of La Rouche are his contentions that the Queen of England is the head of the world's illegal drug trade and that the Democratic party is "pro-gay." In 1986, two La Rouche adherents captured the Democratic party's nomination for lieutenant governor and secretary of state in Illinois. In California, several La Rouche supporters ran in the Democratic primary for elective offices, but they failed to capture any nominations. More important, though, the La Rouche organization succeeded in qualifying an initiative dealing with AIDS (Proposition 64) on the November 1986 ballot. This proposed law would have required all people testing positively for AIDS to be immediately quarantined. California voters rejected the La Rouche initiative in the 1986 general election.

As an example of the unique California political milieu, we might note the political power of the state's homosexuals. While gays have organized politically throughout the nation, it is California where they have had their greatest impact. According to *Newsweek,* no city has a larger homosexual population proportionally than San Francisco (a reported 120,000 out of a total 680,000), and no city has adopted a more tolerant view of homosexuals (*Newsweek,* June 6, 1977:16–26). In San Francisco, there are gay Democratic clubs, gay office seekers and holders, and even gay police. Mayoral candidates in San Francisco must seek support from the gay community to have a chance to win. Gay politics had become increasingly mainstream in California in the 1970s, and, in 1986 they rejected the La Rouche AIDS (and antigay) initiative with a massive 71 percent "no" vote. Indeed, California voters in 1978 rejected an initiative that would have allowed school districts to fire homosexual teachers. However, the looming specter of an AIDS plague, moving from male homosexuals as its prime victims into the heterosexual population, could potentially trigger an antigay backlash.

California has also served as a sanctuary for a wide variety of unusual religious cults and sects, from Aimee Semple McPherson and the Foursquare Gospel Church in the 1930s to Hare Krishna, Scientology, Synanon, or the "Moonies" of the 1980s. The "Flat Earth Society," based in Lancaster, California, rejects the round earth concept and claims 2,800 members! More seriously, the 1978 mass suicide of hundreds of members of the People's Temple Church, a California-based cult, received massive national and international attention. Gurus, con artists, and fanatical leaders have always found willing followers in the Golden State.

Window on the Future

California, inevitably, seems to be in the center of the American political-social swirl: the Watts race riots, the 1960s student protest movement, the anti-Vietnam war crusade, the environmental movement, the antienvironment movement, or the Jarvis-Gann property tax revolt are examples. Bradshaw (1976:1–6) notes, "new issues often seem to demand attention in California long before they emerge in other places." Kenneth Lamott (1971:4) writes, "California is our distant warning system for the rest of the United States. California is our window into the future. California is the center of the whirlpool, where all currents come to a focus."

Clearly, a great many features of American social life and American "pop" culture are California-inspired—fashions, sports crazes, music,

1-4 *Gay parade. A gay and his mother join a march down Hollywood Boulevard.*

Photo courtesy United Press International

food fads, or movie and television programs. California frequently is also the springboard for national trends—hang gliders, scuba diving, cross-country skiing, hot air balloons, off-road vehicles, hot tubs, home computers, walking on hot coals, skateboards, and surfboards are examples. "Val" talk ("grody to the max" and other such expressions), which overnight became a national linguistic phenomenon, was based on the unique speech patterns of San Fernando Valley teenage girls. The "drive-in" phenomenon—movies, restaurants, banks, and photo processing—is particularly Californian. Walt Disney's Disneyland in Anaheim, California, was the first of the modern theme amusement parks that have sprung up around the country.

Much of what has been written about California pokes fun at the Golden State:

> California's major export to the rest of the country has not been its fruits and vegetable; it has been craziness . . . You name it; if it babbles and its eyeballs are glazed, it probably comes from California (Royko, 1979).

Yet, a more serious and significant evaluation is found in Scammon and Wattenberg's (1971:137) observation that:

> California . . . is not really atypical, screwballs notwithstanding, . . . California is . . . a barometric state. Among large states, Illinois and California are the two that vote most consistently like America as a whole.

Looking at California's differences from another point of view, John Naisbitt (1982:6) notes:

> We have learned that there are five states in which most social invention occurs in this country. The other forty-five are in effect followers . . . . Not surprisingly, California is the key indicator state; Florida is second, although not too far behind; the other three trend-setter states are Washington, Colorado, and Connecticut. . . . When we trace back new trends or positions on issues eventually adopted by most of the fifty states, we find that these five states are again and again the places where new trends began. It's difficult to say why, other than to observe that all five are characterized by a rich mix of people. And the richness of the mix always results in creativity, experimentation, and change.

Some of American's leading authors—Walt Whitman, Mark Twain, John Steinbeck, and contemporary novelist Joan Didion—have written about the Golden State. On one point they would all agree, California is indeed a fascinating state.

California has long served as a haven for senior citizen retirees seeking the mild, balmy weather. Many Californians fight the aging process with ferocious determination—jogging, aerobics, fat farms, health food stores, iron-pumping emporiums, and exercise salons are all very much a part of the state social scene. Physical fitness entrepreneurs such as Jack LaLanne, Vic Tanney, and Jane Fonda are state folk heroes. Zsa Zsa Gabor and Ronald Reagan are just two examples of senior Californians who look much younger than they really are. And when death can no longer be denied, there is yet another prime tourist attraction, Forest Lawn Cemetery.

Some of the country's biggest newsmakers are Californians: political leaders such as Ronald Reagan, Gerald Ford, George Schultz, Casper Weinberger, Tom Hayden, Ed Meese, the recently deceased Howard Jarvis, and ex-governor Jerry Brown; show business personalities such as Tom Cruise, Sissy Spacek, Charlton Heston, Ed Asner, Molly Ringwald, and Michael J. Fox; sports celebrities such as Tommy Lasorda, Kareem Abdul Jabbar, Steve Garvey, Joe Montana, and O. J.

Simpson; scholars such as Jonas Salk or Edward Teller; media personalities such as Johnny Carson and Werner Erhard, and notorious criminals such as Charles Manson, Sirhan Sirhan, and Juan Corona. Although other states have their nationally known personalities, unusual cults, extremist political groups, and fads, in terms of overall magnitude, California is in a class by itself.

POLITICAL SIGNIFICANCE

As the most populous state in the nation, California has more voters and potential voters than any other state in the nation. California is inevitably a political power to be reckoned with.

Presidential Nomination Process

In the nineteenth century, delegates selected to national presidential nominating conventions were handpicked by party leaders. These delegates did the bidding of their respective leaders at the convention. Early in this century, in California and other (mainly western) states, reform-oriented Progressives came to political power. Among the various reforms advocated by Progressives (see Chapter 2 for a more complete discussion) was the presidential preference primary system of *electing* delegates. In California, Oregon, Washington, Wisconsin, New Hampshire, and a handful of other states, instead of having party leaders choose delegates, voters were given the power to elect them.

Through much of this century, two states, New Hampshire and California, had the most important presidential preference primaries. The New Hampshire primary, traditionally the first scheduled in presidential election years, has played an increasingly decisive role in providing momentum to presidential candidates and, conversely, in torpedoing the plans of other presidential hopefuls. The California primary has traditionally been the last major presidential primary held prior to the national party conventions. The state's sizable Republican and Democratic delegations made it a great prize for presidential candidates. Winning the California primary could provide a presidential candidate a helpful last-minute surge. As William J. Crotty (1977:214) noted:

> The Golden State's primary was easily the most significant and decisive of all . . . a primary victory in this state awarded the winner about one fifth of the total votes needed for nomination. Historically, candidates who lost California seldom won their party's nomination.

Further enhancing the importance of the California presidential primary historically was the fact that, until 1972, both parties in California operated under a "winner take all" rule. The candidate receiving the most votes in the Democratic or Republican primary won all the state's delegates to the party convention. For example, in 1972 Senator George McGovern captured all 271 California delegates to the Democratic National Convention even though he won only 43 percent of the Democratic primary vote.[5] In 1976, California Democrats reformed their "winner take all" primary, by adopting a proportional representation system. California Republican leaders have kept their "winner take all" system because they believe it focuses more attention and importance on the California GOP primary. It clearly enhanced Ronald Reagan's 1980 and 1984 presidential bids!

Unfortunately, over the last several decades the significance of the California presidential primary has sharply declined. Reforms launched in the early 1970s encouraged more states to adopt presidential primaries, and thus, California's primary is no longer unique. In the contemporary setting, early primary states (e.g., New Hampshire and Florida) and early caucus states (e.g., Iowa and Maine) have become the key battlegrounds for presidential candidates. Getting off to a good start in these states is more than half the battle, and the eventual nominee is almost always known by the end of March. In 1988, a number of southern states will conduct their presidential primaries on the same day in early March. This regional primary will increase the south's importance in determining who will be nominated, and will further weaken the significance of California's. Hence, the June California presidential preference primary has become nearly meaningless— in most cases the decision has already been made.

While various state party leaders have urged moving the California primary back to April or March, thus far, no consensus for change has developed.

General Elections

California has more electoral votes (forty-seven) than any other state. To get elected a presidential candidate must receive a minimum of 269 electoral votes. California's forty-seven electoral votes comprise 17 percent of the necessary margin. California, in effect, is more important to a presidential candidate than the thirteen smallest electoral states combined: Alaska, Delaware, Hawaii, Idaho, Maine, Montana, Nebraska, Nevada, New Hampshire, North Dakota, South Dakota, Vermont, and Wyoming. By the next federal census (1991), California's population growth in the 1980s may translate into two or three additional house seats and forty-nine or fifty electoral votes. California also

---

[5]A coalition of Democratic presidential candidates challenged the results of the 1972 California primary by appealing to the convention's credentials committee— which upheld them. But this decision was later overturned by a floor vote of the entire convention.

tends to be a bellwether state in presidential elections. Over the last sixty-four years (1920–84), California has gone with the presidential winner fifteen times. In only two elections (1960 and 1976) have its electoral votes gone to the loser.

Because of the state's growing political importance and the high visibility of its major officeholders, over the last several decades California politicians have become key players in the presidential and vice presidential nomination process. California nominees include on the Republican side: Earl Warren, vice presidential candidate (1948); Richard M. Nixon, vice president (1952 and 1956), presidential candidate (1960), and president (1968 and 1972); Ronald Reagan, presidential candidate (1968 and 1976) and president (1980 and 1984).[6] Following his landslide 1986 gubernatorial reelection, George Deukmejian has frequently been mentioned as a potential 1988 vice presidential candidate. On the Democratic side, Governor Jerry Brown ran for the presidency in 1976 and 1980 while U.S. Senator Alan Cranston ran in 1984. California is also the most important state for presidential candidates to secure campaign contributions.

Congressional Politics

It has become a cliché to state that power in Congress resides in its committees and committee chairs. Traditionally, seniority has been the main criterion for determining committee membership and chairs. (The member of the majority party with the longest continuous service on a committee automatically became chair until the mid-1970s.)

Over the last fifty years, Democrats have almost always been the majority party in Congress, and southern Democrats, who represented safe, one-party districts, won easy reelection and were able to build substantial seniority. Thus, southern Democrats often chaired key committees in Congress. On the other hand, Congress members from California traditionally had difficulty accumulating sufficient seniority to attain leadership positions. This was due in part to the relative evenness of the Republican-Democratic balance in the state and in part to the older age of the average new California representative (many previously had spent years in the California legislature). Historically, the only really powerful California congressmen were members elected to party leadership positions not directly tied to seniority—for example, Senator Alan Cranston currently holds a Democratic party leadership position in Congress.

---

[6]In 1980, after receiving the Republican presidential nomination, Ronald Reagan seriously considered naming fellow Californian, Gerald Ford (Palm Springs), as his running mate. A president and vice president coming from the same state would have been unprecedented.

In addition, the California House delegation was frequently wracked by strong internal political feuds further dissipating its overall influence in the House. The sizable California delegation inevitably tends to be politically diverse, ranging from militant Democratic liberals from San Francisco and Berkeley to the radical, right-wing Republicans from southern California suburbs. Thus, the state's Democratic and Republican delegations seldom work together as a team (Bottorff, 1986). Although the California House delegation was the largest in the 1980s (forty-five), it was unable to match the power of the more unified, seniority-laden conservative southern state delegations (for example, Texas) or some urban northern delegations (for example, Pennsylvania).

At present, California's traditional weakness in Congress appears to be changing. In the early 1970s, congressional reform forces led by former Representative Phil Burton, augmented by a host of newly elected "Watergate" Democratic freshmen, emboldened by committee chair scandals, and encouraged by the powerful new public interest lobbies such as Common Cause and Ralph Nader's Congress Watch, were able to achieve changes in the formerly rigid seniority system. Today, committee chairs must win biennial approval from the majority party caucus in order to retain their positions. In 1974, three committee chairs lost their positions by votes of the majority party caucus. In 1984 Democrats elected Congressman Les Aspin Armed Services Chair even though he was the *seventh ranking* Democrat on the committee. Clearly, power in the House of Representatives has shifted to an extent from the once fiercely independent senior committee chairs to the majority party caucus, and this, in turn, should help increase the power of California Democrats in the chamber.

Additionally, due to reapportionment-generated "safe" districts, many more California Congress members these days have accumulated the necessary years of service to qualify as chairs of standing committees. On the Democratic side in particular, members from some of the state's major cities (Los Angeles, San Francisco, Oakland, and Sacramento) and several from the rural Central Valley have become almost as well entrenched as their southern or midwestern counterparts used to be. Thus, in 1986, California Democratic House members secured four standing committee chairmanships and twenty-one subcommittee chairs. (Subcommittee chairs sometimes rival standing committee chairs in terms of power and authority.)

In addition to the powerful party leadership role played by Senator Alan Cranston, emerging new leaders within the California House delegation include: Tony Coehlo (Democratic Whip—third ranking in power behind the speaker), Vic Fazio, Norm Mineta, Leon Panetta, Bill Lowery, Tony Beilenson, and, in particular, Henry Waxman and

Howard Berman. The latter duo helped raise campaign funds for nearly a dozen House Democrats from California.

Finally, the rapid population growth of the Sun Belt states has given the region enormous new representational strength in Congress, and California, as a charter member of the Sun Belt team, is helped by the new power equation in Congress.

Supreme Court Politics

California's impact on the U.S. Supreme Court is difficult to assess. Former California Governor Earl Warren served as Chief Justice of the Supreme Court during the tumultuous decades of the 1950s and 60s. The Warren Court issued a number of landmark decisions on a variety of topics (school desegregation, voting rights, reapportionment, and rights of defendants) that strongly influenced the future direction of American constitutional law.

In addition, several significant California-generated legal controversies have served as a backdrop for major U.S. Supreme Court decisions. Perhaps the most famous recent example is the Bakke case. Alan Bakke, a white male, argued that he had been denied admission to the University of California Davis Medical School because of reverse discrimination. In 1978, the Court ruled that Bakke had been wrongfully denied admission to the Davis Medical School under an unconstitutional quota system. The Court also went on to say, however, that race could be used as a criterion for admission to assist minority applicants.

Probably the most significant way California has exerted an influence on the U.S. Supreme Court has been the leadership role played by its own state supreme court, particularly in the 1950s–60s. During those years California's Supreme Court developed an impressive national reputation for innovation. In a number of critical legal areas, the U.S. Supreme Court followed the lead of the California court. As one writer put it:

> In 1961, when the U.S. Supreme Court held that all states were forbidden to use illegally seized evidence in a criminal trial, it cited a 1955 California decision. In 1965, the U.S. Supreme Court struck down Arizona and New York Supreme Court decisions when it announced the *Miranda* rule against confessions from a suspect not informed of his rights. [But] a companion California case was upheld because the state's court had reversed this conviction. California has led, too, in civil rights cases. In 1948, California was the first to strike down a statute prohibiting interracial marriage. Nineteen years later the U.S. Supreme Court followed the California example. And when California voters repealed fair housing legislation in 1964, the State Supreme Court set aside the voters' decision in reasoning followed by a

later U.S. Supreme Court ruling (*Sacramento Bee,* October 6, 1974, section P, p. 1).

However, in more recent years, ideological divisions, jealousies, internal dissension, and many controversial decisions have weakened the court's position. Leaks to the press and alleged politically motivated delays in announcing court decisions culminated in a public investigation of the state supreme court in the summer of 1979. While the investigation was, in itself, inconclusive, the court's reputation was badly damaged. (See Chapter 11.) Finally, the unprecedented rejection of three California Supreme Court justices by voters in the November 1986 elections indicated considerable public dissatisfaction with the performance of the state supreme court.

CALIFORNIA AND THE AMERICAN FEDERAL SYSTEM

California was officially admitted to statehood in 1850. It was the first noncontiguous American territory to become a state. Debate over California's admission as a free state was intense because of the slavery issue and southern fears that political power would tip to the north.

In theory, within the American federal system, the national government has only those few powers that are explicitly delegated to it in the U.S. Constitution, while all other powers are reserved to the states. In fact, under the early leadership of Supreme Court Chief Justice John Marshall (1801–35), the powers of the national government were vastly expanded through the use of the implied powers doctrine. Marshall's immediate successors tended to shift away from federal supremacy to a states' rights position, but in the 1930s during the Great Depression and President Franklin Delano Roosevelt's New Deal, a new court majority eventually returned to the strong national government position. Since 1937, the Court has usually upheld the right of the national government to act in most areas. There are virtually no limits on the subjects that Congress may legislate on.

The balance between national and state government powers has been a continuing bone of contention in the American federal system. While various issues have exacerbated the national-state relationship over the years, one issue in particular generated much of the early conflict—race. From debates at the constitutional convention over the continued importation of slaves, to the bloody Civil War, to the tragedies of the Reconstruction Era and the later "separate but equal" doctrine, to the civil rights struggles in the 1960s, one of the chief legacies of federalism was to provide southern states the legal rationale to maintain their white supremacy systems. However, in 1954 the U.S. Supreme Court reversed itself and ruled in *Brown* v. *Board of Education* that "separate but equal" was unconstitutional and that Topeka, Kansas, school officials would have to integrate their public schools "with all deliberate speed." This decision was later extended to other cities and states and to all public facilities in later court rulings. In 1964 Congress passed the Civil Rights Act which forbade governmental or private employers engaged in interstate commerce to discriminate in hiring. And, in 1965 Congress passed the Voting Rights Act to prevent southern states from attempting to discourage blacks from voting by threatening them with a potential federal takeover of voter registration. Today, racial issues tend to be more national in scope—school busing or affirmative action are examples—the strong states' rights stance of the old confederate states is in sharp decline.

Indeed, the states' rights battle cry has been heard lately more in the western states than southern. In the late 1970s California, Nevada, Alaska, Montana, and Idaho were in the forefront of what came to be dubbed in the press the "Sagebrush Rebellion." At the heart of this squabble was the fact that a large percentage of Western states land was under the control of the federal government (45 percent of California is administered by the federal government), while most midwestern, southern, and eastern states had miniscule federal landholdings. Many western state officials resented federal rules and regulations dealing with this land and on other policy matters. An example of an issue that pitted the West against the federal government occurred during the Jimmy Carter presidency when the federal government for fuel conservation and safety reasons mandated a fifty-five-miles-per-hour speed limit on interstate highways. To "encourage" western states (the major opponents of the measure) to adopt and enforce the new speed law, the federal government threatened to withhold portions of federal highway funds of noncomplying states. Many western politicians argued the law made little sense in the vast expanses of the West. It was mainly because of western pressure that the Reagan administration and Congress agreed to modify this policy in 1986.

Ronald Reagan championed the motto "get government off our backs" when he ran as a presidential candidate in 1976 and 1980 and as incumbent president in 1984. Many of Ronald Reagan's strongest political allies were Sagebrush rebels. After his election President Reagan's appointment of leading Sagebrush rebel James Watt as his first secretary of the interior sent a clear signal to all of Reagan's sentiments on the matter.

In a similar vein, throughout his two terms as president, Ronald Reagan steadfastly promoted his "New Federalism" concept by advocating a shift of powers and responsibilities from Washington D.C. back to state and local governments. However, while generally viewed as a strong states-righter, President Reagan has, at times, promoted some national government issues. The Reagan administration's support for: (1) the federal twenty-one-year-old drinking requirement which many state leaders oppose; (2) exploring and drilling for western states' off-shore oil which has antagonized a number of California and Oregon public officials; and (3) bringing state national guard units under greater federal control (so they can be sent for training to locations in Central America which some governors oppose) are examples.

POLITICAL REFORM AND POLICY INNOVATION

Through much of this century California has been in the vanguard of states promoting political reform. At the turn of the century reform-oriented progressives in California and other mainly western states came to political power. Progressives wanted to promote honest, open, efficient, and responsive government. They saw as their enemy party bosses, party machines, tainted public officials, and avaricious special interests. Central to the Progressive philosophy was the belief that the public—not the politicians or corporate interests—should wield ultimate political power in our society through the ballot box. William J. Crotty (1977:214) discusses this western reform mentality in describing the extension of the franchise in the United States:

> The weight of public opinion in the western states was overwhelmingly against any property limitations on the vote. . . . The contrast between the western states and those in the East was pronounced. The latter were older, more comfortable with the established ways, and more conservative and elitist. . . . Not surprisingly, voting rights for women were granted in the western states first.

Some of these progressive reform ideas such as the direct primary, presidential primary, or direct democracy devices (initiative, referendum, and recall) were adopted later in some states east of the Mississippi River. Clearly, California was in the forefront of reform early in this century. And, while these reforms were not a panacea, on the whole, they did help for a time promote more honest and responsive state government.

In addition, through the leadership of former Speaker Jess Unruh and other state legislators, the California legislature in the 1960s sought to reform itself (see Chapter 7) by raising legislators' salaries, adding professional staff, and refurbishing offices, committee rooms, and chambers. In the late 1960s, the California legislature became the reform model for many other states. Studies by various experts (Walker, 1969; Burns, 1971; Gray, 1973; and Naisbitt, 1982) came to similar conclusions: the California legislature was one of the more, if not the most, innovative state legislative bodies in the nation. And, in 1974, when voters approved the Political Reform Act initiative that among other features sought to regulate lobbyists, limit campaign contributions, and require all political candidates to periodically report on campaign contributions and expenditures California once again was clearly on the cutting edge of political reform. These features were emphasized in earlier editions of this text.

Today, California government's leadership in reform and policy innovation among the states is in jeopardy. Clearly, the most critical political reform issue of the 1980s is finding a way to stop the ever-mounting costs of political campaigns and the attendant advantages gained by major special-interest contributors. A host of states have already passed laws to deal with this problem. Thus far, the California legislature and governor have been unable to reach a compromise on this issue. In the Golden State "the sky's the limit" on campaign spending. Indeed, Speaker Willie Brown recently commented that perhaps the only way this issue will ever be resolved in California will be to find a solution from outside the customary framework of government through the initiative process. Increasingly, the initiative process is being used by politicians and special interests not as a last resort but as a first step in bypassing a constantly deadlocked legislature-governor. The capitol has been rocked by a major political scandal (the Moriarity affair) and a constant string of minor scandals—consultants on state contracts who produce no work; campaign funds used for legislators' personal expenses; legislative votes influenced by special-interest campaign contributions; or legislative staffers working on members' campaigns on state time. These and other scandals have tarnished the once proud image of California as a reform model. In addition, the state Supreme Court and its chief justice from 1978 to 1986, Rose Bird, became the target of massive public outrage. As Mary Ellen Leary (1983) notes:

> The change in California that most intrigues the state's major business economists is that it is becoming less distinctive from the other states, less special.

It should be emphasized: Most California public officials and staff are honest, conscientious, and hard-working, but the system does not seem to be working well of late. On occasion in the 1980s, state government has acted in a bold and creative way—the 1982–83 Medi-Cal reforms, the Hart-Hughes-Honig public school reform measure, the 1985 workfare program, or Assemblyman Lloyd Connelley's toxics legislation are examples. Bowman and Kearney (1986:225) rank California as first among the states in hazardous waste regulation. But these tend to be the exception to the rule. More typical is the legislature-governor's difficulties in 1987 to compromise on the SSC (Superconducting Super Collider) issue to allow California to bid along with other states for this $4.5 billion federal project. In a desperate last-minute effort, the California proposal was submitted, minutes prior to the deadline.

Who is to blame for this malaise? Democrats blame Republican Governor George Deukmejian, and he blames the Democratic legislative leaders and also used to blame the Rose Bird Court. Democratic and Republican leaders blame one another for excessive partisanship. Democrats also blame Howard Jarvis and Paul Gann for exploiting the initiative process, the latter blamed the political establishment with their theme "teach the politicians a lesson," and some demand new reforms for this old (initiative) reform. Elected officials blame the press for focusing on trivial minor scandals and presenting a distorted view of state government to the public. Many public officials blame the special interests who provide large campaign contributions to officials. And reformers blame the U.S. Supreme Court for ruling that campaign contributions are a form of public expression which cannot be limited under the free speech provisions of the First Amendment. Thus, there is no shortage of potential scapegoats.

William Crotty has wisely observed:

> Reform comes gradually and at times painfully slowly. The need for reform has to be demonstrated over and over again, and most frequently it takes a crisis situation to arouse broad public concern to accomplish the desired end. Always they introduce new problems, and the effort to repeal and render them impotent continues unabated by their critics comfortable and powerful within a system that has rewarded them generously.

Perhaps, we are at this crisis point in 1988 in California wherein dynamic and creative leadership will emerge to confront the many political and social issues of the day.

SUMMARY

Economically, socially, and politically California is one of the most influential states in the nation. Technologically, it is the most advanced state in the nation. Historically, California has been a leader among the states on reform and policy issues. By understanding something about the issues and political crosscurrents in California today, we can discern something about the future trends in American national politics.

2

California—Its People and Politics

California, here they come;
Doctor, lawyer, merchant, bum;
They come by car and train and plane,
Straight from Kansas, Georgia, Maine,
Massachusetts, Minnesota,
Iowa and North Dakota,
Rich folk, poor folk, young folk, codgers
Moving westward like the Dodgers.

Richard Armour[1]

THE LAST FRONTIER

For years, California was the last frontier in America, physically and psychologically. Many without hope came to the Golden State, and many others who came brought only hope. Between 1850 and 1986, the state population grew 158 times—from 165,000 to 26 million (see Illustration 2–1). In the same period, the United States only grew nine times. Had the nation grown at the pace set by California, there would be today over 3 billion Americans rather than the present 240 million.

One feature that makes California's growth so startling is its continuously high rate. Only two other states have had similar growth rates—Florida since 1850 and Arizona since 1900. Many states have had short periods of rapid growth, but they then settled down to slow growth. In every case, the rapid growth phase was due to migration—a part of the westward expansion of the United States. What distinguishes California's growth is that it has continued over such a long period of time.

[1]Richard Armour, "I Loved You, California," *Look*, September 25, 1962, p. 54.

2-1 *California's population by decades.*

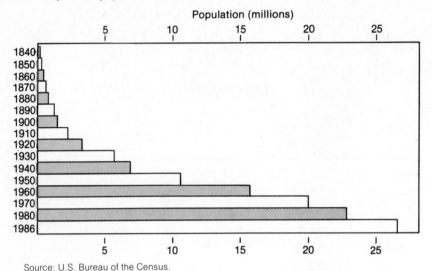

Source: U.S. Bureau of the Census.

For many, California was more than a "last frontier"—it was a *last chance*. Long after the Old West was gone, California remained a place where the young, the poor, and the disadvantaged had a chance to make it. It was also a place to retire—if you'd made it someplace else. Migrants have always outnumbered natives since the Gold Rush of 1849.

THE EARLIEST EXPLORERS

The first people to live in what we now know as California were Indians—descendants of nomadic tribes that crossed the Bering Strait some 25,000 years ago.[2] When Spain made its first serious effort to colonize California in the 1760s, the total Indian population was approximately 140,000.

THE SPANISH-MEXICAN ERA

Early European Explorers

The Spaniards came to the New World looking for riches that had been described in *Las Sergas de Esplandian* by Garci Ordonez de

---

[2]The Chinese were probably the next to explore the west coast of North America. Ancient Chinese implements, including a bronze fan and a bronze coin 3,000 years old, have been found in British Columbia.

Montalvo, published about 1498. In a fanciful tale of adventure, he described the beautiful island of California:

> . . . at the right hand of the Indies there is an island named California, [which] . . . abounds with gold and precious stones . . . .

Of course, no one had ever seen California—it was a myth.

The Spanish occupied Mexico in 1519 (eighty-two years before the first English colony was established in Virginia) looking for the cities of gold and the worldly paradise described by Christopher Columbus. No such cities existed, but the Spaniards believed these tales and kept looking for them for over 250 years.

In 1542, Juan Rodriquez Cabrillo (a Portuguese) sailed along the California coast, passing by areas we now know as San Diego, Catalina Island, Ventura, and Monterey—going as far north as the Fort Ross area. The next year, Bartolome Ferrelo sailed up the coast to what is now the northern border with Oregon. These were the first *Europeans* to discover California.

Another early explorer, Sir Francis Drake, landed north of San Francisco Bay in 1579, named the land Nova Albion ("New England"), and claimed it for England: (Drake's "New England" was discovered forty-one years before the Pilgrims landed at Plymouth.) Essentially, though, California was ignored by the Spanish and other European nations until 1765.

The Mission Period

The mission had been used extensively during the 1600s and 1700s as a colonizing device in Spain's New World colonies. Under the command of Gaspar de Portola, soldiers, Franciscan priests (including Father Junipero Serra), and Baja California Indians reached San Diego in 1769 to establish the first of the California missions.

This began the mission era in California history. Under the direction of Father Serra, missions combined religious conversion of the Indians with practical instruction in agriculture and building. A few missions were quite large, with carpentry shops, blacksmithing, weaving, pottery, and candle making. The last mission was established at Sonoma in 1823 and marks the end of both the Spanish and mission periods.

California was a marginal colony in the Spanish empire. Ruled from Mexico City by a Royal viceroy, little attention was given to, or control exercised over, this vast territory. At most, the Spanish had about 3,000 citizens, soldiers, and missionaries in California. Their control was limited to a narrow coastal strip from San Diego to Sonoma, north of San Francisco. (Ironically, this strip of land today contains most of the state's population.)

The Mexican Period

California was not involved in the Spanish-Colonial Wars of Independence (1808–1820s). In early 1822, when the Mexican Revolution succeeded, Californians easily accepted the new regime. The Spanish governor simply swore allegiance to the new government. But, the new Mexican government was largely concerned with staying in power and devoted little attention to California—even less than had the Spanish.

Under Spanish rule, the missions were important in California. Under Mexican rule, they were dismantled and to some degree replaced by rancheros. Mission properties were sold by the government or given in grants to favored individuals.

During the Mexican period, a thin trickle of outsiders came to the state including whalers, fur traders, and "mountain men." Most visited California and returned home, but a few stayed. Richard H. Dana wrote his famous *Two Years Before the Mast* after sailing to California on a hide and tallow ship in 1834. And in 1841, the Bidwell party arrived by land from the Middle West; opening a new route for thousands of Americans who were to arrive in the next few years.

Bear Flag Revolt

A few Americans, encouraged by the weakness of the Mexican government, anticipating war between Mexico and the United States, and concerned about British designs on California, staged a brief revolt in June 1846. Led by adventurer, John C. Frémont, they seized a herd of horses, captured two Mexican generals, and raised a flag displaying a grizzly bear. Their revolution was cut short by the war between Mexico and the United States, and today all that remains of the revolt is the California state flag.

The Mexican-American War

Most Americans believe that the Mexican-American War was a conflict over Texas. President James K. Polk could probably have secured Texas without war, but Polk wanted much more. Specifically, he wanted California—and *that* meant war. Ironically the major object of the war was hardly touched by battle, since most of the fighting took place in Mexico. With American occupation of Mexico City, the war was over. In February 1848, Mexico signed the Treaty of Guadalupe Hidalgo ceding California (as well as Texas, New Mexico, and Arizona) to the United States for $15 million. This ended the short period of time (1822–48) when Mexico had title to California.

THE AMERICAN ERA

The American era began with the Gold Rush of 1849. This event had an incredible impact on California. In 1840, the total state population was about 116,000, most of whom (110,000–112,000) were Indians. By 1860, state population had reached 380,000. By 1870, it was a half million, but the Indian population had been reduced to about 30,000. The Spanish and Mexicans unintentionally reduced the Indian population through disease and ignorance, but the Americans killed them outright.[3] One of Frémont's expeditions reported:

> We killed plenty of game and an occasional Indian. We made it a rule to spare none of the bucks.

Almost all of the Indian, Spanish, and Mexican cultures were swept aside by the onrushing American civilization. The most obvious remnants today are the names of some of our major cities—San Francisco, San Jose, Monterey, Santa Barbara, Los Angeles, San Bernardino, and San Diego. Several restored missions, Old Town in San Diego and Olvera Street in Los Angeles, and parts of old Monterey have become tourist attractions. The state community property laws are based on the Spanish legal system, and some architecture and furniture reflect a lingering Spanish influence. But while the Constitution of 1849 stipulated that all laws be published in Spanish as well as English, that requirement was dropped in the Constitution of 1879. Essentially, California quickly became as American as Massachusetts, Missouri, or Illinois. In fact, much of the constitution of 1849 was borrowed from the Iowa and New York constitutions.

The Gold Rush

Discovery of gold in January 1848 at Sutter's Mill on the American River started the "gold rush." News of the find spread, and by late May 1848, San Francisco, Monterey, and San Jose were largely deserted for the gold fields on the American River. By 1849, the news had spread around the world, and the gold rush was on. In the mid-1850s, perhaps as many as 100,000 people were at the diggings—over a third of the state population! The value of gold mined in 1852 was over $80 million. Most of the miners came to make their fortune and then leave. Many left penniless, but a few made a fortune. And, more fortunes were made by those who served the mining camps.

---

[3]In 1963, representatives of the remaining California Indians and the U.S. Justice Department agreed on a $30 million settlement for the 64 million acres of land taken from them (47 cents per acre).

2-2 *Gold: Where it all began at Coloma in 1848.*

Photo courtesy California State Library

The gold rush swept aside the pastoral Spanish-Mexican life-style. Roads, stores, mills, and small manufacturing plants were built. Cities such as San Francisco, Sacramento, and Stockton developed during the gold rush period. The miners of 1849 found more than gold, though few realized it at the time. They came to a state whose potential wealth in agriculture, manufacture, trade, and services would far exceed the riches of the mother lode.

The Railroad-Land Boom

When the Central Pacific Railroad joined the Union Pacific at Promontory Point, Utah, in May 1869, California was finally linked to the rest of the nation. Prior to that, those who came to California traveled by sailing ship, stage coach, wagon, horse, or on foot. Most trade

2-3 *Building the railroad. Chinese labor built much of the railroad that linked California to the rest of the nation. Chinese coolies riding a wood-burning train in the Bloomer cut, Placer County, California.*

Photo courtesy California State Library

was carried by sail around the horn or across the Panama Isthmus after completion of the Panama Railroad. But, the ocean route was slow and dangerous. At best, in the mid-1860s, it took twenty-one days to get to California by ship (using the Panama Railroad). The overland stage from Tipton, Missouri, to San Francisco took twenty-five days—subject to delay due to Indian attacks or floods.

Upon completion of the railroad California was opened to massive migration and economic development (it also gave the railroad a stranglehold on the state's economy). Many were drawn to southern California by promise of the health-giving climate. One writer of the time noted:

> The purity of the air of Los Angeles is remarkable . . . The air . . . gives to the individual a stimulus and vital force which only an atmosphere so pure can ever communicate.

Most came in search of inexpensive land. The railroad received over 10 million acres of land from the federal government as a construction reward—much of it in southern California. Wanting to "cash out" (sell the land), Southern Pacific began flooding the country with sales propaganda. Special trains were prepared for land seekers, and as a final inducement, the price of the ticket was applicable to the cost of the land. If an immigrant bought railroad land in California, the trip was free. By the 1880s, 350,000 people had come to the state—half to southern California.

The land boom collapsed suddenly in the spring of 1888. Inflated prices, speculation, and the beginning of a national depression ended southern California's first real estate binge.

Commenting on the crash, a fictional character in a contemporary novel, *Millionaires of a Day* said:

> I had a half million dollars wiped out in the crash and what's worse, $500 of it was cash.

The land boom of the 1880s was significant to the development of southern California. Until then, most migration had been to the northern part of the state—first for gold, then to the San Francisco Bay and Sacramento areas for jobs and land. Few people went to southern California then. Los Angeles was considered to be the last frontier, a tough cow town where in the mid-1850s the murder rate reached one a day, an ominous figure, since the county had a total population of only 5,000! But, landbooms of the 1870s and the 1880s brought thousands of people to the southern part of the state. By the end of the 1880s, southern California was growing at a rate much faster than northern California and continued to do so until the 1970s. But between 1970 and 1985 the pattern has been reversed, with the fifty-one northern California counties growing by 35 percent compared to 26 percent for the seven southern California counties.

Black Gold

Between 1900 and 1940, a series of massive oil discoveries generated further southern California land speculation and population growth. In the late 1920s, offshore drilling and production began at Summerland near Santa Barbara. Until recently California's oil production has been greater than state needs, and millions of barrels were exported each year, mostly to other states. Since 1968, however, production has declined while demand has increased. As a result, California now imports oil.

The Military-Defense Industry Boom

World War II had a great impact on California's population and economic growth. Before the war, the military establishment was not a significant part of the population (less than 1 percent). But at the height of the war, 11 percent were in uniform. Of greater importance, California became a major center for military bases, war production, and shipping.

Almost 2 million people came to California during the war: Some half million were drawn by work opportunities in the war plants; others came to take new jobs created by a booming economy; and finally, many came as members of the armed forces brought in for training. In 1940, before the war, unemployment had been over 12 percent, but by 1944 it was less than 1 percent.

Following the war (1945–47), almost 700,000 servicemen were discharged in California. Remembering the cold, rain, and snow of their Middle West and eastern homes, 300,000 stayed in the Golden State. Thousands who went home soon returned.

THE PEOPLE

Throughout the history of California, the poor and the foreign-born have come seeking their fortunes, sometimes recruited, sometimes escaping grinding poverty or fleeing discrimination. Chinese, Filipinos, Japanese, Dust Bowl migrants, blacks, Mexicans (legal and illegal), and most recently Southeast Asians are prime examples. Indeed, as of September 1984, some 265,000 Southeast Asian refugees had settled in California, 36 percent of the 728,000 total in the United States. According to U.S. Immigration and Naturalization data, about 25 percent of all foreign immigrants to the United States come to California.

Filipinos

Filipinos constitute the single largest Asian group in California—some 489,000 in 1985. Almost 90 percent live in the state's urban areas. The Philippines rank second only to Mexico as a source of foreign immigration into California. Filipinos tend to occupy low-status jobs and earn less than do most other ethnic groups.

Chinese

During the Gold Rush, some 25,000 Chinese came to California. After the rush, many returned to China, but some stayed. Another 20,000–25,000 were brought to California in the 1860s to work on railroad construction gangs. By 1870, perhaps as many as 150,000 Chinese had arrived under labor contracts that came close to being a debt-bondage system. The large number of Chinese (about 18 percent of the state's population at that time) caused much concern to unemployed whites. Due to brutal harassment and lack of opportunity, many

Chinese returned to their native land. The Chinese Exclusion Act of 1881 stopped further immigration. By 1920, there were only 29,000 Chinese in the state. Since then, their numbers have grown steadily to about 395,000 in 1985.

Japanese

Between 1900 and 1920 the number of Japanese increased from 10,000 to 72,000. But even these relatively few immigrants reminded Californians of the earlier "Yellow Peril," and pressures for their exclusion soon began. What particularly irritated many white Californians was the Japanese success in agriculture. While constituting only 2 percent of the population, they controlled more than 11 percent of the state's agricultural land in 1920. In 1924, Congress excluded further Japanese immigration.

After the bombing of Pearl Harbor in 1941, many Californians were more than willing to believe that all Japanese were potential traitors. In 1942, in one of the state's most shameful episodes, all Japanese (citizens and aliens) were rounded up and forced into relocation centers. They were, to all intents and purposes, concentration camps. Released at the end of the war, the Japanese rebuilt their shattered lives and by 1985 numbered about 289,000. Today, the average Japanese in California has a high educational level and an income higher than the state's average.

Vietnamese

The Vietnamese are the most recent group of immigrants who have come to California seeking a new start. There were essentially no Vietnamese in the state in 1970—in 1985 there were 222,000. Their average education is close to the state average, but their annual incomes are among the lowest in the state.

Other Asians

In addition to the aforementioned, there are also sizable ethnic enclaves of Cambodians, Laotions, Koreans, and Pacific Islanders residing in the state.

Mexicans

No one knows for sure how many people of Mexican origin live in California. In 1980, the U.S. Census counted 4.5 million people with Spanish surnames. Of these, 3.6 million were from Mexico (with others from Puerto Rico, Cuba, other Latin American nations, and the Phil-

2-4 *Japanese-American children waiting to be sent to an Owens Valley relocation center.*

Library of Congress; photograph by Russell Lee

ippines). In addition, there are many others who entered the nation illegally. In 1984 the U.S. Immigration and Naturalization Service seized 476,000 illegal immigrants on or near the U.S.-Mexico border. By 1985 about 5 million people of Mexican origin were living in California of whom perhaps some 1.2 to 1.5 million were immigrants. Some 750,000 of these immigrants were documented aliens with the balance being in the state illegally. While some Mexican immigrants work on California farms, many more are employed in manufacturing and personal services.

Mexican-Americans constitute the largest single minority in California—over 19 percent of the state's population. The first wave of Mexican immigrants came to California (and other southwestern states) as a result of the Mexican Revolution in 1910. Exclusion of Japanese and Chinese migrants created a demand for cheap farm labor which was filled by the Mexicans in the 1920s. By 1930, there were probably about 200,000 Mexicans in California, many of them immigrants.

World War II created a tremendous need for farm labor again, and more Mexicans came to California—some of them illegally. These workers were subject to great abuse. This situation led to an agreement

2-5 *Illegal aliens camping out in orange grove.*

Photo courtesy United Press International

in 1951 between the Mexican and U.S. governments to regulate migration and provide some protection to the Mexican workers. Under this agreement, hundreds of thousands of *braceros* worked in California's farm fields. But under pressure from organized labor, the bracero agreement was terminated in 1964.

According to the 1980 census, the typical Hispanic is younger and has less formal education than the average. Only 25 percent have finished high school and less than 10 percent have gone on to some form of college. Hispanics who do not use the English language very well often suffer economic and/or social isolation. While many Hispanics are better off economically than blacks, those who are illegal immigrants may be deported. In times of economic hardship, Hispanics may be the most vulnerable of the disadvantaged. The new Simpson Immigration Reform bill passed by Congress in 1986 providing for strict sanctions against employers who hire illegals but also amnesty and the right to apply for citizenship for illegals residing in the U.S. prior to 1982 may improve the situation.

During the 1970s, a small but growing Hispanic elite began to emerge—teachers, professors, doctors, and lawyers—many of whom have become politically active.

2-6 *Japanese autos and kosher burritos: California's cosmopolitan culture mix can be found in many of its urban areas.*

Photo courtesy of Carl Myers

Dust Bowl Victims

Oklahoma, Arkansas, and other plains states were swept by drought in the 1930s. While total migration to California dropped to an all-time low as a result of the Depression, the "Okies" and "Arkies" came looking for jobs that didn't exist and helped swell the migration numbers again. Many of them went to the Central Valley looking for farm work.

Blacks

World War II's booming economy lured millions of blacks away from their southern homes. About 300,000 came to California during the 1940s—an increase of 272 percent! While the black portion of the state's population climbed steadily in the 1950s–1960s, it has leveled off in the 1970s–1980s.

Today, blacks comprise the second largest minority in California, approximately 8 percent of the state's population. Two out of three live in the central cities—many of them in ghettos—like Watts and Hunter's Point. On average, blacks earn 30 percent less than whites. About one out of seven blacks has had some college, but social, political, and economic equality has not yet been achieved.

On the other hand, a black elite has emerged in the last thirty years—a development accelerated by the 1960s civil rights movement. In the 1970s and 80s, black candidates have won important political offices at both the state and local level.

Future Population Patterns

California has been and will continue to be a haven for ethnic minorities. Scattered over the state are some thirty-three foreign language newspapers. In addition, a number of California radio and television stations broadcast in foreign languages, and some motion picture theaters specialize in foreign language films. To accommodate the Latino population, many counties print ballots in Spanish as well as English, and the State Department of Motor Vehicles publishes driver instruction booklets in various languages.

By the year 2000, population experts predict that the white-Anglo portion of the population which is now 57 percent will have shrunk to under 50 percent. As some ethnic minority leaders have proclaimed, California in the next century will be the first mainland third-world state. As the white population declines proportionately and the black percentage stabilizes over the next several decades, explosive growth will come within the Asian and Latino communities. Much of this growth will be generated by immigration into the state. Los Angeles has become the "Ellis Island of the Nineteenth Century"—approximately one out of six foreign-born people in 1985 became United States citizens in this city. According to U.S. Census Bureau figures, from 1980 to 1986 California counties (Los Angeles, San Diego, Orange, San Bernardino, Riverside, and Sacramento) made the nation's top fifteen for population increases, but in percentage the fastest growing counties were in rural northern California (Nevada, Calaveras, and Lake).

The population growth within the ethnic minority communities helped create part of the stimulus for the English Only language initiative (Proposition 63) of November 1986 approved by nearly 75 percent of voters. Exactly how this initiative will be implemented is not clear at the moment. What is obvious is that some Californians feel threatened by the burgeoning minority population and believe that the best way for these groups to become acculturated is by weaning them away from their native tongues.

POLITICS OF THE PEOPLE

To better understand the present, it is necessary to understand the past. Although there are many fascinating chapters in California's political history, we will concentrate on only a few of the most significant features or individuals that have had a lasting impact on California politics.

California political history can be divided, roughly, into seven time segments:

1.	Democratic dominance	1850–61
2.	Civil War politics	1862–67
3.	Two-party competition	1868–97
4.	Republican dominance	1898–1957
5.	Two-party competition	1958–73
6.	Democratic dominance	1974–1982
7.	Two-party competition	1983–?

Obviously, state's politics are not fixed; over time one party or the other dominates—with some periods of balanced competition. Clearly, California politics are in constant change.

The first two historical periods had little lasting impact on contemporary politics. However, between 1868 and 1897 three features are worth noting: (1) emerging power of the railroad; (2) the Workingman's party of the 1870s; and (3) the Populist movement of the 1890s. They are significant today because they illustrate the continuing struggle for reform; the uncertain results of reform; and the fundamental relationship between politics and economics.

NINETEENTH-CENTURY FEATURES: 1868–1897

The Railroad Era

California's railroad magnates, Leland Stanford, Charles Crocker, Mark Hopkins, and Collis Huntington—the "Big Four," as they were known—dominated California's economy and politics from the 1880s into the 20th century. Controlling transportation into and out of the state, as well as much of it within the state, the owners of the Southern Pacific Railroad used that economic power to gain political control of California. Their greed and corrupt politics gave rise to several protest movements—the Workingman's party, Populism, and the Progressive movement.

Each of the Big Four became a major economic power in the state. Today, their names are institutionalized in a major university, a bank chain, a leading art gallery, and hotels. Moreover, Southern Pacific is still one of the largest private landholders in California.

Workingman's Party

Led by Denis Kearney, the Workingman's party was a response to major social and economic forces in California: high unemployment brought about by economic recession in the late 1870s, and rapid growth of cheap Chinese labor in the state. White animosity toward the "Yellow Peril" grew steadily in California as thousands of Chinese were brought in to work on the railroad. After completion of the railroad (1869), Chinese immigrants looked for other kinds of work, and unemployed white workers resented the new job competition. The Workingman's party strongly opposed the import and use of Chinese labor.

Kearneyism (as it was also known) came to stand for state regulation of railroads, utilities, and banks; a fair tax system; an eight-hour work day; compulsory education; and the direct election of United States senators. (Some of these proposals were later adopted at the California Constitutional convention of 1878–79.)

But as California's economy improved and various portions of the Workingman's program came to be adopted by both Democrats and Republicans, the Workingman's party soon disappeared.

Populists

This late nineteenth-century minor party was a mixture of agrarian reformers, nonpartisans, and socialists. While never achieving significant political power, Populists helped alert the public to many needed reforms. In several instances, they provided the balance of power between Democrats and Republicans. Populists were staunch advocates of women's suffrage; railroad regulation; monetary reform ("free silver"); municipal ownership of utilities; the secret ballot; the initiative, referendum, and recall; direct primaries; income tax; and unemployment relief—all of which are accepted policy today.

Kearneyism and Populism were both clear manifestations of citizen discontent with the existing economic and political system. While neither movement gained sufficient strength to implement its programs fully, each did help pave the way for later successful reform.

TWENTIETH-CENTURY FEATURES

Republican Dominance: 1898–1958

In 1898, California Republicans won control of both houses of the legislature and the governor's office. For the next sixty years, Republicans effectively controlled California government. This long period of Republican control finally came to an end with (1) fundamental changes in the California primary election laws, (2) a bitter internal fight in the Republican party, and (3) an increase in the loyal Democratic vote.

Progressives.   As California government increasingly came under control of the Republican party in the early 1900s, so, too, did the Republican and Democratic parties come under control of the Southern Pacific Railroad and its corporate allies. According to Fremont Older, a leading newspaper reporter of the time, the entire state was controlled by the Southern Pacific (Older, 1926).

> In those days there was only one kind of politics and that was corrupt politics. It didn't matter whether a man was a Republican or a Democrat. The Southern Pacific Railroad controlled both parties, and he either had to stay out of the game altogether or play it with the railroad.

Older's statement should be taken seriously, since his newspaper was one of those on the railroad's payroll!

In addition to Southern Pacific machinations, another corrosive political force emerged in the state during this period—big city bosses and party machines. The most notorious California political "boss," Abe Ruef of San Francisco, was eventually convicted of bribery. But his partners in corruption—labor leaders and corporate executives of Pacific Gas & Electric, Pacific States Telephone & Telegraph, and other major California companies—were never convicted.

The Ruef bribery trial received maximum publicity when the prosecuting attorney was brazenly shot by a witness *in the courtroom.* More publicity developed when the witness was later found dead under mysterious circumstances in his own jail cell. Hiram Johnson, an obscure attorney at that time, accepted the job as a replacement prosecutor and helped secure Ruef's conviction.

Appalled by the railroad's activity, corruption in state and local politics, and the need for social and economic betterment, a small group of liberal Republicans began a statewide campaign to eliminate Southern Pacific control and implement reforms. Some of the state's newspapers actively supported the Progressives. But, there were notable major exceptions, such as the *Los Angeles Times, Oakland Tribune, and San Francisco Chronicle.*

Most Progressives expected a long uphill fight against the railroad and its entrenched allies—the regular Republicans. But the railroad Republicans lost a key vote in the 1909 legislature, and a partial primary nomination system was established. And in the spring of 1910, the railroad made a major tactical blunder by not making an early selection of *its Republican candidate for governor.* While the railroad hesitated, four "regular" Republicans announced their candidacy. When the rail-

2-7 *Hiram Johnson on the campaign trail. No TV or radio in 1910; the candidate appeared in person.*

Photo courtesy California State Library

road decided to support one of those four, the other three refused to bow out of the race.

In contrast, Progressives focused their support on one candidate—the fifth Republican—Hiram Johnson. Building on his Reuf trial publicity and growing voter discontent with the railroad and its stooges, Johnson, a fire-breathing "give-'em-hell" candidate, toured the state with his battle cry, "Kick the Southern Pacific machine out of California politics." Describing Harrison Gray Otis, owner of the *Los Angeles Times,* Johnson said (Delmatier, et al., 1970:168):

> He sits in senile dementia, with gangrened heart and rotting brain, grimacing at every reform and chattering in impotent rage against decency and morality, while he is going down to his grave in snarling infamy . . .

The four regular Republicans split 113,000 votes between themselves, while Johnson won with 102,000. A few months later he defeated the Democratic candidate in the general election. Equally important, Progressive candidates won control of both the state assembly and state senate. This gave them the power to enact the most comprehensive and far-reaching political reforms in California history.

Though Progressives dominated the state for only a few years, their legacy has been enormous. Among their social reforms were:

1. Prohibiting child labor.
2. Establishing workmen's compensation.
3. Expanding and strengthening of the state railroad commission.
4. Providing free school texts.
5. Extending the eight-hour work day.
6. Expanding conservation programs.

These social-economic programs clearly distinguished Progressive Republicans from old-line "regular" Republicans.

More important were the Progressive political reforms, since they involved significant changes in the processes of government. These included:

1. Direct democracy legislation—the initiative and referendum.
2. Recall.
3. Direct primary system and a presidential preference primary.
4. Nonpartisan local elections.
5. Restructured political party organizations.
6. Extended civil service.
7. Cross-filing.

Of these reforms, only cross-filing has been eliminated. The other reforms continue to exert a substantial influence on California politics.

Progressive leaders were mainly middle-class professionals who had a profound distrust of partisan government, powerful corporations, and labor unions. (Mowry, 1951:87–89). In their moralist/individualist fervor, they attacked both private and public corruption.

For a short time, Progressive reforms sharply reduced corruption and special interest poweer in the state. But, in 1916, Hiram Johnson was elected to the U.S. Senate. His departure from state government left Progressives without a leader. By 1921, conservative Republicans were back in power. By the late 1920s, special interests were as active as ever, and by the 1930s and 40s, they had reached new heights of power (see Chapter 5). On the other hand, California, for the most part, has continued in the Progressive tradition of honest government. In contrast to many eastern states, it has relatively honest and open government.

Democrats Denied.   Through the 1920s, Democrats remained the minority party. They had less than 30 percent of the two-party registration and less than 10 percent of the state's legislative seats. The major statewide offices were held by Republicans.

The cataclysmic depression era brought massive economic, social, and political change to the nation and to California. Yet politically, the 1930s continued to be a period of frustration for state Democrats who achieved much less than they hoped for. Beginning in the mid 1930s, California politics began to exhibit the bizarre patterns that have frequently confused and amazed observers. From 1936 through 1956, California appeared to be a "Democratic" state, but it voted "Republican" more often than not. This apparent contradiction was rooted in several significant factors:

1. Democratic voters' weak party identification.
2. Strong ideological divisions within the Democratic party.
3. Weak party organizations.
4. Cross-filing.
5. The state's Republican newspapers.

All of these factors, working together, denied victory to state Democrats for some twenty years and in the rest of the nation helped give rise to California's reputation for "weird" and unfathomable politics.

California's voters—particularly Democratic voters—became famous, or infamous, for their willingness to cross party lines. Thus, while California supported Democratic presidential candidates in four out of six elections between 1936 and 1956, it elected only one Democratic governor (Culbert Olson, 1938) in five elections, and two Democratic U.S. senators in eight elections. Clearly, in elections for major state offices, Republicans had the edge in California between 1936 and 1956. Since a sizable majority of the state voters were registered Democrats, it is equally clear that substantial numbers of them crossed party lines and supported Republican candidates for statewide offices. (Illustration 2–8 charts the growth of Democratic registration from minority to majority status.)

Elections for the state legislature and the U.S. House of Representatives further illuminate the point. From 1932 through 1944 Democrats won a majority of California's congressional seats. But in that same period (seven elections), they won a majority of state assembly seats in only three elections (1936, 38, and 40) and never gained a majority in the state senate. Thus, while the turbulent 1930s and early 40s improved Democratic registration in California, Republicans were able to regain legislative power by 1942 and hold it until 1958.

Democratic voters were willing to desert their party for several basic reasons. First, some voters were recent arrivals to California with no firm attachment to their new state or to the Democratic party, which frequently was different than their party "back home." Second, no precinct workers came to mobilize them as they had in states such

2-8 *Democratic Party Strength, 1930–86*

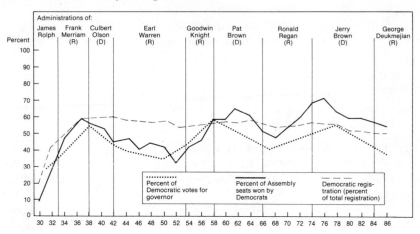

Source: California Secretary of State, *Statement of Vote,* 1930–86.

as New York, New Jersey, or Pennsylvania (see Chapter 6). In addition, the Democratic party was badly divided along ideological, policy, and personality lines. The Depression gave rise to a host of offbeat reform organizations that cut away at potential support for the Democratic party.

Frequently, conservative Democrats simply voted Republican as a matter of political philosophy. The GOP helped by setting up campaign committees of "Democrats for _____." Thus, in the 1940s and 50s there were: Democrats for Warren, Democrats for Eisenhower, and Democrats for Nixon.

Cross-filing further compounded the problems of weak party organization and low levels of party loyalty. Cross-filing allowed candidates from one party to seek the nomination of another party in the primary; voting for the best person, not the party was the progressive view. Typically, Republicans would file in the Democratic party primary, and Democrats would file in the Republican party primary. Voters, ignorant of the listed candidates' party affiliation, assumed that all candidates on their primary ballot were members of their own party.

Many incumbents began winning both major party nominations. By the mid-1940s and early 1950s, 70 to 90 percent of the state legislative elections were essentially decided in the primary. (Winning both major party nominations in the primary meant automatic victory in the general election.) The tactical advantage of cross-filing went to Republicans since they were the minority party—with about 40 percent of the registered voters. Cross-filing let GOP incumbents run for the Democratic party nomination in the primary. The GOP incumbent's name familiarity through favorable press coverage was a substantial advantage over the usually unknown Democratic candidates.

Earl Warren, the most popular Republican governor in California's history, understood the tactical advantage of being nonpartisan. In 1942 he said:

> I believe in the party system and have been identified with the Republican party in matters of party concern, but I have never found that the broad questions of national party policy have application to the problems of state and local government in California.

Four years later he successfully cross-filed—winning the Democratic gubernatorial nomination. Cross-filing was modified by initiative in 1952 and abolished in 1959 by a Democratic legislature and Democratic governor.

Another factor contributing to Democratic failure was the essentially one-party press in the state. Before television became a major source of news, newspapers played a dominant role in California politics. Most of the state's press was Republican. Two of the state's most powerful newspapers—the *Los Angeles Times* and *Oakland Tribune*—were part of the GOP party establishment. Most newspapers not only endorsed Republican candidates, but consistently gave them more favorable news coverage. Frequently the press would either ignore Democratic party candidates or report only unfavorable news about them.

By the mid-1950s, though there were clear signs of a Democratic party rebirth. The effects of cross-filing had been sharply curtailed in the 1954 and 56 elections (the result of a 1952 initiative that required primary election candidates to be identified by party affiliation). Democrats had organized a sometimes effective volunteer group—the California Democratic Council (CDC)—in 1953. Newspapers, sensitive to charges of partisanship, often under new "professional" management, and forced to compete with television, began to present more balanced news coverage.

A quiet, though intense, conflict over control of the Republican party began when Governor Warren resigned in 1953 to become Chief Justice of the U.S. Supreme Court. It erupted into a bruising fight over the governorship in 1958 when U.S. Senator William Knowland sought the office to further his presidential ambitions. Democrats, taking advantage of the split in GOP ranks, won both the governor's office and control of the legislature, spelling an end to the era of Republican dominance.

During this period issues were largely economic—from FDR's New Deal in the Depression through Earl Warren's legacy of construction and new or expanded state programs. California embraced President Roosevelt's New Deal but rejected a whole host of "home-grown" panaceas during the economic dark days of the 1930s. World War II swept aside all issues except victory over the Axis in the early 1940s and brought an economic boom to California through the 1940s and 50s.

Earl Warren presided over most of that economic and population explosion. In ten years (1943–53), the state budget more than tripled; education expenditures increased fivefold; highway construction, tenfold. The Warren administration also increased old age pensions, widened unemployment insurance, provided the beginnings of the state's modern mental health program, and established a new system of higher education. In many ways, Warren's stand on issues and programs added to Democratic frustrations. He promoted many of their policies, and they were hard pressed to criticize him.

Two-Party Competition: 1958–1973

The 1958 elections terminated sixty years of Republican rule in California and were the beginning of a relatively brief period of brisk two-party competition (1958–73). It also ushered in a series of bitter internal GOP party battles between moderates and conservatives, which conservatives finally won. The Republican party's share of registered voters began to decline in this period, dropping to an all-time low by the mid-1970s.

Conservative Republicans, led by Assemblyman Joe Shell, openly challenged Richard Nixon for the GOP gubernatorial nomination in 1962 and won a third of the primary vote. Conservatives, in 1962, then began a concerted drive to capture the GOP. In two years, conservatives gained control of two major Republican volunteer (workers) groups and established a third—United Republicans of California (UROC). In 1964 conservatives took control of the state Republican party when U.S. Senator Barry Goldwater (Arizona) defeated moderate New York Governor Nelson Rockefeller for the GOP presidential nomination.

In 1964, overwhelming approval for Proposition 14, which repealed California's Fair Housing Law banning racial discrimination in the sale or rental of all publicly assisted housing as well as most privately financed apartments in the state revealed California voters' conservative, antigovernment, or racist attitudes. Support for repeal was statewide, with Democrats voting yes six to four and Republicans in favor by four to one. (Later, the state supreme court struck down the initiative as a clear violation of basic federal constitutional rights).

Enter Ronald Reagan—Stage Right.   Ronald Reagan got his first taste of big-time politics in the 1964 Goldwater campaign as a prominent spokesman for both the campaign and conservative causes. Toward the end of the 1964 campaign, Reagan gave his now famous speech, "A Time for Choosing," which set the themes for his political career as governor and president:

> Government has laid its hand on health, housing, farming, industry, commerce, education, and to an ever increasing degree interferes with the people's right to know.

Reagan's sincerity, his apparent knowledge of the issues, his Hollywood star persona, and his ability to project an image of reasonable indignation were attractive to voters. He also impressed state GOP leaders who were looking for a candidate who could defeat incumbent Democratic Governor Edmund G. "Pat" Brown in 1966.

Democrats won in 1958, 60, 62, and 64 over a badly divided GOP. But by 1966, Republicans had largely healed their split. Conservatives were in firm control of their party and were anxious to halt the Democrats' economic and social policies. Among the most contentious issues were fair housing and employment policy, water project construction, minimum wage provisions, and tax increases. Republican voter registration, however, was only about 40 percent of the total, and the GOP needed an attractive candidate who could appeal to conservative Democrats.

Ronald Reagan was that kind of a candidate. Though he had never run for public office, his "amateur" status was turned into a political asset. Reagan ran as a citizen-candidate against the professional politicians in Sacramento.

Pat Brown, on the other hand, was a relatively colorless politician. While he had governed in the competent Earl Warren tradition, it was not enough in an era of profound social and economic change. The Vietnam War badly divided the Democratic party. The emerging civil rights movement—punctuated by race riots in Watts and Hunter's Point in 1965—combined with continuously growing state budgets, added taxes, and a whole host of other controversial issues to make Brown vulnerable in 1966. Liberal Democrats reluctantly endorsed him only after a bitter floor fight in the California Democratic Council. Hurt by attacks from both the left and right, Brown was no match for Ronald Reagan.

Leading a united party against the badly divided Democrats, Reagan defeated Brown by almost 1 million votes out of 6½ million cast, thus beginning a political career that would take him to the White House in 1980 and 1984.

Since 1968, most GOP candidates for major office in California have been conservative—George Murphy, S. I. Hayakawa, Paul Gann, Ed Reineke, Mike Curb, and George Deukmejian. The few moderate Republicans—Houston Flournoy, Ken Maddy, Pete Wilson and Ed Zschav—have felt compelled to woo party conservatives (see Chapter 3).

Democrats, on the other hand, began to divide over the Vietnam War—which exacerbated basic ideological divisions within the party. In particular, the 1968 presidential elections focused on the war—President Johnson's decision not to seek reelection, the nomination contest between Vice President Humphrey and U.S. Senators Robert Kennedy and Eugene McCarthy, the murder of Senator Kennedy on primary election night in California, and riots at the Democratic national convention helped pave the road to victory for Richard Nixon and further weakened the Democratic party in California.

Reagan's administration (1967–74) covered the Vietnam War era, Watergate, and growing concerns over energy, taxes, civil rights, and the apparent failure of government to solve a whole host of domestic economic problems.

Coming into office pledged to "cut, trim, and squeeze" the state budget, Reagan ironically presided over the largest tax increase in the state's history. Some of this increase was mandated by the state supreme court in *Serrano* v. *Priest* to equalize public school funding. Additional tax revenues were also required to meet the state's Medi-Cal and welfare programs (see Chapter 10), as well as to meet the deficit inherited from outgoing Governor Pat Brown. Equally important, Reagan was faced with a Democratic legislature (see Figure 2–8) and had to meet his opponents halfway on some issues. For example, he and Democratic assembly Speaker Bob Moretti hammered out a welfare reform package that became a model for many other states in later years.

Reagan was the state's central political figure while he was governor, yet his personal popularity did not always transfer to other GOP candidates, nor was he able to rebuild Republican party strength in California. Republicans did hold most of the state's minor executive offices between 1967 and 74 (see Illustration 2–9) but only controlled the assembly for two years (1969–70) and never controlled the state senate during the period.

Democratic Dominance: 1974–1982

An emerging pattern of Democratic victories occurred in the early 1970s. When Reagan left office in 1974, he left with a substantial reservoir of public goodwill and support in the state and a strong positive image across the nation. But his personal popularity did not transfer to his party.

Watergate engulfed and destroyed President Richard Nixon and devastated the GOP in 1974. Republicans lost five assembly seats in 1974 (after losing seven in 1972). GOP party registration dropped to an historic low in 1978—34 percent—contributing to further losses of legislative seats. But Watergate did more than damage the GOP.

2-9

Campaign Committee for Proposition 9

Proposition 9, the Political Reform Act initiative of 1974, was placed on the ballot in response to growing public concern over lobbying abuse and campaign contributions, a concern heightened by the Watergate scandals.

Jerry Brown (son of former governor Pat Brown) had been first elected to the minor statewide office of secretary of state in 1970. By vigorously using that office's powers, he built a reputation for political reform, which gave him a decided advantage in the 1974 gubernatorial elections. Increased public concern about political corruption combined with Brown's close ties to Proposition 9, the Political Reform Initiative, on the June 1974 ballot and his name identification gave him an edge over eighteen other candidates seeking the Democratic gubernatorial nomination.

President Nixon's protracted struggle to extricate himself from the Watergate break-in and cover-up failed. Faced with the clear probability of impeachment, he resigned in early August, shattering GOP election hopes for 1974.

Jerry Brown took office in January 1975, an unknown quantity in a time of change. His eight years as governor spanned the balance of the decade as he faced a host of new and vital issues in California in an often unconventional way.

In the 1970s, the state's growing nonwhite population began to politically assert itself. Wilson Riles, the first black elected to statewide office, became state superintendent of public instruction in 1970. He was joined in Sacramento in 1974 by Mervin Dymally, the state's first black lt. governor and March Fong Eu, the first Asian elected to statewide office (secretary of state). Brown's appointments also reflected the growing political strength of women and minorities. While Jerry Brown was governor, more blacks, Hispanics, and women were appointed to major offices than in any previous administration.

The cost of housing emerged as a major issue in the mid-1970s. Later, rapidly inflated housing costs helped fuel the property tax revolt of 1978 and, subsequently, local rent control laws.

While Governor Brown did little about these problems, he and the legislature established the state's Agricultural Labor Relations Board—a major victory for Cesar Chavez's United Farm Workers. Brown also led the fight against the "freeway" establishment—an open challenge to California's long love affair with the automobile and massive freeway construction. Energy policy also became a major concern: rising oil prices, OPEC embargos, the risks associated with nuclear energy (Proposition 15, 1976), and air pollution led to establishment of an Energy Resources Conservation and Development Commission in 1975 (see Chapter 9). The governor also took a hard-line stance on crime asking for substantial prison construction funds. A major change in prison sentencing policy led to a rapid growth in prison costs and population (see Chapter 11).

The 1978 election was a relatively easy contest for Governor Brown against the GOP's bland nominee, Attorney General Evelle Younger. But while Brown was winning reelection in November, Democrats lost seven Assembly seats—restoring Republican strength in the lower house to pre-Watergate levels.

The big story of 1978 was Howard Jarvis's Proposition 13 property tax revolt and the massive voter turnout in June to approve his initiative measure overwhelmingly. The results were profound; in essence, Proposition 13 "rolled back" property tax levels and put a ceiling on them, cutting the average homeowners property tax by about half! Proposition 13 was opposed by many of the state political and economic leaders who saw in it the destruction of local government's tax base, elimination of needed local government services, and a threat to local government "home rule." The voters saw Proposition 13 as needed relief from taxes and a chance to express their feelings about government (see Chapters 10 and 12).

The 1978 elections raised the race issue again with the defeat of two blacks on the statewide ballot—incumbent Lt. Governor Mervyn Dymally by Mike Curb and Yvonne Burke for attorney general by George Deukmejian.

At the same time, election of eight new Republican assemblymembers commited to the spirit of Proposition 13 convinced legislators of the electorate's desire for a reduction in government spending. In this, they found an ally in Governor Brown, whose admonition to the voters to "lower their expectations" was returned by the voters telling California government officials to reduce their goals!

As a general rule, programs that cost money were not received favorably in Sacramento after 1978. Reinforcing the 1978 Proposition 13 message was a special election ballot measure, Proposition 4, limiting the growth of state and local government budgets to amounts required by population increases and inflation. Proposition 4 (the "Gann measure") had no immediate effects since restricted tax revenues fell far short of the expenditures allowed due to high inflation rates and population growth. However, by 1986 the Gann budget ceiling presented California state government with some very real difficulties (see Chapter 10).

The 1980 elections in California were anticlimactic. Yet, they pointed toward a growing conservative vote and a significant change in government's policy agenda. Governor Brown, whose presidential hopes were dashed after losing in Wisconsin on April 1, abandoned the race. In November, President Jimmy Carter was overwhelmingly defeated, receiving only 36 percent of the vote. In a larger sense, Reagan's victory appears to have been personal—a popular governor (1967–72) running against an unpopular incumbent president.

The foundations of a GOP resurgence in California in the 1980s can be seen in the Republicans' net gain of four congressional seats and two assembly seats. They had previously picked up seven assembly and two congressional seats in 1978 and three state senate seats in 1979 special elections. .

The 1970s had been a period of weak Republican strength in California (see Table 3–3, p. 64). According to a Field survey, the proportion of citizens who said they were "conservative" was about 42 percent in the early 70s but increased to 52 percent by 1980. At the same time, Californians who identified themselves as "liberals" grew from 26 percent to 34 percent. Along with becoming more conservative, California also became more polarized in its political philosophy in the late 1970s and early 80s.

Environmental issues—nuclear power, Lake Tahoe, air pollution, and coastal conservation—continued to plague the state. Water, always a divisive topic, became a major issue again when opponents of the Peripheral Canal (a political "strange bedfellow" coalition of Central Valley farmers and northern California environmentalists) defeated

2-10 *Energy from the wind. Whirling windmills, a high tech nonpolluting energy source to serve the needs of California's millions.*

canal legislation by referendum (Proposition 9) in June 1982. The rejected S.B. 90 would have built a canal along the eastern and southern edge of the Central Valley's delta region to deliver more northern water to southern California. Environmentalists lost two battles in November 1982 when a water conservation measure (Proposition 13) was defeated (growers opposed it) and a bottle disposal measure (Proposition 11) was also defeated.

Two-Party Competition: 1983–?

Governor George Deukmejian's narrow 1982 victory over Los Angeles Mayor Tom Bradley was no mandate. He came to the state capitol a lonely Republican surrounded by Democrats in both the legislature and other executive offices. Given the many powers of his office (see Chapter 8), Deukmejian won his budget fights and has clearly dominated California government in the 1980s.

In their gubernatorial rematch in 1986, George Deukmejian easily beat Mayor Tom Bradley by a nearly two to one margin. Bradley attacked Deukmejian on a number of fronts, but only on the toxics issue did the incumbent governor seem vulnerable, and this issue was not enough. Democrats swept to victories in the other executive offices and retained control (though reduced from 1984) in both legislative houses. The election proved a mixed bag: Democrats and environmentalists were victorious with the toxics initiative, and Democrats and Republicans beat back an attempt by fanatic Lyndon La Rouche to exploit the AIDS scare in his Proposition 64. The deceased Howard Jarvis won his last initiative battle with Proposition 62, a follow-up to Proposition 13; but his direct democracy partner, Paul Gann, lost with Proposition 61, an attempt to limit elective officeholders' and public employees' salaries and benefits. And, finally conservatives could take heart that Proposition 63, the English as the official language initiative, won by a massive landslide (nearly three to one). But, some critics were convinced that this initiative won easily because of its less than subtle racist tinge—a continuing facet of the California political milieu.

SUMMARY

California's spectacular population and economic growth, and the very diversity of that population and economy, have produced consistently changing social and political patterns. In the first three decades of this century, politics were Republican. The struggles over policy and power took place within the GOP. The issues at stake concerned the white middle class and involved economic or governmental reform.

But as the population and economy changed during the Depression, World War II, and the great postwar economic boom, the peoples' needs and issues changed, too. In 1958, Democrats gained control in California, and after fourteen years of two-party competition, they became the dominant party. Blue-collar, labor, racial minority, and civil liberties issues moved to the top of the policy agenda.

However, new needs and new issues are emerging in the 80s. The old labels of *liberal* and *conservative* no longer seem to apply, and both political parties are looking for new solutions to the old as well as new issues.

Whatever happens, nothing is immutable in California politics—and change will remain a central feature of Golden State politics.

3

Elections in California: Voters, Candidates, and Campaigns

Elections are a central feature of all democratic governments. If the election process enables citizens to express their choice of meaningful alternatives, government is legitimate. People will believe in its fairness and will support it.

The election process, however, is not neutral. How elections are organized, who can run, who can vote, and the many factors that influence the results are important. Every practice, technique, or law helps some and places a burden on others. Generally speaking, the process tends to support the status quo—the way things are.

Over the years, substantial changes have been made in California's election laws and processes that have profoundly affected the system.

WHO MAY VOTE

Eligibility

To be *eligible* to vote in California, one must be eighteen years old by the time of the election, a citizen, and a resident of the district at least thirty days prior to the election (except new residents in presidential elections). There has been a steady expansion of those eligible to vote. Women, racial minorities, eighteen- to twenty-year-olds, ex-felons, and, as of 1976, even some "mental incompetents" are now eligible to vote in California.

Registration

Each county has a registrar of voters (smaller counties use the county clerk) who maintains a county list of registered voters. Before the state primary and general elections, the registrar of voters will assign deputies to supermarkets, shopping centers, churches, university and college campuses, sports events, and other places where large numbers of people may gather. Most political parties and many civic groups also conduct registration drives. One can even register by postcard. Some fast food restaurants provide registration postcards. It is easy to register in California.

Only one known substantial registration fraud has occurred in contemporary California history. In the 1975 San Francisco municipal elections, there were over 11,000 registered voters who did not actually live in San Francisco. Typically, these illegal voters were city employees who had registered to vote in San Francisco in order to participate in city elections on matters that concerned them—pay and retirement.

In California, registration is semipermanent. Once people have registered, they remain on the list of registered voters unless they are convicted of a felony, die, are declared mentally incompetent by a court, or fail to vote in either the primary or general election *and* move out of the county.

WHO MAY RUN

Eligibility

To be eligible to run for state public office in California one must:

1. Be a citizen of the United States and of California.
2. Be a registered voter of the party whose nomination one seeks. For nonpartisan office (superintendent of public instruction or judge), party affiliation is not required—one can be independent or decline to state an affiliation.
3. Be a resident of the state for at least three years. Candidates for executive or judicial office must have lived in California for five years. Candidates for assembly, state senate, and the Board of Equalization must have lived *in their district* for at least one year.

Qualifying

A potential candidate qualifies for the ballot by first filing a *Declaration of Intent* with the county clerk—saying, in effect, "I intend to run for the office of _____."

Second, the potential candidate must file a petition with a small number of signatures of registered voters who assert they support the candidacy. Candidates' petitions for statewide office must have at least sixty-five valid signatures, while assembly and state senate candidates need forty valid signatures of citizens who belong to the candidate's political party (not a requirement in nonpartisan contests).

Third, the potential candidate must pay a filing fee or substitute an additional petition with more signatures. The filing fee is 2 percent of the annual salary for statewide office; 1 percent for other offices.

It's easy to get on the ballot in California, but getting elected is not easy. For example, in an average election year approximately 350 or so candidates will file for the eighty-member assembly. About 75 of these hopefuls will be third-party candidates with no real chance of getting elected. Another 150 Democratic and Republican candidates will be eliminated in the June primary and, finally, another 80 or so Democrats and Republicans will lose in the November general elections (there usually are one or two popular incumbents who have no opponent).

PRESIDENTIAL BALLOT

Under California law, the secretary of state is required to compile a list of *all potential presidential candidates*. The list must be compiled by January 31 of each presidential election year. Anyone who is actively seeking the nomination or anyone who is "generally advocated for" is put on the list. This law makes it hard for serious candidates to skip the California presidential primary elections. It also makes it difficult for favorite-son candidates to dominate the election. In addition, anyone who is interested may get on the ballot by petition.

As a result, the presidential ballot tends to have many names on it. In 1976 there were eighteen presidential candidates, in 1980, sixteen, and in 1984, fifteen.

BALLOT FORMS

California uses the *office block ballot*—presenting the competing candidates *by office sought* (see Illustration 3–1). This contrasts with states where the *party column ballot* is used. In these states, competing candidates are listed *by party membership*. A single vote at the top of the list is a vote for each of the party's candidates. But in California, it is hard to vote a party ticket. The office block ballot tends to reduce partisanship and accents the candidate as a person.

Ballot Position

Until 1974, incumbents were always listed first in their office block. This helped them get reelected since some people merely vote for the first name on the ballot. However, Proposition 9 (1974) eliminated this

3-1 *Office block ballot.*

1   ## COUNTY OF BUTTE
CONSOLIDATED GENERAL ELECTION—TUESDAY, NOVEMBER 4, 1986

STATE

Governor	Vote for One
GARY V. MILLER, American Independent Governing Board Member, Mt. SAC Comm. College Dist.	3 ➡
JOSEPH FUHRIG, Libertarian Professor of Economics	4 ➡
GEORGE "DUKE" DEUKMEJIAN, Republican Governor, State of California	5 ➡
TOM BRADLEY, Democratic Mayor, City of Los Angeles	6 ➡
MARIA ELIZABETH MUNOZ, Peace and Freedom Educator	7 ➡

Lieutenant Governor	Vote for One
MIKE CURB, Republican	9 ➡
CLYDE KUHN, Peace and Freedom College Instructor	10 ➡
NORMA JEAN ALMODOVAR, Libertarian Author	11 ➡
JAMES C. "JIM" GRIFFIN, American Independent Truck Driver	12 ➡
LEO T. McCARTHY, Democratic Lieutenant Governor	13 ➡

Source: Butte County Clerk, sample ballot, November 1986.

incumbent's advantage. Subsequent court cases and legislation have led to the present system of a random listing of candidates.

ABSENTEE BALLOT

Until 1979, only voters who were ill or who would be traveling on election day could qualify for an absentee ballot. However, a law enacted in 1978 now permits anyone who wants to use an absentee ballot to be able to do so.

Absentee ballots provided the margin for the Deukmejian gubernatorial campaign in 1982. A statewide absentee ballot campaign addressed to GOP voters produced 302,343 absentee ballots—turning defeat at the "polls" into victory election night (see Table 3–1). Absentee ballots accounted for 4.7 percent of the total vote cast in 1972 but, by

TABLE 3-1
Polling Place and Absentee Ballot Votes in the 1982 Gubernatorial Election

	Bradley	Deukmejian
Polling place ballots	3,598,557	3,578,671
Absentee ballots	189,112	302,343
Total	3,787,669	3,881,014

Source: California Secretary of State, *Statement of the Vote*, November 1982.

1986, 9 percent of the general election vote (685,340) was cast by absentee voters.

An even more dramatic use of absentee ballots came in the spring 1983 recall election directed against San Francisco Mayor Dianne Feinstein. Feinstein won the election by an overwhelming majority, and 40 percent of some 140,000 votes cast for her were absentee.

ELECTIONS

Primaries

The partisan primary is designed to select a party's nominee for the general election. (Nonpartisan primaries are discussed in Chapter 12.) California's direct primary was one of the major reforms enacted in the Progressive era and was designed to give more power to the people in selecting their parties' candidates. Prior to adopting the primary, the state's political parties chose candidates in caucuses, or conventions. These were open to fraud and manipulation—insuring that the party leaders would remain in control and often denying the will of the people.

Primary elections are important not only because they determine the party's nominee, but because they often determine in effect the final outcome of the general election. Only a third of California's legislative districts are truly competitive. One party or the other has a substantial majority in two-thirds of the congressional, assembly, and state senate districts. These are "safe seats." Thus, winning the majority party primary is the same as winning the seat. In these races, the general election becomes a formality.

In recent years, as the number and proportion of independent voters has grown, many voters find themselves shut out of the often crucial major party primary elections. In June 1986, nearly 11 percent (10.89 percent) of voters could not vote in the major two parties' pri-

TABLE 3-2
Assembly Incumbent-Held Seats and Open Seats in the 1986 Primary

Incumbent Running	Open
(N = 68)	(N = 12)
# of Candidates - 163	# of Candidates - 64
Av. # = 2.3	Av. # = 5.5

Source: Data, California Secretary of State, *Statement of Vote*, June 1986.

mary because they were either registered as independent or they belonged to one of the third parties.[1]

When an incumbent decides not to seek reelection, there is usually substantial competition for nomination (see Table 3–2). In some districts, as many as a dozen candidates will campaign for the office—particularly in the dominant party's primary. ("Dominant" for Democrats would mean a 60 percent registration and, for Republicans, 45 percent registration.)

In primary elections a candidate will often win with less than a majority of the vote—*a plurality victory*. This happens often in open districts where there is no incumbent seeking reelection. The same situation can happen in statewide elections, too. All but one of the Democratic candidates for statewide office in 1974 won their party's primary with less than a majority of the votes. Yet each of the plurality victors went on to win in the general election.

General Elections

Usually, political excitement is greater in the general election than in the primary. It is the payoff of a long, hard campaign. The issues are more clear-cut, and the opposition is *between party candidates* rather than *within parties* as in the primary. General elections are the finals in each election race.

In about two-thirds of the legislative races, the real decision is made in the primary. However, for statewide elections and for about one-third of the legislative races, the general elections are crucial.

Statewide campaigns for governor, lieutenant governor, other minor executive offices, and the U.S. Senate are usually hard-fought, the outcome is often in doubt, and the victory is frequently narrow, partic-

[1]A 1987 Supreme Court decision dealing with Connecticut election law is likely to have ramifications in other states. The Court ruled that if Connecticut Republicans wanted to allow those registered as independents to vote in their primary, they should be allowed to. The state law requiring that only party registrants could vote in their primary was unconstitutional. Currently, California Republicans are weighing this option—and California Democrats may feel compelled to do likewise.

ularly if there is no incumbent in the race. In 1976, S. I. Hayakawa won his U.S. Senate election with barely half the votes. President Ford captured all the state's 1976 presidential electoral votes with 49.7 percent of the vote compared to Jimmy Carter's 48 percent. In the non-incumbent controller's race of November 1986, Democrat Gray Davis won over Republican Bill Campbell by capturing 51 percent of the vote. But by all measures, the closest victory was George Deukmejian's in 1982 when he won the governor's office with 49.3 percent of the total vote cast, 93,345 votes more than Tom Bradley's 48.1 percent share.

THE ELECTORATE

Partisanship

From 1935 to 1958, California Democrats had a substantial majority in voter registration but were unable to transform it into victory at the ballot box. The difference between party registration and political control is at the heart of the state's reputation for having a fickle electorate.

In a 1983 California Poll survey, only 31 percent of respondents agreed with the statement that it is better to be a firm party supporter than to be a political independent.[2] Partisanship is important to only a minority of the state's voters.

There are three ways one can measure party strength in California. First, how do voters register? Second, what do people say when asked about their party preference? And, third, how do they vote?

Registration

Democratic party registration had averaged about 56 percent since 1960 but in the 1980s it has dropped to 51 percent. Republican registration averaged 37 percent in the same period, declining to a low of less than 35 percent in the late 1970s and early 1980s and finally rising to 38 percent in 1986. Currently, the three official third parties listed on the California ballot comprise a miniscule percentage of voter registrants—American Independent, 1.16, Libertarian, 0.42, and Peace and Freedom, 0.34.

California law permits voters to register as Decline to State if they have no party choice. These nonparty registrants have increased substantially in the last twenty years (to 8.9 percent in 1986). In particular, it appears that many young, first-time voters are uncertain or indifferent about their party affiliation.

[2]Source: *California Poll,* November 1983.

TABLE 3-3
Party Registration and Party Preference, 1970–1982

	1970	1974	1978	1982	1986
Democrats as defined by:					
Voter registration	54.9	56.2	57.1	53.2	50.8
Public opinion poll	50.8	54.6	53.1	50.6	44.0
Republicans as defined by:					
Voter registration	39.8	36.8	34.7	34.9	34.2
Public opinion poll	43.7	41.4	37.7	38.4	45.0

Source: California Secretary of State, *Statement of Vote,* 1970, 1974, 1978, 1982, and 1986 and *California Poll,* 1970, 1974, 1978, 1982, and 1986.

Party Preference.   Democratic-Republican voting strength has varied considerably over the years. From 1970 through 1986, Democratic registration has consistently run higher than Republican registration, although the difference between the two parties has narrowed in the mid-1980s. However, registration figures magnify the Democratic advantage because county clerks are not allowed by state law to prune all the deadwood from voter registration rolls. A more reliable indicator of Democratic-Republican voter strength in the state is the Field Poll. Field (February, 1987) reports that Democrats were the majority party through the 1970s and the early 1980s, but, as of 1986 Republicans had surged slightly ahead of Democrats (see Table 3–3). Whether the Irangate scandal will slow this Republican trend is not clear. Perhaps even more interesting, Field reports that when respondents were offered other options such as independent or third party, the percentage of voters identifying with the major two parties dropped significantly— Republicans, 38 percent; Democrats, 37 percent; independents, 23 percent; and third party, 2 percent. Among those identifying themselves as Democrats and Republicans only about half viewed themselves as firm partisans.

Voting Behavior.   Party strength, as measured by statewide votes, changes markedly from election to election. Between 1966 and 1970, Republicans were stronger than Democrats, winning ten of the thirteen statewide races. But from 1974 to 1986, Democrats were stronger, winning twenty-two out of thirty elections. Such fluctuations over a short period of time suggest that statewide election results are strongly influenced by incumbency, candidate appeal, and issues.

TABLE 3-4
**Total Vote Cast for Candidates for State Assembly between 1974 and 1986,
Democratic and Republican Percentages**

Vote for	1974	1976	1978	1980	1982	1986
Democrats	55.5%	55.0%	53.6%	47.5%	52.5%	52.0%
Republicans	42.4	43.4	44.7	47.7	45.8	47.0

*Excluding districts with no contests.
Source: Data, California Secretary of State, *Statement of Vote*, 1974–86.

On the other hand, if we use election results from the more obscure state assembly races, the effects of incumbency, personality, and issues are significantly reduced compared to statewide races. Over time, these figures seem to be reasonably good measures of basic party strength. The results of these races are provided in Table 3–4. Measured this way, basic Democratic party strength appears to be about 53 percent, while basic Republican party strength appears to be about 46 percent.

Party strength measured three different ways gives us three slightly different answers. Registration figures (because of the deadwood) and assembly voting totals (because of incumbency advantages and gerrymandering) appear to slightly exaggerate Democratic strength. Perhaps the most reliable figure in estimating party strength, at least currently, is survey data, and as of 1987 the two parties are virtually dead even. Statewide races where there is no incumbent (such as the Davis-Campbell controller's race in 1986) hinge much more on the attractiveness of the candidate than on his or her party affiliation. Attractiveness also depends on media coverage—particularly TV. Such coverage is usually available for statewide races but seldom for local or legislative elections.

Ideology.   Illustration 3–2 shows the ideological structure of California voters (based on exit polls). Clearly, most Republican voters (seven out of ten) describe themselves as conservative. Thus, it is not surprising that most Republican candidates are conservative.

Democrats are more divided ideologically; 29 percent in the conservative wing of the party, and 43 percent in the liberal wing. The 18 percent in the middle hold the balance of power.

3-2 *Ideology of California's active voters—Democrats and Republicans.*

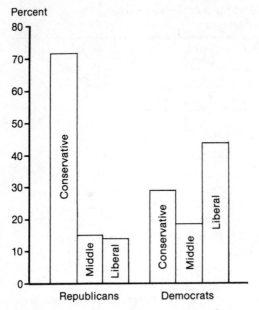

Source: "Political Party Identification," *California Opinion Index,* October 1985.

Demographic Characteristics

Several factors seem particularly significant in Table 3–5:

1. While the sexes used to vote in similar proportions for Democrats and Republicans, this is no longer the case. Fifty-four percent of women favor the Democratic party, and just the opposite, 54 percent of men support the Republican party. Certainly, part of the reason for the difference is the Republican party's opposition to the Equal Rights Amendment (ERA), abortion and comparable worth.
2. Only 12 percent of Republicans belong to ethnic minorities, but 27 percent of Democrats do.
3. Republicans have leads among the youngest (eighteen to twenty-nine) and oldest (sixty-plus) age groups, while Democrats lead with age groups in between.
4. Seventy-one percent of Republicans consider themselves strongly or moderately conservative, but only 43 percent of Democrats consider themselves strongly or moderately liberal.
5. Republicans come from the upper end of the economic scale (two out of three were homeowners), while Democrats do better with the disadvantaged.

TABLE 3-5
Demographic Characteristics of Partisans (1976 and 1985)

	Democrats		Republicans	
	1985	1976	1985	1976
Male	46%	48%	54%	47%
Female	54	52	46	53
18–29	26%	30%	29%	22%
30–39	27	22	21	19
40–49	15	14	15	16
50–59	12	15	14	16
60 or older	20	19	21	27
White (non-Hispanic)	73%	70%	88%	89%
Hispanic	12	17	7	7
Black	12	10	2	2
Asian	3	3	3	2
Strongly conservative	6%	7%	27%	20%
Moderately conservative	23	30	44	44
Middle-of-the-road	18	20	15	22
Moderately liberal	37	32	12	12
Strongly liberal	16	11	2	2
Homeowner	57%	55%	66%	67%
Renter	43	45	34	33
Union household	26%	29%	16%	19%
Non-union household	74	71	84	81
Less than $10,000	15%	37%	8%	30%
$10,000–$19,000	22	36	16	31
$20,000–$29,999	21	15	20	21
$30,000–$39,999	15	3	17	7
$40,000 or more	24	3	33	5
Refused to state	3	6	6	6
Less than high school	10%	25%	8%	14%
High school graduate	25	29	22	26
Some college/trade school	39	29	41	37
College graduate	26	17	29	23

Source: "Political Party Identification," *California Opinion Index*, October 1985.

Regionalism

As in other states, California occasionally exhibits *regional* patterns in its voting behavior. In the Golden State, regionalism is typically north versus south—the south usually considered the seven counties south of the Tehachapi Mountains and the rest of the state making up the north.

Historically, apportionment of the state senate (see Chapter 7), water, and gas tax allocations have been major regional issues dividing California. Additionally, in party primary elections, if one candidate is from the south and another from the north, votes will sometimes divide for the candidates along regional lines (partially due to name familiarity). Both major political parties maintain state central committee offices in each of the two regions. And many state agencies and professional groups maintain northern and southern state offices.

Regionalism as a political factor emerges when other factors are absent or weak—usually in a primary or nonpartisan race and sometimes in a vote for a ballot measure.

George Deukmejian's razor-thin victory in 1982 was based on his southern California vote margin of 141,423, which overcame his northern California deficit of 48,078 votes. In the 1986 reconfirmation election of Chief Justice Rose Bird only two counties of the fifty-eight gave her a majority—San Francisco and Alameda, two northern, liberal Bay area counties. Field reports that Republicans have a 9 percent advantage over Democrats in the south, but in the north Democrats have an 11 percent margin over Republicans.

Voter Participation

As a general rule, Democrats tend to be less politically active than Republicans. Partly, this is because Democrats more often come from the lower socioeconomic categories than do Republicans. Those who are poor, lack education, hold unskilled jobs, or are young often do not see politics as important. They do not have the time, skills, or energy to become politically involved. Many blacks, Chicanos, and poor whites feel that they are not important politically; they are alienated from the system and often do not vote. On the other hand, well-educated, wealthy, professional people usually see politics as important to them. They know they can have an impact on the system, and they vote (as well as participate in politics in other ways). Thus, as we see in Table 3–6, there is a significant difference between the ethnic proportions of California's *total population* and the ethnic proportions of the *voting population*. While whites made up 67 percent of the total population, they represent 83 percent of the voters for an *effectiveness ratio* of 1.25. In contrast, Hispanics, while making up 19 percent of the population, accounted for only 8 percent of the votes cast—an *effectiveness ratio* of .417. Thus, some groups have more political influence than others simply because they have high voter turnouts. Whites, upper-income people, and homeowners tend to be much more involved than Hispanics, blacks, or those with low income.

This difference in turnout helps Republican candidates overcome their minority party status. In recent general elections, Republican

TABLE 3-6
Ethnic Patterns, Total Population, Registered Voters, and Voters, 1980 General Election

	Total Population	Registered Voters	Voted in 1980 General Election
White	15,667,902 (66.6%)	9,100,000 (80%)	7,300,000 (83%)
Hispanic	4,544,331 (19.2%)	1,000,000 (9%)	700,000 (8%)
Black	1,783,810 (7.5%)	680,000 (6%)	425,000 (5%)
Others	1,575,769 (6.7%)	580,000 (5%)	350,000 (4%)
Total	23,667,902	11,361,623	8,775,459

Source: "Ethnicity and the Political Process," *California Opinion Index*, March 1982.

voter turnout has been greater than Democratic voter turnout by about four percentage points. (Less than 77 of every 100 registered Democrats went to the polls. But 81 of every 100 registered Republicans voted.) This higher level of voting by Republican voters helps offset the GOP registration deficit. Republicans also tend to be more active in other forms of political effort—campaign work, financial contributions, and club membership.

Even though a large proportion of elections are decided in the primary, fewer voters go to the polls in the primary than in general elections. The June 1986 primary voter turnout was the second lowest in state history (40.5 percent of those registered voted; in 1928 only 39.6 percent voted). While general election turnout in 1986 was also poor (59.3 percent of those registered voted), there were approximately 2.5 million more votes cast in the November election. And, of course, millions of potential voters do not bother to register. In 1986, 17.5 million Californians could have registered to vote, but only 12.8 million did—of these, only 7.6 million actually voted.

RUNNING FOR OFFICE

Money

"Money is the mother's milk of politics," declared Jess Unruh, past assembly speaker and ex-state treasurer. Any campaign for public office will cost money. Even candidates running for minor office need printed literature. And for bigger campaigns, candidates must spend money for postage, headquarters rent, telephones, bumper strips, advertisements in community newspapers, lawn signs, and staff. Candidates for statewide office also need substantial amounts for TV, radio, and travel. Campaign budgets for ballot measures are almost totally devoted to media costs.

Aside from media, other campaign expenditures are: printing literature for mailings, campaign management firm fees, attorneys and accountants to keep the campaign from stumbling over complex election laws. Campaign mailings have recently emerged as a major factor—particularly in legislative races in major urban areas where TV and newspaper ads cost so much. They are also used statewide to reach selected groups of voters.

In the 1970s and 80s, campaign costs have skyrocketed. This has been due, in part, to the increased use of expensive TV for statewide and regional campaigns as well as expanded use of computerized mailings. Inflation and population growth also contribute to this spending increase. Inflation cut the buying power of the campaign dollar to thirty-five cents between 1960 and 1980; population growth meant there were half again as many voters to contact.

Equally important, California became a competitive two-party state in the 1960s and 70s. Both Republicans and Democrats had to spend more money just to stay "even." Like the international arms race, as each candidate, party, or ballot measure committee spent more money, the opposition felt obliged to spend more too.

Why People Give.   Joe Cerrell, a leading California campaign manager, suggests the following reasons that people give to political candidates:

1. They like the candidate personally.
2. Giving is an ego trip—having the candidate (governor, U.S. senator, or president) ask for money feels good.
3. Insurance—the contributor does business with or is regulated by the government and may need help someday.
4. Investment—the contributor is doing business with or is regulated by the government and needs help now.

Interest groups are by far the largest source of campaign money. According to the Fair Political Practices Commission, about 85 percent of all funds contributed to candidates come from interest groups. Clearly, insurance and investment loom large in motivating campaign contributions.

Motives for contributions to campaigns "for" or "against" a ballot measure are less complex. Basically, these are issue campaigns. In 1972, *Playboy* magazine gave $125,000 to defeat Proposition 18, which would have given local governments power to control obscene materials. In 1978, tobacco companies contributed over $6 million to defeat a ballot measure that would have regulated smoking (Proposition 5). In 1982, the National Rifle Association and its allies spent a record $7.3

million to defeat a handgun control measure (Proposition 15). In 1986 Chevron Corporation spent $251,839 dollars to defeat Proposition 65, the toxics initiative.

Raising Campaign Money.   Asking people to give is probably the most hated part of campaigning. Former Assembly Speaker Bob Moretti once described it as "embarrassing and degrading." Every major campaign has a finance chair who is supposed to raise money. But, large contributions ($10,000—$20,000—$50,000) often require a personal meeting between donor and candidate.

Increasingly, however, campaign contributions come from groups— a single group, such as the state employees; an association of groups, such as United for California (industry and finance); or political action committees (PACs). Essentially, a PAC collects money from its members (individuals or groups) with the understanding that the funds will be combined and then given to candidates sympathetic to the common political goals of the individuals or group.

By the late 1970s and early 80s, PACs and other groups became the major source of campaign money. Leading all other PACs according to the Fair Political Practices Commission (FPPC) spending reports in the 1980s has been the California Medical Association PAC. Other PACs with contributions in the hundreds of thousands are teachers, labor, real estate, state employees, corporations, farm labor, savings and loans, finance, and agriculture.

While large individual campaign contributions probably amount to no more than 5 percent of the total raised statewide, they can sometimes be very important to a specific candidate. Dr. Louis Cella gave $287,000 to Ken Cory's 1974 controller campaign, obviously providing a substantial part of the total spent ($730,000). But the all-time record for individual donations belongs to Jane Fonda, who gave her husband (Tom Hayden) $400,000 toward his 1976 U.S. Senate campaign. In 1982, Fonda gave her husband $215,000 for his assembly race and loaned him another $625,000.

Obviously, a wealthy candidate has an advantage. Multimillionaires like Norton Simon or William Matson Roth can use their own money. Yet ironically, wealthy candidates often have difficulty in getting campaign contributions. Potential contributors think that wealthy candidates should use their own money.

Another useful source of campaign funding is the early loan. Max Palevsky, a liberal Los Angeles Democrat, likes to give campaigns a fast start with a massive early loan.

Large amounts are often raised at cocktail parties, campaign dinners, and lunches. A contribution to the candidate at a cocktail party may be $100 or $150. Campaign dinners may cost $250 or $500 a plate, but many more people come to a dinner—so more money is raised.

Governor Deukmejian raised over $1 million at a September 18, 1982, fund-raising dinner featuring President Ronald Reagan.

An important state like California will also attract outside campaign money. Two 1982 ballot measures brought in significant out-of-state funds: Proposition 15 (hand-gun control) lured $1.2 million from the Washington D.C. National Rifle Association, while out-of-state food packagers spent over $1 million against Proposition 11 (anti-litter). Virtually all of the money spent on behalf of Proposition 64, the Lyndon La Rouche-inspired AIDS initiative of 1986, came from out of state (96 percent).

A recent development in campaign fund raising is the computerized fundraising "personal" letter. The Orange County campaign management firm of Butcher-Forde has raised hundreds of thousands of dollars for initiative campaigns this way.

Amounts Spent.   While inflation and population growth account for part of the reason why running for office in California has become so expensive, the prodigious amounts raised and spent in the last several elections can also be attributed to increased television and mailing costs, heightened partisanship and paranoia. Jerry Brown and his Republican opponent for governor, Evelle Younger, spent $5.9 million running for governor in 1978. By 1986, George Deukmejian and Tom Bradley had spent nearly $11 million as of mid-October with nearly a month left in the campaign! Million dollar races for the state legislature have become commonplace in open districts. The California Commission on Campaign Finance, a private blue-ribbon commission, reported that $57.1 million was spent on 100 legislative seats in 1986 (a 31 percent increase since 1984 and only about 10 percent came from individuals contributing less than $100. In addition, spending on ballot propositions has continued to climb.

How It Is Spent.   How campaign funds are spent depends on several factors. How much money is available? What and where is the constituency? What other resources are available? Is the candidate an incumbent or not?

For most statewide campaigns—governor, attorney general, and so forth—large sums are spent on media (TV, radio, and newspapers).

Media

Television and Radio.   California is a *media* state. It is the center for much of the nation's radio, TV, and movie industry. Over 50 TV and 400 radio stations serve the state.

"Media" in California has come to mean TV, and television advertising is very expensive. Most TV money is spent on the thirty-second

3-3 *Debating the issues. Gubernatorial candidates George Deukmejian (R) and Tom Bradley (D) in a 1982 face-to-face TV debate. No debates were held in 1986—Deukmejian refused.*

Photo by Michael Williamson/courtesy Sacramento Bee

spot—selling the candidate's image, a slogan, and sometimes an issue. Costs vary with the size of the market (Los Angeles compared to Redding); the day (weekday or weekend); the time of day (3 A.M. or 7:30 P.M.); and the popularity of the program "next" to the spot.

In 1982, an early morning spot on Sacramento's KCRA might go for as little as $30—compared to $2,500 for prime-time 7–10 P.M. KNBC (Los Angeles) charged between $5,475 and $11,325 for a thirty-second, prime-time spot. KRON (San Francisco) charged between $2,200 and $3,000 for most prime-time spots—but those next to "Hill Street Blues" cost $7,000.

Television reaches a wider audience than newspapers. While virtually every home has a TV, newspapers reach about eight of ten households in the state. A good part of the media's political influence stems from the lack of competition in providing political news. Equally significant, the media has more credibility with the public than most public officials or candidates.

Newspapers.   Historically, the print press was a power in California's state and local government. Before TV and party competition (before the mid-1950s), a handful of newspapers were major forces—the *Los Angeles Times, San Francisco Chronicle, Oakland Tribune,* and the Hearst *Examiner* papers (San Francisco and Los Angeles). In particular, the *Times, Chronicle,* and *Tribune* were powerful because they dominated the state's Republican party, and trumpeted the GOP position in news columns and editorials.

The historic Republican bias of major state newspapers has been reduced by three factors: first, emergence of TV; second, a new generation of owners and management; and third, William Knowland's disastrous gubernatorial candidacy in 1958.

Television provides substantial competition to newspapers in essentially every area of the state. Thus, since the early 1950s, newspapers no longer have a monopoly on the news. And as a result, newspaper reporting has become less biased.

Over the last twenty years, the *Times, Tribune, Chronicle,* and several other major urban newspapers have come under new management or ownership. The new management has given higher priority to objective comprehensive news coverage. Many newspapers no longer make endorsements in major partisan campaigns. Some purposely present conflicting opinion on the editorial pages. The *Los Angeles Times* has developed into one of the nation's finest newspapers, while the *Sacramento Bee* has long enjoyed a solid reputation for its coverage of state politics.

Because of California's size, each newspaper (some 130 dailies) can cover only a small fraction of the state. Essentially, there are eight news regions in the state, each isolated from the others by distance or mountains. This fragmentation of media influence reduces the power of any one newspaper.

Only three newspapers have a substantial share of the state's total circulation. The *Los Angeles Times* is read in one out of five California homes, while the *Chronicle* and *Los Angeles Examiner* are read in about one of ten homes. No other newspaper has more than 5 percent of the state's total readership. Most newspapers get only a small fraction of their hometown circulation. Even the mighty *Times* gets only one-third of the circulation in Los Angeles County.

Media Impact.   This multiplicity of newspapers and TV stations serving each region is significant. Over 22 million (90 percent) of the state's residents have some choice of news source. And in the Los

Angeles and San Francisco areas, the number and kind of alternatives are staggering. It is important to note that while most of us read only one newspaper, we have several TV stations from which to choose.

The precise impact of TV, newspaper, radio endorsements, and news coverage is hard to assess. However, based on the few studies conducted in California (and elsewhere) there are some general observations that can be made. Newspapers and television appeal to different audiences. Newspapers tend to be read more often by the higher-income and better-educated voter; TV is more often the only news source for the lower-income and less-educated voter. The visual impact of TV is a powerful influence on a viewer who has no other source of information about the subject.

Media, both print and electronic, has become an "agenda setting" power—that is, the issues that concern people are the issues presented in the media.

The press has more influence in local and nonpartisan races than in national or partisan elections. There is some research that also supports the conclusion that the media have an impact on voting for or against ballot measures.

In the long run, media endorsements are probably less significant than day-to-day news coverage and content. Incumbents often get publicity; challengers usually do not. How an issue is presented (offshore oil spills, the state's annual budget, or an increase or decrease in the welfare load) will have an impact on the voters' basic perceptions of the issues.

Public Opinion Polls

Public opinion polls are another key part of major campaigns for public office. However, public opinion polls are expensive. A well-designed statewide poll will cost as much as $30,000 to $40,000. Serious candidates for major public office will try to have at least one public opinion survey taken early in the campaign. Such polls usually are the base for a candidate's strategy.

Candidates use public opinion survey information to:

1. Identify major issues.
2. Assess their own strengths and weaknesses.
3. Assess the strengths and weaknesses of their opponents.
4. Help raise campaign funds and other support.

Candidates who are trailing in the polls will often spend virtually all of their campaign funds on a media "blitz" in order to generate increased name recognition before a scheduled Field Poll for example. The increased standing in the polls is used, in turn, to convince potential contributors that the campaign is gathering momentum. It becomes, in short, a cycle of money—media—name recognition—increased support in polls—more money—more media—more name recognition, and so on.

Incumbency

If there is anything like a "sure bet" in politics, it is the incumbent. In 1986, not a single incumbent was beaten in a statewide race or in a Congressional or state legislative contest. Several reasons account for the high success rate of incumbents: name recognition, advantages of office, better access to campaign dollars, and for legislative candidates, gerrymandering.

Name Recognition. Governors, attorney generals, and U.S. senators are often prominent in the news. What they do *makes news*. In a very real sense, their names become household words. Challengers running against a statewide incumbent have to overcome at least four years of publicity given to the incumbent. For example, in 1986 no Republican challenger even bothered to file against Democratic Treasurer Jess Unruh.

However, in very high visibility contests an incumbent can on occasion be defeated. Sometimes a bitter primary battle can contribute to defeat in the general election. Governor Pat Brown (1966) and U.S. Senator John Tunney (1976) are examples of this.

A massive national disaster or political scandal will also badly damage incumbents. In office, they are considered to be at fault or to blame for what happened. The Depression of the 1930s and Watergate scandals of the early 1970s clearly hurt incumbents who were in no way involved in either of the problems.

Office Advantages. Most legislative incumbents do not get the publicity given to statewide officeholders. The advantages the former enjoy are substantial, however. All state legislators have district offices and staff who are busy year-round. This staff varies in size according to the legislator's interests, seniority, and powers. But there will be at least an office director, secretary, and an assistant. Many incumbent legislators are assisted by unpaid interns. (For more detail, see Chapter 7.)

District staff spend most of their time doing casework and assisting constituents who need help, and who will remember this help when they vote, it is hoped. Problems may range from lost social security checks to revoked drivers' licenses.

Lawmakers try to be in their districts on weekends when the legislature is in session and full-time during recess. Their days and nights are packed with breakfast, lunch, and dinner meetings; coffees and teas; Rotary, Kiwanis, Chamber of Commerce, and union meetings; schools and churches; PTAs and Boy Scouts; League of Women Voters; American Association of University Women; and dozens of other community groups concerned with government policy. The incumbent "reports" on the Sacramento scene and soon builds an image as a hardworking, effective lawmaker.

Incumbents can send out newsletters, press releases, questionnaires, and letters of congratulations to constituents for honors and achievements. On the average, each lawmaker gets more than $15,000 worth of publicity per year at taxpayer expense.

Money. Incumbent legislative candidates usually raise about four times as much campaign money as do their challengers. A recent detailed examination of campaign contributions by Common Cause found that interest groups usually give most of their money to incumbents. Here and there, a "cause" interest group (National Rifle Association, for example) or party organization may give money to the challenger. But mostly, the challenger has to depend on friends, local business or commercial contacts, or personal funds.

Reapportionment. State legislators customarily draw district lines each decade to guarantee easy elections for incumbents (See Chapter 7). There are only a handful of truly competitive districts in the state.

Public Figures

Some candidates who are not incumbents but who are public figures also enjoy the advantage of *name recognition*. Actors, TV personalities, and sports figures can often build a successful political career on their name recognition.

Ronald Reagan is an obvious example. A well-known Hollywood actor, Reagan was able to use his movie and TV fame as a springboard to political success.

TV newscaster Stan Statham, a Republican, was able to overcome a 59 percent Democratic party registration to win a seat in the state assembly in northern California. Baxter Ward, a muckraking TV newscaster, won a seat on the Los Angeles County Board of Supervisors, and another broadcast personality, Robert K. Dornan, won a west Los Angeles congressional seat. Bill Press, Los Angeles television newscaster, is a candidate for the Democratic U.S. Senate nomination in 1988, while Bruce Herschensohn, another southern California newscaster, finished second in the Republican U.S. Senate primary of 1986.

Offspring of famous people also have an advantage. Governor Jerry Brown's campaign for secretary of state in 1970 and his campaign for governor in 1974 were substantially helped by the fact that his father

3-4 *Lobbyists and Campaign Contributions*

"Gentelmen, California already has off-track gambling
I've bet $338,000 on the reelection of 14 members of this Commitee!"

Dennis Renault, Sacramento Bee

(Pat Brown) had been governor. John Tunney's U.S. Senate victory in 1970 was due, in part, to his father's fame as a boxing champion.

S. I. Hayakawa, who achieved national fame in battling student demonstrators who were protesting against the Vietnam war and racism was later elected to the U.S. Senate (1976). Tom Hayden, a leading student activist in the 1960s, capitalized on his notoriety (and Jane Fonda's name and money) in attacking John Tunney in the Democratic primary, winning a third of the votes in June 1976. Later, in 1982, he won a seat in the state assembly.

To an extent name recognition can sometimes can be bought. Thus, Congressman Ed Zschau, a relatively unknown Republican office-holder prior to his statewide challenge to Democratic incumbent Alan Cranston in 1986, was able to build substantial name recognition over a relatively short period of time. To do this, Zschau ran a blitz of TV ads in the early spring in an attempt to familiarize voters with his name (he even had to educate voters on how to pronounce his last name). Zschau's massive spending helped him win the Republican primary, and he came within an eyelash of beating incumbent Cranston in the fall election.

REFORMS

Reform has been an integral part of California's political culture and history. There are two kinds of reform, substantive/policy and procedural. The most notable Progressive reforms were procedural because they affected the way the political system functions: how we select our public officials and the powers they exercise.

Overall, American (and California) reformers have had the general goal of opening the political system to increased popular participation. Extending the right to vote to an ever greater proportion of the population, promoting the initiative, referendum, and recall, and establishing the direct primary are examples.

Since the 1974 Watergate scandals, political reformers have focused on campaign costs, campaign contributions, and lobbying regulation. The assumption is that our public officials would represent the "people" better without the corrupting influence of interest group campaign contributions. More than any other single event, Watergate set the stage for the political reform movement of the 1970s; perhaps the Moriarity scandal will serve the same purpose in the latter 1980s.

Proposition 9

Clean politics, campaign reform, lobby regulation, and conflict of interest are terms familiar to all politically aware citizens. Virtually all elected California officeholders publicly have argued that they favor reform in these areas, but getting them passed by officeholders (in effect, "winners under the existing system") in the highly charged partisan atmosphere at the capitol has been impossible.

In 1974 in the Watergate era, Proposition 9, an initiative jointly sponsored by Common Cause, People's Lobby, and Secretary of State Jerry Brown qualified for the June primary ballot. Supported by a wide range of civic and community groups, and by some politicians as well, and opposed by nearly all of the major interest groups operating in the state, it was overwhelmingly approved by voters.

Provisions of Act

The Political Reform Act of 1974 (P.R.A.) had four major goals: limiting campaign expenditures, requiring disclosure of campaign expenditures and sources, limiting lobbying expenditures (see Chapter 5), and prohibiting conflicts of interest. In addition, the act established a

3-5 *Free Speech versus Campaign Finance Regulation*

Courtesy of Dennis Renault, Sacramento Bee.

Fair Political Practices Commission to administer it. In this chapter, we will focus on the campaign finance regulations of P.R.A.

After the act was adopted, it was attacked in the courts by those who opposed limits on campaign spending. The U.S. supreme court struck down expenditure limits on initiative measures in 1977. Since then all other such limits were removed. The court also struck down the restrictions on lobbyists making, or arranging for the making of, campaign contributions.

Campaign Disclosures. Under P.R.A. all campaign contributions and expenditures of $100 or more must be reported by all candidates for state and local elective office. The contributor's name, address, occupation, and employer's name must be given. This information must be filed both forty and twelve days before and sixty-five days after election day. Thus, if local newspapers report the information, it is at least possible for voters to learn the funding sources of candidates and propositions before the election.

Fair Political Practices Commission. This commission has five members: the chair and one other are appointed by the governor, and the attorney general, secretary of state, and controller also each get to appoint a member. Members serve four-year terms.

The Fair Political Practices Commission is empowered to establish rules needed to implement the act, hear complaints, hold hearings, and investigate where needed. A major task of the commission is to receive and file reports from lobbyists and campaigns. Given the number of lobbyists, candidates, ballot measure campaigns, etc., the commission can reasonably expect over 20,000 filings in an election year.

Impact of the Reform Act

Disclosure. Because of P.R.A. California citizens since 1975 can, if they are interested, discover who is giving to which candidate and how the candidate is spending those funds. While this data has not been earthshaking in a few campaigns, candidates have put on the defensive in explaining why they received money from Group x. The attempt of reformers to try to limit campaign spending has not succeeded because of court rulings. Since these spending records are public, some politicians have used them to put pressure on the special interest groups for more campaign money. "You gave $5,000 to assemblyman X and only $2,000 to me—what's the matter?" This is an all-too-common refrain at the capital these days.

Inexperienced candidates have often found the paperwork (reports, records, etc.) a substantial burden on their small staffs. In contrast, experienced candidates (usually incumbents) have had less difficulty with the act (see Table 3–7).

The act also had substantial impact on some specific campaign activities. Most notable was the increased use of paid legal and account-

---

TABLE 3-7
Impact of Campaign Disclosure and Lobbying Provisions of the Political Reform Act of 1974 (a Survey of Candidates)

	Increased	No Effect	Decreased
Advantage of incumbents	59%	34%	7%
Role of special interests	36	46	19
Citizen awareness of the role of money in politics	50	47	3
Honesty in campaigning	30	64	6
Level of political information among voters	27	65	8

Source: Putt & Springer (1977).

ing personnel, increased use of paid campaign managers and other staff, and increased use of professional advertising.

Enforcement. After giving incumbents and other candidates time to learn the new law, the FPPC has begun to strictly enforce the act. In recent years, it has imposed substantial fines on those who flagrantly violate the law. For example, in 1980, the commission levied a $36,000 fine against Senator Bill Greene for falsely reporting the source of campaign contributions. In 1983, the FPPC hit the California Republican party with a $25,000 fine for failing to properly identify the source of campaign contributions in 1979 and 1980. The commission has also gone after local politicians running afoul of the law. Former Mayor Roger Hedgecock of San Diego was accused of laundering funds. And, in 1986 the FPPC filed suit against Sacramento County supervisor William Bryan for *$2.9 million* accusing him of "violating virtually every major provision of the act."

On balance, the act has been a limited success, but, as we have noted previously, the critical problem remains unresolved; campaign costs.

Public Financing of Campaigns. At present, the public finances political campaigns in two ways. Under federal law, presidential candidates receive matching funds from the U.S. Treasury in the primary and outright grants in the general election. And more indirectly as discussed earlier in this chapter, incumbents in California have the advantage of newsletters, district offices, and district staff paid for by the state.

Direct public funding. As concern over ever larger campaign expenditures increases, so has the pressure for direct public funding of campaigns. Assembly Speaker Willie Brown and ex-speakers Leo McCarthy and Jess Unruh have all identified public campaign financing as a critical state issue.

Several proposals have been made for public financing of campaigns in California, but none have yet been approved in the legislature. Supporters argue that public financing combined with limits on contributions and expenditures is the only way to keep campaign costs within reason and minimize the influence of special interests. Skyrocketing campaign costs, it has been argued, keep many potential and highly qualified candidates from seeking public office.

Opposition to public financing comes from those who fear it will destroy direct public involvement in politics; those who see public financing as encouraging kooks, idiots, and ideologues to run; and Republican leaders contend the public has repeatedly voiced opposition to public funding of campaigns. There is concern that limiting a person's right to give a large campaign contribution is, in effect, limiting his or her freedom of expression. There is also fear that public financing will strengthen the two major parties, whose candidates would easily qualify, but weaken or destroy the minor parties, whose candidates would probably not qualify for financing.

But even if all of the political and legal problems were solved, several difficult administrative problems remain. First, would public campaign funding be provided in primary elections? Primary campaigns are important. They often are the real election. Thus, if used, public finance should be made available in primary elections. But the requirements for running for assembly or state senate are so minimal at present that almost any registered voter can get on the ballot and would be eligible for this money.

After a candidate qualifies for public financing, how much should be provided? The answer depends on several factors, the most significant being the number of voters in the constituency. But as we also know, statewide and regional campaigns can make very effective use of TV and radio, while local campaigns usually have to use direct mail. So a campaign may actually cost more per voter in an urban assembly district than it does in a statewide race.

If an incumbent gets the same amount to spend as his or her challengers, the incumbent has a very real advantage. Having been able to send newsletters to the voters in the previous two or four years, having a district office to help constituents, and having had the advantage of press coverage for two or four years, the incumbent has a big headstart on challengers.

Attempting to put together a public finance law that meets court and constitutional standards, does not alienate taxpayers ("My tax dollars will be going to provide money to that no-good crook!"), treats Democrats, Republicans, and third party candidates fairly, disallows transferring of funds from one candidate to another, provides for assistance in primary and general elections, and equitably limits but encourages relatively small contributions from private contributors and interest groups is not an easy task. As we noted previously, an initiative may be the only realistic hope to achieve this objective, and in June 1988 a common cause campaign spending reform initiative has qualified for the primary election.

Recent Campaign Issues

Slate Mailers. Increasingly popular, the slate mailer has become a vehicle for "getting the message" to the voter. Typically, those who prepare the mailer contact candidates and campaign managers for contributions in exchange for endorsement in the mailer. Candidates have charged that they were told what their contribution would be—if they didn't pay, their opponent would and often received the endorsement. According to Richard Nevins (Board of Equalization), when he refused to pay $40,000 one of his opponents appeared on the "slate."[3]

One particularly large slate mailing in Los Angeles was titled "Democratic Voter Guide," but it listed Republican candidates too. Another 1982 slate, mailed as an "official" state Democratic party document, took positions on several ballot measures that had not been approved by the party.

Absentee Ballots.　Clearly, George Deukmejian's use of absentee ballots in his narrow 1982 victory has increased interest in this voting option. Does marking the ballot at home pose a threat to the privacy of the vote? What are the chances of vote fraud? Does the device favor the more highly motivated voters—more often Republicans? Or does it favor those who are not willing to make the effort to go to the polls but who would vote at home—more often Democrats?

Dirty Campaign Tactics.　Every two years, newspaper writers and television commentators are almost sure to say, "the election campaign this year is the dirtiest in our nation's history."

Richard Reeves, noted political columnist, says dirty campaigns will continue because they are successful.[4] He has also charged that California is in a sense responsible for dirty campaigns because state's politicians were responsible for developing the thirty-second spot TV commercial and computerized letter. But attempts to regulate or legislate on the subject have largely failed. Even so, almost twenty states have laws of some kind designed to curb unfair campaign tactics.

Essentially, the problem of campaign regulation centers on the First Amendment guarantees of free speech. According to several decisions by the U.S. Supreme Court, if state laws restrict political advertising, mailings, or other forms of communication, those restrictions must be narrowly and specifically aimed at false statements. Further, the Supreme Court has ruled that candidates for public office or elected public officials place themselves in the public spotlight. They may be attacked and criticized to a far greater extent than private citizens.

Nor does there appear to be a way to legislate against false, misleading, or ego-inspired statements a candidate may make about him- or herself. The normal concept of "consumer protection" does not apply, again because of the prime importance in a democracy of the free and unrestricted flow of campaign materials. At present, the most effective regulation of campaign practices and materials appears to be community standards rather than law.

[3]*Los Angeles Times,* June 18, 1982.
[4]*Sacramento Bee,* December 3, 1982.

SUMMARY

As we have seen, the ways in which election laws work are not neutral. While almost anyone can file for public office in California, few can command or attract the resources required for victory.

Primary elections are often more important than the general.

Interestingly, voters also seem to be becoming more conservative and more ideological in their voting. Fewer and fewer voters are strong party voters and increasing numbers view themselves as independents. Republicans and Democrats at present are nearly equal in political strength in the state. In part, the new conservatism appears to be simply the end of the Depression-born Democratic New Deal coalition. But the new conservatism also appears to be rooted in some fundamental changes in the state's economic structure and in the end of the state's "go-go," "growth-is-beautiful," visions. As the state turns inward, it may continue to exhibit fundamental changes in political goals. Ronald Reagan, Jerry Brown, and George Deukmejian certainly attracted votes with their anti-government postures.

These themes are easy to present on TV—they are essentially negative images. But if our candidates keep on telling us that government is bad, and keep on showing us how dirty politics can be, will many voters continue to participate?

4

Direct Democracy—Power to the People?

At the turn of this century, the United States was swept by the Progressive political reform movement (described previously in Chapter 2). Though the movement was national in scope, affecting to varying degrees cities and towns in nearly every state, there is little question that the Progressive impact was felt most keenly in a few midwestern states, such as Wisconsin and Minnesota, and in the western portions of the United States in what had formerly been strongholds of a nineteenth century political reform—Populism.

Progressives wanted to clean up politics, control politicians, and curb excessive special interest power. In California, the chief special interest target of Progressives was the Southern Pacific Railroad. According to former newspaper editor Fremont Older (1926:14), in 1896 Southern Pacific dominated the legislature, courts, municipal governments, county governments, and the newspapers of California. Southern Pacific, in turn, was the recipient of state and federal largesse— cash subsidies, no rate regulations, a sympathetic railroad commission, massive land grants, and favorable loans.

To combat this political and economic power California Progressives sought to provide citizens with a greater voice in governmental decision making. Clearly, no reform elements in the Progressive program were more important than their holy trinity—the initiative, referendum, and recall. Underlying these three reform proposals was the belief that *ordinary* citizens using the petition process and voting booth ought to have the ultimate decision-making power.

4-1 *"Direct Democracy" in Action. The November 1986 ballot contained five initiatives, 61–65.*

61	**PUBLIC OFFICIAL, EMPLOYEE, CONTRACTOR COMPENSATION.** Limits compensation of state and local public officials, employees and individual contractors. Fiscal impact: Net fiscal impact is unknown. This measure would result in unknown savings to state and local governments estimated to be about $125 million in the first year at state level and roughly the same at local level. These savings, however, could be offset and could even be outweighed by the need to pay vested sick and vacation leave at a one-time cost of about $7 billion.	**YES** **NO**
62	**LOCAL TAXATION.** For new and increased taxes, local governments and districts need two-thirds popular vote—special taxes; majority—general taxes. Fiscal impact: Prevents new or higher general taxes by local agencies without voter approval. Could reduce local agencies' existing tax revenues, if their voters do not ratify the continuation of new or higher taxes adopted after August 1, 1985. Provisions imposing penalties and requiring voter approval cannot be applied to charter cities.	**YES** **NO**
63	**OFFICIAL STATE LANGUAGE.** Requires Legislature and state officials to ensure English as official state common language. Provides for private enforcement. Fiscal impact: No direct effect on the costs or revenues of the state or local governments.	**YES** **NO**
64	**ACQUIRED IMMUNE DEFICIENCY SYNDROME (AIDS).** Declares AIDS virus carrier a contagious condition, subject to quarantine and reportable disease regulation. Fiscal impact: The measure's cost could vary greatly depending upon its interpretation by health officers and courts. If existing discretionary communicable disease controls were applied to AIDS, given the current state of medical knowledge, there would be no substantial change in state and local costs. If measure were interpreted to require added disease controls, costs could range to hundreds of millions of dollars per year depending on measures taken.	**YES** **NO**
65	**TOXIC DISCHARGE AND EXPOSURE RESTRICTIONS.** Prohibits discharge of toxic chemicals into drinking water and requires warnings of toxic chemicals exposure. Fiscal impact: Costs of state and local enforcement are estimated at $500,000 in 1987 and thereafter would depend on many factors, but could exceed $1,000,000 annually. Costs would be partially offset by fines collected.	**YES** **NO**

Source: Butte County Election Department

DIRECT DEMOCRACY: A WESTERN PHENOMENON

Currently, some twenty-three states provide for the initiative, and in many of these same states the referendum and recall are also allowed. Moreover, some of the twenty-seven states that offer no statewide direct democracy options do allow for the initiative, referendum, or recall at the local level.

Unlike some Progressive reforms (the secret ballot, direct primary, or presidential preference primary) that have been adopted in the great majority of states, direct democracy enjoyed an initial burst of adoptions by states in the early part of this century and a few others have adopted the initiative in the intervening years, but over the last fifteen years no new state has adopted the initiative. This is particularly striking in light of the enormous interest in the initiative process generated

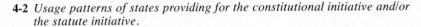

4-2 *Usage patterns of states providing for the constitutional initiative and/or the statute initiative.*

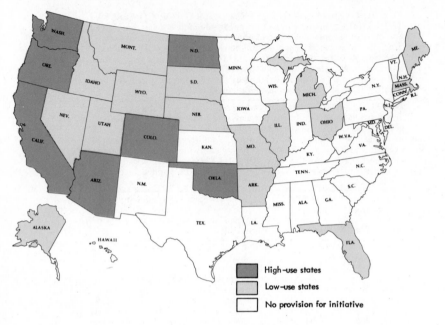

by Proposition 13 Jarvis-Gann property tax relief measure of June 1978. However, it is interesting to note that no state with the initiative has abandoned it. Once in place it stays.

Clearly, direct democracy devices have been adopted primarily in the western states. Only six states (23 percent) out of the twenty-six east of the Mississippi River currently provide for the initiative, compared to seventeen (71 percent) out of the twenty-four west of the Mississippi River (see Illustration 4–2).

The Progressives' middle-class reformism, their antipathy toward the two major establishment parties, their suspicions of officeholders, and their reliance on ordinary citizens to exercise ultimate political power have helped shape the ebb and flow of California politics ever since. California voters tend to be wary of politicians. And while the Progressive movement has faded from the California political stage, reform-oriented public interest lobbies, such as Common Cause, the Public Interest Research Group, and the League of Women Voters, continue to strive on the contemporary scene to promote reforms in tune with Progressive goals. In a sense, Paul Gann and the late Howard Jarvis, authors jointly and separately of more than a dozen initiatives in the late 1970s–80s, struck a particularly Progressive theme in their Proposition 13 campaign of June 1978—"teach the politicians a lesson."

PROCEDURES

Initiative Procedures

The *initiative* allows citizens the opportunity to propose and to approve laws. There are two types of initiatives—statute and constitutional. California and most of the other western states provide for both initiative options. The statute initiative gives citizens the power to make changes in the laws, and the constitutional initiative allows citizens to amend the constitution.

The basic steps in the California initiative process are: (1) interested citizens draft a proposed measure; (2) the measure is submitted to the Office of the Attorney General for titling and summary; (3) proponents pay a $200 fee; (4) petitions are circulated among voters with backers having 150 days to qualify their petition; (5) the secretary of state's office determines whether the proper number of valid signatures has been collected within the time frame and if so it automatically goes on the state election ballot.[1] If the initiative has more aye than nay votes, it becomes the law. Additionally, if provisions of two or more propositions approved at the same election conflict, the measure receiving the higher affirmative vote prevails.

In order to further protect this citizen weapon from the "politicians," Progressives also made it difficult for the legislature to amend an approved initiative. Constitutional initiatives may be changed only through passage of another initiative. Statutory initiatives can be amended by a majority vote of the legislature and submission to the electorate, unless the initiative specifically permits amendment without voter approval.

Finally, initiatives are subject to review by the courts, if challenged by opponents. For example, the anti-school-busing Proposition 21 of 1972 was ruled unconstitutional by the California supreme court. Proposition 9, the Political Reform Act of 1974, underwent a series of challenges in the courts with some portions being declared unconstitutional. Proposition 13, the property tax relief measure of June 1978, was immediately challenged but was quickly upheld by the California supreme court. Initiatives at variance with the U.S. Constitution may also be declared unconstitutional by federal courts.

California initiatives may cover only one topic, but this is some-

---

[1]Strangely enough, even though California gained several hundred thousand people between 1982 and 1986, the number of signatures that will be needed in 1988 and 1990 to qualify statute and constitutional initiatives is less than it was in 1982! This is because in 1986 only 43.3 percent of those who could have voted (17,561,000) did vote (7,617,142). And, based on the 1986 total vote cast for governor (7,443,551), to qualify a statute initiative (5 percent) in 1988 and 1990 will require *372,178* valid signatures, and to qualify a constitutional initiative (8 percent) will require *595,485* valid signatures.

times hard to define. Thus, Proposition 9, the Political Reform Act of
1974, and Paul Gann's Victim's Bill of Rights initiative of June 1982
were challenged in court on the contention that they encompassed
more than one subject. The court must determine whether an initiative's provisions are reasonably germane.

Referendum Procedures

The *referendum* gives citizens the opportunity to "veto," in effect,
bills recently passed by the legislature and signed by the governor.
Briefly, the process works as follows: (1) the legislature passes and the
governor signs a controversial bill; (2) certain citizens strongly oppose
the new law and decide to attempt to qualify a referendum for the ballot
before the law goes into effect sixty-one days after the legislative session; (3) citizens attempting to qualify a referendum have only ninety
days after the governor has signed the bill to collect the necessary
number of valid signatures—5 percent of the total vote cast for governor in the preceding election (372,178). And, if sufficient signatures are
secured the measure goes on the ballot. Finally, certain types of bills
are excluded from the referendum process: calls for special elections,
tax levies, urgency measures, and appropriations measures.

Recall Procedures

The *recall* gives citizens the power to remove incumbents from office using the petition/election procedure. For a statewide recall, valid
signatures of qualified voters equaling 12 percent of the total vote cast
for that particular office must be gathered. Thus, the signatures of
893,227 voters would have to be collected within 160 days to place a
recall of Governor George Deukmejian on the ballot between 1986 and
1990.[2] And, unlike the initiative and referendum, which are normally

---

[2]At the state level, the petition effort to recall an officeholder theoretically could
begin on the first day of the officeholder's term. If the correct number of valid signatures is collected, a special election would then have to be called. The ballot for a
statewide recall, except for judges, would be divided into two parts. On the top half
of the ballot the list of charges brought against the incumbent would be set forth, as
well as the incumbent's defense of his or her position. Then the question would be
posed: *Shall_____be recalled from the office of_____?* On the bottom
half of the ballot, the various nominees for the office (to be placed on the ballot as a
candidate one would need to secure the signatures of 1 percent of the vote cast for
that particular office in the last election) would be listed. Not surprisingly, the challenged incumbent may not qualify as one of the candidates on the bottom portion of
the ballot. If there are more no votes than yes votes, the incumbent remains in office,
and votes on the bottom half of the ballot are not counted. Additionally, the state
must reimburse the incumbent for the expenses of the campaign. If there are more
yes than no votes, the officeholder is removed from office, and the candidate with the
most votes on the bottom portion of the ballot is elected and serves out the remainder
of the recalled officeholder's term.

voted upon in the June or November statewide elections, recalls that qualify are usually described in one-item special elections. At the local level, required signatures range from 10 to 30 percent depending upon the population of the local district.

In the next few sections we shall consider the recall and referendum, and after this we shall focus our main attention on the initiative, the most important of the direct democracy devices.

RECALL USE—STATEWIDE

No recall effort directed against a statewide officeholder has ever qualified for the California ballot. Indeed, only a handful of statewide officials in the various recall states have ever been removed from office, and these all occurred many decades ago. Some states have awesome signature requirements—for example, Kansas requires 40 percent. The few abortive statewide recall attempts (directed primarily against governors) have always fallen far short of securing the necessary signatures. However, several California legislators many decades ago were removed from office in recall elections.

Several factors contribute to this notable lack of recall use at the state level. First, massive numbers of signatures are required to qualify the recall petition for the ballot, far more than are required for initiatives or referenda. To collect the sizable number of signatures necessary to qualify a statewide recall requires a monumental effort. Second, as with impeachment, the recall petition conveys to some citizens a kind of radical, desperate action that may be disquieting to potential petition signers. These people might feel that the normal channels for throwing out the rascals (the next regular election) is preferable to the recall process. Third, recall proponents have long noted that some citizens seem to be confused by the term "recall"—they think it means "remember" rather than removal.

While it is easy to minimize the importance of statewide recalls in California since voters here have never had to face one, the development of direct mail petitioneering in the late 1970s suggests the statewide recall is at least conceivable under the right circumstances. Certainly, former Chief Justice Rose Bird took the various right-wing recall efforts launched against her seriously since many of these same people had been successful in qualifying conservative initiatives for the ballot using direct mail.[3] If nothing else, the four separate recall efforts aimed against her were like an early artillery barrage designed to "soften up" the enemy in preparation for the final assault (the recon-

---

[3]Among the leading targets of recalls were the following state politicians: Governor Culbert Olson, five recall attempts; Governor Jerry Brown, four; Governor Pat Brown, three; Governor Ronald Reagan, three; and, Chief Justice Rose Bird, three.

firmation election). Currently, Arizona Governor Evan Mecham, it appears, will be forced into a recall election in early 1988.

RECALL USE—LOCAL

The local recall is available to a greater or lesser extent in thirty-six states. Twenty-one states, including California, provide for recall of nearly all local public officials; fifteen allow for recalls of only certain officials or only in home rule cities; and the other fourteen states do not provide for local recalls. The percentage requirement needed to qualify local recalls for the ballot varies considerably. In Texas and Florida some small, rural districts require only 5 percent of registered voters, while in Chattanooga, Tennessee, recall proponents need to secure 50 percent in order to recall the mayor.[4] Though the local recall is used sparingly, if ever, in the states that allow for it, in a few mainly western states—Oregon, Nebraska, Alaska, Idaho, Michigan, Nevada, Washington, and California—the device is used occasionally.

In California, there appears to have been an upturn in local recall elections recently. Typical local recall issues in the 1970s and 80s have tended to center around: (1) planned-growth or no-growth advocates versus prodevelopment interests, (2) the firing of a popular local official and its aftermath, (3) local officials voting pay raises for themselves, and, (4) "back to the basics" versus modernist education philosophies on local school boards. Of course, not all local recalls deal with important issues. Thus, two members of the Paradise city council faced major recall drives in 1981 because they had voted to ban parking on the city's main thoroughfare on the day of that community's annual Gold Nugget Days parade.

Local recalls seem most plentiful in smaller, rural communities where local residents tend to take a keen interest in the politics of their community, and in the suburbs of Los Angeles and the outlying southern California counties of Riverside, San Bernardino, Orange, and San Diego where the local recall has deep historical roots.

At the local level where the recall has been used successfully, targets have frequently been prominent officeholders, such as mayors,

---

[4]In California, requirements for local recall qualification are as follows:

Number of Voters	Percent to Qualify	Days to Qualify Petition
Less than 1,000	30	40
1,000–5,000	25	60
5,000–10,000	25	90
10,000–50,000	20	120
50,000–100,000	10	160
100,000 or more	10	160

supervisors, city council members, or school board members. In the last analysis, whether the recall process has been used or abused frequently depends on "whose ox is being gored."

Criticism of Recalls—State and Local

Critics of the recall process cite any number of problems inherent with the device, including: intimidation of officeholders by disgruntled minorities, heightened acrimony, and partisan hanky-panky. For example, certainly part of the motivation to recall Ronald Reagan as governor in 1968 was an attempt to discredit his presidential ambitions. The point is that politics and the recall process are inextricably linked.

Recall campaigns tend to be dirty and mean since the recallee's integrity is inevitably at stake. In small communities, recalls have frequently polarized towns and alienated neighbors. On the other hand, the ability of citizens to be able to use the recall helps encourage responsiveness of public officials and discourage incumbent arrogance.[5] Thus, as with the other democratic devices, there are distinct pro and con trade-offs with the device.

REFERENDUM USE

Nearly all states providing for the initiative also provide for its alter ego, the petition referendum. However, the pattern in these states is similar; very few referendums have ever qualified for the ballot over the last three or four decades. Indeed, New Mexico has *never* had a referendum successfully qualify for its ballot.

Before proceeding, we should note that there are two other kinds of referendums in addition to the petition referendum, the compulsory and the advisory referendums. When the legislature passes a constitutional amendment or bond issue, these measures are automatically placed on the next election ballot and are called compulsory referendums which voters may approve or reject. Advisory referendums are nonbinding measures on the ballot, which are posed by city councils or boards of supervisors to assess the mood of a community.

Used in virtually every state of the union, compulsory referendums can sometimes be of considerable importance, particularly on bond issues for schools, jails, veterans, or parks, but the constitutional amendments are often highly technical and legalistic. Should counties be required to have an elective district attorney? Should postsecondary education personnel be under civil service? Should local government employees be required to live in the city where they work? Should a

---

[5]Michigan voters recalled two state senators in 1983 after their legislature voted a 38 percent income tax increase.

board of chiropractic examiners be authorized to adopt rules and regulations governing chiropractors? These are typical compulsory referendums presented to the voters.

Finally, advisory referendums are used infrequently at the local level by city councils and boards of supervisors to put nonbinding questions on the ballot in order to get a sense of direction from the community. Unlike reputable surveys though, questions posed on the ballot can be designed to elicit a response from the voters. For example, Chico residents were asked the following in November 1986: "Should a large scale apartment and housing development be built next to Upper Bidwell Park, causing tremendous impacts [sic] on our park and causing costly urban sprawl?" Yes or No? Needless to say, Chicoans did not like the idea. In some communities foreign policy questions have been asked of voters—aid to the contras, or disinvestment in South Africa. Does this lead to voter overload and frivolous voting, or does ascertaining community sentiment on these foreign policy issues help contribute to a national dialogue? Both sides have good arguments.

Petition Referendums

From 1961 to 1981, 36 initiatives, 208 compulsory referendums, and *0* petition referendums qualified for the California ballot. While the petition referendum was used occasionally in the early decades after its adoption, it has been a rare phenomenon since the 1940s. Petition referendum use in California by decade is as follows:

Referendums Qualifying for Ballot by Decade	Number of Petitions
1912–19	11
1920–29	11
1930–39	11
1940–49	1
1950–59	1
1960–69	0
1970–79	0
1980–86	4

As we can note, while the use of petition referendums declined precipitously from 1940 to 80, there has been a modest revival of the technique in the 1980s. Two questions come to mind: first, why have so few petition referendums (as compared to initiatives) qualified for the ballot? Second, why has there been an upturn in petition referendum use in the 1980s?

Clearly, one key reason for the lack of referendum use (as contrasted to the initiative) has been the time constraints placed on referendum backers. Referendum proponents have only ninety days to collect 5 percent (372,178) of state voters' signatures to qualify their measure for the ballot, and the stopwatch starts running as soon as the governor signs the bill. Thus, Republicans were furious in 1981 when Democratic Governor Jerry Brown signed the reapportionment bill a few minutes before midnight. This meant that Republicans were robbed of one precious day in their qualifying quest; they had only eighty-nine days to collect signatures. To have any realistic hopes of qualifying a referendum, a group has to begin anticipating action while a measure is progressing through the legislature. Initiative proponents, on the other hand, can be organized and ready to roll as soon as their initiative is certified by the secretary of state. In the past, groups as politically adept as the California Real Estate Association have been unable to qualify their petition referendums for the ballot because of the time constraints.

Petition referendums sometimes develop when the legislature and governor go too far out on a limb on an issue. While the California legislature tends to be responsive to public opinion, occasionally on highly emotional moral issues—abortion, race relations, sexual practices, death penalty, gun control, and the like—legislators may vote their consciences and not their constituencies. This can provide the necessary ingredients for a referendum effort.

Interestingly, in the 1980s, the two issues generating referendum activity were not moral issues: water—the proposed construction of a Peripheral Canal to transfer "surplus" northern California water around the Delta region to southern California—and reapportionment—Republicans charged that the Democrats had drawn election districts to help themselves and destroy the GOP.

The epitaphs written by experts on the petition referendum's demise seem premature at the very least. Two new factors have helped fuel referendum efforts: the new technology in signature collecting (see discussion in next section) and the continuing decline of public confidence in our public officials.

Surprisingly, the four referendums of June 1982 qualified with relative ease for the ballot. Republicans collected an unprecedented 2,767,203 signatures for their three referendums on reapportionment (congressional, state senate, and assembly). Peripheral Canal proponents had difficulty keeping their professional petition circulators paid since they were collecting signatures so rapidly. Voters in the June 1982 primary rejected the legislative-passed bills on all four referendums.

While the four referendums dealt with a set of fairly unique problems and though it does seem unlikely that there will be many referendums in the years immediately ahead, for occasional controversial issues, the referendum is certainly a realistic option today. And, at the

4-3 *Paul Gann (left) and the late Howard Jarvis (right) celebrating the victory of Proposition 13, a property tax relief measure, in June 1978.*

United Press International

local level, referendums have been employed by planned growth advocates to override city council and supervisorial actions.

Finally, is the referendum worth keeping? Proponents note that the referendum helps keep government accountable and responsive to the public. Opponents note that the petition referendum discourages legislators from taking principled stands against public sentiment. As with the other direct democracy devices, there are good arguments for and against the direct democracy techniques.

INITIATIVE

There are sharp differences in initiative procedures among the states. For example, some states have *no* circulation period requirements;

they only require that petitions be submitted four to five months prior to the general election. Florida has a four-year circulation period; California has 150 days; and in Oklahoma, initiative backers have only 90 days to collect signatures.[6] In many states there are geographical requirements stipulating that petitions must be signed in a certain number of state counties. (California has no such requirement.) Most initiative states require 5 to 10 percent of the state's registered voters to qualify the petition, but North Dakota has a 2 percent requirement and doesn't require that signers be registered voters. Some states forbid professional petition circulators, though this law has never been tested in court. In Missouri, an average of 30 percent of all signatures are invalidated, and in Florida, initiative proponents must pay for this signature validation process. While differences in initiative use in various states may hinge on formal qualifying requirements, for the most part, initiative use seems more related to political-social factors than anything else.

Initiatives in California

It is interesting to note that while there was a drop-off in the number of initiatives qualifying for the California ballot in the 1940s, 50s, and 60s, there has been a remarkable upsurge in the number of initiatives circulating and qualifying in the 1970s and 80s. In Table 4–1, the number and percent of initiatives circulating, qualifying, approved, and rejected are listed by decade.

Approximately three times as many initiatives circulated in the 1970s as in any previous decade, and that trend continues into the 1980s. Of the total number of initiatives that have circulated in the state since 1912, nearly one-third have been launched since January 1, 1970. Exactly why so many initiatives have circulated over the last several years is not altogether clear, but it appears to be related to: (1) a continued decline in public confidence in governmental leaders and political institutions, (2) the enormous popularity of particular initiatives (the Jarvis-Gann property tax relief measure) which encourages imitative efforts, (3) the inability of the legislature to respond on certain issues, (4) the many professional petition firms in the state whose raison d'être hinges on constant initiative activity, and (5) the mushrooming growth of single-issue groups and PACs. This spectacular increase

---

[6]Michigan's attorney general in 1974 argued that a state statute that required initiative proponents to turn in all signatures within a 180-day period was unconstitutional and that signatures could be collected over a four-year period between gubernatorial elections. From 1974 until 1986 initiative proponents in Michigan had assumed they had four years to collect signatures. The issue was brought to court in 1986 and the court ruled that the 180-day time frame was constitutional. This ruling removed from the ballot a utility regulation initiative and a death penalty initiative.

TABLE 4-1
Number and Percent of Initiatives Submitted to Voters

Decade	Number Titled by Attorney General as Eligible for Circulation	Number and Percent Qualifying	Voters' Action	
			Adopted	Rejected
1912–19	45	30 (67%)	8 (27%)	22 (73%)
1920–29	51	35 (69)	10 (29)	25 (71)
1930–39	66	35 (53)	9 (26)	26 (74)
1940–49	42	19 (45)	6 (32)	13 (68)
1950–59	17	10 (59)	2 (20)	8 (80)
1960–69	44	9 (20)	3 (33)	6 (67)
1970–79	180	24 (13)	7 (29)	17 (71)
1980–86	147	24 (16)*	12 (55)	10 (45)
Total	592	186 (31)	57 (31)	127 (69)

*These twenty-four ballot measures include two initiatives which qualified for the ballot but were removed by the court prior to their being voted upon—the Sebastiani Reapportionment Initiative and the Balance the Budget Initiative.

Source: This table, though modified and updated, is adopted from Eugene Lee, "California" in *Referendums: A Comparative Study of Practice and Theory,* ed. Daniel Butler and Austin Ranney (Washington, D.C.: American Enterprise Institute, 1978), p. 91.

in initiative activity is not just a phenomenon of California but characterizes political patterns in a number of initiative states.

What types of issues, generally, are brought to voters via the initiative? Clearly, they run the gamut, but often they comprise some of the most controversial issues of the day—the death penalty, political reform, property taxes, property rights and racial exclusion, marijuana penalties, pay TV, school busing, farm labor rights, state lottery, tort reform, nuclear energy safety, and homosexual teachers. While most initiatives, of course, never qualify for the ballot, the titling, summarizing, and circulation of an initiative provides individuals and groups a chance to begin public discussion of an issue. It is a legitimizing process.

The initiative process allows voters an opportunity to express their opinions on a host of controversial issues as a sort of "court of last resort." Not surprisingly, the subject itself is of considerable controversy. From the very first years immediately after the adoption of the initiative to the present, there have been persistent criticisms of the process. Many legislators dislike the initiative because it takes power away from them and dilutes representative government. Knowledgeable observers worry about the public's capacity to vote thoughtfully on initiatives. Even the initiative process' most vehement supporters recognize problems with the device. Let us examine some of the criticisms of the initiative and then consider some of the counterarguments to these criticisms.

Drafting Phase

Criticisms.   One of the major complaints critics level against initiatives is that they tend to be poorly or hastily drafted. Most legislative bills move slowly through the legislative labyrinth. In the legislature, bills are repeatedly scrutinized, polished, and amended by various legislative committees. The initiative comes to the voter full-blown, without the give-and-take found in the legislative process. Literally anyone, including cranks and crackpots, can submit an initiative idea and then begin circulating the petition forms. In 1974, two private citizens alone proposed thirty separate California initiatives! Finally, given this situation, initiatives can be unclear, bizarre, lengthy, complicated, and, potentially, unconstitutional. Over the years, a number of initiatives which had been approved by voters were declared unconstitutional by the courts.

Rebuttal.   Direct democracy supporters would concede there is some truth to these charges, but there is another side. If an initiative is patently harebrained, it is unlikely to win acceptance from the voters in the signature-gathering campaign. While many initiative proposals have circulated, over the last several decades, few have qualified for the ballot and fewer have passed (see Table 4–1).

It may be true that some initiatives are not well thought out or are poorly drafted, but, in fairness, for years the legislature has been guilty of passing legislation hastily without careful scrutiny, especially during the last week or two of a session when there is inevitably a tremendous backlog of bills. It should also be noted that a growing number of initiatives are drafted by legislators (i.e., the "experts") after their proposed bills have been rejected by the legislature, or by skilled attorneys who specialize in political law such as the Chip Nielsen law firm, which has been on the pro or con side of most initiatives qualifying for the California ballot over the last decade, and Barry Fadem. When Fadem drafted the lottery initiative, he used survey data, analysis of other states' lottery laws and word-by-word study of the initiative draft— much as committee consultants might. Of course, groups must have the financial wherewithal to hire these attorneys. Furthermore, given the fact that legislators are expected to vote on thousands of bills and resolutions each year, few can give more than cursory attention to many of these votes. Voters, on the other hand, have only a few initiatives that they have to vote upon. And having voters directly decide critical issues is part of the "democratic" evolution in America.

Finally, while some initiatives have been declared unconstitutional by the courts, so too have measures passed by Congress or the state legislatures. Obviously, the final word on constitutionality must come from the courts and one is never really sure until a measure is tested in court.[7]

Qualifying Phase

Criticisms.   Critics of the initiative process contend that in order to amass the requisite number of signatures necessary to qualify a statute or constitutional initiative in the time allotted, it is necessary to have either enormous financial resources or a large mass organization. Hence, it is argued that the initiative, rather than being an important citizen weapon, is in reality a tool of narrow, special interests—the petroleum industry, automobile manufacturers and dealers, land developers, building interests, and the like.

Under the original provisions of the Political Reform Act initiative of 1974, groups would have been limited in how much they could spend to qualify a measure for the ballot (25 cents times the number of signatures necessary to qualify). These limits were struck down by the state court as being unconstitutional, since they violated the free speech provisions of the First Amendment to the U.S. Constitution. The state court noted the U.S. Supreme Court's action striking down campaign expenditure limits in *Buckley* v. *Valeo*.

Large mass-member organizations, such as the California Teachers Association or the California State Employees Association, can mail out petition forms to their many members, but smaller groups cannot hope to qualify an initiative relying only on their own membership. Wealthy groups can hire expensive professional petition firms to collect their signatures for them. The current reigning dean of petition solicitors is the F. G. Kimball Company of Westlake Village, California. Over the last few decades the Kimball Company has helped qualify dozens of initiatives and referendums. Solicitors working for Kimball are advised to approach people waiting in lines or walking slowly (according to Kimball, the best single place they found for collecting sig-

---

[7]Perhaps most distressing to direct democracy advocates, former Chief Justice Rose Bird argued that on legal challenges of qualified initiatives, the Court should declare them constitutional or unconstitutional *prior* to their being voted upon by the public. She said this would save proponents and opponents millions of dollars in futile campaigns. Moreover, she felt this might deflect some of the hostility directed against the court when they declared an initiative unconstitutional after an overwhelming majority of citizens had already voted for it. The defeat of Rose Bird and two other liberals on the court (Justices Reynoso and Grodin) in their reconfirmation elections in November 1986 probably means that the newly constituted court will not likely follow the path on initiatives that Justice Bird proposed.

4-4 *Getting signatures on a petition*

natures in 1981 was the King Tut exhibit in Los Angeles). If a voter is wary, petition circulators are taught to emphasize that signing one's name does not necessarily mean agreement.[8] Signing the petition merely helps put the measure on the ballot so that voters can have a chance to express themselves on the issue at the next election. Frequently, petition firms do not collect all the signatures required for a particular initiative campaign as this might cost initiative proponents several hundred thousand dollars (approximately 53 cents per signature). Usually, the petition firms guarantee a certain number of signatures—75,000 or 100,000—to augment an unpaid volunteer effort.[9]

The newest kind of petition firms are those specializing in signature gathering through computerized mass mailings. After extensive pre-

[8]In Sacramento in 1986 the rights of petition solicitors and opponents of an initiative became a court issue. Local Sacramento environmentalists launched a petition drive to stop an agricultural area (North Natomas) from being rezoned to business-commercial. The rezoning would also have accommodated the proposed new arena for the National Basketball Association professional team, the Sacramento Kings. Environmentalists brought suit contending that their petition seekers were harassed by outraged sports fans and others favoring development, and that they were unable to collect enough signatures because of the intimidation.

[9]The Kimball Company's success streak (forty-three petition campaigns where they delivered the agreed upon number of signatures for a client) was broken in 1986 when two different initiative efforts they worked on failed to qualify.

sampling, petitions are sent to a carefully culled list of potentially sympathetic citizens whose names have been conveniently stored on computer tapes.

Undoubtedly, the most famous of these new petition-by-mail firms is the Butcher-Forde Company of Orange County. They first used the device successfully in the John Briggs 1978 death penalty initiative drive. Since then, targeted mass mail has been used in a variety of other initiative campaigns—property tax relief, income tax indexing, and anti-rent control. While the cost per signature in a mass-mail petition campaign is three to four times higher than with clipboard petition firms, some mail campaigns have generated enormous return contributions more than making up for the higher initial cost. Moreover, citizen enthusiasts can help circulate the mailed petition among their family and neighbors, further augmenting the number of signatures.

The mass-mail firms have become particularly adept in persuading people to open their envelopes, read, and sign the enclosed petitions. The color of the lettering on the envelope, a bold printed warning such as "OFFICIAL DOCUMENT ENCLOSED," and an accompanying letter warning the reader of a looming catastrophe have been used to get readers to respond.[10] While critics of this new signature-gathering process complain that only one side is presented to prospective signers, defenders argue that this procedure is more sensible than urging distracted people walking through shopping centers to sign petitions. With mail petitions voters are able to consider the issue at home at their leisure.

Critics of the initiative process contend that the legislature better represents the unorganized, the minorities, the young, and the non-voters in our society, while the initiative serves the interests of the voting white middle-class. This view is debatable. Legislators clearly respond to *voters* and to *special interest* campaign contributions. While "public interest" propositions, such as the smoking initiatives of 1978 and 1980, the bottle deposit initiative of 1982, and the handgun initiative of 1982, were beaten—in part because of the awesome spending of the opposition—they came much closer to being approved in the initiative arena than they had in the legislature.

Critics of the initiative process argue that there are many opportunities for deception in gathering signatures. In some early initiative campaigns, "dodger cards" reportedly were used to cover up the attorney general's summary of the measure. Petition signers can then be misled on the details of the initiative. People's Lobby founder, the late Ed Koupal (Duscha, 1975) stated:

---

[10]In one direct-mail initiative campaign in 1980 relating to police funding, solicited voters received an envelope which read: "In reference to police matter at" and the recipient's address. A window on the envelope showed that the matter was referred by a police sergeant and declares the matter to be URGENT-URGENT-URGENT.

Generally, people who are getting out signatures are too goddamned interested in their ideology to get the required number in the required time. We use the hoopla process.

First, you set up a table with six petitions taped to it, and a sign in front that says, SIGN HERE. One person sits at the table. Another person stands in front. That's all you need—two people.

While one person sits at the table, the other walks up to people and asks two questions. We operate on the old selling maxim that two yeses make a sale. First, we ask them if they are a registered voter. If they say yes, we ask them if they are registered in that county. If they say yes to that, we immediately push them up to the table where the person sitting points to a petition and says, "Sign this." By this time, the person feels. "Oh goodie, I get to play," and signs it. . . . people don't ask to read the petition and we certainly don't offer. Why try to educate the world when you're trying to get signatures?

Rebuttal.   While money and/or large organizations can help in qualifying initiatives, they are not, as it has been argued, indispensable. Clearly, over the last several elections, small, less affluent groups have scored some impressive victories in signature-gathering campaigns. For example, the bottle deposit initiative of November 1982 (Proposition 11) qualified for the ballot largely through the efforts of the small, but determined, California Against Waste. Similarly, the handgun initiative of November 1982 (Proposition 15) and the oil profits tax initiative of June 1980 (Proposition 11), the English Only Initiative (Proposition 63) and the AIDS Initiative (Proposition 64) of November 1986 qualified for the ballot on a shoe string. They used volunteer signature collectors in their successful qualification campaigns.[11]

The point is that small, less affluent groups have been able to qualify initiatives for the ballot without enormous financial resources or large-scale mass organization. Grassroots appeal and ingenuity can be critical factors.

Campaign Phase

Criticisms.   Clearly, the most frequently heard criticism of the initiative process is the role that big money plays in direct democracy campaigns. Undoubtedly, enormous sums have been spent by proponents and opponents in initiative campaigns. In 1976, nearly $4 million

[11]Paul Gann, "People's Advocate" founder, after successfully masterminding Proposition 13, the property tax relief measure, to victory in June 1978, launched a new government-spending-limit initiative on election day, November 7, 1978. Under his ingenious scheme, Gann placed volunteer signature gatherers at polling places (carefully positioned more than 100 feet away from the polls). As people finished voting, they would walk a few paces over to the colorfully marked card table of the Gann volunteer and sign the new initiative.

was spent on the nuclear power initiative and over $3 million on the farm labor initiative. An historic high point (or all-time low?) was recorded in the general election of 1978 when several cigarette companies raised and spent more than $6 million to defeat the antismoking initiative of November 1978 (Proposition 5). This spending record was short-lived—the handgun initiative (Proposition 15) of November 1982 established the new record of $7.1 million. Additionally, in 1982, the bottle deposit initiative fight was the fourth most expensive initiative campaign in state record—$6.7 million.[12]

A more serious objection is the considerable advantage wealthy groups have when pitted against less affluent groups in an initiative campaign. Obviously, the side with the most money can buy more billboards, newspaper ads, TV spots, and the like to help influence the electorate. In some initiative campaigns, the spending disparity between proponents and opponents has reached outlandish proportions. For example, in 1972, opponents of Proposition 20 (the coastline initiative) spent five times as much as the proponents—$1.1 million versus $210,000; public employee groups spent nearly $2 million in their campaign on the state employee salaries initiative, while opponents spent a paltry $37,000. In 1978, cigarette companies spent more than ten times as much as anticigarette forces in the Proposition 5 campaign.

Critics of the initiative emphasize that these direct democracy campaigns are frequently managed by professional public relations firms. These firms have little interest in informing or educating voters; their goal is to win elections. Public relations firms using techniques pioneered originally in advertising campaigns for commercial products (toothpastes, mouthwashes, and underarm deodorants) have transferred them to the campaign arena. Distortions, gimmicks, deceptive slogans, half-truths, and outright lies have characterized many initiative campaigns. Though public relations firms also manage some statewide candidates' campaigns, their impact is greater in initiative campaigns because voters do not have the usual candidate or partisan cues to guide them in this type of election.

Examples of confusing claims and counterclaims are extensive in the history of California initiative campaigns. In 1972, advocates of "tax relief" Proposition 14 argued that a yes vote would reduce taxes, and opponents of Proposition 14 countered that a no vote would reduce taxes. State employee ads in 1972 proclaimed, "It's your money, keep state pay in line, vote Yes on 15." In reality, a yes vote would have made it easier for state employees to receive salary increases. Advocates of the measure argued that "keeping state pay in line" referred

---

[12]Professors Owens and Wade (1985) argue that when inflation and population increase are factored in there has been no substantial increase in spending on initiative campaigns since the 1950s.

to having state employees paid at a level commensurate with what they would earn in the private sector! Opponents of Proposition 20 of 1972 argued that a yes vote would lock up the coast from the people; proponents argued that they were trying to save the coast for the people. Opponents of the 1982 bottle deposit initiative audaciously portrayed themselves as "concerned environmentalists" worried about the future of recycling centers if Proposition 11 passed. Opponents of the toxics initiative (Proposition 65 of November 1986) argued in their media ads that they were opposed to the measure because there were too many exemptions in it. They deceptively implied that they wanted a tougher law.

In the Jarvis-Gann property tax relief measure, (Proposition 13), voters were inundated with bewildering sets of figures on the number of state, county, and city employees who might be laid off or the amount of money citizens would receive if Proposition 13 were to pass. Pro- and antismoking forces waged a bitter campaign in 1978 and 1980 over how much it would really cost to be implemented. In short, potential opportunities for razzle-dazzle, hocus-pocus politics are considerable in initiative campaigns.

Rebuttal.   Campaign spending on initiatives has risen steadily, it is true, but so has spending on candidate races. While the side with the most money obviously has a distinct advantage, it is not necessarily insurmountable. Indeed, in several recent initiative campaigns, the side spending the most money lost. Gene Lee (1978:113) notes that from 1972 to 1976, in the sixteen initiative campaigns of that period, the side spending the most money in the campaign won eight times and lost eight times. In several campaigns spending was incredibly lopsided (highway patrol, 100 percent–0 percent; state employee salaries, 98 percent–2 percent), and yet they lost. Proponents of the nuclear freeze initiative of November 1982 spent $3.5 million to persuade voters to support the measure; opponents spent $6,041 to defeat it. The initiative was approved 52 percent to 48 percent. What this suggests, of course, is that an expensive, professional campaign is helpful, but it will fail if it runs counter to substantial public sentiment.

There does appear to be some evidence that lopsided spending to *defeat* a measure can be critical. Only rarely can the underfinanced side persuade voters to vote yes. For example, on the smoking, bottle deposit, and handgun control initiatives, early polls taken at the beginning of the campaign period indicated there was substantial support for these measures among voters who had decided. However, opponents employing their superior financial advantages in expensive campaigns were able to persuade the undecided voters that these initiatives would be costly to consumers, were confusing, and would mean more governmental red tape and regulation. In campaigns such as these, the no vote becomes the safe, conservative option for perplexed voters worried about change. However, in 1983, San Francisco voters approved a tough no smoking ordinance even though tobacco companies outspent their foes ten to one, and, in 1986 toxics initiative foes far outspent proponents when urging voters to vote no. They lost.

As noted previously, the court has struck down expenditure limits on initiative campaigns, and in addition, efforts to limit the size of individual or group campaign contributions in an initiative campaign are fraught with constitutional problems. In 1980, the Berkeley city council adopted an ordinance limiting individuals and groups to a maximum of $250 in local initiative campaigns. (The ordinance was aimed primarily at real estate interests who were gearing up to defeat a rent control initiative.) This law, in turn, was challenged in the courts by real estate interests. The Berkeley ordinance was upheld by the California state supreme court on a narrow four to three vote. It was then appealed to the U.S. Supreme Court. The latter Court, in a decisive eight to one vote, overturned the California court decision declaring the law unconstitutional. The U.S. Supreme Court majority argued that the Berkeley ordinance violated free speech and free association rights, and that there was inconclusive evidence that "big money" was the decisive factor in initiative elections.

One additional factor that has helped, to an extent, to narrow the financial imbalance in initiative campaigns has been the "fairness doctrine." The Federal Communications Commission has ruled that when one side vastly outspends the other on radio and television spending, the less affluent side must be provided free radio and television time by the various stations at a ratio of one to three (one minute of free time for every three minutes bought by the wealthy side). This may mean that in the future the monied side will spend more of their campaign budget on direct mail, billboards, and newspaper and magazine ads since the latter are not regulated by the fairness doctrine.

Voting

Criticisms.   Critics of the initiative process believe that most voters are woefully uninformed about the host of complex, lengthy propositions confronting them. The Political Reform Act of 1974 contained more than 22,000 words; it is unlikely that many voters read all (or any) of its various provisions. Other initiatives, such as Governor Reagan's 1973 property tax proposal or the 1978 Jarvis-Gann property tax limit, were highly technical and complicated and, hence, difficult for the average voter to grasp fully.

It is argued that voters have a difficult enough time knowing something about the races at the top of the ticket; expecting them to have informed views on a host of propositions including initiatives at the bottom of the ticket is not realistic. Further reinforcing this view, pollsters have repeatedly noted that there is enormous ignorance and confusion among voters during initiative campaigns. According to pollster Mervin Field, as late as mid-October 1986 only 11 percent of voters had heard of the Jarvis Initiative (Proposition 62) to plug up loopholes in Proposition 13.

Concerns have been voiced by initiative critics that given the absence of party cues, voters will more likely follow the lead of newspaper endorsements.[13]

Rebuttal.   Few supporters of the initiative process would deny that *some* initiatives are long and complex, and voters are faced with a host of difficult voting decisions. Yet most voters expressing a preference at the top of the ballot do take the time and, evidently, feel competent enough to vote on initiatives at the bottom of the ballot. The more controversial and widely discussed the proposition, the greater the vote cast. In November 1982, approximately 7.7 million Californians voted in the gubernatorial election, and only a few hundred thousand less (7.4 million) voted on the bottle deposit initiative or on the handgun control initiative. In June 1978, 6,607,000 votes were cast on Proposition 13— 750,000 more than were cast in the gubernatorial primary.

While it is true that some earlier Field polls have indicated little voter awareness of particular initiatives during the campaign period, most voters know about the more controversial initiatives. Thus, in September 1982, Field reported that 66 percent of California voters had heard about the bottle deposit initiative; 51 percent the nuclear freeze initiative; and 80 percent the handgun control initiative. In October 1986 Field reported that 77 percent of California voters had heard of Proposition 63, the English Only Initiative, and more than half had heard of the Toxics and AIDS Initiatives.

One factor helping account for low voter awareness of initiatives during the campaign derives from the typical strategy of an initiative campaign: "Save your campaign money until the last week or two and then spend it all in a last-minute blitz." Additionally, the public receives its *California Voters Pamphlet* just a few weeks prior to the election. It is likely that some voters learn about the initiatives when reading through portions of the pamphlet.[14] The point is that the over-

[13]Magleby (1984) argues that since voting turnout in the June primary is low, initiatives should be voted upon only in the November general election.

[14]In a suit brought by the Center for Law in the Public Interest, plaintiffs argued that the ballot arguments written by the legislative analyst are supposed to be "clear and concise." They argued in their suit that the language used in describing the initiatives is unreadable to a majority of California citizens and is pegged more to a thirteenth- or fourteenth-grade level. The case is pending.

whelming majority of California voters have heard of and know about the well-publicized initiatives when they cast their ballots. Indeed, placing some highly controversial initiatives on the ballot may actually help encourage voter turnout.

LEGISLATIVE FAILURE

One final summary criticism of initiatives should be noted. It is asserted that when various groups or individuals are forced to resort to the initiative, the legislature has, in effect, failed to do its job. A prime legislative objective is to resolve group conflict. If a legislature is unable to reconcile group differences and groups resort to initiatives, the legislature, it is argued, has obviously failed. The inability of the legislature and governor to pass satisfactory property tax relief culminating in the passage of Proposition 13 of 1978, the property tax relief initiative, is a good example. However, in fairness to the legislature, this view of legislative failure seems overly simplistic.

Initiatives develop when a group or groups fail to receive satisfactory legislative action. Issues such as malpractice—pitting doctors against lawyers against insurance companies—or coastline planning—pitting developers, builders, and labor unions against environmentalists—are difficult for the legislature and governor to resolve successfully. Inability to pass satisfactory compromise legislation should not necessarily be construed as failure but may merely reflect the relatively even balance of power of the various contending groups in the legislature.

Overall, there appear to be several possible directions one might take in revising the initiative process. One course would be to make it more difficult to launch initiatives (a counterreform to Progressivism). Thus, proposals have been made to increase the qualifying percentages, require signatures to be gathered in public places, prohibit petition companies from collecting signatures, shorten the circulation period, require that initiatives be signed by at least one-third Democrats and one-third Republicans, raise the initiative filing fee, or reinstitute the indirect initiative (this would allow the legislature to debate the merits of a qualified initiative and approve it or reject it—if rejected it would automatically be placed on the next ballot).

While many legislators, journalists, and academics would welcome these sorts of changes in the initiative process (indeed, some would prefer to abolish the process entirely), the California public strongly approves of the initiative process. According to a February 1983 Field Poll 86 percent of California voters agreed that "Initiative and referendums allow the public to decide issues where public officials are hesitant to act for fear of offending certain groups." Sixty-six percent of

Field's sample agreed that "citizens ought to be able to vote directly on important issues and policies instead of having their representatives voting for them." In November 1979, Mervin Field (California Poll:7904) asked Californians the following:

> Some states allow proposition elections and others do not. California is one of the states that does. Do you think proposition elections are a good thing for Californians, a bad thing, or does it make much difference to you?
>
> | | |
> |---|---|
> | Good thing | 85% |
> | Bad thing | 4 |
> | Not much difference | 11 |
>
> In general, do you feel you are more affected by the outcome of candidate elections or by proposition elections?
>
> | | |
> |---|---|
> | Candidate elections | 22% |
> | Proposition elections | 74 |
> | No difference | 4 |

Indeed, David Magleby (1984) reports that 71 percent of California *nonvoters* believed that direct legislation was a good thing for state citizens! Given the overwhelming public support for the initiative process in California and the watchful vigilance of some of the public interest lobbies, attempts to make it more difficult to propose initiatives have foundered.

A second direction in initiative revision would be to make it even easier to qualify initiatives for the ballot. However, the prodigious number of initiatives circulating and the substantial number of initiatives qualifying suggest there is no compelling need to review the initiative process in this direction, and there is little support for such an effort.

Finally, a third avenue of initiative revision would be to attempt to make the process work more equitably for all Californians. In this vein, two prime problem areas could be addressed: (1) the amount of information citizens have in making their voting decisions on ballot propositions and (2) the "big money" factor.

To address these problems, legislation has been proposed which would require the legislature to conduct hearings throughout the state on qualified initiatives. At these hearings, experts and interested public could testify pro and con on proposed initiatives. Hopefully, publicity and information would be generated. Undoubtedly, the question of whether the public can handle initiative issues by voting competently will continue to be a hotly debated subject.

The role of big money in initiative campaigns is the second significant problem. There is no question that lopsided spending provides advantages to the monied side—particularly when they want the voters to vote no.

Legislation has been introduced to forbid special interests from hiding behind innocuous and/or deceptive campaign committee titles such as Californians Against Regulatory Excess (Tobacco firms). Thus, under the proposed format, instead of television commercials opposed to the bottle deposit initiative being sponsored by Californians for Sensible Laws, the real interests paying for the commercials—soft drink companies, breweries, grocery chains, and labor unions—would have to be so designated. This proposed reform is, of course, rife with constitutional problems.

Attempts to limit spending on initiative campaigns have been consistently struck down by the courts.[15] One interesting suggestion has been made: allow initiatives in California to circulate for a longer time period—for example, for one year. This might encourage more groups to collect signatures through mainly volunteer efforts rather than with paid solicitors.

In summary, the initiative provides a last resort to the public to bypass a stymied or recalcitrant legislature and/or governor. Initiatives do allow for decisive decisions on particularly sensitive, hard-to-resolve issues. Reforms can and should be made in the initiative process. However, we argue that the direct initiative should be retained. It is a deeply engrained feature of the California political scene. While there are trade-offs, the pros outweigh the cons in our minds.

Finally, adoption by the voters of Proposition 9 (the Political Reform Act of 1974) and Proposition 13 (property tax relief) highlight the most important advantage of the initiative: it allows voters to defy the establishment and to collectively thumb their noses at the powers that be. With both propositions, the major figures in the political establishment came away with egg on their face. In the last analysis, we feel this is a healthy feature. What came to be the motto of the proponents of Proposition 13—"show the politicians who's boss"—certainly is in the spirit of the Progressive surge at the beginning of this century and is a healthy feature of California democracy today.

SUMMARY

Because of the power of various special interests, the legislature at times has had difficulty reaching satisfactory compromises on highly controversial issues. Without the initiative, California voters would not have realized lobby or campaign reform, would have no coastline commission, or property tax relief. Moreover, the significance of initiatives

---

[15]Assemblyman Tom Bates introduced legislation in 1985 which would set *voluntary* spending limits on initiatives with hopes of using moral suasion to get both sides to agree.

cannot be measured solely by the number qualifying and winning approval of the voters.

A threatened initiative can "encourage" the legislature to act. Successful qualifying of the nuclear initiative, the farm worker initiative, and the property tax limitation initiative provided the necessary stimulus to the legislature to pass legislation on these topics to head off the initiatives. And, the threat of a new initiative effort proceeding after the bottle deposit initiative was defeated in 1982 prompted the bottlers and soft drink and brewery industries to agree to a compromise bill passed in the legislature in 1987.

Some issues, such as medical malpractice, handgun control, no-fault auto insurance, or abortion, perhaps cannot be resolved legislatively and hence may have to be resolved eventually through the initiative process. Also, issues that directly effect the legislature, such as campaign spending reform reapportionment or the unicameral proposal, will have to be eventually decided by the initiative.

5

Interest Groups and Lobbyists: In the "Good Ole Days" and the Contemporary Setting

From the state legislature's first session in December 1849 in temporary San Jose quarters to the elegant refurbished capitol of contemporary Sacramento, interest groups and "legislative advocates" (a legal euphemism for lobbyists) have been an integral part of the California political scene. In fact, according to former President Pro Tem of the Senate Hugh Burns, they preceded the legislature.

> Don't forget that the lobbyists were here [in the State Capital] even before we got here. The history shows us that at one of the first [legislative] sessions [in the state's history] in San Jose, the lobbyists had come to town before the legislative members and had taken up all the rooms in the hotels, and there was no room for the members to stay.
>
> That probably gave rise to the first expression about getting in bed with lobbyists—there was no other place to sleep. (*Sacramento Bee,* July 14, 1969:5)

Indeed, it has been argued with some justification that, for much of California's political history, lobbyists have tended to dominate the legislature and the rest of the state government as well. While interest groups and lobbyists have been active and are influential in all the state capitals and Washington, D.C., there seems little question that California has been and remains a strong lobby state (Zeigler and von Dalev 1971:127).[1]

---

[1]In a recent comparative three-state study (Wiggins, Hamm, and Bell, 1984, pp. 23–24) the authors note that interest groups are more likely to be involved with bills moving through the California legislature than were interest groups in Iowa or Texas in their respective legislatures.

Given the sorts of decisions that are made by the legislature, governor, commissions, and state bureaucracy, it is not surprising that businesses, trade associations, labor unions, government employees, and literally hundreds of other groups find it necessary to be represented at the state capital. Indeed, one recent study (Briscoe and Bell, 1985) reports that over one-third of all bills introduced in the 1981–82 session of the California legislature came from the so-called Third House in capitol politics—lobbies.

INTEREST GROUPS AND LOBBYISTS

Interest groups are organizations of people who seek to influence government to make "favorable" decisions on their behalf. Not all groups are "interest" groups; only groups that have a desire to get something from government are. Thus, the Chico Model Train Club under normal circumstances is not an interest group, but when the Club attempted to persuade Amtrak to provide train service to Chico, or when it petitioned the Chico city council for funds to refurbish the train station, it was acting as an interest group.

People join interest groups for a variety of reasons. For years, scholars have noted that Americans tend to be joiners who enjoy socializing with other like-minded people. Many citizens become involved in group activity to improve their economic condition. Through joint effort, pressure can be exerted more effectively on government— businesses, farm groups, trade associations, labor unions, or professional associations are examples of the types of groups seeking to improve the economic life of their membership. However, public interest/ cause groups that have blossomed on the state and national political scene in the 1970s and 80s are interested in promoting broader, common issues. Members of these latter "good guy" groups (e.g., the Sierra Club, League of Women Voters, PTA, NAACP, or Common Cause) do not join to improve their own economic status but to fight for "worthy" causes. Some groups emphasize the special opportunities members can enjoy if they join—medical or dental insurance, group travel programs, and so on. Sierra Club members, in addition to joining an environmentally active group, get to participate in various hikes and excursions and are sent a monthly magazine detailing outing news and attractive deals on camping equipment. Farm Bureau members, AMA doctors, American Political Science Association professors, and others keep abreast of developments in their respective fields in part through publications sent by their groups. Finally, some members join labor unions or employee groups not so much because they want to, but as a condition of their employment.

Lobbyists are hired by interest groups to represent their organization's viewpoints in Sacramento. Thus, in addition to our official elected representatives, lobbies provide the public an alternative form of functional representation. Since virtually every citizen belongs to at least some group that lobbies at the state capitol—business, labor, environmental, racial, seniors, children, women, animal lovers, local governments, employee groups, churches, and many others—they have another voice at the capitol in addition to their legislative representatives. Not surprisingly, well-organized, well-financed, prestigious groups (e.g., bankers, insurance interests, real estate brokers, doctors, attorneys, retailers, or petroleum interests), have always found ready access in Sacramento; disorganized poor, low-status groups frequently have more difficulty gaining a serious hearing.

Overall, lobbyists perform several critical functions. First, they serve as the eyes and ears for groups of citizens at the state capitol—the watchdog function. Since few in the public can really follow what's going on at the different levels of American national, state, and local government (further complicated by the separation of powers format), lobbyists are employed to help keep track of what is happening and report these activities back to their respective groups. Second, they champion "their" group's interests at the capitol. They attempt to get measures favorable to their group passed and unfavorable measures killed. In doing this, they use a variety of techniques to influence decision-makers. Third, they provide information to legislators on pending legislation or tell the legislator what the group members' views are. It is important to remember that the right to lobby is, in effect, guaranteed by the First Amendment in the Bill of Rights—the right of citizens to petition their government for redress of grievance.

INTEREST GROUPS AND LOBBYISTS IN HISTORICAL PERSPECTIVE

Southern Pacific Era and the Progressive Reaction

During the latter part of the nineteenth century and the first years of the twentieth century, Southern Pacific Railroad dominated California government. But in the early 1900s, the Progressive reform movement swept the country. These reformers sought to eliminate corruption in government (see Chapter 2). California Progressives fought zealously to eliminate the corrupt power of Southern Pacific Railroad from California's state government.

Artie Samish Era

During the 1930s and 40s, Artie Samish, was the dominant lobbyist in California. Physically, Samish was a newspaper cartoonist's dream:

the perfect stereotype of how a lobbyist should look—straw hat, large cigar, enormous paunch, and loud tie.

Samish became the most infamous state government lobbyist of his time. With only a modest formal educational background and a short stint as a clerk in the state senate, Samish went into lobbying. He quickly became the king of Sacramento lobbyists and, as his lobbyist reputation grew, more businesses and special interests vied for him to represent them, further enhancing his political power. At the height of his power, Samish represented more than a dozen major California interests. His power was so immense that the governor of California, Earl Warren, stated, "On matters that affect his clients, Artie unquestionably has more power than the governor" (Velie, August 13, 1949:13). Samish could raise enormous sums from his grateful clients to bankroll campaigns (in what he called his "select and elect" system) and to "wine and dine" and provide other amenities to public officials. Samish understood the legislative process, had many influential friends, represented many wealthy interests, and had a network of paid tipsters.

The lurid, corrupt overtones and flamboyance of the Samish era are largely gone from the Sacramento lobby scene today. Contemporary lobbying is more honest and today's lobbyists more businesslike. No contemporary lobbyist has the dominant power Samish had in the 1940s. However, the conviction in 1986 of W. Patrick Moriarity, owner of a fireworks company, for providing lavish gifts, bribes, and prostitutes to various state and local government officials to prevent communities from banning fireworks sales, and the conviction of former assemblymember/lobbyist Bruce Young suggest that old style lobbying is not completely dead.

REASONS FOR STRONG LOBBIES

By establishing rules, regulations, and taxing policy, state government has traditionally had a strong influence over certain kinds of businesses: banks, insurance companies, mortuaries, dairies, petroleum industries, liquor interests, utilities, horsetracks, agribusiness, real estate, construction, and land development. Many of these groups have actively sought government regulation to protect themselves from competition. These interests and others have found it vitally important to be represented in Sacramento. Historically, five key factors contribute to the strong lobby nature of California politics as contrasted to other (particularly eastern) states: (1) Progressive reforms that weakened political parties, (2) interest group campaign contributions, (3) coterminous development of statehood and lobbies in the western states, (4) the nonprofessional quality of the pre-1966 California legislature, and (5) low public visibility.

Weak Political Parties

Progressive reforms, such as cross-filing, civil service, the direct primary, prohibitions on preprimary endorsements, and the direct democracy devices, served to weaken political parties and, concomitantly, encourage special interests. Special interests using the initiative process could also hire professional campaign management firms to collect signatures and run their initiative campaigns if the legislature should be unresponsive. Ironically, Progressive reforms designed, in part, to curb special interest power often have served to augment their influence.

Interest Group Campaign Contributions and Gratuities

Because political parties are weak, candidates for partisan offices have to plan their own campaigns and raise their own financial support (the latter has increasingly come from interest group political action committees, PACs). As campaign costs have spiraled, so too has group influence. In California, many officeholders feel more indebted to their interest group backers than their party, and most legislators raise only token amounts from their districts and constituents. Lobbyists for special interests can afford to wine and dine and provide other gratuities to officeholders.

Coterminous Development

The industrial revolution and the development of corporate America occurred during the same period of time that western territories were attaining statehood. As Harmon Zeigler and Michael Baer (1969:37) note:

> In the western states, however, political systems and interest groups developed simultaneously. Interest groups did not have to fight existing political institutions; they shared in the development of the political system; lobbyists and politicians "grew up" together. Furthermore, the political traditions of the western states—nonpartisanship, open primaries, a high rate of participation—invite interest groups (along with everybody else) to compete for the stakes of politics.

Nonprofessional Legislature

Third House advocates lobby all the state governmental institutions—assembly and senate, governor and administration, bureaucracy, commissions and courts—but the legislature is the centerpiece of lobbyist maneuverings. Through 1966, the California legislature was a nonprofessional, part-time institution. California state legislators were poorly paid, inadequately officed, and understaffed. Indeed, this was the situation in every state legislature in the country at the time. Indeed, some contemporary state legislatures are still strictly non-professional. For example, New Hampshire continues to pay its state legislators $100 per year; Massachusetts still does not provide offices for its rank-and-file members; and a great many contemporary state legislatures have virtually no professional staff.

Low Pay.   Prior to 1966, the meager legislative salary lawmakers earned did not cover their living expenses while in Sacramento, trips back to the district, house payments or rent, food, clothing, and other miscellaneous expenses. The low legislative pay served more as a token of civic gratitude than as a living wage. The view was that the public-spirited citizens who ran for the legislature were, in effect, donating their services in much the same manner that most city council members, school board members, or planning commission members do currently. Some legislators served only a few terms and then "graduated" into the lobbyist ranks and quadrupled their former legislative salaries. Others returned to their previous occupation to recoup their losses, and some ran for higher office.

The imaginative techniques some legislators employed to survive financially in the "good ole days" are legendary. Some economized by renting rooms at downtrodden Sacramento hotels. One legislator used to save money by hitchhiking back and forth to his Los Angeles constituency.

But, of course, the normal and accepted means many legislators used to cut costs in this earlier period was to live off the lobbyists' largesse. Indeed, a few of the less scrupulous legislators not only survived financially but prospered. Some lobbyists (not all by any means) were more than willing to pay for hotel bills, buy meals and drinks, take legislators on expensive travel junkets, provide tickets to sporting events, or give them gifts of money. Rather than returning to their empty hotel rooms after a long, arduous day at the capitol, many legislators found it more appealing to have lobbyists take them out for an evening on the town. Bars and restaurants near the state capitol did a booming lunch and dinner business. The Derby Club, Moose-milk, the Caboose Club, and other regular luncheon meetings of lobbyists and legislators were Sacramento institutions. Additionally, a few lobbyists were known to provide female companionship for some of the temporary-bachelor legislators.

In the 1940s, Artie Samish paid his top staffers $3,000 to $4,000 per month as contrasted to a legislator's $1,200 *annual* salary! At the height of his powers, Samish did not even bother to go to the state capitol building to testify before committees or buttonhole legislators. Instead, legislators would come to Artie Samish. He would host lavish

5-1 *The Cattle Pack, a California cattleman's lobby, hosts lawmakers at an annual breakfast. Meeting with legislators at mealtime is a traditional lobbying technique.*

Photo courtesy Sacramento Bee

luncheon buffets in his hotel suite and would provide the finest wines, liquor, and gourmet food to his legislator guests. After lunch, there would be card games for interested legislators and lobbyists. At the very least, this socializing provided Third House agents greater access to legislators than was available to lobbyists who could not afford to entertain. It helped pave the way to lasting friendships. At its worst, social lobbying may have bought some legislators' votes.

Shrewd lobbyists could direct legal business to a lawyer-legislator's law office, buy insurance from an insurance agent-legislator, invest in real estate from a real estate broker-legislator, or do business with a business-owner-legislator. A favorite device of savings and loans and banks was to place local legislators on their boards of directors. It provided the bank with increased status and gave the legislator extra income with a minimal amount of work.

Many lobbyists ingratiated themselves with the legislator's staff—particularly the secretaries—by taking them to lunch or giving them gifts. Skillful lobbyists quickly discovered where a particular legislator's interests were—sports, dining, hunting, golfing, cards, drinking, and the like—and would then try to capitalize on the knowledge.

Inadequate Facilities.   In the early years, California legislators did not have private offices. Many legislators used their desks on the floor to conduct legislative chores—dictating letters, reading mail, discussing bills with lobbyists, being interviewed by reporters, or chatting with visiting constituents. Experienced lobbyists thrived in this bedlam. Bills could be killed or amended or lost in this confusion, and few would know the difference.

Lack of Staff.   Lobbyists were not only friends and confidants of legislators, they were also prime sources of information. Since legislators could not possibly be expert on all the subjects with which they had to deal, lobbyists provided legislators with this much-needed information. Lobbyists helped draft legislation or provided questions sympathetic legislators might use at committee hearings. Freshmen legislators were particularly grateful to lobbyists when asked to carry a bill (i.e., to be its author), since this was the way lawmakers established a legislative record.

Low Public Visibility

Until the last decade or two, the major metropolitan dailies of California tended to give short shrift to Sacramento doings. They preferred to concentrate their efforts on national or international news along with a heavy smattering of local news. Sacramento was viewed by the major metropolitan dailies as a hot, dusty valley town with few cultural refinements, inhabited primarily by political hacks, local satraps, and faceless bureaucrats. And it was.

The closed, secretive nature of the legislative system of this bygone era further played into the hands of the lobbyists. On the senate side, committee chairs were able to control action of their committees and either pass along or kill bills arbitrarily. Not surprisingly, lobbyists would often concentrate their efforts on the upper house because it was smaller, its power more diffused, turnover minimal, and partisanship imperceptible. In both houses, committees frequently met in executive session (closed), or met prior to the hearing at a local bistro to iron out differences. In addition, there was no official record kept of committee votes.

In most cases, lobbyists asked a legislator or other public official for just a few votes each year. These were usually technical bills on esoteric subjects where there was little public opinion but which might mean millions to the lobbyist's clients. This is how one author (Berg et al., 1976:146) described the process:

> If, for example, a lobbyist needs a "no" vote on a bill before a particular legislative committee, he or she drops by the office of those members who

5-2

BEHIND THE GREEN DOOR

Dennis Renault, Sacramento Bee

are . . . friends and explains the bill in one or two sentences. The lobbyist asks if the legislator is getting any mail on the subject, and wonders in a seemingly questioning way whether a "no" vote would hurt the legislator back home. When it is clear that there has been little or no mail on the subject (generally only a handful of bills in each session generate the mail), the lobbyist says, "This one means a lot to my principals. If I don't beat it I'll lose the account (or my job). I'd personally appreciate it if you can give me a vote. And I'll let our people in your district know how helpful you've been to us and make sure they give you some help (that's money) in your next campaign."

LOBBY REFORM

Essentially, there are three prime ways lobbyists today persuade legislators: (1) with facts and expertise, (2) through the political power of the group—voting potential and campaign workers, and (3) with financial power—campaign contributions; wining-dining; use of well-paid, well-connected professional lobby talent; and honoraria.[2] Obviously, the first two categories above are relatively noncontroversial parts of the governmental process. It is the third category that has always been the most controversial. Thus, there have been periodic attempts throughout this century to reduce the impact of wealthy special interests in the state's political processes, but only modest progress has been made. In this century in California, four reform periods stand out: (1) the Progressive era, (2) the Samish scandal aftermath, (3) the Unruh legislative modernization drive, and (4) the post-Watergate period. It is possible that in the late 1980s we are on the verge of a new reform era. The Moriarity affair, spiraling campaign costs, negative "hit" pieces, and scandals surrounding legislative contracts and consultant payments may help provide the impetus for new reforms at the capitol.

There is little doubt that the style of contemporary lobbying is different from earlier lobbying; however, there is considerable dispute as to whether the changes that have taken place have *really* made any significant differences.

Lobby Reform—Progressive Period

As noted, Progressives early in this century made the first concerted attempt to limit special interest influence. For example, the Progressives placed in the constitution a prohibition on any transport company (Southern Pacific was the obvious target) giving any public official a free ride (no pun intended). They also established a state railroad commission to set rates charged by Southern Pacific and other public utilities. Progressive reform, though, was directed more against political parties, politicians, and special interests rather than lobbyists. The impetus to control lobbyists came some forty years later in the wake of the Samish revelations.

Lobby Reform—Samish Aftermath

In 1949, *Collier's Magazine* published a classic muckraking journalism, "The Secret Boss of California" (Velie, 1949). The article, based on a freely given interview with the then-notorious California

---

[2]Honoraria are fees paid to officeholders by lobbies for speeches given at interest-group meetings. While a long-time feature of congressional politics, honoraria have only recently become an important aspect of Third House influence in contemporary California. There are a number of advantages groups and officeholders gain from honoraria: for example, interest group members get to lobby key legislators in informal settings, and officeholders can augment their legislative salaries for speeches (normally drafted by legislative staff) that they present. Over the last year or two, several legislative leaders have earned more in honoraria than they have in salaries.

lobbyist, Artie Samish, described how he exerted influence over the state legislature and state bureaucracy. Included within the text of the article was a famous color photograph of the gargantuan Artie Samish seated in a chair with "Mr. Legislature," a wooden puppet, being manipulated by Samish. "Said the big man: And how are you today, Mr. Legislature?"

The *Collier's* series for the first time brought to the attention of the California public the behind-the-scenes stranglehold Artie held over state government. After publication of this article, there was a public clamor for reform of the lobbying process.

Governor Warren, responding to the Samish scandal commented that, "Disreputable lobbying practices are impairing the efficiency of state government and besmirching the creditable work of the vast majority of our legislators, offices and employees" (Samish, 1959).

In response to the Samish scandal, in 1949, the legislature passed the Collier Act (named after its author John Collier, not the magazine) which was patterned after the Federal Regulation of Lobbying Act. The Collier Act required lobbyists to register, file monthly financial reports of contributions and expenditures over ten dollars, and list bills they were supporting or opposing. Because of the confusion in implementing the Collier Act, a year later (1950) the Ervin Act was passed to strengthen and clarify the Collier Act provisions. In 1951, Samish was indicted, convicted of income tax evasion, and sentenced to federal prison. While the Collier and Ervin Acts were of some modest help in opening up the lobby process, in fact, little really changed.

Lobby Reform—Unruh Period

Proposition 1A.   In November 1966, California voters approved several major constitutional amendments (Proposition 1A) which significantly changed the legislative process. These amendments gave the legislature authority to set its own session length and salary schedule.

While Proposition 1A did not deal directly with lobby reform, the impact of these changes was keenly felt in the Third House. Speaker Jess Unruh contended that poorly paid legislators were fair game for lobbyists. He argued that lobbyists could influence lawmakers if legislators were dependent upon them for gratuities. If legislators were paid reasonable salaries, better educated, more competent citizens would run for the legislature, and they would be better equipped to stand up to the lobbyists. Higher legislative salaries would mean that lawmakers would be freed from depending upon their original occupations to sustain them, and there would be less need for special interests to hire legislator-lawyers or retainers. Full-time legislators would be able to devote their complete attention to complex legislative issues.

5-3 *Artie Samish and "Mr. Legislature."*

Photograph by Fred Lyon, Collier's Magazine, August 13, 1949.
© 1949 by Crowell-Collier Publishing Co.

Adoption of Proposition 1A has affected legislators and lobbyists in several ways. First, since the legislature began meeting year-round, some legislators, and many lobbyists as well, have found it more convenient to move their families to Sacramento. This has meant fewer lobbyist-legislator dinner outings. As better educated, more politically astute legislators began to get elected, lobbyists have had to change their *modus operandi* to relate to this new breed of legislators. New legislators were more likely to be influenced by lobbyists with expertise in a subject area rather than simply an unlimited checking account. While the practice of lobbyists picking up tabs continued, the dependency relationship had been altered. The development of a professionalized legislature helped encourage the concomitant development of a professionalized lobby corps.

Prior to 1966, many legislators had been anxious to "graduate" into the lobby ranks in order to make a more respectable salary. In the more professionalized arena of the contemporary capitol, several ex-lobbyists actually sought and won seats in the legislature.[3] While a few recent legislators, such as former assemblymembers Frank Murphy and John Knox or former State Senators Dennis Carpenter and John Briggs, have voluntarily retired from the legislature to become lobbyists, not as many as formerly seem to choose this path today. Unfortunately, legislative salaries have not kept up with inflation. Legislators would need to earn $55,000 in 1987 (they currently earn $37,100) to equal their $16,000 salary of 1966. The lure of "big money" in lobbying may entice growing numbers of legislators to leave legislative ranks in the years ahead.

Clearly, legislators have become the coequal partner in the legislator/lobbyist relationship. While lobbies are still critical in funding campaigns, no one lobby can beat a legislator or deliver the votes of their members. Increasing numbers of legislators in the majority and minority parties look to legislative leaders of their respective parties for campaign contributions, not just lobbies. Lobbyists need legislators as much as legislators need lobbyists.

Other Unruh Innovations.   Two other Unruh innovations also helped alter the lobbyist-legislator relationship: the development of a professional cadre of legislative staff, and increased partisanship (see Chapter 7). By adding professional staff, legislators no longer had to rely solely on lobbyists for expertise; they had a new, more neutral source of information. A more partisan legislature meant that legislators could be buffered to an extent from special interest pleadings.

Reapportionment.   Prior to 1966, and the U.S. Supreme Court's *Reynolds* v. *Simms* "one person, one vote" decision, which forced states to use population as a criterion for representation in both houses of American state legislatures, lobbyists focused most of their lobby effort on the upper house.

Since most special-interest lobbyists tended to be defensive, fending off attacks on their groups, it was more convenient to work with a few key senators in killing assembly-sponsored measures. Powerful northern rural senators held a stranglehold over committees dealing with urban problems. Since the northern rural senators received little district input on these issues, they could trade favors with lobbyists on

---

[3]Jean Moorhead Duffy is one of the more unique politicians on the state political scene. Her professional career includes the following milestones: first, a nursing instructor at California State University Sacramento; next, a lobbyist for California Nurses' Association; then, election to the assembly as a Republican assemblymember for two terms, followed by a switch to the Democratic party and reelection to the assembly; marriage to former Republican assemblyman-lobbyist Gordon Duffy; and finally in 1986 retirement from the assembly and the launching of the Duffy and Duffy contract lobby firm.

bills helping their districts, and given the small population size of these northern rural districts, a modest campaign contribution in a relatively low-cost campaign could be crucial.

Lobby Reform—Post-Watergate

The Political Reform Act of June 1974—Proposition 9.　The most recent development in legislator-lobbyist relations came with the adoption of the 1974 Political Reform Act (Proposition 9) by the voters. The act was an omnibus reform measure dealing with several different reform areas. It affects lobbying directly and indirectly.

Overall, the act required lobbyists, legislators, and administrators to provide more extensive information about their dealings (particularly financial) *and* also sought to reduce the influence of wealthy, special interests at the state capitol.

The act, it should be noted, was an initiative generated, in part, by the Watergate scandal, legislative inaction, and rumors of corruption at the state level.

The act was opposed by many of the most powerful political interests in the state, including the AFL-CIO, Teamsters, California Medical Association, Building Trades Council, Taxpayers' Association, Real Estate Association, Growers Association, Chamber of Commerce, Farm Bureau, United Professors, State Employees Association, the Executive Committees of the Democratic and Republican State Central Committees, and Peace and Freedom party. Many other special interests would have joined the anti-reform act forces, but felt it was hopeless to oppose a "motherhood"-type measure in the post-Watergate period. In any case, opposition to the reform measure proved futile; voters gave overwhelming approval to Proposition 9 by a nearly two to one margin (it received a majority vote in all fifty-eight California counties).

Included among the key features of Proposition 9 reforms are: (1) *all* lobbyists are required to register (the Fair Political Practices Commission established a definition of lobbying based on time spent attempting to influence public officials, number contacted, and compensation received); (2) lobbyists can spend no more than ten dollars per month per public official—legislator, staff member, administrator, or commissioner; (3) detailed reports must be filed periodically with the Secretary of State's Office and the Fair Political Practices Commission dealing with who has been lobbied, subjects discussed, and how much has been spent; and (4) the Fair Political Practices Commission has overall responsibility for enforcing the act. Additionally, several other reform features of Proposition 9 impinge indirectly on lobbyists, special interests, and public officials. There is a tough *campaign disclosure* law requiring candidates to file regular spending reports on all contributions and expenditures twice during the campaign and once after the election. There are also conflict-of-interest regulations. All state public officials are required to annually disclose their income.

Originally, the act set spending limits on all statewide campaigns (including ballot propositions). Also, as initially adopted, lobbyists were forbidden from conferring with their clients about which public officials should receive campaign contributions (enforcing this provision would have been difficult), and they were also prohibited from making campaign contributions.[4] These features of the act have since been declared unconstitutional by the courts, thus weakening the act.

Since voter approval of the reform act in June 1974, lobbyists have grudgingly accepted its reform requirements as a *fait accompli,* and they have been concerned about not violating any of the regulations. Soon after its adoption, however, a number of key lobbyists joined together in the Institute of Governmental Advocates to fight Proposition 9 in the courts. Some lobbyists and special interests have probed for loopholes in the law. Thus, it is difficult to keep track of the $10 limit on lobbyists if one pays with cash rather than credit at a restaurant. Interest group executives can entertain legislators lavishly without the budgetary restrictions of the lobbyists. It is also reported that some Third House advocates may ask a legislator to pay by check for the amount of a lunch tab over the $10 limit (for example, let's say 77 cents) but then the lobbyist will hand the legislator a check for $1,000 as a campaign contribution. Former FPPC Chairman Tom Houston has argued that the $10 spending limit is unenforceable. Clearly, there probably always will be ways for the opportunistic or devious to get around such laws.

Hence, the debate on the reform act continues. Let's consider some of the major pros and cons of the act as it relates to lobbying.

Critics.   Opponents contend that the $10 monthly limitation on lobbyist spending is meaningless—or worse, insulting. They argue that only the naive believe that legislators' votes are exchanged for dinners, drinks, or other gratuities. It is argued, too, that the limitation has impeded the lobbyist-legislator exchange of ideas. Prior to June 1974, legislators and lobbyists met at local restaurants and discussed matters in a convivial setting away from ringing phones and endless interruptions. Critics of the reform measure say this useful exchange of information has been curtailed. Some have argued that the law restricts many ethical lobbyists while providing opportunities for the unscrupulous.

---

[4]It was obvious at the outset that this feature would have a limited impact since the group represented by a particular lobbyist or its PAC could still provide campaign contributions and thus gain the good will of that politician for that lobbyist. Proponents argued that this made the lobbyist less of a "bag man" in the process.

In attempting to enforce the $10 limit, the Fair Political Practices Commission ran into a score of practical problems in the 1970s, ranging from the sublime to the ridiculous:

1. Must a lobbyist whose young daughter is invited next door to a legislator's daughter's birthday party report the gift on the reporting forms?
2. Does a male lobbyist have to report gifts he gives to his wife if she is a member of the legislative staff?
3. Must lobbyists report that they invited a legislator, perhaps a long-time friend, to their house for dinner?

Not surprisingly, many lobbyists and legislators resent Proposition 9's intrusions into their private lives.

Critics of Proposition 9 attack the alleged "police state," "big brother is watching you," syndrome created by the act. An annual audit of lobbyists, it is argued, is excessive. The Fair Political Practices Commission, it is charged, is yet another layer of bureaucracy. Worse though, these unelected commissioners tell elected representatives how they should act. The Commission has repeatedly levied fines against legislators and lobbyists for failing to comply with provisions of the act. As one might expect, there have been many run-ins between the commission and legislators and lobbyists. Drafting regulations implementing the Political Reform Act has not been easy. Conflict of interest issues, campaign expenditure reporting, legislative staff involvement in campaigns, campaign procedures, and a myriad of other issues have frequently pitted the FPPC against candidates, officeholders, staffers, administrators, and lobbyists. The claim is made that there is an implicit assumption in the act that many legislators, staff members, administrators, and lobbyists are guilty of all sorts of wrongdoing but in reality, only a very small minority are.

Finally, critics charge that the FPPC requires too much paperwork. Indeed, spokespersons for many of the groups supposedly helped by the reforms of Proposition 9—the League of Women Voters, the PTA, and the Sierra Club—have complained that the extensive paperwork entailed in the act has worked to their disadvantage. Wealthy groups have the staff or can hire professional accountants to keep track of lobby expenses and fill out the complicated forms; poorer groups do not have this ability.

Supporters.   Proponents concede there have been some problems in administering the act, but they argue there are similar problems in implementing any major, complex piece of legislation. Establishing rules and guidelines and dealing with problems of administration never contemplated by the authors of the act are always difficult. For the most part, the FPPC has succeeded, its supporters argue. Guidelines

have been established, compliance achieved, and legislators and lobbyists have learned to live with it. Indeed, Dan Lowenstein, former
FPPC chairperson, is concerned that lobbyists have become so used
to the act and its various provisions that it may no longer have the
impact and vitality that it once did.

Above all, supporters of Proposition 9 contend it has greatly helped
improve the tone of lobbying in Sacramento. The extensive entertaining, posh excursions, and lavish gifting have been reduced. At the very
least, on its most innocent level, "wining and dining" buys access and
helps promote friendships—and access and friendships are the name
of the game in Sacramento. Money spent for entertaining is not ex-
pended whimsically by special interest groups; it is a calculated investment similar to a campaign contribution. Proponents of the act
argue that the $10 limitation is strict but reasonable. The big expense-
account lobbyists have somewhat reduced opportunities to gain influence because of their extensive gift giving.

Reform backers argue there is no attempt in the reform act to muz-
zle lobbyists or reduce legislator-lobbyist interaction as its critics argue. Even if Lobbyist X's $10 minimum has been expended for the
month on a legislator, the lobbyist can still have long discussions at
lunch or dinner—the only difference is that each would have to pay for
his or her own check. In any case, it would seem that whatever initial
fears legislators may have had about being listed on lobbyists' forms
have been dispelled. The FPPC reports that hundreds of thousands of
dollars are spent by lobbyists each year entertaining legislators, staffers, and administrators.

Finally, are interest groups on a more equal footing these days?
There is no question that "public interest" groups such as Common
Cause, the Sierra Club, the Planning and Conservation League, the
League of Women Voters, and consumer groups have a substantial impact on policy. Historically, "do gooder" interest groups used to have
difficulty being taken seriously. The Political Reform Act has helped
contribute to this new balance. No one ever suggested that the Political
Reform Act was a panacea. The hope was that it would contribute to
opening the political process, reduce (to an extent) the influence of
wealthy special interests, and ameliorate some of the more outrageous
practices of the past.

At first, the FPPC tended to rely mainly on voluntary compliance,
but today the commission emphasizes enforcement. In the 1980s a
number of legislators, lobbyists, and other local public officials have
been fined by the FPPC for various infractions. Getting fined by the
FPPC may sting a bit, but it seems to have little long-term effect on
the perpetrators. In any case, the FPPC's continued presence in Sacramento's political waters has helped change the political game.

Over the last several years, the FPPC has sponsored a number of further reform proposals which have subsequently been adopted by the legislature. These proposals: (1) prohibit officeholders from using campaign funds for personal use; (2) prohibit state officials from leaving their government posts and then returning to represent clients on matters they had been involved with on the state payroll; and (3) prohibit legislators from accepting campaign contributions in the capitol building.

The lobby reforms that have taken place over the last several decades have made contemporary lobbying in Sacramento a more professional and reputable endeavor. Undoubtedly, the style of lobbying has changed, and the substance of lobbying has also changed to a limited extent. Interest-groups and their lobbyist agents have a right to promote the governmental goals of their respective groups. Hopefully, political clout will rest on a variety of factors, not simply monetary resources, in the years ahead.

THIRD HOUSE POLITICS
Interest Groups

The most recent compilation of interest groups in California (April, 1985) by the secretary of state indicates that currently there are nearly 1,100 separate organizations registered. The various groups represented include:

Business	34%
Health	15
Local Government	10
Education	10
Insurance/finance	6
Agriculture	5
Labor	4
Legal	3
Utilities	2
Miscellaneous/"public interest"	11

Lobbyists

Few contemporary lobbyists knew early in their careers that they would eventually become legislative advocates. There is no prelobby undergraduate major, graduate school training for aspiring lobbyists, or even an apprenticeship program. Rather, the people who become lobbyists invariably wind up there by chance or accident. Certainly, in the public mind, politicians are viewed suspiciously, but lobbyists have an even more notorious reputation. This is unfortunate, since most contemporary lobbyists are bright, well-educated professionals who are honest and ethical.

Essentially, people gravitate into the lobby ranks from two prime sources: (1) from within the governmental milieu or (2) from within the particular interest group or business.

Governmental Milieu.   Currently, several dozen ex-legislators and an assortment of other ex-officeholders serve as lobbyists for various interests in Sacramento. Some ex-officeholders become lobbyists not voluntarily, but because they have lost elections. Others leave the legislature voluntarily seeking "greener" pastures. While ex-legislator lobbyists comprise a small portion of the total number in the lobby corps, it should be emphasized that these advocates tend to be contract lobbyists associated with lobby firms normally representing a number of clients of key special interests. Obviously, ex-legislator lobbyists trade on their friendships with former legislative colleagues and their intimate knowledge of the legislative process. Ex-legislator lobbyists have a special relationship with their former colleagues (it would be awkward to keep an "old buddy" waiting for an appointment in the outer office). Ex-legislators, better than anyone else, understand the pressures, tensions, and frustrations in the legislator's job. But, because of the rapid turnover in legislative membership and the periodic reshuffling of administrative posts, the ex-legislator lobbyist cannot trade on old friendships for very long.

Other lobbyists coming from within the governmental milieu include ex-legislative staffers, former bureaucrats from different executive departments, and student interns. As with former legislators, these individuals know the players, understand the process and informal "rules of the game," and have frequently developed a policy expertise. Some enterprising individuals have persuaded key legislators to recommend them to an interest group looking for a lobbyist. A strong recommendation from Committee Chair X that Group Y should hire Lobbyist Z is not casually overlooked. Lobbyists coming from within the governmental milieu comprise several hundred of the more than 800 Sacramento lobbyists.

Some interests announce (via the "grapevine") that they will be selecting a contract firm to represent them, and they request bids from prospective lobbyists which would include items such as: costs, expertise, special access, strategies to be employed, and experience. Some multipurpose contract lobby firms do legal work, association management, and newsletter production for their clients.

Group Milieu.   The majority of lobbyists attain their positions from within the group they represent. Many corporations have public affairs divisions staffed by attorneys who represent them in Sacramento. Employees with skills in public relations, politics, sales, or advertising are

5-4 *Lobbyist registration. A typical page from the secretary of state's Lobbyist Directory.*

1985-1986 LOBBYISTS

OAKES, JOY M.
1228 N Street #31, Sacramento, CA 95814   (916) 444-6906
Sierra Club

OAKLEY, RICHARD C.
925 L Street, Suite 915, Sacramento, CA 95814   (916) 446-2433
Air-Conditioning and Refrigeration Institute
Pacific Texas Pipeline Company
Rick Oakley and Associates

OGLESBY, ROBERT P.
520 Capitol Mall, Suite 802, Sacramento, CA 95814   (916) 447-7752
Butterfield & Butterfield
CP National
Orrick, Herrington & Sutcliffe
Waste Management, Inc.

OHLSON-SMITH, AUDREY
1127 11th Street, Suite 450, Sacramento, CA 95814   (916) 442-5895
California Teachers Association

OLSEN, CHARLES H.
719 Ocampo Drive, Pacific Palisades, CA 90272   (213) 454-2053
1127 11th Street, Suite 824, Sacramento, CA 95814   (916) 446-6105
California Association of Health Facilities
California Confederation of the Arts, Inc.
California Optometric Association
Charles H. Olsen Associates
H. F. Ahmanson and Company
Home Health Services and Staffing Association
Knudsen Foods, Inc.
Lawndale, City of
Pacific Water Quality Association, Inc.
Pierson Esq., David C.
Robert M. Berry, Realty Inc.
Southern California Rapid Transit District
T. N. Truax Enterprises
Ticketron, a Division of Control Data Corporation
Upjohn Healthcare Services, Inc.
Williams-Kuebelbeck and Associates

obvious possibilities. Some corporations or businesses assign key executives to their Sacramento beat. Individuals going into lobbying from within a corporation, business trade association, or public interest usually represent that single client, though a few have eventually branched out into contract lobbying after a successful initial period with a single client. Generally speaking, the major asset lobbyists offer to legislators and administrators in this category is specialized expertise in their business or trade association.

The Job—Salaries, Workload, Costs.   It is difficult to generalize about the salaries of lobbyists since they vary considerably. A few, such as James "Judge" Garibaldi or Donald Kent Brown, make several hundred thousand dollars a year lobbying, while a few others (for example, the lobbyist for the League of Women Voters or the PTA) receive no salary and virtually no expense money. Most full-time California lobbyists are paid far better than California state legislators, and many working for the top professional lobby firms in Sacramento earn salaries in excess of $100,000 a year.

To earn their salaries, lobbyists put in long, tiring days, especially when the legislature is in session. They must keep track of countless details. A typical morning of the average lobbyist might include: an early trip to the Bill Room to pick up the amended versions of several bills he or she is following; a hurried discussion with a legislator in the hallway about a bill coming before that legislator's committee; a walk over to the office to check the mail, answer some telephone calls, or edit the group's newsletter due to be sent out; a conference with group executives on pending legislation; a short coffee break with a fellow lobbyist to discuss testimony for an afternoon committee hearing; a deadly dull Senate Finance Committee hearing; and last, lunch with a committee consultant to discuss a bill that the committee consultant's boss, the committee chair, will soon be introducing.

Then comes the afternoon. . . .

Most lobbyists seem to enjoy their work. It is financially rewarding, meaningful, important, and provides reasonable job security. For the most part, there is an unwritten rule among lobbyists that once a lobbyist has secured a client, other lobbyists are expected not to try to win that client away. The emergence of the new high-powered, professional lobby firms anxious to secure new clients probably means the beginning of a more competitive situation. Thus, there have been a growing number of occasions when an interest group has dropped one lobbyist and hired another to further its legislative goals.

Types of Lobbyists.   Currently, there are over 800 registered lobbyists in California who, in turn, represent almost 1,000 different groups. In addition, Sacramento's many volunteer lobbyists do not have to register, nor do legislative liaison officials (in effect, lobbyists) in state agencies. Some groups are represented by many lobbyists, and some lobbyists represent many groups—it all depends. A growing portion of lobby business in Sacramento is conducted by the many new professional advocacy firms (115). These firms usually have two to five lobbyists and generally represent ten to twenty different clients.[5] The major utilities of California generally have large corps of lobbyists (Pacific Gas and Electric, seven; Southern California Gas, four; Pacific Telephone and Telegraph, six; San Diego Gas and Electric, five), while some major corporations are represented by a single lobbyist (e.g., Hal Broaders represents Bank of America).

Interestingly, there has been a dramatic increase in women lobbyists at the capitol. Through the 1960s, there were only a handful of women lobbyists, and generally they represented the "do-gooder" groups—Humane Society, League of Women Voters, PTA, or the American Association of University Women. By the mid-1970s, women comprised 6 percent of the lobbyists, and by 1986, 20 percent. Moreover, a growing number of women lobbyists are employed by the high-powered professional lobby firms. At the same time, the number of black or Latino lobbyists has remained low. (Blacks currently comprise less than 2 percent of the state's registered lobbyists.)

[5]A-K Associates, one of the state's largest lobby firms, has seven lobbyists and dozens of clients. The client list includes:

A-K Associates, Inc.
American Adventure, Inc.
American Ambulance Association
California Ambulance Association
California Association of Large Suburban School Districts
California Association of Medical Products Suppliers
California College of Podiatric Medicine
California Dental Service
California Executive Recruiters Association
California Independent Telephone Association
California Radiological Society
California Rice Industry Committee
California Society of Pathologists
Committee on the Unitary Tax
Continental Telephone Company of California

Council of American Survey Research Organization
Director of Timber Counties Coalition
Escrow Institute of California
Golden Gate Bridge, Highway and Transportation District
Hemet Valley Flying Service
Ingemanson Enterprises
International Fire Management
Northwestern National Insurance Company of Milwaukee
Pathology Practice Association
South Lake Tahoe, City of
Stratos Tanker, Inc.
Thousand Trails, Inc.
Tobacco Institute
Vietnam Veterans of America
Western Surety Company

Source: Secretary of State Lobbyist Registration 1985–86.

Lobby Spending

Interest groups in California expend considerable sums of money in their lobbying efforts. On the average, over the last several years groups have spent more than $30 million per year (tax deductible as a business expense) in lobby expenditures to influence policymakers. Organizations that spend substantial sums of money on lobbying view this expense as a prudent and wise investment. A lobbyist operation at the capitol (lobbyist salary, office, and staff) costing a few hundred thousand dollars a year could help influence decisions that might mean millions of dollars for the affected group! A growing number of groups are finding it useful to have lobbyist representation in Sacramento.

Some groups channel most of their funds into lobbying and provide substantially lesser amounts for campaign contributions; others parcel out roughly equal amounts for campaign contributions and lobbying. According to the FPPC, the ten leading interest groups in terms of amount of money spent to influence legislative or administrative action in 1983–1984 were:

Pacific Gas and Electric	$14,357,288
Pacific Telesis Group	5,643,428
Western Oil & Gas Association	1,879,119
California Medical Association	1,517,447
Southern California Gas	1,327,351
Chevron	1,126,207
California State Employees Association	1,060,179
General Telephone Company	930,743
San Diego Gas	833,968
California Teachers Association	807,108

Clearly, over the last decade there has been a steady increase in the number of people lobbying and the number of groups represented. Any number of factors probably contribute to this phenomenon: first, the increasing complexity and heterogeneity of California society and economy; second, more people have been registered as lobbyists since the adoption of the Political Reform Act because of the Fair Political Practice Commission's definition of lobbyist; third, there has been a substantial increase in the number of single-issue lobbies such as those concerned with the death penalty, abortion, or tax reform; and fourth, increased efforts by entrepreneurial lobbyists who actively seek new clients among businesses or corporations either unrepresented at the state capital or represented only in a large trade association.

Finally, any group has the right to be represented by a lobby as long as it pays its $25 registration fee. However, are all groups *truly* represented in Sacramento? And even if they are represented, is it anything more than token representation? For example, Pacific Gas and Electric (PG&E) spent more than $14 million in attempting to influence decisions between 1983 and 1984 and it has seven lobbyists representing it

5-5 *Assemblyman Tom Hayden joins two Hollywood notables (his wife, Jane Fonda, and actress Kristi McNichol) in demonstrating for toxic waste controls.*

in their governmental relations division. These seven lobbyists explain and defend this multibillion-dollar corporation's views to legislators, administrators, and commissioners. But who represents the views of the consumers of PG&E's gas and electricity? The Tobacco Institute can spend thousands of dollars a year and hire A-K Associates, one of Sacramento's top lobby firms, to represent them, while the American Cancer Society has a single lobbyist. Because of this wealth disparity, some less affluent groups have resorted to unconventional tactics to be heard. Housewives, the self-employed, consumers, the poor, and the unemployed are some of the groups that traditionally have had little, if any, direct representation in Sacramento. It is true today that these groups are at least better represented than they used to be, but they have a long way to go.

Techniques of Lobbying

In addition to campaign contributions, wining-dining and honoraria, lobbyists representing groups such as the CTA, AFL-CIO, or CSEA have an advantage because of the vote potential of these large mass-membership organizations. The Teamsters are a good example; they are a large, wealthy mass-member group with many potential voters.

5-6 *"Over the top" at Rancho Seco nuclear power plant. Nuclear power protestors urge shutdown of plant.*

Photo courtesy Sacramento Bee

While many critics of the lobby process are concerned about the influence Third House advocates derive from the money and mass memberships of the groups they represent, few would object to the role lobbyists play in providing information to public officials. Lawmakers must be generalists, but lobbyists can concentrate on particular policy issues and can play a critical role in helping provide the specialized information necessary for decision making. Because they are in constant touch with group members, lobbyists can also convey to public officials the view of the membership. Public interest lobbies and less affluent groups can compete equally with the wealthy special interests in expertise.

Effective Lobbying—Beyond Money and Political Power

First and foremost, an effective lobbyist has a keen understanding of the complex issues facing his or her client group. A skilled lobbyist is able to explain clearly and concisely the main facets of an issue to a legislator, administrator, staff member, reporter, or another lobbyist. Advocates impart this information in the lobbies of the capitol (this is how lobbyists originally got their name) as legislators rush to committee hearings or floor sessions, in the capitol cafeterias, in nearby coffee shops or cocktail lounges, at Sacramento tennis courts or golf courses, in memos and reports, or in formal testimony presented at committee hearings. (However, most important decisions have been made prior to committee hearings.) Good lobbyists learn quickly that to be effective they must be brief, succinct, and to the point. The effective lobbyist knows how to read the legalese of bills, spot flaws, look for key points or problems, and suggest amendments. The effective lobbyist is equally at home at a luncheon meeting at the Sutter Club; in a quiet, informal, frank discussion in a legislator's office; or in a formal presentation of testimony at a committee hearing.

Second, an effective lobbyist understands the legislative process and the formal rules governing that process. Effective lobbyists provide input at all phases of the process: bill origination, bill drafting, assignment to committee, selection of committee members and chairpersons, scheduling of bills, floor action, conference committees, the governor, implementation by administrative agencies, court action, and initiatives.

Many of the skills effective lobbyists possess come only with experience. How many votes are necessary to get a bill out of the assembly Education Committee? Are the votes there, or should a bill be held over? How do you avoid a hostile committee? Should one agree to a particular amendment? What are the deadlines?

Third, the effective lobbyist knows not only the formal rules but the informal, unwritten rules as well. For example, a cardinal rule in Sacramento is, if a lobbyist determines he or she will have to oppose a bill, the lobbyist is honor-bound to go to the bill's author and discuss the reasons for opposition with that legislator *prior* to committee hearings. The legislative author of the bill might suggest some amendments to the bill in hopes of persuading the lobbyist not to oppose the measure.[6] Indeed, it is entirely possible the legislator may have no strong commitment to the bill but may have introduced it in behalf of an interest in his or her district. The legislator might very well say something like, "Go check with the lobbyist sponsoring the bill and see if you can iron out your differences. Whatever you decide is fine with me."

Among other key unwritten rules is that a good lobbyist will never threaten a legislator with defeat. In the first place, he or she probably

---

[6]Briscoe and Bell (1985) report that one of the unwritten rules of the game at the capitol is that if a bill's author agrees to a lobbyist's request for amendments to a bill, the lobbyist is not supposed to continue to oppose the bill. A deal has been made.

could not deliver, and in the second place, today's opponent may be tomorrow's ally.

In Sacramento, lobbyists are expected to give the people they are trying to influence "the straight scoop." Obviously, lobbyists present their group's views in the most favorable light, but they must also be able to explain the pros and cons of a bill to a legislator. A lobbyist that knowingly lies to or misleads a legislator would not only lose that legislator's support henceforth, but would also lose face with (even access to) other legislators. The Sacramento inner circle of legislators, staff, lobbyists, and reporters is small and intimate. Word of an important transgression spreads rapidly. If a lobbyist should happen to give a legislator the wrong information, mistakenly, about a bill's effect, the advocate would be expected to get to the legislator and clear up the point as quickly as possible. In short, honesty, discretion, and keeping commitments are essential elements of lobbying in the California state capitol.

Fourth, the effective lobbyist usually tries to become a friend of the legislator and get on a first-name basis with that person. An effective lobbyist makes an effort to know about the special interests of the legislator or administrator—whether they involve sports, hunting, or antique pipe organs. Many of the more successful lobbyists of the 1980s trade on the sports interests of the new generation of legislators, and invitations to play tennis, racquetball, or golf are as popular lobbyist-legislator activities today as gin rummy and poker were a few years ago.

Fifth, effective lobbyists work cooperatively with their lobbyist colleagues. They often trade information and help one another. Moreover, on any issues of consequence, coalitions of lobbies work jointly to support or oppose measures. Effective lobbyists know how to exploit the power of their group.

Sixth, effective lobbyists help orchestrate the local membership and grass roots organization with the capitol operation. If a group has a solid middle-class, well-educated, politically savvy, and well-distributed mass membership (e.g., the California Teachers Association, real estate brokers, Common Cause, doctors or state employees), it can alert its members to potential problems at the capitol and generate a substantial statewide mail or phone-in campaign that can have an effect. Obviously, lobbyists work closely with legislators whose districts encompass significant elements of the lobbyist's group.

Teachers, motorcycle club members, real estate brokers, and the physically handicapped are among the groups that have descended on the capitol in all-out efforts to win policy concessions. Demonstrations and speeches (always covered by the press and television reporters) are usually held on the steps of the capitol. After these gatherings,

5-7 *The late Howard Jarvis delivering boxes of letters to Sacramento lawmakers urging budget and tax cuts in 1979. This is "grass roots" on a grand scale!*

Photo courtesy Sacramento Bee

members are urged to seek out the legislators and let them know what the problems are. Some groups try to "mau-mau" legislators at committee hearings in the hopes that angry glares, raucous cheers or jeers might intimidate fence-straddling lawmakers.

FURTHER REFORMS IN THE LOBBYING PROCESS

What additional measures, if any, should be adopted to further reform the lobbyist process? First and foremost, the most essential reform would be to provide some form of public financing of state election races to further reduce the monetary power of particular special interests. Ideally, influence should hinge on voting power, information and expertise rather than just "big bucks." The goal should be to help groups compete on more even terms. The reforms enacted in California have helped to an extent to improve the lobby process, but there is still much to be done.

SUMMARY

Lobbying is an essential and indispensable part of the American governmental process—citizens petitioning their government. Lobbyists and special interests have been inextricably linked with California government throughout state history. Interest groups are necessary and vital to democratic government, but some pose a potentially grave threat to democratic institutions through their money influence, entertaining, and "me-first" attitude. Unfortunately, there is an unequal distribution of resources among different groups. The various lobby reforms that have been launched in California have helped reduce the potential for evil, but further reforms are needed.

6

Political Parties in California: The Perennial Power Vacuum

In theory, the Supreme Soviet is the highest deliberative lawmaking body in the Soviet Union; in theory, the British monarch presides over the British Commonwealth of nations; and in theory, California's political parties are directed and coordinated by a three-tiered system of state conventions, state central committees, and county central committees. But in reality, none of this happens. For the most part, California's official party organizations play only a minor role in influencing and shaping state politics.

The main reason California's political parties have traditionally been so weak and ineffective hinges largely on the key historical feature we have referred to frequently in this text: the Progressive reform movement of the early 1900s. Progressives were concerned about the rise of corrupt city and state political machines and their boss leaders in the various states. San Francisco was already under the sway of the Boss Reuf Machine, while the Republican and Democratic parties, as well as the institutions of government in California at that time were the pawns of the Southern Pacific Railroad. Fremont Older (1926:14), a leading newspaper reporter of the time, noted:

> The Southern Pacific Railroad dominated not only the Republican party, but also, to a large extent, the Democratic organization. Virtually every one of influence supported the railroad, because it was in control—and thus the sole dispenser of political favors.

In return, the Southern Pacific Railroad received enormous subsidies from government. To this day, this corporation remains California's largest single private landholder.

PROGRESSIVE PARTY REFORM

The reforms enacted by the Progressives made it difficult (some might say impossible) for California political parties to perform their traditional functions: recruiting candidates, endorsing and supporting office seekers in primaries, taking stands on issues, raising campaign funds, organizing campaigns, moderating differences among conflicting group demands, and achieving compromises in the general election. Significantly, most of the political reforms instituted by the Progressives remain intact. Progressive reforms still shape contemporary California politics.

Primary Election Reforms

To remove Southern Pacific tentacles from the state's political parties and to expand the role of voters in the nomination process, Progressives successfully fought for the enactment of the direct primary system. Under this system, voters *elect* party nominees rather than having party leaders, at what were often rigged conventions, *select* party nominees. Indeed, adoption of the direct primary system allowed for the nomination and election of Hiram Johnson to the governorship in 1910. A Republican convention would not have nominated Hiram Johnson as its gubernatorial candidate.

California was also one of the first states to adopt a presidential preference primary for electing delegations to national nominating conventions. Under the presidential preference primary system, delegates selected to go to the national party conventions were popularly elected—not just hand-picked by party leaders as they had been formerly.

Antiparty Reforms

Cross-Filing.   Among the more important party reforms passed by Progressives, which helped shape California politics, was cross-filing. Under cross-filing, candidates for partisan office were allowed to file not only in their own party's primary but in the opposition party's primary as well. And the candidate's party affiliation was not indicated on the primary ballot. Progressives believed that voters should not be limited to their own party's candidates in the primary, but rather, they should be able to vote for the best candidate—regardless of party. Unfortunately, the opportunity to vote for other parties' candidates in the primary depended on candidates' decisions whether to cross-file.

From the 1930s well into the 50s, cross-filers (usually well-entrenched incumbents) were frequently able to capture both parties' nominations in the primary. In the November general elections, these candidates would go on the ballot as hyphenated Republican-Democratic (or vice versa) candidates. Earl Warren and Pat Brown, former California governors, were both successful cross-filers. On the whole, cross-filing tended to give Republicans greater tactical advantages than Democrats. Republicans were usually better organized, had more newspaper support, and had better financial resources than Democrats.

Nonpartisan Elections.   Progressives also established nonpartisan local elections in California. Local issues, it was argued, such as road repair, park maintenance, or dog leash laws are not partisan, and parties should not intrude in the local election process. Voters should make voting decisions based on candidate qualifications rather than party designation. On the other hand, as Eugene Lee noted (1960), nonpartisan local elections provide activist business community members ("Main Street" types) distinct advantages they would not have had with partisan voting. Conservative businesspeople know each other through service club memberships and volunteer community activities, and could effectively coordinate political activities. Not surprisingly, nonpartisan local elections further weakened local party grass roots organization (see Chapter 12).

Party Organization Checks.   Progressives placed into the state election code a very detailed framework under which parties were to operate. The state election code spelled out in precise detail items such as when the parties could meet, for how long, and how they should be structured. For example, party chairs could not even succeed themselves in office. And, initially, county central committees were not linked to the state central party committee, nor was their provision for party organization below the county level.

Endorsing.   One reason political parties in some eastern states were so powerful was because they could provide endorsements to trusted party candidates (those who had "paid their dues") in the primary election or at state party conventions. In these states, those seeking partisan nominations would vie for the support of the party organization with endorsement of a particular candidate meaning almost certain nomination. The party could provide campaign advisers, financial assistance, and legions of precinct "foot soldiers" to go door to door for those endorsed.

Given their weakened condition, California political parties never really got into the practice of endorsing party candidates in the primary. The nonendorsing tradition extended to nonpartisan races as well. Some interpreted the section of the Election Code stipulating that all judicial, school, city, and county elections were to be *nonpartisan* as formally precluding party involvement. Over the years some party activists argued that parties not only had the legal right to make pre-primary endorsements in partisan races, but they had a moral obligation to help "quality" candidates secure the nomination. And on occasion, a particular county central committee might endorse a party candidate. But for the most part, parties stayed out of these contests. To clarify the matter (and to limit obstreperous local party groups), a law was passed in 1963 which prohibited parties from endorsing in partisan contests. Elected party officeholders have seldom been enthusiastic about having the party endorse.

In 1979, a private citizen, Samuel Unger, brought suit against a Democratic county central committee when it endorsed a local school board candidate. Unger argued this was a clear violation of the law, and his position was upheld in court. Three years later, Unger again went to court (dubbed in the press as "Unger II"), but this time Republicans were his target. Unger charged that the state Republican party had been involved in the "recall Rose Bird" campaign, and that this was a clear violation of the Election Code.

While Unger II was pending, the Committee for Party Renewal, comprised of academics, some Democratic party officials, and a few Republican and Libertarian activists concerned about California's weak parties, brought suit in federal court contending that the endorsing prohibition was an infringement on parties' freedom of speech. On April 16, 1984, Federal Judge Marilyn Patel ruled that: (1) parties could endorse in partisan primaries, and (2) parties could organize themselves as they saw fit. She abstained for the time (because of the pending Unger II case) on whether parties could be prevented from endorsing in nonpartisan races. In 1984, the state Supreme Court, while noting personal misgivings, ruled five to two that nothing in state law prohibited parties from endorsing or campaigning against candidates in judicial races. Unger lost round two. Reacting to this decision, the legislature passed a constitutional amendment prohibiting parties from endorsing in nonpartisan races, which voters approved in November 1986, 56 percent yes, 44 percent no. Obviously, there is still much legal confusion on this issue.

Excluding the legal question, *should* political parties endorse in partisan primaries—or in nonpartisan elections? While most party activists would say "yes" to both, but their sentiment is stronger for party primary elections. Party advocates argue that every organization in California previously had the right to publicly endorse/support their choices *except* the organizations most vitally concerned with the outcome—parties. Besides the free speech/right of association arguments, party proponents note that the inability of parties to endorse has led to a number of abuses: special interest power, slate mailer entrepreneurs, and occasional bizarre candidates. Why shouldn't a party have the right to warn its members that a particular candidate who has filed in its primary is a Klan member, or Nazi, or La Rouche supporter? Endorsing would revitalize the parties.

On the other hand, endorsing could lead to factionalization. Would the unendorsed bolt the party? Would endorsing cut down on the number of primary candidates and thus, voter choices. Would California party members be inclined to go along with the party's endorsees? Some might, but many would not. Would endorsing lead to bossism, packed meetings, and behind the scenes maneuvering? Legislative party leaders might want a nomination to go to a capitol insider (staffer), while local activists might favor a popular mayor. Do we really want parties further politicizing judicial contests or local races? In short, party endorsing is a two-edged sword. The potential for bitter conflict is always present.

Ballot Reforms

Progressives championed the adoption of the Australian secret ballot in order to help discourage vote fraud. Additionally, Progressives instituted the office-block system on the election ballot. The office-block system made it more cumbersome to vote the straight party ticket (see Chapter 4). Voters are forced to vote separately for each of the offices. This tends to weaken party-ticket voting.

Civil Service Reforms

In many eastern seaboard states or midwestern industrial states during the nineteenth century and in a few today, party organizations tend to be comprised of state and local government employees whose jobs depend upon their party's staying in power. Government jobs in these states are dispensed to party activists and relatives as patronage and not on the basis of merit or qualification. Progressives promoted the concept of civil service reform. Qualifications and test scores are used to determine who receives government jobs. The traditional work force of eastern party organizations—government employees—are absent from California political parties.

For much of this century, amateurs and volunteers have been the mainstays of California political party organization. While volunteers occasionally play instrumental roles in local campaigns—staffing headquarters, walking precincts, collecting signatures, distributing flyers at supermarkets, stuffing and addressing envelopes, putting up signs, and performing other tasks of the campaign—in statewide and legislative races the focus tends to be on money, mailers, and media (see Chapter 3).

Social Setting

Further compounding the weakness of California political parties and discouraging effective state party organization has been the population flux within the state—migration into and movement within the state. In eastern states, party machines tended to rely on coalitions of ethnic voters—Irish, Italian, Polish, Jewish, Puerto Rican, Slavic, or black neighborhoods. People living in these ethnic neighborhoods often knew their precinct captains by name. If someone had a problem—a pothole in the street in front of their apartment, trash not picked up, a traffic ticket, or children in trouble with the authorities—residents knew they could turn to their precinct captain for assistance in cutting through government red tape. In return, voters were supposed to support the party machine in the polling place. Today, the government—through food stamp programs, welfare checks, unemployment relief, and social security—has taken over this function.

This pattern never really developed in this state. However, it is true that in a few distinctive areas in California—such as the Irish, Italian, Chinese, or gay and lesbian neighborhoods of San Francisco, the Jewish population concentration in West Los Angeles and Hollywood (Littwin, 1977), the Mexican-American barrios in East Los Angeles, the black precincts in Oakland-Berkeley (Jacobs, 1976), or the Watts-Compton area—popular local politicians have put together effective political organizations in some ways reminiscent of the old-fashioned political machines. The Waxman-Berman organization in the Jewish neighborhoods of West Los Angeles or the Dymally organization in Watts, are examples. But, they are also strikingly different from the old-style political machines since they largely depend upon volunteers, not ward heelers, for the organizational work force. Vote fraud is virtually nonexistent.

Interestingly enough, the antiparty mood of California now appears to be part of the national picture: increasing numbers of voters do not feel committed to any political party. Political action committees of special interests, not political parties, are the major funding source for politicians' campaigns.

POLITICAL PARTY ORGANIZATION

State Central Committee

The State Central Committee (SCC) is the key party unit for Democrats and Republicans. Once every two years, each party's full State Central Committee convenes in Sacramento. At these party conclaves, members thrash out issues, elect party leaders, hear from national and state officeholders and aspirants, and develop strategy for upcoming campaigns.

State Central Committees usually marshall their relatively modest resources by providing assistance to candidates in marginal districts or to new candidates (Republicans have traditionally had more success in raising campaign money and parceling it out to their nominees.) Workshops are conducted to encourage more effective campaign organization. However, the candidate has the prime responsibility for the campaign, not the party.

Throughout most of this century, incumbent officeholders have dominated and controlled their respective party's State Central Committees. Incumbents knew one another, had more prestige than their nonofficeholder colleagues, and could each appoint many additional members to the SCC. Historically, little was done by the SCC without the incumbents' blessings.[1]

While officeholders continue to influence the SCCs, the Democrats, particularly, have reformed their party organization to provide a greater opportunity for grass roots influence. Today, instead of merely appointing members, local Democratic units elect approximately one half of the members on the Democratic SCC.

---

[1]The weakness of the official party leaders vis-à-vis the elected party officeholders was highlighted in a sharp internal conflict within Democratic ranks in 1982. The dispute revolved around the party's official positions on certain ballot measures. Democratic party officials wanted to send out a slate mailer to California Democrats urging them to vote for the party's nominees in the general election. Because party leaders were short of funds to finance such a mailing, they decided to ask Democratic Speaker Willie Brown for help in getting the mailer out. Brown agreed, and the mailer sent out included recommendations on certain ballot propositions upon which the Democratic party had never taken an official stand: textbook loans to private schools amendment (Proposition 9), the bottle deposit initiative (Proposition 11), and the water conservation initiative (Proposition 13). Indeed, on the latter two initiatives in particular, there was strong rank-and-file sentiment among Democratic activists in support of the measures. However, the mailer (*The California Democratic Leadership Ballot Guide*) recommended that Democratic voters vote against the bottle deposit and water conservation initiatives and for the textbook amendment.

Why did the mailer recommend such controversial positions? Money. In order to finance the mailer, Speaker Brown turned to various special interests who had a keen interest in the 1982 elections. Big business and big labor put up $30,000 for a "no on 11" recommendation, agribusiness forces put up $30,000 for a "no on 13" recommendation, and private school interests contributed $15,000 for a "yes on 9" recommendation. While many Democratic officials expressed dismay and shock over these proposition recommendations, their inability to do anything once again emphasized the weakness of the party organization.

This same confusion occurred again in 1984 over the Democratic party's stand on the lottery initiative. A slate mailer was sent to some Democratic voters urging them to vote for various Democratic candidates, but there was no mention of the lottery initiative which the party had officially gone on record as opposing.

6-1 *Supporting their candidate. Delegates to the 1983 state Democratic convention demonstrate for "Favorite Son" Alan Cranston.*

Photo by Richard Gilmore/Courtesy Sacramento Bee

Briefly, this is how the two parties select members to their respective state central committees:

Republicans (approximately 1,000 delegates)	Democrats (approximately 1,700 delegates)
1. All elected party officeholders.	1. All elected party officeholders.
2. Each elected officeholder gets eight additional appointments.	2. Each elected officeholder gets five or six appointments depending on office held.
3. National party committee members.	3. National party committee members.
4. Immediate past chair.	4. Immediate past chair.
5. Chairs of all county committees.	5. Members elected from county committees.
	6. Members elected from assembly district caucuses—five per caucus.
	7. Presidents of the CDC and Young Democrats.

Day-to-day operations of the two parties are handled by the state chairs, other elected party officials, and executive committees of the state committees. Unlike the more cohesive Republicans, an extensive set of unofficial caucus groups operates within the Democratic party structure—blacks, Hispanics, feminists, gays, youth unions, and even business and professions. This "balkanization" trend has been criticized by some party leaders as being counterproductive.

To an outsider, it might seem strange that the anonymous leaders of the two party organizations would spend thousands of dollars of their own money campaigning for an office that is unpaid and which requires countless hours of work. Not surprisingly, party officials tend to be wealthy, socially prominent individuals able to devote time and energy to party work. There are a few prominent attorneys from well-connected Los Angeles or San Francisco law firms who sometimes seek party posts. Their close ties to incumbents have advantages for their law firms. For the most part, though, party work is a labor of love with one major side advantage—the chance to hobnob or feud with major elected party officials. While some state party leaders have attempted to use their party position to run for elective office, this strategy has seldom succeeded.[2] Few rank-and-file party members know these party leaders.

Few would argue that the State Central Committees play a leading role in California politics, but new attempts to invigorate these historically moribund party organizations are underway. Occasional state chairs (for example, Charles Manatt on the Democratic side or Gaylord Parkinson on the Republican side) have succeeded in overcoming some of the obstacles to strong party organization and have provided effective party leadership. State chairs, however, must tread warily in their politicking (former Democratic chair Dick O'Neil was roundly censured by Republican *and Democratic* state senators when he attempted to intervene in a leadership squabble in that house).

There has been a longtime simmering feud in Democratic ranks between party leaders and elected officeholders. Democratic party leaders have felt that they should have a greater voice in overall party decision making. This dispute became particularly acrimonious during Betty Smith's tenure as state chair in the early 1980s. One Democratic Assemblymember called her a "moron" for expressing satisfaction with a party platform which he believed did not address contemporary realities. Speaker Willie Brown was critical when Chairman Smith expressed some criticism of Justice Rose Bird and stated:

> Any party leader who utters words of that nature certainly is not as interested in the legislative leaders as she should be. I want to say this directly to the party leadership. You should never, never, never be accepted or tolerated by any Democrat when you in any manner offer any aid or comfort

[2]In 1986, Republican state chairman Mike Antonovitch resigned his party position when he ran for the Republican nomination for U.S. Senator. Antonovitch finished third in the Republican primary, and in 1987 former Democratic Chair, Nancy Pelosi, has succeeded Sala Burton (deceased) for Congress from San Francisco.

to those who would destroy the independence of the judiciary. (*Sacramento Bee*, January 27, 1985, p. A-3.)

The vehemence of the Brown attack on Smith is not atypical of the way Democratic officeholders have viewed attempts by party leaders to assert themselves. Though Smith was chastised then, many Democratic candidates later refused to publicly take a position on the Bird confirmation election some even openly opposed her in the fall 1986 campaign.

Republicans, on the other hand, have frequently chosen party chairs who have previously held elective office—ex-Assemblyman Robert Naylor, ex-Assemblyman and Supervisor Mike Antonvitch, Congressman Ed Reinecke, and Congresswoman Clair Burgener. These ex-officeholders are members of the "club." Also, Republican chairs seem more willing to accept their subordinate role in party decisionmaking.[3]

California Republican and Democratic Presidential Primary Systems—1984

California Republicans continue to operate under their "winner take all" system (the candidate receiving the most votes in the primary elects all of his or her delegation). Criteria, such as party work, candidate loyalty, monetary contributions, and regional and affirmative action balance are frequently used by Republican candidates in selecting their delegations. There is some current discussion in Republican ranks to abolish their "winner take all" system in 1988 and go to a proportional system for electing delegates.

Since the tumultuous 1968 Democratic National Convention, California Democrats have experimented with several different systems for selecting convention delegates. Overall, in the 1970s, California Democrats focused on two objectives in their delegate selection changes: (1) achieving ethnic and gender balance in the delegation (national party guidelines mandated this change); and, (2) democratizing the selection process by abolishing their winner-take-all system and broadening the grass roots input into the selection process by electing delegates pledged to presidential candidates at local caucuses. For the most

---

[3]Occasionally, there has been tension between elected officeholders and GOP leaders. In 1987, William Park, formerly vice-chair of the party, assumed he would become chairman as this had been the tradition in Republican ranks. However, elected officeholders became fearful that Park, a toxics dumpsite operator repeatedly cited by the Environmental Protection Agency for violations, would not be a good symbol for the party. Park was defeated in his bid to become state chair of the Republican party by Robert Naylor, a former assemblymember and assembly minority leader. Park complained that Republican volunteers were being steamrollered by elected officeholders.

part, these objectives have been achieved. Democratic delegations to national conventions since 1968 have reflected the racial and gender diversity of the state's population.

Not surprisingly, these Democratic reforms—especially the grass roots input—generated internal party criticism. It was argued that many of the delegates who were chosen were picked only for affirmative action reasons, were inexperienced in convention politicking, or had not been active in party efforts.

Because of these criticisms, California Democrats again revised their delegate selection process in 1984. The primary format worked as follows: first, the various candidates' steering committees selected slates of delegates pledged to their presidential aspirant in the forty-five congressional districts (each district has from 3 to 8 delegates depending upon its Democratic strength); second, from these lists, 209 of California Democrats' 345 total delegates were chosen; third, the remaining 136 delegates were reserved for party leaders, party office-holders, and for affirmative action balancing. Since California Democratic activists seem relatively satisfied with the delegate selection process format of 1984, their 1988 presidential primary may be unique: no new changes!

However, as noted in Chapter 1, so long as the California presidential primary comes as late as it does among the various state primaries, the chance that it will have much impact on the candidate selected becomes increasingly remote. So there is some interest in moving the primary date ahead to March or April.

County Central Committee

At the bottom rung of the state political party structure is the *County Central Committee.* As with the other party units, County Central Committees have seldom been noted for their political effectiveness. While some voters may know the names of their assembly member, state senator, or county supervisor, they are far less certain of knowing the names of people who comprise their party's County Central Committee. Individuals run for County Central Committee positions by first securing the names of a few sponsors from within party ranks in order to qualify for the ballot and, second, running against other party competitors in the June primary.

Since most individuals running for the County Central Committee have little name recognition, there is no real campaign or media coverage of the race—voting and success frequently hinge more on one's ballot position than anything else. For the most part, most California voters receive the party message on TV or radio or through the mail, not in person. Indeed, in many rural counties, party leaders have difficulty finding enough people to run in order to fill empty slots on the

Central Committee, and many committees wind up having to appoint members to fill out terms.

The prime duties of the County Central Committee are to assist local party candidates running for office, and, in effect, maintain the party presence in a particular area.

County Central Committees may sometimes find themselves sharply divided over how much effort they should expend to assist the campaign of a particular local candidate, since the County Central Committee historically has no real voice in that individual's nomination. In many states, candidates must, in effect, "pay their party dues" (be active in the local party, contribute money, work in the office) before they can hope to get the nomination of the party. Interestingly, in another state influenced by the Progressives, Colorado, state law requires that a candidate must receive at least 20 percent of the vote in a pre-primary party caucus meeting before being allowed to file for office in the primary. Clearly, this helps keep Colorado party "jokers" out of the deck. But in California, local party organizations must accept the will of the voters, and at times, they do this with some reluctance.

On very rare occasions, County Central Committees can play a decisive role in local politics. If an uncontested party nominee should die before the primary, or if the nominee selected should die before the fall general election, the County Central Committee is given the responsibility of choosing a replacement.

Finally, we should not conclude our comments on weak party organization in California without briefly paying tribute to the small corps of volunteer activists in each party. Unpaid, unrewarded, and overworked, these party activists can be found in virtually every California community. They keep the party presence alive at the local level. Since most of their contemporaries spend no time on party activities, California party activists are a unique subset of the state population.

As noted in Chapter 3, the majority advantage Democrats held over Republicans in California dating back to the 1930s is now virtually gone. Surveys and election results indicate that in terms of vote turnout, the two parties are nearly even. Democratic legislative majorities are mainly a product of incumbency advantage and gerrymandering.

The central debate in Democratic party circles revolves around whether the party should soft-pedal or abandon its New Deal, activist tradition. Neoliberals in the party argue that Democrats must broaden their appeal to attract the new baby-boomer generation of voters. They urge the party to champion new issues and new programs. Meanwhile, traditional liberals in the party in the labor movement, the black and Hispanic communities, and feminists want the party to adhere to its activist principles.

Republicans, who have been a fairly cohesive minority, may face far greater intraparty differences now that the party has reached parity with the Democrats in California. At their most recent (1987) convention GOP archconservatives were angered when the party rejected a tough antiabortion plank, supported sex education and said nothing about school prayer, vouchers or cutting taxes—standard issues for right wing Republicans.

POLITICAL PARTY SUBSTITUTES

Because of the traditional weakness of the state's political parties, other organizations have emerged in California to provide traditional party functions.

Extraparty Groups—Republican

In 1934, a group of moderate Republican leaders (including Earl Warren) decided the state GOP needed to project a more centrist image. The California Republican Assembly (CRA) was organized to help the more progressive elements in the party survive the primaries and get elected. CRA was an *unofficial* party group and hence not bound by the legal prohibition on endorsing in the primary.

CRA soon came to play a pivotal role in state Republican nomination politics. It could provide financial assistance, campaign expertise, manpower, and the prestige of its endorsement behind its candidates. Local CRA committees interviewed and questioned prospective Republican legislative candidates prior to their filing for office. After surveying the field, the local committee placed its stamp of approval on a specific candidate. In statewide races, CRA had a special selection panel which interviewed prospective Republican candidates and discussed with them their stand on key issues of the day. Richard Nixon got his start in politics by winning a CRA endorsement in a southern California congressional district.

As CRA's prestige grew, many prospective Republican candidates who failed to win endorsement would decide not to file for office. The CRA-endorsed candidate would face little or no intraparty opposition and could often poach on the Democratic side under cross-filing and capture that party's nomination.

Though CRA began as a voice of moderate Republicanism, over the years it became increasingly conservative. Yet it was not conservative enough for some in the organization. These ultra-right-wingers pulled out of CRA to form a new extraparty group—United Republicans of California (UROC). In 1964, yet another Republican extraparty group, the California Republican League (CRL), was formed to support moderate Republican candidates. None of the Republican extraparty groups plays a decisive, or even modest, role in GOP nomination politics anymore. Thus, Bob Naylor garnered more support than any of the other Republican U.S. Senate candidates in 1986 at the CRA endorsing convention; but he finished seventh out of twelve in the primary.

Extraparty Groups—Democratic

The California Democratic Council (CDC) was organized in 1953. The CDC, while not as important in Democratic nomination politics as CRA was in Republican, was, nevertheless, a significant factor in its heyday. Democratic aspirants actively courted the group, and CDC's nominating conventions became a critical juncture for Democratic candidates. Unlike the CRA or UROC, which were comprised of relatively small groups of party activists, CDC, for a time, was a relatively large mass-member organization.

In 1976, a new extraparty group emerged on the California political scene—Tom Hayden's Campaign for Economic Democracy (CED). Hayden had gained considerable media notoriety for his leadership in the anti-Vietnam War movement in the 1960s and early 70s as one of the founders of Students for a Democratic Society (SDS). Hayden became more of a celebrity when he married popular film star and anti-war activist, Jane Fonda.

Organized initially from the volunteer corps that worked for Hayden in his unsuccessful bid to unseat incumbent John Tunney as the Democratic candidate for U.S. Senate in 1976, CED was partly a Hayden campaign organization, a liberal interest group active in lobbying, a caucus within the Democratic party, a local grass roots organization encouraging and coordinating local activists' campaigns, and an endorsing group (though it has primarily endorsed only CED members).

CED members were elected to local office in a dozen or so communities (mainly college towns like Chico, Davis, and Santa Cruz) throughout the state. CED championed issues such as rent control, solar energy, land use planning, toxic waste safeguards, and the nuclear freeze.

In 1985, a coordinated, well-financed conservative counterattack helped defeat several CED local government incumbents up for reelection. Republicans have found that raising the Hayden spectre can help fill their party's campaign coffers.

Only July 22, 1986, Tom Hayden announced that CED was closing down and that a new organization, Campaign California, was taking its place. Hayden said that CED had successfully focused on the problems of the 70s, but that a new organization was needed to grapple with contemporary societal problems. CED officials noted that too much energy had gone into local issues and into electing or reelecting local CED candidates. "Four seats on the Chico City Council don't do much about toxics pollution," said Hayden (*Sacramento Bee,* July 23, 1986). Hayden said that more emphasis would go into statewide and national issues in the new organization, and that it would focus on four prime media centers in California—Los Angeles, San Francisco, San Jose, and Sacramento. Hayden also stated that there had been confusion about the meaning of "economic democracy" in the CED, Campaign for Economic Democracy. "Some thought that it implied the organization favored a public solution for every private ill, and this was not the case," he said. Hayden promised Campaign California would be more supportive of the private entrepreneur than CED. All CED members were automatically transferred to the new group.

Critics of CED were jubilant with the announcement. They felt it showed that CED's efforts to elect their members to local office, after some initial successes, had, for the most part, failed. To appeal to California's broad mass of citizens CC had to moderate its program.

What role Campaign California will play in the immediate future is not clear, but the Hayden organization was a major factor in collecting enough signatures to qualify the November 1986 toxics initiative for the ballot. Whether Hayden's radical past will continue to haunt him and the organization he leads remains to be seen.

Problems of Extraparty Groups

All of the extraparty groups, have fallen upon hard times. Each group has its own individual set of problems, but there are some common difficulties as well. CRA and CDC were able to exert maximum leverage when they had a monopoly on the endorsing function within their respective parties and when cross-filing was in vogue. Competition has lessened the value of CRA and CDC endorsements.

Extraparty groups tend to attract issue-oriented people, and hence these groups seem to be particularly susceptible to angry wrangling over platforms or the wording of resolutions. CDC's ranks were decimated by bitter divisions over U.S. involvement in the Vietnam War. Many in the group felt the organization should not undercut Democratic President Lyndon Johnson by openly opposing the war.

CRA and UROC have tended to take more conservative positions than the Republican rank and file, and the CDC and CED tended to be more liberal than average Democratic voters. Democratic and Republican officeholders forced to seek compromises in the political arena have sometimes been criticized by their respective extraparty group's zealous adherents suspicious of a "sell out."

Another reason for the demise of the extraparty groups is that the campaign workers these groups can offer candidates—door-to-door canvassers, envelope stuffers, placard placers, and so on—have become less consequential in the era of automated statewide campaigns.

Firms can be hired today to do the drudgery work of politics, from addressing envelopes to putting up signs, and television is the most significant factor in statewide campaigns. However, there will always be a place for local party activists even in an era of automated campaigns.

Extraparty groups still provide forums for candidates running for office to make speeches and get some publicity. Their endorsements receive some press coverage at least, though since 1966 they must print a disclaimer ("not an official party group") on all flyers. The groups take controversial stands on leading issues of the day and thus encourage public dialogue on these matters, but their impact on the nomination process is virtually gone.

KINGMAKERS

In addition to extraparty groups, small informal groups of the very wealthy have at times attempted to influence candidate selection—particularly in Republican nomination politics. These "Lords of the Lettuce," as one disgruntled Republican candidate called them, attempt to use their pooled "big bucks" as leverage to encourage or discourage Republican statewide prospects. On the Democratic side, statewide aspirants traditionally woo "big labor" for campaign contributions.

PROFESSIONAL CAMPAIGN MANAGERS

Another prominent feature of the California political scene emerged in the 1930s: the professional campaign management firm. The now legendary husband and wife public relations firm of Whitaker and Baxter was the first to employ modern advertising techniques in political campaigns. For a fee, the firm provided expert advice to their clients on the overall management of a campaign, including raising money, planning, and wording and placement of ads. Whitaker and Baxter concentrated primarily on ballot proposition elections.

Between 1933 and 1955, Whitaker and Baxter managed seventy-five different campaigns and won seventy. They usually managed attractive ballot measures and relied on a sympathetic press to carry the message to the voters.

After World War II, others, such as Spencer and Roberts, Baus and Ross, and Murray Chotiner, joined the field. The weak party structure, the size of the state, the concomitant need to use mass media to reach voters, and the many ballot proposition campaigns encouraged the development of professional campaign management. Today, there are dozens of firms and other professionals running campaigns.

Professional campaign management firms in contemporary California work for candidates as well as ballot propositions and usually with

6-2 *Computerized political mailings. Candidates now use high-speed computerized electric typewriters to prepare "personalized" campaign letters.*

Courtesy International Business Machines Corporation

only one party's candidates. They include the Republicans Spencer and Roberts, Woodward and McDowell, George Young Associates, and Baus and Ross, and the Democrats Joe Cerrell, Sandy Weiner and Co. and Winner-Wagner. The Winner-Wagner Company runs not only political campaigns but also does contract lobbying. Specialization seems the order of the day. While one professional management con-

6-3

Courtesy Sacramento Bee

'AC-*CENT*-TCHU-ATE THE NEGATIVE/E-*LIM*-INATE THE POSITIVE; LATCH *ON* TO THE DEROGATIVE/DON'T MESS WITH MR. IN-BETWEEN!"

sultant may be hired for overall supervision of the campaign, subcontractors will often be used to do radio and TV spots, or buy time in the media, compose ads, select billboards, dig up dirt on the opponent, or send direct mail.

In addition to the public relations firms, there are hundreds of campaign consultants and media experts who offer their expertise to candidates for a fee or salary. For example, U.S. Senator Pete Wilson spent $1,166 for a one-day communications seminar with Leonard H. Roller, Inc. Roller provided intensive training in press conference psychology and how to respond to "unfriendly" questions. Consultant Don Penny works with candidates on style, content, and delivery of speeches. Media expert Maxwell (Bud) Arnold specializes in television filming of candidates. Major candidates look to media professionals, not the official party organization, for their campaign advice. Indeed, one 1978 GOP gubernatorial candidate, Ken Maddy felt compelled to hire a public relations firm to assist with his campaign in order to give it credibility with major contributors and the media.

From the early years of professional campaign managers to the present, there has been considerable concern raised over the success rate of these "hired guns" in the election process and also of the deterioration in the quality of campaigns. Candidates, it has been charged, are being sold to voters in much the same way that mouthwashes, toothpastes, or underarm deodorants are being advertised. As Michele Willens (1981:413) stated in describing the 1982 gubernatorial primaries:

> Statewide elections in California have become outrageously expensive media-mad escapades . . . Mike Curb, George Deukmejian, and Tom Bradley will each spend millions of dollars, with most of the money going into brief appeals sandwiched between the likes of "Laverne and Shirley," and "Magnum P.I."

Whether these public relations firms—through sloagns, half-truths, and television spots—have lowered the quality of American campaigns continues to be debated. And just as major television network spokespersons argue that the trivia, banalities, and sexual sniggering of many typical top-rated television shows are there because this is what the public wants, so too, public relations specialists say their techniques must be used to reach the typical, apathetic voter. Of course, whether a particular campaign consultant gets hired and fees charged are largely determined by his or her recent won/loss record. In order to stay in business, campaign professionals must win a reasonable number of campaigns and, to do so, they often must play hard ball with aggressive attacks, heavy use of TV spots, and last minute hit pieces. Campaign consultant Richie Ross, in justifying a particularly mean campaign he directed, said that the bottom line was that "we won." To win, campaign pro Bill Butcher has said that he would do anything for his candidate that was not strictly illegal. Pollsters concur: the public is far likelier to remember a sharp attack by a candidate than anything else. It is this fierce winning at whatever the cost that bothers critics.

What, if anything should be done about these "hired gun" professionals? Former Fair Political Practices Commission Chair Dan Stanford has proposed that political consultants be required to register with the state and agree to abide by an ethical code. There has been no action on Stanford's recommendation as yet. There also would seem to be no constitutional way to prevent these professionals from directing campaigns, but the extent of their involvement would likely be reduced if effective limits on campaign spending could ever be achieved. At present, running state campaigns can be very profitable. But, too much of the blame for the poor quality of campaigns is given to the professional consultants. What is needed is for candidates to take charge of their own campaigns.

Of course, there is no secret formula to winning a campaign. The quality of the candidate, the issues, and the mood of the electorate will all contribute to the outcome, not just the consultants hired.

Last, it should be noted that what started as a uniquely California phenomenon, professional campaign managers, is now a major feature of national campaigns and elections in many other states.

SPECIAL INTERESTS AND PACs

Special interests and their political action committee (PAC) contributing arms also serve as party substitutes. At the federal and state level, PACs provide more money to candidates than do the parties. Thus, in describing a new animal lovers PAC (ROAR-PAC) being put together by Senate Pro Tem David Roberti, Martin Smith (1983:99) states:

> The decision by a leader of the California legislature to turn to a single-issue constituency for support of this point of view is further evidence of the decay of political parties. They no longer provide the most effective means of raising money or communicating with like-minded voters.

(See Chapter 5 for a more complete discussion of special interests and lobbying.)

PARTY IN GOVERNMENT

Legislative Leaders

Though the official party organizations provide only a modest amount of money to legislative candidates, (the Republican party does far better on this score than the Democratic party), an increasingly important funding source for party nominees is legislative party leadership. Beginning with Jess Unruh in the 1960s, reaching a crescendo in the early 1980s with the Leo McCarthy-Howard Berman speakership fight, and continuing to the present with Speaker Willie Brown, Senate Pro Tem David Roberti, and Republican minority leaders Pat Nolan and Ken Maddy, campaign money has been transferred from legislative party leaders to "deserving" nominees. This builds up IOUs between recipients and legislative leaders. Obviously, it is easier for legislative leaders to ask colleagues for a vote as a quid pro quo since they have been partially responsible for that member's election. Legislative party leaders used to steer clear of involvement in their own party's legislative primaries, but in the increasingly partisan legislature of the 1980s, they are playing an ever more critical role. Legislative leaders encourage candidates to run in some open districts either because they believe the potential candidate can win or to keep the other side "honest" (i.e., provide an entrenched incumbent of the other party with an opponent that will keep him or her occupied in the fall election. Party leaders can provide their choices with campaign staffers and financial backing for their races. Given their access to Sacramento lobby money and campaign experts, the "anointed" legislative candidates have enormous advantages.

Legislative Voting

Given the antiparty traditions of California politics, it is not surprising that political parties in the Sacramento arena have not historically displayed the same rigid disclipline evidenced in some of the eastern state legislatures. One, of course, must be wary when comparing party voting in the state legislatures. As Keefe and Ogul (1977:300) note:

> There are wide differences in party competition among the states. There are southern states where Republican politicians come in contact with the legislature only by visiting the state capital and northern states where Democratic legislators have a status only a notch above that of the interloper— so dominant are the major parties in their localities.

Nearly all of the roll-call studies comparing state legislatures come to the same conclusions: first, several eastern state legislatures such as New York, Connecticut, Rhode Island, Massachusetts, and Pennsylvania have unified, cohesive legislative parties; and second, the California legislature is invariably grouped at or near the bottom of the list in terms of the number and percentage of party-division votes. For example, Jewell and Patterson (1966:420–21), while noting some fluctuation over the years, rank the California legislature as one of the least partisan state legislatures. In a similar vein, Professor Hugh Le Blanc (1969:33–57), in a comparative study of twenty-six different state upper houses, ranked California's senate at the very bottom of the list— Rhode Island had a 100 percent cohesion score; Pennsylvania, 82 percent; and California, 17 percent.

During most of the twentieth century in California, personality, skill, and political savvy were far more important to an ambitious member wanting to get ahead in the legislative arena than was party affiliation. Moreover, many legislators were hyphenated Republican-Democrats (successful cross-filers) who owed little debt to either party for their election. California legislators quickly discovered it was far more important to have been on the winning side in a fight for speaker or president pro tem than belonging to a particular party if one hoped to become a committee chair. On controversial issues, the California legislature, more often than not, tended to be divided along rural-urban, north-south, or special interest factional lines rather than party.

There is little doubt that the number of party votes has increased over the last decade. In each house, majority and minority caucuses attempt with varying degrees of success to unify party members on at least some controversial votes, though there are few binding positions taken. Additionally, the increasingly important fundraising role of the speaker, president pro tem, and other majority and minority leaders has injected a more partisan tone in the contemporary legislature. However, while parties are more important in the present-day California legislature, they are still far less unified than the eastern states.

Governor as Party Leader

The California governor, Republican or Democrat, is the real leader of his or her respective party. The more popular governors in California history, however, governors such as Earl Warren, Goodwin Knight, Pat Brown, and the legendary Hiram Johnson, have tended to deemphasize party. Those stressing partisanship have not been very effective. While recent governors, such as Ronald Reagan and Jerry Brown, have been important spokespersons for their parties, each stressed independence from and often disdain for traditional party politics.

Furthermore, the elected plural executive in California has been another factor promoting bipartisan state politics. Normally, at least a few state executives belong to a party different from the governor's.

THIRD PARTIES

Third parties have intermittently played interesting but seldom crucial roles in California politics. In this century, there have been a number of significant third-party efforts including the Hiram Johnson Progressives, Upton Sinclair's Socialist party of the 1930s, and contemporary third parties such as the Peace and Freedom party, American Independent party, and the Libertarian party.

The problems facing third parties in California plague third parties nationally: little money, overemphasis on a single issue, few "name" candidates, lack of organization, and popular issues borrowed by the major parties.

While some states have made it difficult for third parties to qualify for the ballot, this has not been the case in California. Under the provisions of the California Elections Code, to qualify for a place on the California ballot, a new third party must either: (1) register at least 1 percent of California voters (76,172) into the party or (2) get 10 percent (761,720) of the voters to sign a petition asking that the party be placed on the ballot.[4] Given the enormous number of signatures entailed, this latter option has never been used.

[4]Based on 1986 voter registration data.

In 1976, the California legislature further modified its election laws to allow third-party *candidates* another option. Third-party candidates could qualify by simply getting 1 percent of the registered voters' names on a petition requesting that the particular candidate be placed on the ballot. Third-party candidates qualifying for the ballot under this option are listed on the ballot as independents without any accompanying party affiliation designation. In 1976, presidential candidates of the Communist party and the Socialist Workers party, qualified as independents under this provision.

Additionally, staying on the ballot in California is even easier than qualifying. To remain on the ballot, a party must first, maintain a registration of at least *1/15th* of 1 percent and, second, have at least one of their candidates running for statewide office receive a minimum of 2 percent of the votes cast. The *1/15th* of 1 percent means that in 1987 a third party had to maintain only (4,571) registrants to stay eligible. There are usually enough disgruntled voters within the two major parties plus third-party voters to secure in one or two of the statewide races the necessary 2 percent to keep the party on the ballot for the next election.

Peace and Freedom Party

The Peace and Freedom party was born out of the frustrations many Americans felt with the interminable Vietnam War. When Democratic party leaders President Lyndon Johnson and 1968 Democratic presidential candidate Hubert Humphrey sought to continue the American presence in Vietnam until an honorable peace had been achieved, disgruntled Democrats saw the Peace and Freedom party as a viable alternative for opposition to the war.

Membership in the party has declined steadily since the end of the war, and, the number of candidates they have running in state legislative and congressional races has declined in the 1980s. The prominent radicals of the 1960s are no longer involved in the party. Attempts by some Democratic legislative leaders to increase the $\frac{1}{15}$ of one percent to $\frac{1}{2}$ of one percent and thus eliminate the Peace and Freedom Party from the ballot (they tend to siphon away Democratic votes) was beaten back by third party, Republican and press opposition. Illustrative of the depths to which this once proud, socialist third party had fallen came in the 1974 gubernatorial elections, when the Peace and Freedom party's gubernatorial candidate, Elizabeth Keathley, became so upset with the party's lack of visibility and news coverage that she campaigned in the nude on a Venice beach in southern California (to get more exposure?). What had once been a serious radical effort had, by the mid-1970s, degenerated into a comic farce.

American Independent Party

For much of its early history, this party's leadership had a strange sort of love/hate relationship with George Wallace. In 1968, George Wallace, the presidential candidate of the party (though he was not an official party member), garnered 13 percent of the national vote. The American Independent party has always had a staunch, ultraconservative program. They frequently criticize Republicans for "me-tooing" the Democrats. Since 1968, there has been a steady decline in the AIP vote percentage in the United States and in California. A succession of conservative "second-stringers" (John Schmitz, Lester Maddox, John Rarick, and the Reverend Bob Richards) have carried the AIP presidential banner into oblivion.

Finally, it should be noted that though the AIP has never come close to electing any of its candidates in a California election and only two party members were running for a Congressional or state legislative race in 1986, A.I. party registration has continued to edge upwards over the years. At present, the AIP has almost three times as many registrants as either the Peace and Freedom or Libertarian parties. A cynic might wonder whether the AIP "success" is more an artifact of their name—Independent—than their growing popularity. It is possible that some new registrants are confused and believe they are registering independent rather than into this archconservative third party.

Libertarian Party

The Libertarian philosophy can, perhaps, be best summarized in a single word—"against." Libertarians are opposed to nearly all governmental activity. Libertarians argue that those who want a particular service—education, health care, mail delivery, or parks—should pay for it individually. Libertarians favor the dismantling of Social Security, Occupational Safety and Health Administration (OSHA), regulatory commissions, and nearly every governmental program currently in existence. They also adamantly oppose new governmental programs, such as gun control laws or a national health care system. Libertarians are enthusiastic supporters of virtually all tax reduction schemes. They favor reduced military spending, getting the United States out of the United Nations, and bringing all American forces stationed abroad back home.

Not surprisingly, the Libertarian emphasis on a strict laissez-faire, profit-motive approach has a strong appeal to some ultraconservatives in the corporate community. Whether these same businessmen would support some of the more controversial economic views of the Libertarians, such as opposing the Chrysler bailout, support for free trade and indifference to cheap Japanese imports, or opposition to fair trade laws or agricultural price supports, is probably another matter.

Libertarianism also has an appeal to the other end of the ideological spectrum, the ultraliberal. Libertarians are opposed to any victimless crime laws. So long as one is not harming another, he or she should be allowed total freedom. Thus, Libertarians oppose laws that attempt to regulate sale or use of such drugs as marijuana, cocaine, or heroin. Libertarians favor legalized prostitution, oppose obscenity laws, and believe that the state should not get involved in regulating sexual activity between consenting adults. And, Libertarians oppose the draft. Thus, Libertarians attract supporters from both ends of the political spectrum.

Libertarians made impressive gains in the 1970s. They are an official party in over half of the states today. In 1978, over 1.3 million votes were cast for some 200 different Libertarian candidates running for various offices across the country. In 1982, Libertarians had candidates running in many of the state legislative and congressional districts in California. In Alaska, two Libertarians were elected to the state legislature.

Libertarian voting strength has already begun to ebb in California and nationally. Party registration is also declining. The two Libertarian Alaska state legislators have since been defeated. Symbolic of the party's decline, Norma Jean Almodovar, an admitted ex-prostitute and the Libertarian candidate for Lt. Governor in California in 1986, started a poster-of-the-month club as a means of gaining some publicity for her campaign. Every month a new pin-up poster of Almodovar appeared and, as promised, each month more was revealed of the real candidate. In the midst of her "hard-fought" fall campaign, Almodovar went to Denmark to attend an International Hookers Convention. Clearly, the Libertarian party has fallen on hard times, and Ronald Reagan and his Libertarian theme rhetoric would seem the chief culprit.

Third-Party Significance

While California's third parties fade into obscurity, third parties can occasionally play an interesting "spoiler" role in legislative races. In close elections, a Peace and Freedom candidate can drain a small, but significant, percentage of liberal-left votes away from the Democratic candidate. This can throw the election to the Republican candidate. As an example, in 1972 in the 27th Senatorial District, voting results were as follows:

Stevens (Republican)	136,515
O'Neil (Democrat)	132,616
Perrick (Peace and Freedom)	5,450

Peace and Freedom voters *probably* would have voted for the Democrat if they had not had the Peace and Freedom option.

Libertarians can have the same potentially adverse effect on Republican candidates. The 1982 Twelfth Senate District race is an example:

McCorquodal (Democrat)	79,457
O'Keefe (Republican)	76,327
Wilson (Libertarian)	8,613

Hence, the generous provisions of the State Elections Code allowing nearly moribund third-party corpses to remain in a state of suspended animation on the California ballot can create special problems for Democrats and Republicans in a few marginal districts. Democratic legislators in particular have complained about the phantom candidates (they seldom show up at public forums) of the Peace and Freedom Party who "steal" votes from Democrats.

Of course, even the spoiler's role is diminished if third parties do not even field candidates in many legislative races, as was the case in 1986. The number of third-party legislative candidates in the November 1986 general elections were as follows:

	Libertarian	Peace and Freedom	American Independent
Congress (45)	19	11	0
State Senate (20)	3	4	0
State Assembly (80)	27	21	2

REFORMING POLITICAL PARTIES

Should California political parties be further reformed, or perhaps more accurately re-reformed? Clearly, the Progressive reforms have succeeded in relegating the official parties to a relatively modest role in California politics.

The weakness of the official state party organizations will not be easily overcome with a few cosmetic changes; the problems are too deeply engrained in the California political culture. However, there are some indications that the party organizations are beginning to stir a bit. New rules broadening participation of rank-and-file Democrats in elections to the State Central Committee, new interest by party leaders in strengthening their organizations, a new optional checkoff box on state income tax forms to allow taxpayers the opportunity to contribute to the party of their choice (little money has been raised this way), new opportunities for the parties to formally endorse their preprimary choices, renewed interest in moving California's presidential primary to an earlier date, and stronger ties between the Democratic and Republican party organizations and the satellite, exparty groups surrounding each are all indicative of this trend. Yet, none of these changes will probably do much to strengthen California political parties in a meaningful way. And, California Democrats and Republicans face a new dilemma: Should independents be allowed to vote in their primaries? The Supreme Court ruled in a Connecticut case in 1987 that if one party or the other wants to invite independents to vote in their primary, state law cannot prohibit it. Republicans, for the most part, seem much more enthused about this than do Democrats.

Finally, do weak structural parties give elected party officials too much flexibility to "do their own thing?" Will state voters be enthusiastic in supporting stronger parties? Have heightened partisanship and more cohesive legislative party voting led actually to more problems? How much influence should organizational party leaders have over publicly elected party officeholders? For every reform, there are negative trade-offs and unanticipated consequences. Attempting to assess the usefulness of a particular reform and its trade-offs is a never-ending task.

SUMMARY

Historically, the two major parties have been weak because of Progressive reforms and the mobility of the state population. Third parties have not been a significant factor over the last several decades except as potential "spoilers." Partisanship is on the increase in the California legislature. Elective officeholders are the real leaders of the two state's parties, but the internal state party organizational leaders are attempting to play more assertive roles. New reforms in political parties may strengthen these organizations.

7

The California Legislature: Cinderella or Frankenstein?

Overall, state legislatures perform four major tasks in the American federal system: (1) lawmaking, (2) oversight, (3) representation, and (4) education. Let's briefly consider each of these functions.

LEGISLATIVE TASKS

Lawmaking

Lawmaking is traditionally considered as *the* critical task of the legislature. Every year thousands of bills, constitutional amendments, and resolutions are introduced in the various state legislatures for consideration. As the policymaking arm of state government, state legislatures are restricted only by the federal and state constitutions, judicial review, and the governor's vetoes in their deliberations. Legislators spend untold thousands of hours in the tedious, laborious job of working over legislation—bill assignment, subcommittee hearings, full committee hearings, fiscal committee hearings, testimony, amendments, and the like.

In a sense, the rites of legislative bill passage can be compared to a giant pinball game. Bills (pinballs) bounce madly from one committee to another over to the other house and then, perhaps, back again. Most bills, like pinballs, get sidetracked along the way. And as in pinball where the same metal balls are used game after game, legislative bills that die in one session are likely to be reintroduced the next session, or the next. Prime sources of the substantial stream of legislation include: special interests and lobbies, governors, state bureaucracies, legislative staff, local governments, political parties, constituents, and even legislators at times.

The legislature is the public arena where various competing interests thrash out their policy differences. The prime lawmaking objective is to seek compromise among the bewildering array of conflicting demands.

Oversight

The oversight function is another important legislative task. Being a counterbalance to the governor and keeping track of the state bureacracy is a formidable undertaking. Most state legislatures have difficulty being a coequal branch with the governor. State legislatures tend to be divided by personal, regional, and/or party divisions further complicated by two house divisions. The many legislative members have difficulty competing with the single governor for media attention. However, state legislators can make bureaucrats tremble—particularly when the budget of an agency is being reviewed.

Representation

No task is performed so zealously by state legislatures as the representative function. Legislators, keenly aware of looming reelection battles, are anxious to serve their constituents. "Bringing home the bacon" and the "pork barrel" are traditional features of American legislatures.

Two classic dilemmas of representative government are: (1) should legislators merely echo the sentiments of their constituents when voting, or should they follow their own judgment or conscience; and (2) should legislators reflect a typical cross-section of the adult population of a state—racially, socially, and occupationally—or should they represent the most able elements of a state's population?

Education

Finally, state legislatures serve an important educational function. The legislature provides a major public forum for discussion of the critical issues of the day. It is the one branch of government where the decision-making process is, to some extent, public, and while the public portion of the legislative process is the tip of the iceberg, citizens can at least see the tip.

Legislative investigations of vexing public issues help focus attention on these problems. Moreover, through newsletters and speeches, legislators help keep local citizens informed on developments at the

7-1 *Legislature in session. However, most of the day-to-day work is done in committees.*

Photo courtesy Sacramento Bee

state capitol. Of course, given the public's absorption with daily living problems and other distractions, the educational function does get sidetracked frequently.

FORMAL STRUCTURE OF THE CALIFORNIA LEGISLATURE

Patterned after the bicameral Congress and like forty-eight of the other state legislatures (Nebraska is the sole exception), the California legislature has two houses—the assembly and senate. The upper house, the senate, has forty members elected to four-year staggered terms (half are elected every two years). The lower house, the assembly, has eighty members who serve two-year terms. From 1923 until 1965, the legislature operated under the federal plan: representation in the assembly was based on population; in the senate, representation was based on area (counties). Since 1965, the U.S. Supreme Court has required *both* houses of American state legislatures to be apportioned on the basis of population.

One must be a registered voter, a U.S. citizen, an inhabitant of California for three years, and a resident of one's district for one year to be eligible to run for the California legislature.

While the bicameral structure and committee framework of the California legislature remain basically unchanged from the first legislative session after statehood was attained to the present, other facets have changed. In the 1960s, the California legislature was transformed from a rural, "horse and buggy" state legislature into a modern, full-time professional legislature. Or to use the phrase of one state expert, the California legislature became the "Cadillac of American state legislatures."[1]

THE PROFESSIONAL LEGISLATURE

For much of the nineteenth and twentieth centuries, American state legislatures were the dustbins of the American federal system. State legislatures were fettered by antiquated state constitutions, outflanked by the national government's new social programs, confused by bureaucrats, dominated by full-time, professional governors, and beholden to lobbyists for meals and sustenance. Further compounding the difficulties facing state legislatures was the problem of representativeness. Prior to 1965 state legislatures were usually dominated by rural legislators who were usually indifferent, if not openly hostile, to urban needs. As population steadily shifted to urban centers in various states during the twentieth century, these rural solons fought a bitter rear guard action to maintain control. State legislatures came to be labeled in the press as antiquated institutions—a not-very funny national joke.

Several events occurred in the 1960s and early 70s which helped lead a number of state legislatures to modernize and professionalize. One key factor was the series of reapportionment decisions issued by the U.S. Supreme Court in the early 1960s, culminating in *Reynolds* v. *Sims* in which the Court ruled *both* houses of American state legislatures were to be apportioned on the basis of population. The rural stranglehold on state legislatures was effectively broken.

Background to Reform

Until the early 1960s, California's legislature was much like that of other states. Legislators were poorly paid, and met only part of every year. State legislators had inadequate offices, haphazard procedures, and very few professional staff. Through 1965, the California legislature's working conditions were controlled extensively by the state constitution. For example, legislative salaries ($6,000 annually) and the

[1]Whether one should view this as a compliment or criticism depends on one's personal perspective.

7-2 Jess Unruh. He led the legislative reform movement in California.

Photo courtesy Sacramento Bee

length of session (120 days for general sessions in odd-numbered years and 30 days for budget sessions in even-numbered years) were locked into the constitution. To change either feature required amending the constitution, an always difficult endeavor. First, the amendment would have to be approved by a two-thirds majority vote in each house (opportunities for grandstanding were legion), then signed by the governor, and, finally, the toughest hurdle of all—submitted to an always wary public for final approval. Not too surprisingly, raising legislators' (politicians!) salaries was a difficult notion to sell to the public.

In order to deal with these constitutional problems as well as remove obsolete portions from the document, the legislature adopted a concurrent resolution in 1963 establishing a Constitutional Revision Commission. The commission made its report to the legislature in February 1966 and recommended revisions of articles dealing with the legislative, executive, and judicial branches of California government. These proposed constitutional revisions were submitted to voters as Proposition 1A of November 1966.

Under the provisions of Proposition 1A legislators would set their own salaries and determine for themselves the length of the legislative session. The legislature had previously passed a pay raise bill raising their salary from $6,000 to $16,000 upon public approval of the measure. To assuage the public, legislators were to be limited to a 5 percent salary increase per year, and any pay hike approved by the legislature would not become effective until the next legislative session.

1A—The Successful Campaign

The leading proponent of Proposition 1A, and the person most instrumental in getting the constitutional revision approved, was Speaker Jess Unruh (recently deceased). To gain support for 1A, Unruh received support from several key sources: (1) he secured the cooperation of the "other party"—many key Republican legislative leaders gave solid support to the effort; (2) he persuaded lobbyists to join the campaign ("take a lobbyist to lunch" became a legislative theme) and warned them that their failure to provide 1A with political campaign contributions would be long remembered; and (3) he garnered the support of much of the state's press by promising the legislature would pass new, strict conflict of interest rules upon adoption of 1A. Unruh campaigned tirelessly the length and breadth of the state championing the measure.

Unruh argued that improving legislative salaries would help attract brighter, better educated people to the legislature. Low pay, he believed, tended to discourage able citizens from running for office and made it nearly impossible for many blacks and Hispanics to run for office. Inadequate pay virtually guaranteed that legislators would be dependent on lobbyists for meals, lodgings, and other sundries. Further, Unruh contended that pay should be based upon the responsibilities of the job, and, hence, legislators deserved more money. Improved legislative salaries would allow legislators a chance to concentrate their full-time attention on their legislative chores.

In November 1966, California voters, by a solid three-to-one margin, voted approval of Proposition 1A. After the overwhelming vote of approval for Proposition 1A, Speaker Unruh was invited to address university groups, public forums, and other state legislatures on the topic of legislative reform and the California success story. In addition, delegations of legislators from other states came to visit the California capital almost like pilgrims visiting Mecca to discuss with their California colleagues how this "miracle" might be achieved in their states.

Since the passage of 1A, salaries for California legislators have increased several different times. As of December 1986, they earned $37,105 per year. In addition, California legislators enjoy other "perks" (perquisites) of office.

Perks

California legislators receive $75.00 daily (Monday-Sunday) for living expenses while the legislature is in session. This generally adds a $16,000 or so tax-free supplement to legislator's incomes. This sum alone is greater than the salary total for legislators in about half of the other states. Among the other perks (most were adopted when the constitution limited pay increases) are: (1) $350.00 monthly for car leasing; (2) a gasoline credit card providing free gas and maintenance service on the leased car; (3) money for district office rent; (4) a telephone credit card; (5) office supplies and office furniture; (6) money for five constituent newsletters and/or questionnaires per session; (7) medical, vision, and dental insurance programs valued at $2,692 per legislator; and (8) a generous retirement system.

Staff Augmentation

Prior to the 1960s the California legislature had a small professional staff. Besides some clerical, secretarial, and housekeeping staff, there were only a handful of professional staff including the:

1. *Legislative Counsel* (1913), which provides bill drafting and amending services to legislators. Presently, there are some sixty attorneys engaged in this highly technical work.

2. *Auditor General* (1955), which uses some fifty auditors to provide independent postaudits of state agencies to insure that funds are spent according to law.

3. *Legislative Analyst* (1957), which has nearly sixty program and budget analysts who provide fiscal expertise to legislators. Their annual publication "Analysis of the Budget Bill," in effect, sets the parameters of legislative debate on the budget. Under its first director, Alan Post, and his successors, William Hamm and Elizabeth Hill, the analyst's office has maintained a reputation for fairness and nonpartisanship.

During the Unruh speakership years in the 1960s, there was a rapid expansion in numbers of assembly legislative staff. The senate, though proceeding more cautiously in staff development, also added new legislative aides during this period. However, over the last several decades, the assembly has had a substantially larger staff than the senate. In the 1980s, under the leadership of Senate President Pro Tem David Roberti, the upper house has added many new staffers. Today, there is little difference between the two houses in size and quality of staff.

Unruh and other legislative reformers argued that professional staff could provide legislators sorely needed policy expertise. A skilled professional staff, it was contended, would allow legislators to concentrate on their more important legislative chores (staff could handle the more routine tasks), and equally significant, these aides would be able to provide legislators a more "neutral" informational source, freeing them from dependence on the bureaucracy or the lobbyists.

Committee Consultants.   Prior to the 1960s, only a few assembly and senate committees had professional consultants. Today, all standing, select, or subcommittees have at least one (and most have three to four consultants). The critically important fiscal committees have dozens of consultants who assist members. Assembly Ways and Means and senate Finance committees also have a formalized majority/minority staff arrangement much like Congress.[2] Committee consultants have prime responsibility for doing bill analyses, coordinating testimony at committee hearings, and, finally, carrying out other tasks assigned by the chair.

Because legislators serve on many different policy committees and must be knowledgeable in many areas, committee staff provide an indispensable expertise to members. In the late 1960s–1970s assembly committee staff were viewed as professional, nonpartisan experts; some staffers even retained their positions after elections when the chairmanship of a committee changed. In the 1980s, committee staff have become more political. They are expected to owe their allegiance to the chairman and speaker and be loyal footsoldiers of the majority staff. If they don't comply, committee chairs can fire them summarily.

Research Staff.   In 1962, the assembly Legislative Reference Bureau was established, and this office two years later was transformed into the assembly Office of Research. The office has three prime responsibilities: providing long-range and short-range research, lending expertise on a variety of technical subjects to members and other staff, and doing a third-reading analysis of pending bills. Ostensibly nonpartisan, from time to time over the last several decades, the minority party has viewed the consultants in this office as "surplus" majority staff and highly partisan. To help allay concerns about partisanship, the office today is responsible to a *bipartisan* Committee on Policy Management for its overall direction. On the senate side, the senate Office of Research, though smaller, operates similarly. Additionally, on some research projects, the legislature has found it convenient to contract with private consulting firms to carry out more specialized research.

---

[2]Under Republican assembly minority leader Pat Nolan's direction, minority consultants are assigned to the various standing committees to provide Republican members unofficial staff assistance.

Personal Staff.   Members of the assembly and senate are also provided administrative assistants, field representatives at the district offices, and clerical staff. Because of their larger districts, senators have larger personal staffs than do assembly members. The legislator's personal staff performs a variety of functions: answering constituent mail and phone calls, helping people in the district cope with the bureaucracy, working on legislation, doing research, keeping abreast of newspapers in the district, sending out press releases and newsletters, and attending district functions.

Leadership Staff.   Assembly and senate party leaders (the speaker, speaker pro tem, senate pro tem, majority floor leaders, minority leaders, caucus leaders, Rules members, etc.) are provided additional staff for their expanded leadership duties and responsibilities.

Party Staff.   Both houses have dozens of majority and minority party consultants who provide extra assistance to members of "their" party. This staff is primarily concerned with ensuring that their members get reelected. Thus, assembly Democratic majority consultants have recently been focusing their prime efforts on Democratic members' district office operations. Are they run efficiently? Are constituents aware of their presence? Do these offices respond to constituents' queries effectively? Are members keeping in touch with local sentiment?

Prior to the adoption of Proposition 9 (the Political Reform Act), party staff often provided campaign assistance to members while on the state payroll. Today, this practice is illegal and has been sharply reduced. When majority or minority staff go off to work on a campaign, they must take a leave of absence and go off the state payroll. When personal staff and/or party staff volunteer to work on campaigns, they are supposed to do it after hours. Obviously, though, trying to decide what is legitimate legislative work and what is political campaign activity can pose vexing problems for staffers and members. Certainly, over the last decade, party staff have helped contribute to the more partisan tone in the legislature. Whether party staff, whose salaries are paid for by the taxpayers of the state, provide a necessary and legitimate form of assistance to members is a subject of much controversy.

Housekeeping Staff.   Overall administration of the two houses is handled by their respective rules committees. Other housekeeping staff include: the chief clerks of the two houses, who keep track of floor session details; the sergeants-at-arms staff, who provide routine ("gofer") assistance to members; mail room assistants; the secretarial pools; bill room employees; and messengers.

Interns.   In addition to its regular legislative staff, there is another source of assistance available to California legislators—interns. Perhaps the most prestigious of the internships are the assembly and senate Fellowship Programs under the auspices of the Center for California Studies, California State University, Sacramento. Each year, after extremely rigorous competition, each house selects twelve Fellows. These Fellows work as junior staffers providing further research assistance to members and regular staff. Fellows receive a modest stipend for their efforts.

Additionally, a number of colleges and universities have programs allowing students to work in the legislature for academic credit. Interning is one of the very best ways for young people to learn about the legislature, gain valuable job experience, and possibly find staff employment at the capitol.

Procedures

As the California legislature has become more professional, there has been impressive progress in streamlining and routinizing the legislative process to make it more orderly and less vulnerable to behind-the-scenes maneuvering. In the "good ole days," floor sessions were chaotic. Members used to have to use their floor desks to do their legislative office work, and anyone who wanted could get a floor pass. Today, access to the floor is strictly limited to members and their secretaries. Each legislator has his or her own microphone, and floor debates usually proceed smoothly. Unfortunately, chaos still prevails in the closing days of sessions because of the backlog of bills and because many members see distinct advantages in having their bills voted upon at the last minute when members are so preoccupied. In the assembly, an electric roll call system is used to record votes, though the senate still uses the more time-consuming oral roll call.

Committees frequently used to meet in closed-door, executive session. A few committees used to meet ahead of time to decide their course of action, and some powerful committee chairs used to totally control the actions of their committees. Vote switching and "ghost" voting were commonplace. Activities such as these are increasingly uncommon in contemporary Sacramento capitol politics. The two-year session, public announcement of hearings, orderly procedures, and the right of anyone so desiring to testify, all help contribute to a relatively open process.

To keep track of the legislative flow, the senate and assembly publish several important documents: the *Daily Journal* (contains the official proceedings of each house and the roll calls on all votes taken); the *Files* (announcements of committee hearings and listing of bills scheduled for action); and the *Weekly History* (an index of legislative subjects and a record of actions taken on a bill). Bills, constitutional amendments, and resolutions are printed and made available to the legislature and the public as soon after introduction as possible. In addition, the legislature has computerized; capitol and district offices can instantaneously access the status of pending legislation. As chief clerk of the assembly, James Driscoll (1986:163) commented, "The California legislature maintains the most complete and sensitive information system of any legislative body in the world."

EFFECTS OF PROFESSIONALIZATION: CINDERELLA OR FRANKENSTEIN?

What effect has this professionalizing trend had on the California legislature? Overall, it is difficult to *prove* that the legislature has passed more innovative legislation or that public issues have been more successfully resolved since the legislature became professionalized. At the very least, however, the legislature has developed a greater capacity to legislate thoughtfully. Nevertheless, the debate on the merits of professionalization continues. Currently, State Senator H. L. Richardson has proposed a constitutional amendment that would reduce legislative salaries and return the legislature to a part-time operation. The point is, have we created a monster? Is the legislature more productive these days? Is the public getting its money's worth? Admittedly, answers to these questions are subjective. Recognizing this fact, let's examine the arguments of the two sides on this dispute.

Cinderella Case

Proponents of legislative professionalization argue the California legislature has changed markedly, and for the better, over the last twenty years. The legislative reforms enacted have meant substantial improvements in a number of key areas.

Member Qualities.   Clearly, contemporary California legislators are better informed and better educated than they used to be. Nearly every member of the present-day legislature has completed at least some college work, and many have advanced graduate degrees. These members have the ability to deal with the complex problems confronting California. Contemporary California legislators tend to come from four major professional occupational backgrounds: attorneys (usually 35 to 40 percent of each chamber), former local politicians, ex-legislative staff, and small business people.

Prior to 1966, when the legislature was part-time and legislative salaries were minimal, California legislators were mostly middle-aged,

TABLE 7-1
Minority and Female Members in the California Legislature, 1965–1987

| | In the Legislature* | | | | In the State Population |
| | 1965 | | 1987 | | |
	Number	Percent	Number	Percent	Percent
Asian	0	0%	0	0%	7.5%
Blacks	2	2	8	7	7
Hispanics	0	0	6	5	21.6
Women	1	1	17	14	51

*Latino and black women legislators are double counted.

white, male, Anglo-Saxon Protestants. Many of the legislators who served were the well-to-do who could afford to be away from their jobs for a few months each year, and who did not have to live off their meager legislative salaries. Professionalization of the legislature has helped broaden opportunities and has encouraged heretofore un- or under represented groups within our society to seek a legislative position (see Table 7-1). Obviously, a host of reasons help account for the increasing numbers of minority members and women getting elected to the California legislature—reapportionment, growing political awareness in minority communities, and more minorities going to law school or working on legislative staff—but the increased pay, status, and career potentials in the legislature have helped break down the formerly white, "Gentlemen's Club" atmosphere.

Turnover. One of the frequently cited criticisms of nonprofessional state legislatures is the problem of constant turnover in membership and the instability this creates. While there are reasons for extensive turnover (usually about one-fourth of the state legislators are freshmen in an average session), the most frequently noted is low pay. As Keefe and Ogul comment (1977:131), "Burdened by low pay, high costs, and the frustrations of the job, members serve a brief tour of office and drop out."

However, it is true that even in the professionalized California legislature, there is usually substantial turnover in membership, although not as great as in a nonprofessional legislature. As one might expect, the assembly has greater turnover than the senate. In 1966, the average tenure for an assemblymember was 7.8 years. Twenty years later after professionalization and improved working conditions had been implemented, the average assembly tenure in 1986 had declined to 7.4 years! However, tenure did increase in the senate going from 7 in 1966 to 9.4

in 1986. In addition, on average, more than half of all senators have previously served in the assembly, so there is clearly more legislative experience in this chamber.

Why do members leave the excitement and glamour of the high-status California legislature? Of course, some leave involuntarily; they lose elections. Others suffer burnout. The constant campaigning, fund-raising, endless commuting between home and the capitol, relatively low pay,[3] pressures to attend district social functions, long periods away from one's family, and decline in collegiality are some of the factors mentioned. Yet very few leave the legislature to return to the peace and quiet of their former occupations. Particularly in the assembly, there are few careerists in the chamber. Most members wait impatiently for a good opportunity to run for higher office.

Legislative-Governor-Relations. Present-day governors have found the professional legislature a more formidable adversary. Veto over-rides and gubernatorial appointment rejections do seem more commonplace these days, but since so many other variables are involved on votes they are not very satisfactory indicators of legislative independence.

Impressionistically speaking, since 1966, governors and speakers have frequently been locked in fierce conflict—Pat Brown versus Unruh, Reagan versus Moretti, or Jerry Brown versus McCarthy. Legislative leadership seems increasingly assertive. Governor Jerry Brown, perhaps, suffered the most at the hands of his own party colleagues in the Democratic-controlled legislature (see Chapter 8). Governor Deukmejian has frequently found himself pitted against Speaker Willie Brown, but he also must contend with a far more assertive senate leader than is customary, David Roberti, president pro tem.

Certainly, governors no longer casually get involved in legislative leadership contests as they once did. Contemporary California governors must work harder than their predecessors to achieve results in the present-day, professional legislature.

Frankenstein Case

Twenty years ago the California legislature embarked on its professionalizing trend. Are the results positive? Critics would contend that, if anything, the legislature works less well today than it did prior to 1966.

---

[3]Because of inflation, a contemporary legislator would have to earn in salary and per diem a sum of $64,471 to enjoy in purchasing power legislators received in 1967 after Proposition 1A was first implemented. Unfortunately, in 1987 with salary and per diem combined, today's legislator earns only about $53,000.

7-3 *There is never enough time. Lobbyists and interested bystanders hover at the gates to the assembly floor during the last-minute maneuverings to enact or defeat legislation as the session draws to a close.*

Photo courtesy Sacramento Bee

A host of criticisms are leveled against the contemporary, professionalized California legislature: (1) it is unresponsive to the public (initiative proponents have had to take the lead in promoting legislation); (2) it has become polarized and paralyzed by aggressive partisanship; (3) its newer members are political "technicians" (often former legislative staff) who think only in terms of their political survival and raising campaign contributions; (4) it is wasteful and profligate—too much staff, overly opulent offices, etc.; (5) legislators have become prima donnas, not of the people but apart from them; (6) legislators are becoming increasingly "Sacramentoized" losing touch with the people back home; (7) last-minute tricks, conference committee hocus-pocus, and hijacked bills are commonplace; (8) policy and research staff have become politicized; and (9) special interests and PACs dominate the process.

Larry Margolis, former director of the now defunct Citizens Conference on State Legislatures, which ranked California as the "best" legislature in the early 1970s, argues that the California legislature's premier ranking is in jeopardy.

While California's legislature remains near the top in terms of member benefits among state legislatures,[4] its record in resolving state problems does not seem very much different from less professionalized state legislatures. Reformers assumed that if legislators were provided

---

[4]Currently, five state legislatures provide higher annual salaries than does the California legislature.

the necessary tools they would inevitably do the job. This has not always happened.

POLITICS OF THE LEGISLATIVE PROCESS: THE ASSEMBLY

The speaker of the California assembly is unquestionably the most powerful single member of the lower house and, indeed, of the legislature. Let us consider his role in the lower house.

The Speaker's Powers

The speaker is second only to the governor in terms of influence within the California governmental milieu. In the assembly, the speaker has total control over: (1) selection of standing committee chairs; (2) selection of select committee chairs, vice chairs, and sub-committee chairs; (3) assignment of members to committees (Rules Committee is the single exception); (4) assignment to subcommittees, joint committees (i.e., the assembly members), and select committees; (5) selection of the other majority party leadership positions—majority floor leader, caucus chair, speaker pro tem (presiding officer), and party whips; (6) control of assembly floor action; (7) chief rule enforcer; and (8) through the Rules Committee chair, determination of matters such as the location of the member's capitol office, whether the member might get an extra secretary, or even whether a member will be allowed a second district office. Virtually nothing of significance happens in the assembly without the speaker's approval.

Electing the Speaker

Before Jess Unruh's tenure as lower house leader, speakers were elected by a vote of the entire membership every two years after the general election. This was the most important single vote of the session for members. Candidates for speaker would promise choice committee assignments to members in return for their support. Not infrequently, the governor might throw his support to a particular legislator. Party affiliation was a relatively minor factor in speakership elections. Usually, Democratic and Republican assembly members would vote for one of their own party's colleagues—but not always. If a member were on the winning side in a speakership contest, that legislator could expect to be rewarded, but if a member were on the losing side. . .

Unruh modified, in effect, the way speakers were to be elected. In 1964, Unruh successfully secured an agreement within the Democratic party caucus that obligated all members of the majority party to vote on the floor for the candidate receiving the most votes in the majority caucus (i.e., Unruh). This meant the minority party, in effect, had no real voice in the speakership vote. The formal vote of the entire assembly became meaningless.

In the years since Unruh's speakership, the battle for speaker has *usually* taken place in the majority party caucus, but on several different occasions, majority party speaker candidates have either covertly or overtly sought votes from minority party members. For example, after losing the speakership vote to Leo McCarthy in the Democratic caucus in June 1974, Willie Brown tried again after the November 1974 general elections. Brown appealed to Republican assemblymembers for support (and they gave it to him) and to disgruntled Democrats in the lower house. In his second try for the speakership Brown fell a few votes short of the necessary forty-one votes. After losing Willie Brown and the other eleven Democratic mutineers (labeled by the press as the "Dirty Dozen") were punished by Speaker McCarthy—smaller offices, reduced staffs, and no chairmanships. Interestingly, in 1981, after Howard Berman and Leo McCarthy had fought to a standstill in the battle for speaker within Democratic ranks, Willie Brown offered himself as a compromise candidate. Once again, to round up the necessary forty-one speakership votes, Brown appealed to Democrats *and* to Republicans. In fact, Brown received more Republican votes than Democratic votes in 1981. While there has been criticism in Democratic ranks of these appeals to the minority party for votes and in the concessions given to them to win their support, the point is that speaker candidates are after forty-one votes and partisanship is secondary.

In addition to the traditional bartering of committee assignments and chairs to get pledges of speakership support, Unruh added another dimension—campaign contributions. As a powerful legislator and former chair of several "juice" committees (committees where powerful financial interests had policy interests) and a good arm-twister, Unruh was able to raise a substantial Democratic assembly campaign kitty. This money, in turn, was dispensed to "deserving" Democratic incumbents or grateful new Democratic candidates in open districts. Interestingly, 1970s Speaker Leo McCarthy faced his most serious leadership challenge in December 1979 because of the speaker's campaign war chest. Howard Berman, once the speaker's top lieutenant and majority floor leader, sought to topple McCarthy from the speakership because, it was claimed, McCarthy was amassing campaign funds for his own future state race in 1982—not to assist assembly Democrats in marginal districts. Current Speaker Willie Brown, as noted, has been particularly successful in raising campaign funds and transferring this money to his party colleagues to help them get elected. The speaker's ability to raise large campaign contributions is a critical factor in determining who gets elected as leader and provides this person with decisive leverage over "grateful" colleagues. Thus, Legi-Tech reports

7-4 *California Assembly Speaker Willie Brown, 1980–? In discussing his vast legislative powers, Speaker Brown once kiddingly referred to himself as the Ayotollah of the lower house.*

that in 1986 the Willie Brown campaign committee raised nearly $2,000,000, most of which was transferred to Democratic candidates in marginal districts. Clearly, the prime requisite for legislative leadership these days is not policy expertise or leadership style; it's fundraising ability. Also, in the 1980s the speaker and minority leader have become increasingly involved in the party's June primary through providing money and staff assistance to their choices (frequently ex-assembly staffers or capitol insiders) at the expense of local officeseekers. Critics complain that no longer do districts send representatives to the capitol, but rather, the capitol selects representatives for the districts.

Selection to Committees

Since the speaker appoints all committee chairs and selects nearly all committee members (except for Rules), his or her appointment powers are virtually total. The assembly committee selection process is therefore quite different than the mainly seniority system used in its federal counterpart, the House of Representatives. The congressional chair selection process is marked by relatively little politicking, (except perhaps in the caucus vote), little backstabbing, and an almost ironclad guarantee that the chair will be a congressional veteran in his or her 50s or 60s (and sometimes 70s or 80s) with years of acquired expertise in a particular subject matter.

In the assembly, seniority counts for little, though freshmen normally would not be selected as committee chairs. Party affiliation is of more consequence, though traditionally the minority party gets a few of the committee chairs, depending on the numerical size of the minority party, their cooperativeness, and other variables. But seldom would minority members chair the most important assembly committees. The speaker's selection criteria generally include: (1) loyalty, (2) competence and ability, (3) political philosophy, (4) party affiliation, (5) friendships, and (6) occasionally, seniority. Obviously, the more secure in power the speaker, the less the emphasis on loyalty for committee selections. Assembly committee chairs are frequently legislators in their thirties or forties, and often only in their second or third term. The assembly system is more political than the House of Representatives, but new ideas and young, dynamic individuals can also quickly assume leadership positions.

The speaker will generally use the same criteria listed for chair selection for committee selections. Obviously, the speaker wants to retain solid, safe majority party dominance of the major policy committees. Also, unlike chair selections, members are sent forms by the speaker, and they are asked to rank their choices for committees. Selections to committees (except for Rules whose members are elected from the two party caucuses) depend heavily on the interests, background, and district of the legislator. A legislator representing a rural district would probably want to get on the Agriculture or Water Committees; a former school teacher would probably want to get on the Education Committee; an ex-insurance agent on the Finance and Insurance Committee, and so on. Speakers can usually accommodate a request or two per member—if they want to.

If a freshman legislator has a particular policy expertise, he or she is expected to take part immediately in committee deliberations, unlike Congress where newcomers are expected "to be seen but not heard."[5] Since freshman assemblymembers are used to a very short apprenticeship period—a few months at most—speakers must constantly face the challenge of raised committee chair expectations. With a limited number of chairmanships to divvy up, speakers must inevitably contend with disappointed majority party members. To cope with this problem, Speaker Brown has nearly doubled the number of standing committees he inherited in 1980, and he has expanded the size of a number of major "juice" committees. While making little sense on a public administra-

---

[5]Traditionally, one freshman from a "class" is selected for hazing on the floor by senior colleagues when the newcomer presents his or her first bill.

tor's flow chart and creating time conflicts for members when two of their committees meet simultaneously, Speaker Brown's actions make much political sense.[6]

The majority floor leader is second-in-command and is responsible for shepherding key bills of the majority party through the legislature. The caucus chair and whip work to forge unified party stances on major issues. The speaker pro tem is the presiding officer, and usually a highly respected senior member of the majority party. Finally, Rules and Ways and Means Committee chairs are other key figures in the assembly leadership group.

The Speaker—Rule Enforcer

The style and tone of the assembly is set by the speaker. From items as mundane as dress standards to serious breeches of legislative ethics, the speaker plays the central disciplining role. The speaker alone has the power to punish members. As with any social organization, in addition to formal rules, there are many unwritten rules and customs that develop over the years to facilitate group processes. Among the unwritten rules in the California legislature are items such as: honoring commitments; keeping one's word; never attacking a colleague personally in public; supporting committee integrity by not attempting to withdraw a bill from committee; granting a colleague's request for reconsideration of a bill; never testifying in opposition to another member's bill; and never calling public attention to necessary, but embarrassing, features of the legislature such as absentee voting. Clearly, some rules do change over time. Dress code standards have evolved to more informal attire. In the old days members would not campaign against one another, but many do today. Indeed, some lobbyists complain that contemporary members no longer can be counted on to honor a commitment.

Attempts to pry bills out of committees have become increasingly commonplace. And, personal attacks also occur more frequently these

---

[6]When asked by a student if it was his political philosophy that enabled him to form a coalition with Republicans to win the speakership in 1980, Brown answered:

Not at all, political philosophy has very little to do with the speakership. My political philosophy is probably light years away from the Republicans. . . . That crop of Proposition 13 babies voted for me across the board in 1980. Some of the liberal Republicans did not vote for me for one reason or another. . . . when people vote on the speakership, they vote for very basic things—sometimes, for things like chairmanships, vice chairmanships. They vote for parking stalls. They vote for offices [with] windows. They vote for slots [seats] on committees . . . There are all kinds of reasons, unrelated to philosophy. Because, after all, the speakership is in many cases not burdened with any philosophical bent, with any philosophical views. The speakership is a house management responsibility. (*Political Pulse*, December 13, 1985, p. 2) days. In 1986 conservative Republican Assemblyman Gil Ferguson introduced a resolution to oust Democratic Assemblyman Tom Hayden (1960s student activist and anti-Vietnam War leader) from the legislature for allegedly violating the state constitution by aiding and abetting the enemy (Hayden had visited North Vietnam during the war). Though his resolution was defeated by a united Democratic vote, Ferguson's bitter personal attack and other similar attacks by other members on other issues indicates that members are no longer as interested in operating by the formal niceties of the unwritten rules.

It is also true that members don't socialize with each other and don't get to know each other as well as they did in the past. Less time is spent together on the assembly floor and more time is spent in the individual member's offices with their personal staffs. By early Thursday afternoon most of the southern California legislators will be jetting back home not to return until mid-Monday of the following week. In the "good ole days" many members stayed in Sacramento for a few months until the session was completed.

While a rule violator or maverick can be cold-shouldered by colleagues or not included socially, it is the speaker who is the ultimate disciplinarian. Depending upon the severity and frequency of the offense, a speaker can remove a member from a good committee, sack the member from a chair position, move the member to a smaller office, not allow a legislator extra staff, not honor a member's request for expense money to attend an out-of-state meeting, or ultimately, attempt to reapportion the legislator out of his or her district. (Reapportionment takes place every ten years with the federal census.)

Technically speaking, of course, the state constitution stipulates that each house judges the qualifications and elections of its members, and on a two-thirds vote a member can be expelled. But expelling a member is a remote possibility. In fact, there is no blackballing of members in the legislative club—voters, not legislators, determine membership. Legislative leaders must put up with the "accidents of democracy" washed upon the legislative shore. On the few occasions when state legislatures have attempted to exclude a legally elected member, the courts have generally sided with the aggrieved legislator.

Obviously, a legislature comprised of many mavericks would be unmanageable and unproductive. On the other hand, maverick legislators, by refusing to pay homage to the leadership, by challenging stuffy traditions, and by adhering to their principles, add a breath of fresh air to the sometimes stale legislative atmosphere.

Clearly, there are risks and liabilities for speakers if they find they must discipline a member. Heavy-handed disciplining is resented by many members. But the greatest risk to the speaker is in his role as campaign champion for the majority party. If it appears that he may not be effective in promoting the reelection of majority party members, he may be replaced. The Berman-McCarthy speakership fight is the most recent case in point. Howard Berman and other Democrats challenged Leo McCarthy's speakership because they felt McCarthy was more concerned with his own pending statewide election (1982) than with the reelection needs of Democratic assembly members. In the January 1980 Democratic assembly caucus, Berman received twenty-six votes; McCarthy had twenty-four. But McCarthy refused to step down because, he argued, his "term" as speaker was for two years. McCarthy's followers refused to support Berman in any floor vote, and Republicans sat back enjoying the Democratic fight. Since Berman couldn't get the necessary forty-one votes needed on the floor, McCarthy remained speaker. But McCarthy had lost a majority of the Democrats.

Thus, the speaker, normally the driving force in the assembly, became virtually powerless in 1980. McCarthy had great difficulty forcing freshmen Republicans—"Proposition 13 babies"—to operate within usual assembly traditions. Motions challenging committee chairs by forcing bills out of committee were frequently proposed by conservative Republicans. Freshman Republicans created additional problems by demanding to sit together as a group on the assembly floor rather than in the seats assigned them. Attempts by McCarthy to discipline the Bermanites were quickly short-circuited. Berman forces threatened to vote for Republican Carol Hallett for speaker, and McCarthy had to back off. A Democratic civil war raged in the assembly between the McCarthy and Berman camps with thousands of dollars raised and spent by the two sides to elect "their" people and defeat the "others" in the June primary and November 1980 general election.

McCarthy formally conceded to Berman after a November 1980 Democratic caucus vote, and he stepped down from the speakership. Negotiating teams from the two camps met to settle on the terms of surrender. The Berman team, evidently, was unwilling to make sufficient concessions to the McCarthy forces about chairs and other items. Hence, McCarthyites cast about for a compromise alternative to Berman. Willie Brown, who had eventually become a loyal member of the McCarthy team, now saw his opportunity. Meanwhile, several Republicans announced they were going to support Berman (undoubtedly, hoping to get some key posts in the assembly). In order to secure the necessary forty-one votes, Brown sought the support of Republican Minority Leader Carol Hallett. Hallett agreed to support Brown and was able to deliver most of the votes of her caucus, and Brown, in turn, agreed to a series of concessions with the Republican leader. Brown was elected speaker in January 1981. In the Democratic caucus, the vote was Brown, twenty-three; Berman, twenty-three; and one abstention—but Republicans gave Brown twenty-eight additional votes.

The concessions Brown agreed to further weakened an already weak speakership. Among the points Brown accepted were: (1) the speaker would no longer assign bills to committee—the Rules Committee would handle this function; (2) the minority leader would be consulted and have a voice in selecting Republican committee chairs and committee assignments; (3) increased numbers of Republican staff would be hired; and (4) Republicans and Democrats would be provided equal funding for reapportionment.

Many experts believed that the events of 1980 meant that the "Imperial Speakership" was dead. However, after a tenuous two-year coalition speakership, Willie Brown received the unanimous support of assembly Democrats in 1982 and reasserted the speaker's traditional powers. In 1982, Republican votes were no longer needed on the speakership issue. Hence, Brown felt under no compulsion to consult with the then Republican Minority Leader Robert Naylor about Republican committee assignments.

Battles between Democrats and Republicans in the assembly, particularly over the budget and reapportionment, caused Brown to refuse to name *any* Republican assembly member to a committee chairmanship. And, in the 1985 and 1987 sessions Speaker Brown named only a token number of Republicans to chairmanships—four in 1985 and one in 1987. Never before had the minority party been given so few committee leadership positions. While the speaker no longer assigned bills to committee, the speaker controlled a majority on the Rules Committee which handled this function. Epitaphs for the speaker had been too hasty; little had changed.

Yet in the constantly changing California political scene, a major new threat developed to the resurgent speakership: Paul Gann's Legislative Reform Initiative. Responding to the "excessive power" of the speaker, the dominance of the majority party, and legislative "wastefulness," direct democracy wizard Paul Gann, with the encouragement of key Republican assemblymembers, qualified his new initiative for the June 1984 ballot. After being approved by California voters, Democrats challenged the initiative in court contending that the legislature, not the voters, had the sole power to establish its own rules under the Separation of Powers. The court ruled in favor of the Democrats and declared the initiative's proposed rule changes unconstitutional. Less clear was whether the 30 percent legislative budget cut authorized by the initiative was unconstitutional. In any case, assembly and senate majority Democrats through judicious shifting of budget items into other state agencies and some internal economizing, were able to argue they were in compliance with the Gann Initiative.

Finally, while the speaker is a powerful political figure within the assembly, the office has not been a good launching pad to other state elective positions. Some former speakers, such as Jess Unruh and Bob Moretti, developed reputations for being overly partisan or ruthless which hurt their gubernatorial quests. Indeed, McCarthy seemed lucky to survive his troubled speakership by getting elected lieutenant governor. His Republican counterpart, assembly Minority Leader Carol Hallett, lost her bid for lieutenant governor and was later rejected by the Democratic-controlled state senate in April 1983, when Governor Deukmejian tried to appoint her as state parks director. Clearly, skills in building a forty-one-vote coalition in the assembly and the managerial-political skills required to remain speaker do not necessarily transfer to a campaign for statewide office.

The Speaker and the Minority Party

The minority party has a similar leadership hierarchy: floor leader, caucus chair, and whip, with duties that roughly correspond to those of the same positions in the majority party. Perhaps what is most unique in the minority party leadership structure is the paucity of real power of the minority leader.

The size of the minority membership, the political climate, personality, the skills of the minority leader, and other factors, help determine the extent to which the speaker consults the minority leader. If the minority leader is too cooperative, this may alienate minority colleagues. On the other hand, if the minority leader is too aggressive, this reduces opportunities to trade favors with the speaker and hampers the overall effectiveness of the minority leader.

In 1984 Assembly Republicans ousted their soft-spoken, conservative leader, Robert Naylor and elected a far more doctrinaire conservative, Pat Nolan. Nolan was a charter member of what the press called the "cavemen" faction of the Republican assemblymembers, most of whom won election in the Proposition 13 sweep in 1978. Many expected the articulate Nolan to constantly badger Speaker Brown and the majority Democrats. Instead, Nolan has worked out a modus vivendi with Speaker Brown. Nolan promised that he would not be disruptive and would not pull any surprises if, in return, Brown delegated the power to Nolan to select Republicans to chairmanships (if any), vice chairmanships and all committee assignments. Brown agreed to this arrangement, and some of the bitter rancor in the lower house has been reduced by this political "odd couple." Thus, at Nolan's request Speaker Brown removed Republican assemblyman David Kelley from one of his key committee memberships because he had been uncooperative in the caucus. Nolan now has power over his Republican troops that (along with his fund-raising abilities) allows him to exert strong leadership with the minority party.

POLITICS OF THE LEGISLATIVE PROCESS: THE SENATE

Prior to the U.S. Supreme Court-ordered reapportionment of 1966, the California senate was a much different legislative body than the assembly. The motto in Sacramento used to be, "the assembly proposes— the senate disposes." The senate, on the whole, tended to be less innovative, more conservative, more northern and rural-oriented, less partisan, and less professional. Typically, conservative measures would be voted out of the senate and killed in assembly policy committees and vice versa—liberal measures would be torpedoed in senate committees. Since 1966, however, differences between the two chambers have narrowed perceptibly, though some still persist. The senate has become more southern in orientation and more urban-surburban.

Clearly, the senate is the more prestigious body. It has the sole responsibility for approving the governor's appointees. Senators serve four-year terms rather than the two-year terms of assembly members. Hence, senators get a "free-ride" political advantage in the middle of their term. They can run for higher office and still hold their senate seat. Assembly members who want to move up to other offices must gamble with their political careers, since they cannot file for another state office and the assembly simultaneously. There are half as many senators (forty) as assembly representatives, and therefore, they are better known. Individual senators also have more power and independence in their chamber than assembly members do in the speaker-dominated lower house. Finally, assembly members run for the senate when there is an opportunity; senators would never voluntarily run for the assembly.

"Old Guard"

The president pro tem of the senate is the chair of the Rules Committee, but this officer is merely one of five votes on the committee. The pro tem's influence rests less on formal authority and more on informal persuasion. An occasional pro tem (for example, Hugh Burns) has been nearly as powerful as most assembly speakers. Most pro tems, however, are not. Current Pro Tem David Roberti has been a strong leader in the senate because of his ability to raise substantial campaign funds, his good working relationship with Democratic colleagues on Senate Rules, and his willingness to impose discipline on disruptive colleagues. On two separate occasions Roberti has had to punish members who plotted to remove him as pro tem. Several years ago, Senator John Garimendi was sacked from his party leadership position when he attempted to unseat Roberti, and in February 1987

Democratic Senator Dan Boatwright and Republican floor leader John Seymour were removed from key assignments because they had plotted a coup. Currently, Roberti is confronted by a seven-member conservative group within the Democratic membership which could conceivably vote for a Republican pro tem if pushed, and a liberal bloc which would be displeased by any concessions made to conservatives. One thing is certain: Pro tems must constantly look over their shoulders for potential opposition while speakers usually grow more secure in their positions.

Election of the pro tem comes on a vote of all members of the senate. Party affiliation, while of considerable consequence, is not crucial, though the likelihood of the senate electing a minority party pro tem seems extremely remote. Generally, once in office, a speaker is rarely challenged; his or her position usually becomes more secure over time. The pro tem is in a much more precarious position, since senate leadership is a collective enterprise.

The other four members of the Senate Rules Committee are nominated by the two-party caucuses and tend to be veteran members. Again though, there is no ironclad tradition that overlooked members of a party caucus will not look for support from the opposition party.

In the "good ole days," powerful senior senators tended to chair, dominate, and overlap on a few key committees. Seniority was an important criterion for promotion to chairs. Many "old guard" senators believed that new senators ("young Turks") had to be properly trained into senate traditions and customs before they could be given important assignments.

In 1966, Pro Tem Hugh Burns faced an unprecedented situation: twenty-two of the forty senators (a clear majority) were new to the chamber. These twenty-two (fourteen were former assembly members) had been elected in the aftermath of the 1966 reapportionment. Burns treated all twenty-two as "freshmen," giving no preferential treatment to the former assembly members in the group. The disgruntled freshmen and other Burns opponents coalesced to eventually oust Hugh Burns. Today, power is more diffused in the senate.

Changing Patterns of Senate Leadership

The election of Hollywood Democrat Dave Roberti to the position of president pro tem in 1980 signaled a new, more partisan era in senate leadership. Roberti's immediate predecessor, James Mills, who served as senate leader during much of the 1970s, had been elected primarily as a compromise choice of various warring factions in the upper house. Though Mills was challenged frequently by various senate contenders for the pro tem spot, no rival was able to put together the necessary twenty-one votes required to replace him.

However, Mills's coalition fell apart after the November 1980 election. In this election the highly respected dean of the California senate, Al Rodda, lost his reelection bid to Republican challenger John Doolittle in a stunning election upset. In addition, several other senior Democratic senators went down to election defeat due to the efforts of archconservative Republican State Senator H. L. Richardson. Richardson was able to raise enormous sums of money from the Gun Owners of California and law-and-order organizations which he could lavish on his approved list of Republican senate candidates.

Senate Democrats, believing they needed a stronger, more partisan, and more skilled political fundraiser as their leader to counter the Richardson factor, dumped Senator Mills as pro tem in November 1980 and replaced him with Dave Roberti. Senator Roberti has tended to be more combative in style than his predecessors. Roberti has crossed swords with former Democratic Governor Jerry Brown, with current Republican Governor George Deukmejian, and with Speaker Willie Brown. Dave Roberti and his Democratic colleagues on Rules have been highly critical of some key Deukmejian nominees and no longer give rubber stamp approval to gubernatorial appointments. President Pro Tem Roberti has attempted to make the senate into a truly coequal branch with the assembly. For example, symbolic of this new leadership style, Roberti insisted that his office be equipped with the same number of false fireplaces and chandeliers as his assembly counterpart, Willie Brown, in the refurbished state capitol. Roberti has also raised money and provided campaign assistance to all incumbent senate Democrats (no matter what their record) challenged by Republican opponents in the general elections or by other Democrats in the primaries. While Richardson has effectively organized gun owners into a powerful financial force, Roberti has made similar efforts with another special interest group—pet lovers in ROAR-PAC. Roberti has helped lead the fight to stop medical experiments on animals.

Senate Republicans have been sharply divided between a moderate faction led by Bill Campbell and Ken Maddy and a far-right faction led by H. L. Richardson. In 1983, Campbell and Maddy were deposed as minority leader and caucus chair. Policy differences and personal animosities helped fuel the ouster effort. Senator Jim Neilsen, a northern, rural Republican, became Republican leader, and John Seymour took over as caucus leader. In 1987 the Nielsen-Seymour team was dumped after Senate Republicans lost a Senate seat to Democrats in a special election they thought they should win. (Ken Maddy and John Doolittle were elected.) Like a Notre Dame football coach who loses too many games, legislative leaders who fail to get sufficient numbers of party colleagues elected will be ousted quickly. One trend seems clear: the senate is becoming a more partisan chamber.

One last feature of senate leadership should be noted. Technically, the presiding officer of the senate and theoretically one of its leaders is the lt. governor. Since presiding over the senate is a minor, routine duty, most lt. governors have spent little time with the gavel. Indeed, former Lt. Governor Mike Curb spent only a few rare moments during his entire stint as lieutenant governor presiding over the senate.

Additionally, in cases of ties, the lt. governor can cast the deciding vote—but this seldom happens. Clearly, the lt. governor is not one of the powerful leaders in the upper house. (See Chapter 9 for a more complete discussion of the lt. governor's role in state government.) A constitutional amendment to remove the lt. governor as president of the senate was rejected by voters in 1982.

POLITICS OF THE LEGISLATIVE PROCESS: REAPPORTIONMENT

No single issue has exacerbated legislators' personal relations more over the years than reapportionment. Every decade after the U.S. census is taken, state legislatures (in a few states, reapportionment commissions) are required to redistrict congressional, upper house, and lower house district lines based on population shifts into and within the state over that past decade. No issue is more important to legislators since it directly touches on their political survival. But to the public, the issue is at best of secondary interest. One expert has suggested that to allow the legislature to do its own reapportioning is like putting the "fox into the chicken coop." Though the U.S. Supreme Court has required election districts to be equal in population since 1965, there is much that can be done by skilled manipulators to give advantages to one party over the other and virtually guarantee their majority status for the foreseeable future. Strategies such as concentrating the registration strength of the opposing party into a few districts, forcing the other party's incumbents to run against each other, or giving the other party's incumbents substantial new territory to represent have been used. At times obstreperous majority party colleagues have been axed in the process as well. The point is that the majority party has traditionally felt it has the "right" to take advantage of its position in the redistricting.

Reapportionments in California have always been bitter, but the last two reapportionments in the 1970s and the 1980s have been particularly long, bruising battles. In the 1970s, though Democrats had majorities in the two houses, they had to contend with Republican Governor Ronald Reagan, who refused to accept the various Democratic plans submitted to him. After several years of impasse, the court finally stepped in and did the reapportionment.

In 1981, after months of behind-the-scenes maneuvering, the solid Democratic majorities in both houses passed on to Democratic Governor Jerry Brown their reapportionment plan against strong Republican opposition. Strongest concerns were directed against the congressional reapportionment plan (the plan was the work of former Congressman Phil Burton). Going from forty-three to forty-five congressional seats and with Democratic-Republican balance virtually even in the 1980 delegation, Burton devised a redistricting that he proudly believed would give the Democrats at least twenty-seven members and the Republicans about eighteen. Perhaps most outrageous for Republicans was the strangely shaped district Phil Burton devised for his brother John (also a San Francisco congressman). Burton hoped to use his "success" in getting more Democrats elected from California to help him move up the leadership ladder in the House of Representatives. In addition, Republicans believed the senate and assembly plans, while not quite as bad as the congressional reapportionment, were still grossly unfair.

After Governor Brown signed the bill, Republicans did what they had threatened to do—they sought to prevent its enactment through a referendum. Democrats argued that they, as the majority, had the right to draw the lines, and their plan upheld the principle of "one person, one vote." After Republicans had qualified their referendum Democrats challenged them in court. Democrats contended that reapportionment was a legislative matter not subject to referendum and that the newly designed districts must stand or it would create enormous havoc (the June primary was looming). Democrats argued that if the old districts were retained for the 1982 election as Republicans wanted, the one person, one vote principle would be denied and there would be two new House seats to be allocated.

A unanimous state court upheld the Democratic position on House of Representatives districting, and by a four-to-three margin voted in favor of the new assembly and senate districts. However, the court did state that reapportionment was subject to referendum. If a majority of voters approved of the referendum effort by voting no in the June primary, the legislature would have to redraw legislative district lines after the November 1982 election.

Voters in the June 1982 primary election overwhelmingly rejected the Democratic devised reapportionment plans, 65 percent no to 35 percent yes. After the primary, Republicans and Common Cause, a public interest lobby, agreed to jointly sponsor an initiative for the November ballot which would have established a new independent reapportionment commission. Since polls suggested there was much public displeasure with the legislative treatment of this issue and with the massive vote against the Democratic plan, it was assumed that the independent commission proposal would pass fairly easily. In November 1982, voters rejected the independent reapportionment commission initiative. Thus, Democratic majorities redrew, to an extent, the original district lines, but this time they attempted to placate Republican incumbents. The revisions were quickly passed and signed into law.

However, one disgruntled Republican, Assemblyman Don Sebastiani of Napa, still believed the reapportionment plan was unfair. He drafted a new reapportionment initiative to undo the "unfairness" of the Democratic bill. In short order, Sebastiani qualified his initiative. Republican members, initially cool to the Sebastiani plan, reluctantly agreed to support it in a show of party unity.

After considerable pressuring from Democratic and Republican legislators (Democrats even held up the budget for several weeks on the issue), Governor Deukmejian announced that he was scheduling the Sebastiani initiative for a special December 1983 election. Democrats were furious since they believed this was a Republican trick. Democratic leaders knew they would have much greater difficulty turning out their voters in a December special election than would Republicans. Moreover, Democrats noted that the one issue special election would cost the state approximately $15 million to administer.

Democrats challenged the initiative in court, contending that the state constitution mandated that reapportionment be done only *once* every ten years and that the initiative was therefore unconstitutional. They argued it would be utter chaos to have the plan constantly open to change. Republicans argued that the right of citizens to make laws through the initiative process should be supreme, since under our system, power is vested in the people. In September 1983, the court, by a six-to-one margin, accepted the Democratic argument and declared the Sebastiani initiative unconstitutional. Then, in 1984, Governor Deukmejian successfully qualified a new reapportionment reform initiative. Deukmejian's proposal would have had a panel of retired appellate court judges do the reapportioning, and perhaps more important, if approved by voters this panel was to reapportion for the 1986 elections. A hard-hitting Democratic media campaign led to the initiative's defeat in the November 1984 election. In 1986 the U.S. Supreme Court ruled that partisan gerrymandering was unconstitutional in a case brought by Democrats (the minority party) in Indiana. Exactly how the court will determine whether partisan gerrymandering has occurred in a state or locality has not been addressed by the court as yet. The time, expense, and agonies of the reapportionment process of the 1980s have convinced many Republicans legislators and some Democrats as well that some sort of "independent" reapportionment commission is needed—1991 looms.

POLITICS OF THE LEGISLATIVE PROCESS: MECHANICS

Illustration 7–5 shows the flow of bills through the California legislature. While the various "nuts-and-bolts" facts are included in the dia-

7-5 *California's legislative process.*

Initial steps by author

Idea

Sources of bills: legislators, legislative committees, governor, state and local governmental agencies, business firms, lobbyists, citizens.

Drafting

Formal copy of bill and "layman's digest" prepared by Legislative Counsel.

Introduction

Bill submitted by senator or Assembly member. Numbered and read for first time. Assigned to committee by Assembly or Senate Rules Committee. Printed.

Action in house of origin

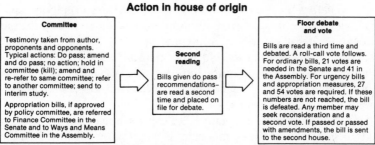

Committee

Testimony taken from author, proponents and opponents. Typical actions: Do pass; amend and do pass; no action; hold in committee (kill); amend and re-refer to same committee; refer to another committee; send to interim study.

Appropriation bills, if approved by policy committee, are referred to Finance Committee in the Senate and to Ways and Means Committee in the Assembly.

Second reading

Bills given do pass recommendations– are read a second time and placed on file for debate.

Floor debate and vote

Bills are read a third time and debated. A roll-call vote follows. For ordinary bills, 21 votes are needed in the Senate and 41 in the Assembly. For urgency bills and appropriation measures, 27 and 54 votes are required. If these numbers are not reached, the bill is defeated. Any member may seek reconsideration and a second vote. If passed or passed with amendments, the bill is sent to the second house.

Disposition in second house

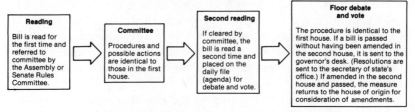

Reading

Bill is read for the first time and referred to committee by the Assembly or Senate Rules Committee.

Committee

Procedures and possible actions are identical to those in the first house.

Second reading

If cleared by committee, the bill is read a second time and placed on the daily file (agenda) for debate and vote.

Floor debate and vote

The procedure is identical to the first house. If a bill is passed without having been amended in the second house, it is sent to the governor's desk. (Resolutions are sent to the secretary of state's office.) If amended in the second house and passed, the measure returns to the house of origin for consideration of amendments.

Resolution of two-house differences (if necessary)

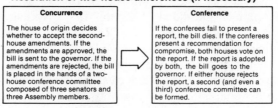

Concurrence

The house of origin decides whether to accept the second-house amendments. If the amendments are approved, the bill is sent to the governor. If the amendments are rejected, the bill is placed in the hands of a two-house conference committee composed of three senators and three Assembly members.

Conference

If the conferees fail to present a report, the bill dies. If the conferees present a recommendation for compromise, both houses vote on the report. If the report is adopted by both, the bill goes to the governor. If either house rejects the report, a second (and even a third) conference committee can be formed.

Role of the governor

Sign or veto?

Within 12 days after receiving a bill, the governor can sign it into law, allow it to become law without his signature or veto it. A vetoed bill returns to the house of origin for possible vote on overriding the veto. It requires a two-thirds majority of both houses to override.

Urgency measures become effective immediately after signing. Others usually take effect the following January 1st.

gram, the essence of the process, frankly, cannot be depicted neatly on a flowchart.

In any given session, thousands of bills, resolutions, and constitutional amendments are introduced in the California legislature. While many bills are killed or held for further study, about 2,000 will pass both houses and be signed by the governor. A few bills are the inspiration of individual legislators or their constituents who have researched a particular issue, but most bill ideas are generated by interest groups, local governments, legislative staff, and executive agencies. Most legislators want to author legislation. They are usually receptive to carrying bill proposals from different groups. Indeed, freshmen legislators consider it a favor if a group provides a bill for the new member to sponsor. Some legislators refuse to "author" a bill with which they do not agree; other legislators introduce nearly everything offered them, though they may make only half-hearted efforts for bills on which they are ambivalent.

Status among one's legislative colleagues hinges, in part, on the ability of members to steer important legislation through the houses— being able to explain your measure, knowing when to accept amendments, knowing how to provide leverage, and knowing how to persuade your colleagues. In capitol parlance, a legislative lightweight is one who "couldn't even get a Mother's Day Resolution through." (In the 1977 session, the legislature passed a resolution honoring grandparents!) Of course, a legislator's reputation is enhanced by being able to help kill a bill skillfully, too.

Each proposed bill is first sent to the legislative counsel's office, which drafts it into proper legal form and indicates the proposed changes in the existing law. The bill is then "placed across the desk" and given a number and dated. After this first "reading," the bill is assigned to a policy committee by the Rules Committee. Most of the time, assignment of bills is routine and bills are sent to the obviously *appropriate* policy committee (agriculture bills to the Agriculture Committee, etc.). However, there are occasions when a bill might go to several different committees and assembly and Senate Rules committees hold hearings with a bill's author to decide which committee should get the bill. Power to assign to a *particular* committee can be instrumental in a bill's passage or defeat. For example, a farm labor bill favoring the organizing rights of farm workers could be sent to the Agriculture Committee (comprised of rural legislators sympathetic to farmer's needs) or the Labor Committee comprised of large city liberals sympathetic to the union movement.

Key policy decisions are made in committee. If a committee rejects a bill, it is "dead" for the rest of the legislative session. If a committee unanimously recommends that a bill be passed by the complete house, it almost certainly will be. In short, the committee process is vital to proposed legislation.

Upon receiving the bill with the author's request for a hearing, the committee chair sets the date for hearing usually as soon as possible, and has it published in the *Assembly* or *Senate File*. The California legislative process does not allow chairs to refuse to hear a bill or seriously delay scheduling hearings on measures that they oppose. Prior to the hearing, the author and lobbyist supporting the proposal will work to secure the approval of committee members, in some cases, by securing cosponsors. Once a commitment is given by a legislator, it is supposed to be honored. Lobbyists opposing the bill are expected to inform the author that they will oppose the measure. Frequently, the bill's author will invite lobbyists for and against a measure to get together ahead of time to see if compromises can be worked out. Ideally, for the bill's author, agreeing to certain reasonable amendments may suffice to head off opposition and guarantee passage of the bill. Nothing is more welcome to a bill's author than to have no opposition offered; this virtually guarantees passage.

Legislators who know their constituents are solidly opposed to a bill are highly unlikely to be persuaded by a lobbyist, colleague, or party leader to support the measure. However, most bills generate little public sentiment. These technical bills may be exceedingly important to particular interests but are seldom discussed in the press, and hence, legislators have considerable latitude in voting.

To the uninitiated, hearings can often be anticlimactic and disappointing. Meeting times can be delayed because there is no quorum; observers who may have traveled hundreds of miles for a hearing may be told that a bill has been held over (put off); or expert witnesses may present testimony to committee members who are either not there, not paying attention, sleeping, or conferring with one another. The reason for this seemingly bizarre behavior by legislators is usually not due to lack of interest, but because legislators have usually already made up their minds on the issue.

Committee members may have already discussed the bill with experts, lobbyists, and staff; read the reports and bill analyses; sat through endless hearings on the bill in previous years; know the governor's and legislative party leader's stands; and checked for district impact. Thus, hearings usually do not provide legislators with new information. They tend to be more for the public record and to generate publicity—though on occasion a few legislators on the fence can be swayed one way or the other by expert testimony. Some groups, in an all-out effort to get committee approval, will pack the committee hearing room with their supporters in hopes of intimidating committee members to support a bill. This sometimes is helpful, but it can backfire too.

After arguments are presented for and against the bill, committee members can propose amendments that probably, but not necessarily, will be accepted by the bill's author. If the bill's author is unwilling to

7-6 *Republican Governor George Deukmejian signs into law the California Workfare Reform bill, 1984—an outstanding example of bipartisan legislative effort that does happen on occasion. With Governor Deukmejian (center, seated) are former Republican Assemblyman Ernest Konnyu (left, seated), Democratic Assemblyman Art Agnos (right, seated), Republican State Senator Jim Nielsen (left, standing) and Democratic State Senator John Garimendi.*

Courtesy Sacramento Bee

accept the amendment, the legislator runs the risk of having the bill defeated in committee. Thus, the member usually accepts the proposed amendment. Sometimes authors must offer clarifying amendments to soften opposition.

After action on the bill is completed in committee, a member of the committee will move to report the bill out "do pass" or "do pass as amended." A majority of aye votes is necessary to report a bill out; abstentions or "taking a walk" (to avoid voting) count, in effect, as no votes. The chair may hold the roll open if members have been called away or have not arrived at the hearing. If sufficient aye votes are not there, a member may move to hold the bill over so that the bill's author can have more time to persuade some of his or her colleagues to support it.

If the committee wants to kill a bill gently or if it deals with a new subject, the committee may recommend the bill for interim study. Occasionally, bills are reported out of committee without recommendation (a tactic rarely employed). Any bill having *any* fiscal impact (nearly every important bill) must go to assembly Ways and Means and senate Finance after clearing the policy committee.

After clearing committee, the chair presents a report to the house indicating what the committee recommends, and it is read a second time. The committee's proposed amendments are always accepted, and then the bill is engrossed (a check for accuracy). The next step is the final (third) reading of a bill where the bill's author makes a presentation on the floor, as do its opponents (if there are any). (Noncontroversial measures can be placed on the consent calendar for pro forma approval.) Most "do pass" or "do pass as amended" legislation will be approved on the floor and sent to the other house, though a few will die. On some occasions, a bill's author, seeing formidable opposition to the bill, may ask to have it sent back to committee for further study.

Certainly, one of the best ways to assess the status of a committee chair is to see what happens to measures clearing his or her committee. Skillful chairs normally have little difficulty getting bills with a "do pass" recommendation approved on the floor. Weaker or less astute chairs sometimes have measures rejected on the floor.

A clear majority, forty-one votes in the assembly and twenty-one votes in the senate, is needed to pass a bill. Two thirds, fifty-four votes, are needed in the assembly and twenty-seven votes in the senate for the budget, constitutional amendments, and urgency measures. The bill then goes to the other house for another round of hearings and committee action. Measures passed by both houses but in substantially different form will be threshed out in conference committees. Finally, the last hurdles in the process are the governor's signature and the bill's adminstrative implementation.

POLITICS OF THE LEGISLATIVE PROCESS: PARTISANSHIP

As previously noted, political parties in the California legislature have, historically at least, had little of the discipline and cohesiveness of parties in many eastern state legislatures. Unlike Congress, where all committee chairs are of the majority party, the California legislature generally provides the minority party with a few chairs. The great majority of issues the legislature must vote upon are technical, noncontroversial, or nonpolitical. However, while there are only a few issues that engender party voting in the California legislature, these few do tend to be the most crucial of the session—reapportionment, election of legislative leaders, or the budget. The budget in particular impinges on a host of policy questions from funding for prison reform to upgrading public schools to providing welfare for the less fortunate.

Party-line voting occurs infrequently at the capitol, but there does seem to be more party bloc voting these days than there used to be—perhaps because of the legislative leaders' abilities to raise campaign contributions and transfer them to their deserving brethren. However, attempts by party leaders to impose party discipline must be done sparingly; otherwise, these party leaders would face increasing opposition within their caucuses.

POLITICS OF THE LEGISLATIVE PROCESS: ROLES

Occasionally, legislators are faced with a classic dilemma—should they vote their own personal convictions (in political science terminology, the trustee role) or should they vote the way their constituents want them to vote (the delegate role)? For the most part, the great majority of legislators tend to be in tune ideologically with their districts and rarely have to confront this issue. Of course, few issues engender much local opinion anyway. Moreover, ascertaining the real views of one's constituents—not just a few inspired letters or a couple of local newspaper editorials—can be difficult.

In any case, there are good arguments that can be made for legislators adopting either the delegate or trustee role. In California, many freshmen legislators tend to take the delegate role in the early years of their service at the capitol, but the longer members serve, the more likely they are to believe that they know more about issues than their constituents. Legislators sit through endless committee hearings, talk to staff and lobbyists, and read the reports. How many constituents do this? A senior legislator is likely to say, "if the public doesn't like the way I vote, let them vote me out of office."

REFORMING THE LEGISLATURE

Clearly, no issue looms as large on the legislative agenda as campaign finance. The California Commission on Campaign Financing reports that a whopping $57.1 million was spent on campaigns for the 100 state legislative seats up for election in November 1986! This means that in the *average* legislative race more than a half-million dollars was spent. This is a 31 percent increase over 1984, and 1988 races will increase another 30 to 40 percent if nothing is done. The Moriarity scandal and other recent campaign finance flaps indicate that the massive amounts of money raised for campaigns does buy access and influence at the very least and decisions at the worst. Until this issue is addressed satisfactorily (and it is admittedly very complicated), the California legislature's reputation as a dynamic, reform leader among the state legislatures is seriously threatened. And, unfortunately, it is unlikely that California legislators (winners under the present system) will be able to work out the necessary compromises on items such as contribution and expenditure limits, public financing of campaigns, and transferring of funds.

Other reforms that have been proposed include: (1) increasing legislative salaries and concomitantly limiting the amount of money legislators receive in consulting, lawyering, and speaking engagements; (2) establishing a unicameral (single-house) legislature; (3) having an independent commission do reapportioning; (4) limiting the number of terms a legislator might serve (to encourage more turnover); (5) limiting the number of bills a legislator might introduce during a particular session; (6) reducing the number of legislative committees; (7) establishing an independent commission to set legislative salaries; (8) allowing committee members to elect their own chairs; (9) extending assembly terms to four years; (10) ending the legislative log jam at the close of the session; (11) paying the leaders of each chamber higher salaries than rank-and-file members; (12) forbidding legislative aides from working in political campaigns—even on their own time; (13) reducing the power of the speaker; (14) opening caucuses to the public; and (15) shortening sessions to allow legislators more time in the district.

SUMMARY

California has one of the most modern, professional legislatures in the nation. It has served as a model for other state legislatures in their modernization efforts. However, there is considerable dispute in academia and media circles whether professional legislatures do anything very differently from nonprofessional legislatures.

The speaker and Senate Rules Committee hold the key to legislative power in the California legislature through their ability to select members to committees, pick committee chairs, and discipline members.

8

California's Governors— The State's Central Political Figures

Unquestionably, executives have become *the central political figures* in contemporary governments. Even in democratic governments, the executive proposes, implements, and coordinates policy. At all three levels of government in the United States—national, state, and local— the day-to-day activities of government most often focus on the executive. Indeed, the very word—executive (to execute)—suggests action and authority.

Executive preeminence, however, has not always been the case in the United States. In the thirteen original colonies, governors acting as the king's agent held most of the power. Following the American Revolution, partly in reaction to the king/governor's authoritarian position, governors were stripped of many of their powers. In a number of states, governors became, essentially, figureheads with little or no power. The same pattern existed at the national level. Indeed, under our first constitution, the Articles of Confederation, there was no chief executive for the national government. *At the end of the eighteenth century, legislatures were the dominant political institutions.*

But the chaotic, aimless drift of the new government under the Articles soon convinced the Founding Fathers that there was a need for some kind of executive authority. And when the new constitution was drafted, the office of president was created.

Over time, the need for continuous program direction and policy coordination and the need for someone to "manage the store" while the legislature was not in session (which was most of the time) forced the states and the nation to establish minimal executive authority. And given the part-time, amateur politician composition of state legislatures

204

in our early history, the gradual emergence of full-time professional executives was inevitable. By the latter half of the *nineteenth century, governors had become the dominant figures in state politics.* Those from large electoral vote states were frequently considered prime presidential timber. Between 1876 and 1932, eight of fifteen presidents were former governors. However, the Great Depression of the 1930s—which gave rise to the New Deal—and the emergence of the United States as a world power following World War II substantially enlarged the national government's powers. In turn, states and their *governors declined in national politics.*

Though governors may not be as prominent in national politics as they once were, *they remain key political figures within their own states.* As Duane Lockard, a political scientist who served in the Connecticut state senate, once observed (1963, pp. 367–68):

> People increasingly speak of a law being "passed by the govenor." In sarcasm, the storekeeper tosses coins into a can labeled "Sales Tax" and says, "A penny for the governor."

However, over the last ten years governors appear to be making a comeback as prime presidential candidates. Both President Jimmy Carter (the first former governor to be elected chief executive in over forty-four years) and his successor, Ronald Reagan, former governor of California, ran campaigns that attacked Washington D.C. and the federal bureaucracy. And, in 1988 one of the prominent contenders for the Democratic presidential nomination is a former governor—Bruce Babbit (Arizona) and another is a current governor, Michael Dukakis of Massachusetts. And, Governor Mario Cuomo, Democratic governor of New York could conceivably be drafted as presidential nominee at the convention. Governors, it would seem, are back in vogue.

Governors of large electoral vote states—New York, Texas, Illinois, and California—are inevitably prominent in national politics. Interestingly, the national stature of California governors increases their political powers *within* the state. Political and community leaders are often reluctant to oppose a potential president. On the other hand, the lure of the presidency, which involves spending substantial time and energy in running for the White House, can lead to charges of neglected duty at home in California. Jerry Brown was hurt by his failed presidential quests in 1976 and 1980. Governor George Deukmejian took great care early in his administration to avoid any appearance of running for president. Although in his second term he did openly speculate about running as the "favorite son" of California Republicans in the June 1988 presidential primary to head off a divisive and costly Republican presidential brawl in the state and also possibly to enhance his chance to get a vice-presidential bid (because of his California bloc of votes). For whatever reasons, Governor Deukmejian decided in spring of 1987 not to run as a "favorite son" candidate in the 1988 California primary.

The size and complexity of California enhance the governor's powers within the state. California is too large and diverse to be dominated by any single regional group or leader. Thus, there is no single urban or regional power base from which someone can challenge the governor. In recent years, most successful candidates for governor have held some other statewide office at the time of their election. Since 1934 (twelve elections), only two governors did not—Culbert Olson (1938) and Ronald Reagan (1966). The other six became governor while holding another statewide office: two were lieutenant governors, three were attorney generals, and one was secretary of state.

Through circumstance, custom, constitution, and law, the governor of California is chief executive, chief legislator, voice of the people, and head of the party. Combined, these make the governor the most powerful executive in the state and a powerful national figure as well.

FORMAL POWERS AND AUTHORITY

Constitutional

There is no single source of executive authority in California's constitution. Article V is devoted to the executive and sets forth the basic powers of the governor, lieutenant governor, and attorney general including qualifications, terms of office, and salary provisions. But other articles of the California constitution also contain executive provisions.

California, like most states, has a system of *plural executives*. Historically, statewide elections of several administrative officials are a legacy of the antigovernor feelings rooted in early colonial experience. The constitutional division of executive power into several positions means that no one person exercises all executive authority. It is, in a sense, a kind of checks and balances system within one branch of government. The governor is only one of seven elected state executives. (The other executives are discussed in Chapter 9.)

Qualifications for and Terms of Office

The constitution stipulates that to be eligible to serve as governor one must be a registered voter, a citizen of the United States, and a resident of California for at least five years prior to election. Elected to a four-year term, the governor currently receives a salary of $85,000 a year and an expense allowance of about $45,000 a year.

Because Governor Jerry Brown opposed increasing his own salary

8-1 *California's governor is the state's major political figure. Governor George Deukmejian giving his "State of the State" message to the California legislature, January 10, 1983. Assembly Speaker Willie Brown* (left) *and Senate President Pro Tem David Roberti* (right) *listen.*

Photo by Richard Gilmore/Courtesy Sacramento Bee

($50,000), by the time George Deukmejian was elected in 1982 the California Governor's salary had fallen behind all other large, urban states governors' salaries and behind many rural state governors as well. In 1982, thirty-eight states paid their governors more than California did. Since 1982, the California governor's salary has been raised to $85,000. Currently, California ranks sixth among the states (Alaska, New York, Texas, Michigan and North Carolina governors earn more) in chief executive pay.

While there is no formal constitutional limit on the number of terms a governor can serve, most early governors served only one term. The last governor to be defeated after one term was Culbert Olson in 1942. Since then, every governor has been reelected to a second term. Earl Warren won a third term, and Ronald Reagan would probably have won a third term had he wanted it. Pat Brown tried for a third term in 1966 and lost. There appears to be more than idle speculation that Governor Deukmejian may be interested in seeking a third term in 1990.

Major Powers

Among the fifty states, California's governor clearly ranks as one of the most powerful. One recent study of state governors ranked California's as the sixth most powerful out of all fifty. Voters in 1922 approved a ballot measure that gave the governor substantial new budget authority, and today the four most significant legal powers of the California governor are budget, veto, special sessions, and appointments.

Budget. In theory, the legislature has the "power of the purse," but in fact, since 1922, the governor has had the authority and the responsibility to prepare the annual state budget and to *present it to the legislature* every January (see Chapter 10).

The budget is a statement of both anticipated revenues and expenditures. Until 1983, it was believed that the state budget had to be "balanced"—that is, expenditures could not exceed revenues. But a combination of political and economic circumstances in 1982 and 1983 produced the state's first unbalanced budget. The constitution prohibits the state legislature from passing any bill which would spend money (an appropriations bill) before the budget has been passed. (The only exception is an *emergency* bill recommended by the governor and passed by a two-thirds majority in both houses.)

The annual state budget is, in effect, a dollars-and-cents statement of governmental priorities and programs. Of course, there are also moral/ethical policies which are not included in the budget. But since most major policies require the spending of some money and since all state expenditures are in the budget, it is the budget that engenders the most dispute in the state capitol.

Placing the budget at the top of the legislative agenda and giving the governor authority to prepare it puts the governor in the driver's seat. Executive policies and programs come first, while the individual legislator's ideas are considered later and must conform to the limits of the budget. If the legislature should try to ignore the budget's priority or spending limits, the governor has the power of the veto.

Veto. One of the governor's most important legislative powers is the exercise of the veto—or the threat of its use. The California governor has two kinds of veto—the *general veto* and the *item veto*. (The "pocket" veto was abolished in 1972.) To override a veto requires an absolute two-thirds vote in both houses of the legislature.

The general veto. Applies to any bill passed by the legislature. The governor can reject any legislation within twelve days of passage by sending it back to the legislature. Normally, the governor makes a short statement of reasons for vetoing the bill.

The item veto. Applies only to an appropriation bill—typically the annual budget. By using the item veto, the governor does not have to choose between accepting or rejecting all of the budget bill. The item veto allows the governor the opportunity to remove the parts he or she does not like and approve the rest. Moreover, the item veto allows the governor not only to *eliminate* a particular part of the appropriation but also to *reduce* it as well. Thus, if the legislature puts an appropriation into the budget which the governor does not like, it can be eliminated. If the legislature increases an appropriation which the governor had in the budget, it can be reduced to the original figure. (The governor may not, however, increase any appropriation after the legislature has passed an appropriations bill.)

Recent governors have vetoed approximately 7 percent (about one out of fourteen) of the bills passed by the legislature. Governor Reagan, facing a hostile legislature in his second term, vetoed more than 12 percent of the bills sent to his desk. In one particularly difficult year (1972), he vetoed over 16 percent. Governor Jerry Brown, in his efforts to slow budget growth, vetoed over 10 percent of the bills sent him in his first three years as governor. In his first term, Governor George Deukmejian vetoed more than 10 percent of the bills reaching him (on the average about 245 legislative vetoes per year).

Over the last several decades California governors (with the exception of Jerry Brown who had eight veto overrides directed against him in one month, July 1979) have rarely been overridden. Indeed, U.S. presidents have been far likelier to be overturned by Congress than California governors by the state legislature. The many overrides inflicted on Jerry Brown were a temporary aberration, not a new pattern of legislative assertiveness.

Governor Deukmejian's battles with Democratic legislative leaders, particularly in his first year when the state faced an enormous deficit, meant endless wrangling between the two branches. To promote his budget priorities, Governor Deukmejian averaged 419 item vetoes per year in his first term. The staunchly conservative assembly Republicans could almost always be counted upon to hold the line for the governor to prevent a two-thirds vote override. Throughout his presidency Ronald Reagan has urged that the federal Constitution be amended to provide the president the substantial power the California governor (and twenty-two other state governors) possess—the item veto also requires a two-thirds legislative vote to override.

Special sessions.   The governor can call the legislature into a special session at any time. During special sessions, legislators can only consider those issues presented by the governor. This enables the governor to control the issue agenda. Before 1967, governors would call special sessions for one of two basic reasons: (1) the legislature was not in session, and there was an important issue which the governor thought required immediate action; or (2) the governor wanted the legislature to consider an issue which it ignored while in regular session.

Between 1863 and 1966, the legislature met only for limited periods of time. Thus, in emergencies or for political reasons, the governor could call a special session. Between 1849 and 1970, the legislature was called into special session fifty-three times. (The record was set in 1940 when Governor Culbert Olson called five sessions.)

Since 1973 the legislature meets in a two-year session beginning on the first Monday in December of even-numbered years, and it must adjourn by midnight November 30 of the following even-numbered year. Because the legislature meets nearly year-round there are fewer opportunities for a governor to discipline legislators by calling them into special session. Today, the only real reason for a governor to call a special session is to force legislators to consider an issue on which the governor wants action. For example, Governor Reagan called a special session of the legislature in 1973 to force consideration of his tax reform proposal. The legislature was opposed to it, and though called into special session for this express purpose, it ignored (in effect, rejected) the governor's proposal.

More important, legislation passed by a special session becomes law in ninety days. Legislation passed in a regular session does not become law until the following January 1, unless passed by a two-thirds vote in both houses. Since it is difficult to get a two-thirds vote (called an "urgency measure"), the governor can use the special session when only a simple majority is available.

Governor Jerry Brown called a special session in 1975 to get passage of housing and malpractice legislation. And in January 1978, Brown called a special session to consider property tax relief. That special session ran concurrently with the regular session and was designed to focus the legislature's attention on what had become a very hot political issue. Had the legislature been able to reach agreement on some reform, it would have gone into effect immediately and perhaps might have eliminated much of the support for Proposition 13 in June 1978.

In February 1983, Governor Deukmejian called a special session to solve the state's immediate borrowing problems. The requested legislation (AB 28X) was quickly passed and signed into law by the governor (see Chapter 10 for details). And, in 1986 Governor Deukmejian called the legislature into special session in an attempt at resolving a prison siting conflict in Los Angeles.

Appointments.   The governor's appointive powers add substantially to the influence of the office. Generally, we can categorize appointments as follows: (1) key administrative (full-time), (2) part-time commissions and councils, (3) judicial, and (4) executive-political.

Key Administrative.   The governor nominates or appoints about 230 key administrators. Among these are some 170 administrative positions; agency secretaries, deputy secretaries, and agency directors. Another 60 positions are on important boards and commissions. Salaries for these positions are often quite substantial. For example, Jesse Huff, Deukmejian's director of finance, receives a salary of $87,552 as does chief of staff Michael R. Frost. Each earns $7,552 more annually than their boss—the governor (see Chapter 9 for further discussion). Salaries for other administrators range from about $50,000 to $75,000.

Most of these positions are subject to confirmation by a majority vote of the state senate. Traditionally, senators have gone along with a governor's nominations to key administrative positions since these people are supposed to reflect the governor's policies, not the senate's. This has been an important philosophical issue in recent years with governors Ronald Reagan, Jerry Brown, and George Deukmejian often in disagreement with the state senate on policy.

In recent years, particularly in the latter part of the Jerry Brown administration and in the first term of the Deukmejian administration, the state senate has become increasingly critical of the governor's appointments. Many of the most important nominations made by Governor Deukmejian were rejected in the state senate. One of Deukmejian's key aides, Michael Franchetti, was originally nominated to be director of finance, but he was turned down by the Senate because of alleged dirty campaign activities. In the first fifteen months of his administration, seven other major appointees of Deukmejian besides Franchetti were rejected by the senate including his nominees for directors of parks and recreation, industrial relations, corrections, fish and game, veterans' affairs, general services, and office of economic opportunity. These nominees were rejected by senate Democrats for alleged excess partisanship, fiscal irregularities, and insensitive comments about racial minorities or sexual orientation. There is also a growing interest by the legislature in overseeing the ways in which policy is administered (see Chapters 7 and 9). As policy variations develop and as different political forces exercise influence, different agencies may be authorized to administer a program or programs within the same policy area. For example, California's agricultural policy is largely administered by three different agencies: the director of the Department of Agriculture and Food, the five members of the Agricultural Labor Relations Board (ALRB), and the board's general counsel. Under the Jerry Brown administration, all of these positions were filled by people with a similar orientation to agricultural policy: "pro-small farmowner" and "pro-farm worker" (United Farm Worker's Union).

But in 1983, newly elected Governor Deukmejian appointed a department director, and an ALRB general counsel and Board members who were much more "progrower" and "anti-farm labor." Holdover Brown appointees who had fixed terms of office were frequently in conflict with Deukmejian's new appointees: Gradually the growers gained a larger voice in part of the government's agricultural adminis- tration, but the UFW held onto power on the ALRB for a time.

Similarly, different points of view led to establishment of the state's Energy Resources Conservation and Development Commission during the Jerry Brown administration. The commission now shares energy policy authority with the much older Public Utilities Commission.

Since many commissioners are nominated to terms of office which overlap that of the governor or may have terms of office longer than four years, it may take a governor several years to gain a majority on a particular board or commission. A one-term governor (four years) may never gain control of several commissions and boards—for ex- ample, the University of California Board of Regents. (Regents are ap- pointed to the board for twelve-year terms. This unusually long term was specifically designed to remove the board from political pressure.) But every governor since 1943 has served more than one term and has been able to place his stamp on the state's administration—eventually.

Commissions and Councils.   There are over 2,300 people who serve part-time on over 300 commissions and boards. They are usually paid a flat daily fee for each meeting ($50 to $100) and are often reimbursed for expenses. These commissions and councils review state policy in specific policy areas and make recommendations for change to the ap- propriate department or directly to the governor or legislature. A few have direct authority to license practitioners of certain occupations and professions and to change policy. Licensing is critical to practitioners, such as barbers, auto repair mechanics, car dealers, doctors, lawyers, and teachers.

A typical cross-section of these commissions and councils would include: the California Commission on Aging, the Cancer Advisory Council, Commission on Fair Employment Practices, the Medical Quality Review Committees, the Student Aid Commission, the Com- mission on the Status of Women, and the many county fair boards (see Chapter 9).

Judicial.   Whenever vacancies occur, the governor appoints judges to the California state supreme court and appellate courts, (subject to confirmation by the Commission on Judicial Appointments) and to su- perior and municipal courts. Usually a two-term governor will get to nominate almost half of all state judges during his tenure.

While all judges must stand for election at the end of their terms, most are appointed initially (see Chapter 11). Judges typically serve until death or retirement; very few are defeated for reelection. Thus,

TABLE 8-1
Judicial Appointments, 1959–1985*

	Percent Minorities†	Percent Women	Total Number
Edmund (Pat) Brown, Sr.	7%	2%	621
Ronald Reagan	7	3	645
Edmund (Jerry) Brown, Jr.	24	14	800
George Deukmejian	20	11	272

*Excluding state supreme court.
†Black, Chicano, and Asians.
Source: Governor's office and the *Los Angeles Times,* December 5, 1982.

most judges serve long after the governor who appointed them has left office, and a governor's initial appointment is much more important than any subsequent election. One of California's most respected judges, Justice Stanley Mosk, was originally appointed by Governor Pat Brown in 1964. Brown was defeated for reelection in 1966, but twenty-three years later Mosk is still active on the state supreme court and was reelected to a new twelve-year term in 1986.

Judicial appointments are frequently partisan—governors usually appoint judges who are members of their own political party. But more important to the governor is the appointee's social philosophy, judicial/legal reputation, specific views on issues relative to the position, and the demands or needs of interest groups, legislators, and community leaders.

Perhaps Jerry Brown's major judicial legacy was his successful effort to appoint women and minority judges. Table 8–1 compares his appointments with those of the two previous governors, Ronald Reagan and Pat Brown, and his successor George Deukmejian.

Executive/Political. The governor also has the authority to fill vacancies for a number of important executive/political positions including: the state's two U.S. senators, elected state executives, and county supervisors. Governors do not often have an opportunity to make these appointments, but when they do, they can be very significant. The untimely death of state treasurer Jess Unruh in 1987 gave Governor Deukmejian the opportunity to select the new state treasurer. Seven of the thirty-nine U.S. senators from California were initially appointed by a governor. And each year the governor will probably make several county supervisor appointments.

Governors can use appointments to secure support from legislators or key interest groups. For example, the 477 appointments to the District Agricultural Associations are typical patronage. Appointments to many minor commissions, councils, and boards are also often used to reward the party faithful, the governor's supporters, or to gain support from various organizations or groups.

Appointments can also become a sore point in executive-legislative relations. Legislators, particularly state senators, expect to be consulted about appointments. Former state senate minority leader William Campbell was offended by Governor Deukmejian's refusal to appoint Glen Craig as California highway patrol commissioner. And on the first day he was sworn into office, Governor Jerry Brown was criticized by two Hispanic legislators because they had not been consulted about Brown's appointment of an Hispanic (Mario Obledo) as health and welfare secretary. Of course, for every pleased nominee, there are probably a dozen other disgruntled hopefuls who were not selected. Nominating can be a two-edged sword.

As part of the "team," appointees often help the governor win political support. Governor Deukmejian's 1983 appointment of Dave Stirling as general counsel to the Agricultural Labor Relations Board was designed not only to bring that board's policy more into line with the governor's thinking but to reward farmer-grower support for Deukmejian.

Sometimes appointees' help is more direct. About two dozen Brown appointees took a week off without pay and traveled to Maine to assist the governor's 1980 presidential campaign. More than fifty appointees made campaign contributions to Brown's 1982 U.S. Senate race and, the governor's appointment of Peter G. Mehas, formerly assistant superintendent of the Clovis Unified School district in Fresno County, at the beginning of his second term was designed, in part, to reassure the education community.

Governors often try to balance appointments to commissions and boards. Thus, in late 1976, Brown appointed two very different people to the University of California Board of Regents. One, Verne Orr, a fiscally conservative Republican and director of finance for Governor Reagan, and the other appointee, Vilma S. Martinez, general counsel for the Mexican-American Legal Defense and Education Fund, had been a strong critic of the University's programs for Chicano students. Governor Jerry Brown particularly, and Governor George Deukmejian to an extent have made substantial efforts to nominate minorities and women to key state administrative positions. (See Table 8–2 for a comparison.)

California governors have been reasonably successful in appointing qualified people. The state court system and the administrative bureaucracy have had national reputations for ability and integrity.

Just as the governor can appoint, the governor can also remove someone whose actions or judgments run counter to the administration's policy or needs. The removal power is weaker, however, than

TABLE 8-2
Comparing Ethnic and Gender Appointments to the Court—Governors Jerry Brown, 1975–1982, and George Deukmejian, 1983–1986

	Brown	Deukmejian
Women	29%	12.5%
Hispanics	9	3.1
Blacks	7	3.8

Source: *Sacramento Bee*, November 14, 1982 and governor's office.

the appointive power.[1] About two out of three gubernatorial appointments serve for fixed terms. Persons appointed to fixed-term positions cannot be removed before the end of the term without good reason—such as illegal activities or gross incompetence. A single error, personality clash, or difference in philosophy are not considered good reasons for removal. Furthermore, the governor's removal powers in many instances are limited by due process. That is, the governor may not remove someone from a middle administrative level without following prescribed procedures.

Minor Powers

Clemency.   The governor has the power to pardon criminals, commute sentences, and issue stays of execution. In doing this, the governor has the advice of the California Adult Authority and his clemency secretary—but the final decision is the governor's. This *minor power* has sometimes produced *major problems* for governors. The most publicized issue in this regard is that of the death penalty. Both Governors Pat Brown and Jerry Brown opposed the death penalty on moral grounds. State voters, on the other hand, clearly support the death penalty. Both Browns were politically damaged by their opposition to the executions. Governor Deukmejian's firm support for the penalty and his tough "law and order" stance works to his advantage politically.

Extradition.   The governor has the power to extradite persons who live in California but are charged with a crime by another state. Persons charged with such a crime by another state can be forcibly transported to that state with the approval of the governor. Normally, California's governors automatically approve extradition. However, on

[1]B. T. Collins, Governor Jerry Brown's chief of staff, is reported to have advised the incoming Deukmejian chief of staff, perhaps half-jokingly, to get an undated resignation letter from every appointee.

rare occasions, a governor will not. Thus, Governor Jerry Brown refused to extradite Indian activist Dennis Banks to South Dakota because he believed that Banks would not get a fair trial in that state. Following George Deukmejian's election as governor, Banks fled from California fearing he might be extradicted by the new governor.

Military.   The governor is commander-in-chief of the state National Guard. In times of emergency, such as earthquakes, floods, or riots, the governor may call out the guard to help provide transport, deliver food or medical aid, and keep order. When riots occur, the governor may use the guard to help local police. Currently, President Ronald Reagan and Democratic governors of several states are locked in a dispute concerning deployment of national guard units for training in Honduras near the tense Nicaraguan border. Democratic governors have objected to having "their" national guard units sent to Central America because of the danger, because they believe it is provocative, and because they disagree with Reagan administration Central American policy. They contend that since these troops have not been federalized by presidential emergency powers, they have authority to refuse to send them.

Ceremonial.   As head of state, the governor is, in effect the personal representative of California. For example, it was Governor Deukmejian who entertained Britain's Queen Elizabeth in the capitol when she visited California in 1983. Governor Jerry Brown took advantage of the national press coverage surrounding the first landing of the experimental space shuttle Columbia by awarding the pilots the "Order of California" when they landed in the state. Such events are good publicity.

The governor's mansion is symbolic of this ceremonial function. A new mansion was planned and built during the Reagan years (1967–74) at a total cost of about $1.3 million, but Governor Jerry Brown refused to live in it—saying it looked like a runaway Safeway Supermarket. Thus, he lived in an inexpensive downtown Sacramento apartment during his two terms. The new mansion became a factor in the 1983 budget crisis when Governor Deukmejian asked to be allowed to live in it and senate Democrats refused. Later, the Democrats relented, but then the governor changed his mind too—saying he preferred to live elsewhere. Perhaps the mansion had become more symbolic of California government than anyone intended!

PERSONALITY AND CIRCUMSTANCES

In the long run, a governor's effective leadership is based not only on constitutional powers, but also on personality, style, energy, and cir-

8-2 *Republican Governor George Deukmejian* (center) *and his wife* (right) *campaigning in behalf of Republican State Senate candidate, Sandy Smoley* (left).

Courtesy of Sacramento Bee

cumstances. How a governor gets along with legislators, what he wants to do, which party controls the legislature, the nature of emerging issues, and the political ambitions of others—all have a substantial impact on the power of the state's chief executive.

Party Leader

Governors of California automatically become leaders of their party. However, not all governors have enjoyed playing the role of party leader, and some have not been successful at it. The most successful governors appear to be those who have been able to be party leaders and yet rise above partisanship.

Generally, California governors pay relatively little attention to their party's statutory organizations—county and state central committees—since these organizations tend to have little political significance (see Chapter 6). For example, Governor Warren would often go to football games rather than attend State Central Committee meetings.

Voters

Republican governors tend to have a more philosophically unified party than Democratic governors. Democratic governors must lead a party that spans a wide ideological range. Thus, 40 percent of California Democrats consider themselves conservatives, another 40 percent consider themselves liberals, and the remaining 20 percent tend to be swing voters. No Democratic governor can afford to ignore either wing of the party, much less alienate it.

Jerry Brown's conservative-liberal mix came from his view that California was entering an era of limits—that government could not tax any more or regulate any more than it now does. Part of his political philosophy clearly came from his own nonmaterial lifestyle.

Thus, just as Democratic voters are split on the issues, so too are Democratic leaders. As former Governor Jerry Brown recently observed, he had to "paddle his (political) canoe first a little on the right and then a little on the left." But such a tactic can lead to criticism of being "wishy-washy"—and Brown was charged with doing more than one flip-flop on an issue.

In contrast, Governor Reagan (1967–74) was clearly *the spokesperson* for most of his state party. Unlike Democrats, California Republicans tend to have a more unified political philosophy—about two-thirds view themselves as conservatives. Thus, Reagan's leadership of his party could be more strongly ideological.

Current Republican Governor, George Deukmejian follows in the Reagan pattern—staunchly conservative but willing to compromise on occasion. Because Deukmejian's victory over Democratic mayor of Los Angeles, Tom Bradley, in the 1982 election was narrow, and because he was a former legislator and capitol insider, many assumed that Deukmejian would be eager to seek compromises with the Democratically controlled legislature. In Governor Deukmejian's first year as state executive "the" issue was how the budget deficit should be addressed. Democrats insisted on new taxes and Deukmejian refused. Eventually, Deukmejian was able to persuade Democratic legislators to go along with his plan of "rolling over" part of the debt until the following year and counting on an improving economy to resolve the deficit problem.

In 1986, Governor Deukmejian and Mayor Bradley had a rematch in the gubernatorial election. Deukmejian's successes on budget and "law and order" issues, his "common sense" approaches, and his low-key style in governmental management contrasted sharply with the frenetic, flippant style of his predecessor, Jerry Brown. Voters seemed to welcome the change. In their rematch, Governor Deukmejian beat Bradley by a nearly two to one margin. The only issue which the governor proved vulnerable on—toxics—was not of sufficient enough importance to persuade independents and conservative Democrats to support Bradley. A Field Institute survey of voters leaving the polling place found that 87 percent thought that things were going "pretty well" or "fairly well" in the state.

Presidential Candidate

As previously noted, California governors are almost always considered *automatic* candidates for president or vice-president these days. Complicating any potential vice presidential plans of Republican Governor George Deukmejian is the fact that his replacement as governor would be *Democratic* Lt. Governor Leo McCarthy. Sometimes a governor's national ambitions can work against him. Governor Jerry Brown's futile efforts in his second run for the presidency in 1979–1980 damaged his political image. He failed to attract much support, lost four successive primaries, and was out of the state campaigning for sixty-three days. Many voters resented this absentee leadership. The national attention given to California governors adds a new variable to the governor's power equation. But, Brown's 1980 efforts, which required him to spend sixty-three days out of the state in the first three months of the year, left him with a $600,000 campaign debt and four consecutive primary defeats, and badly damaged him in California.

Popularity and Lame Ducks

A governor's popularity, measured by election success or opinion surveys affects his powers. Generally speaking, a governor's popularity increases following his first election. Thus, after winning in November 1982 with 49 percent of the vote, Deukmejian's popularity grew. The proportion of citizens who rated him as doing an excellent or good job increased from 27 percent in March 1983 to 36 percent in June.

But a governor's popularity usually begins to decline after he has held office for several years. Jerry Brown's popularity grew after his narrow 1974 victory, but by 1979, more people felt he was doing a poor job than felt he was doing an excellent or good job (see Illustration 8–3).

Declining popularity combined with the approaching end of his second term in office (popularly known as being a lame duck) reduced Jerry Brown's powers. In contrast, Governor Ronald Reagan's popularity continued through his second term, and George Deukmejian's voter approval ratings have increased in his second term.

Legislative Relations

Much, perhaps most, of the governor's time and energy is devoted to legislative relations. Getting the budget passed (see Chapter 10), getting desired legislation approved and unwanted legislation rejected, and getting administrative appointments approved is certainly the core of any governor's workload.

8-3 *Jerry Brown and George Deukmejian's Job Ratings as Governor*

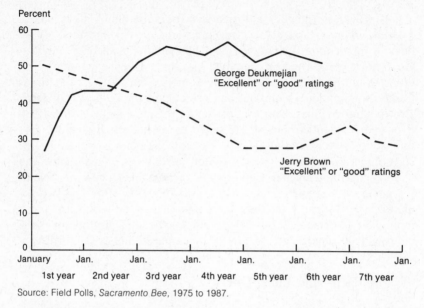

Source: Field Polls, *Sacramento Bee,* 1975 to 1987.

A number of factors influences how well the governor achieves these legislative goals. Aside from constitutional-statutory authority and personal-political popularity with voters there are several other important factors. Among them are partisan makeup of the legislature, personal relations with legislators, the governor's goals, and the goals of legislators, and other major state officials.

Personal Relations with Legislators

Aside from voter appeal and general popularity, a governor's personal relations with legislators are important. If the governor supports a bill, it is easier to get a legislator's vote if the legislator and governor are "friends."

Neither Ronald Reagan nor Jerry Brown had the same warm personal friendships with lawmakers that Earl Warren, Pat Brown, or Goodwin Knight enjoyed. Both Reagan and Jerry Brown became governors on "anti-politician," "anti-Sacramento," and "anti-government" positions. Legislators were also offended by both Reagan's and Brown's "holier-than-thou" attitudes toward lawmakers and civil servants.

Governor Jerry Brown also had personal problems with lawmakers. As secretary of state, he irritated many legislators with his political reform activities—in particular his support for Proposition 9 (the Polit-

8-4 *Governor George Deukmejian discussing the budget bill with Democratic and Republican legislative leaders and staff in the governor's conference room.*

Courtesy of Sacramento Bee

ical Reform Act). Many legislators also felt that Jerry Brown's election was based more on his father's record and name than on any demonstrated ability. Some felt the governor was "flaky," because of his interest in Zen, his antimaterialist attitude, and his nonpolitical friends.

Shortly after taking office, Governor Deukmejian offended senate GOP leaders when he did not give them advance notice of an important executive order freezing state hiring and cutting state spending by 2 percent. As Senator Ken Maddy observed in 1983:

> This place [the legislature] runs principally on ego and images of power . . . the key to [Deukmejian's] success is going to be the relationship he develops with the legislature and certainly with Republicans who have been his supporters. . . . If that relationship is slighted by him or his staff, it's going to be a difficult time."

The substantial friction between Deukmejian and Democratic legislative leaders that characterized his first term abated only slightly in his second term. Complicated issues such as the state's mental health system, financing public schools, prison siting, tort reform, and Gann state spending limits indicate that relations between the governor and Democratic legislative leaders will continue to be strained. As Richard Zeiger, editor of the *California Journal* noted (December 1986):

Deukmejian followed into office a governor who sent the public on a rollercoaster ride of ideas about how government should operate. The thrills were sometimes fun, but they wore thin. Now the public seems satisfied with Deukmejian's staid approach to government. But California's voters, at least in recent times, have not been loyal to any one style for long. George Deukmejian wants to see if he can break the trend.

Finally, the hints dropped that Deukmejian may seek a third term as governor discourage the "lame duck" syndrome.

Campaign Support

One of the most effective ways for a governor to build good personal relations with legislators is by providing them campaign support. This applies, of course, only to candidates in one's own party. Governors are expected to hit the "rubber chicken" circuit—appearing at fund-raising dinners and praising local party candidates' fine qualities. Legislative candidates—incumbents or aspirants—like to be seen rubbing elbows with the governor. It makes them look important to the home folks. Helping the incumbent legislator raise money at a dinner that features the governor as guest speaker puts the legislator in political debt to the governor. Both understand that the governor may collect that IOU during the next legislative session.

Partisan Balance

Democrats have controlled the legislature since 1959. As a result, Democratic governors have had a "built-in" majority to work with. Conversely, Republican governors have to build a majority vote for each of their programs. Increasingly, the number of partisan issues seems to have grown—labor relations, welfare, taxation, the size of government, and most prominently, the budget.

Democratic governors Pat and Jerry Brown, while having Democratic legislative leaders and majorities to work with, had many conflicts with the legislature—frequently over personality disputes. Republican Governors Ronald Reagan and George Deukmejian have battled with Democratic legislators more frequently on policy/ideology issues. In any case, the separation of powers and an assertive and professional state legislature virtually guarantee governor-legislature antipathy.

With the increasing importance of the annual budget bill (see Chapter 10) and the constitutional requirement of a two-thirds vote for approval of it, a militant minority in either house can effectively block budget approval. This has given the Republicans (particularly in the assembly) a strong voice in policy formation.

Personality and Style

California's last three governors (Reagan, Brown and Deukmejian) have exhibited remarkably different personalities and political style.[2] Perhaps most marked is the contrast between the two Republicans, Ronald Reagan and George Deukmejian. Both were elected as conservative, tight-fiscal candidates. Both inherited budget deficits from the outgoing Democratic governors. Both faced legislatures controlled by Democrats. Yet while Reagan promised to "cut, squeeze, and trim" the budget, his first budget was 10 percent higher than the previous (Pat Brown) budget, and he presided over two of the state's largest tax increases. He quickly learned to negotiate and compromise with legislators.

Deukmejian, on the other hand, immediately adopted a hard line by setting a budget ceiling of $22 billion. He was far less flexible than Reagan in his first year as governor.

Deukmejian is clearly more concerned with the details of administration—drawing on his experience both as attorney general and as a member of the state legislature. The contrast between Reagan and Deukmejian is substantial.

Administration Goals

Every governor takes office having made campaign promises and having a personal set of policy and political objectives. Some goals require legislative cooperation—welfare reform, more public school funding, prison construction, new energy or environmental policy—in short, more money or expanded governmental activity. These kinds of goals require new legislation or support for budget expenditures; the governor cannot do it by himself.

Other goals, such as reduced governmental regulation or more "friendly" interpretation of state laws by governmental agencies, can be accomplished without legislative approval by a governor's appointees to such agencies as the Public Utilities Commission, Department

---

[2]Perhaps no event symbolizes so eloquently the Jerry Brown legacy as his official governor's portrait. All former governors' photographlike portraits are on display on the first floor of the capitol building. These paintings show serious and somber former officials standing stiffly beside the capitol building or working in their offices. Jerry Brown's portrait is only of his face. Unlike the other lifelike paintings, the artist commissioned by Brown to do his portrait appears to be a representative of the expressionist school of painting. The painting stands alone in splendid isolation hidden away from the other governors' portraits on the third floor of the capitol building. It has become a favorite "in spot" for capitol guides to show to the waves of tourists coming to the building.

of Corporations, Air Resources Board, Department of Industrial Relations, and so on.

And, of course, the governor's budget powers and item veto give him great leverage over the legislature in the budget process (see Chapter 10).

But in fact, every governor has a set of goals which require different legislative-administrative strategies. Every governor finds negotiation and compromise necessary. Keeping track of bills, state agencies, legislators, boards, commissions, and judges is a tremendous task, and no governor does it alone.

OFFICE OF THE GOVERNOR

The governor is more than an individual; *the person* elected in November *soon becomes an institution*. No one individual can hope to manage California. In playing their many roles and in meeting their many responsibilities, governors must delegate authority to others. And obviously, they need some oversight of that delegation of power. To do this, California governors have a staff of approximately 100 aides. Basically, that organization falls into two parts—staff and cabinet.

Staff

Because the basic tasks of the governor remain largely the same over time, regardless of the office's occupant, the major staff positions are essentially the same in every administration. These major staff positions reflect the ongoing concerns every governor has:

Executive secretary acts as chief of staff, coordinating the governor's staff.

Legal affairs secretary is concerned with the problems of clemency, pardons, and extradition. He or she tends to be involved in other areas as needed.

Press secretary is the link between the governor and the press and, hence, the public.

Legislative secretary is in charge of liaison with the legislature.

Appointments secretary is in charge of screening applicants for the many appointments the governor makes.

In some cases, staffing changes with circumstances. Reagan's concern with higher education led him to appoint an education secretary, Alex Sherriffs. Sherriffs had been a professor of psychology at University of California-Berkeley but became disenchanted with higher education in California. Given the high turnover in Governor Deukmejian's major staff in his first term, second term staffers are nearly all new to their positions. Governor Jerry Brown appointed a space advisor, former astronaut Rusty Schweikert, and an arts advisor, Jacques Barzaghi.

Reagan depended on his staff of specialists and department heads for policy recommendations. He seldom bothered with detail. Brown, much the opposite, devoted considerable attention to detail, looked to his assistants for information, and expected debate among staff—if the subject interested him. However, as time went by, Brown's interests in managing government declined, and he became less involved in legislative issues. Deukmejian combines the Reagan and Brown styles. Clearly a detail person, Deukmejian studies the issues with care and takes considerable time to adopt a position, but he also delegates much decisionmaking to his staff.

Cabinet

The governor's cabinet is composed of five super agency secretaries plus the directors of industrial relations, food and agriculture, finance, and the governor's executive secretary. The cabinet is designed to facilitate policy development and program coordination. Each of the five secretaries represents the many departments, commissions, and boards that make up his or her agency (see Chapter 9). Since no governor can hope to deal with each of the several hundred agencies, departments, commissions, and boards in California government, the cabinet serves as a way of delegating responsibility. Conspicuously absent are two major departments, justice and education. Since their department heads are independently elected, the governor has no direct control over them (see Chapter 9).

SUMMARY

The governor *dominates the executive branch* of government. The legal-formal powers of budget control, veto, appointment, authority to call special sessions of the legislature, and a host of minor powers provide the state's chief executive with a formidable political arsenal. The less tangible but no less real authority of public popularity and party leadership further enhances gubernatorial powers. This is particularly true in California because of the national stature of its governor. Finally, the governor's appointment powers exert an influence on state government and politics long after that governor is gone. Undoubtedly, the governor is the *central political figure* in California.

Yet the governor is also a person—a personality—about whom each of us can have some personal feelings and attitudes. This *personality dimension* is seldom found in other state political figures, such as legislators, administrators, or judges, because they are identified with a larger group. A legislator is one of 120 lawmakers; a judge is one of 1200 judges. But the governor *is the governor*—there is only one. So the office takes on a personality—the personality of the incumbent. This usually serves to the advantage of the governor because people feel that they "know" this person. They feel comfortable in referring to the governor as Jerry or Ronnie or Duke.

9

Administration: Executives, Civil Servants, and Citizens

While the political spotlight most often shines on the governor as the state's chief executive, hundreds of other executives are busy in the day-to-day administrative processes of government. Voters elect a lieutenant governor, five department heads, and four members of the state Board of Equalization. The governor appoints about 170 other important administrators. There are also a few hybrid agencies made up of a mixture of elected officials and appointed administrators. There are also some "predetermined" boards of major importance. In addition, there are some 232,000 state employees who do the work—from digging ditches to filling medical prescriptions. The vast majority of these state employees are hired under civil service or a merit plan.

How these executives and civil servants do their jobs is important to all Californians. Few of us have direct contact with elected public officials; fewer even know their names. But nearly all, citizen or alien, have frequent direct contact with state employees.

PLURAL EXECUTIVE

Having five independently elected partisan executives plus the four elected members of the Board of Equalization (every voter gets to vote for one board member depending upon which of four separate districts in the state he or she lives) plus a nonpartisan superintendent of instruction helps create some interesting internal tensions within the executive branch. Lt. Governor Leo McCarthy and Secretary of State March Fong Eu both announced they were seriously considering being candidates for Democratic nomination in the U.S. Senate race in 1988. Attorneys general and lt. governors in California have traditionally

TABLE 9-1
Comparing California's Plural Executive with Other States

Office	California Elects	A Majority of Other States Elect
Lieutenant governor	Yes	Yes
Attorney General	Yes	Yes
State treasurer	Yes	Yes
Secretary of state	Yes	Yes
Superintendent of public instruction	Yes	No
State auditor	No	Yes
Controller	Yes	No
State Board of Equalization (four members)	Yes	No

Source: *The Book of the States*, 1982–83.

used these offices as launching pads for gubernatorial bids. Jerry Brown used the favorable publicity he generated as secretary of state to run successfully for governor. Jerry Brown's former chief of staff and ex-assemblymember Controller Gray Davis has indicated he will be seeking higher office. Speculation is that Governor Deukmejian's appointment to replace deceased Treasurer Jess Unruh may have the inside track on replacing Governor Deukmejian when he leaves office. The bitter feud in which Superintendent Bill Honig and Governor Deukmejian have engaged recently over public school funding has been called by some political insiders the opening shots of the 1990 governor's race. Even some of the newer members of the Board of Equalization have openly hinted of their higher political ambitions. California governors (and U.S. senators) must constantly look back over their shoulders at their ambitious rivals in the other executive offices.

As one can see in Table 9–1, California, like other states, elects many of its executives. However, California elects more of these executives than most states.

Duties and responsibilities of the various offices in the California plural executive are listed in eight separate constitutional articles.

Lieutenant Governor

The lt. governor's role in state government resembles the vice-president's role at the national level. As one California governor observed, the duties of the lt. governor are "to preside over the senate and each morning to inquire solicitously after the governor's health."

These are hardly monumental tasks. Yet there are some duties of significance. And in some ways, the lt. governor has more power within the state setting than the vice-president has at the national level.

Unlike the vice-president who becomes president only on the death or disability of the president, the lt. governor becomes *acting governor* whenever the governor leaves the state. (Also, the lt. governor becomes governor on the death or resignation of the governor.) Since California governors travel out of state frequently (particularly in campaigns for the presidency), the lt. governor can sometimes have an opportunity to exercise power.

Significantly, unlike the vice-president, the lt. governor is not chosen by the head of the ticket to be a running mate in the election. The lt. governor is elected independently from the governor in the party primaries, and each runs independently from the other in the general election. Occasionally, the Republican (or Democratic) candidates for governor and lt. governor will run cooperatively as a team in the general election. Usually, though, the governor and lt. governor nominees of the party run substantially separate efforts. Yet the lt. governor has often become governor. Of all the statewide executives, the lt. governor has, perhaps, the best chance of becoming governor. And the odds may be getting better as California's governors are now "natural" candidates for the presidency or vice-presidency.

For the first time in the twentieth century, voters in 1978 elected a governor and lt. governor of different parties. As a result, substantial conflict developed between the two. In the spring of 1979, when Democratic Governor Jerry Brown was out of state campaigning for the presidency (he was away more than 200 days in his two-term stint as governor), Republican Lt. Governor Mike Curb nominated a judge to the appellate court. When Brown returned, he withdrew the nomination and substituted his own. Curb objected, asserting that once he had nominated a judge the governor could not return to the state and withdraw the appointment. (Under pressure from Curb, Brown hastily made over thirty additional justice nominations in less than a week and then left the state again!)

Both the governor and lt. governor appealed to the California state supreme court to resolve the question: Who exercises the governor's power and authority when the elected governor is out of state? Curb argued that when Governor Brown was out of state, the lt. governor (Curb) was automatically acting governor and inherited all of the powers and authority of the office. Brown argued that until the judicial nomination had been approved by the Commission on Judicial Appointments (see Chapter 11) the appointment could be withdrawn. Brown argued that so long as he could be in telephone communication with his office and staff, he was still governor.

The court, in December 1979, upheld the lt. governor's powers and authority as acting governor whenever the elected governor is out of the state.[1] Technically, a lt. governor serving as acting governor can sign or veto bills. But, in practical terms he or she follows the governor's instructions in this capacity. Lt. Governor Leo McCarthy has signed bills when Governor Deukmejian was out of state, but he does not exercise independent judgment on these bills. On the other hand, when Mike Curb was lt. governor and serving as acting governor he wanted to act on several bills that were waiting for executive decision. However, when he requested these bills from Brown's staff, they were unable to "find" them.

In 1982 and 1986, California voters again elected a governor and lt. governor of different political parties. Lt. Governor Leo McCarthy emphasized that he would not try to imitate Curb's confrontational style as lt. governor. Indeed, Curb's obstructive behavior as lt. governor, contributed to his defeat in the bitter Republican gubernatorial primary of 1982 against George Deukmejian. Four years later, Curb decided to reenter the elective arena by running for lt. governor (his campaign manager, Bill Roberts, had been Deukmejian's in 1982—déjà vu). Curb promised Deukmejian and other Republican leaders he would be loyal to Governor Deukmejian. He argued that his election would give Deukmejian a freer hand in considering a run for higher office because as a Republican acting governor, he would hold the office for the GOP. After capturing the Republican primary against former ally Senator H. L. Richardson, Curb launched an all-out drive to defeat Democratic incumbent Leo McCarthy. McCarthy was able to effectively exploit issues initially raised by Deukmejian in his 1982 campaign against Curb. Curb, it was noted, had not registered to vote until he was thirty, and his suspect draft status during the Vietnam War had allowed him to avoid military service. Questions were also raised about payola and his record company finances, and whether he had sung background and had written musical scores for several X-rated movies. In addition, after leaving elective office in 1982, Curb had openly disparaged the office of lt. governor. Curb said it was a waste of time and taxpayer money. These issues plus Deukmejian's tepid endorsement helped allow Leo McCarthy to easily defeat Curb in 1986.

As acting governor, the lt. governor usually performs only routine functions such as serving on rare occasions as the Senate's presiding officer. Not surprisingly, senators do not view the lt. governor as "one of the gang." Typically, the governor and lt. governor have an agreement about the lt. governor's actions while the governor is out of state.

---

[1] However, the court also ruled that Brown could withdraw the nomination at any time *before confirmation.*

9-1 *California's plural executive.*

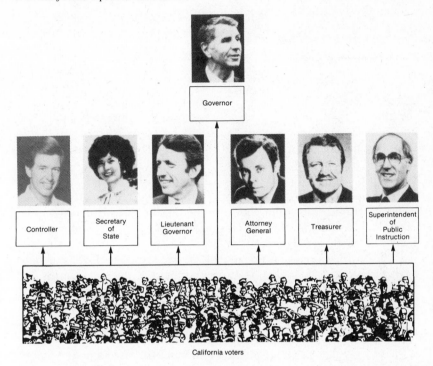

California voters

But emergencies can happen. Lt. Governor Glenn Anderson, acting governor while Pat Brown was on vacation in Greece, had to make socially crucial and politically sensitive decisions about National Guard deployment at the start of the 1965 Watts riots.

On those rare occasions when the state senate is locked in a twenty to twenty tie vote, the lt. governor is authorized to cast the tie-breaking vote. For example, Lt. Governor Mervyn Dymally flew from Denver to Sacramento to cast a tie-breaking vote on the "consenting adults" bill in 1976.

The lt. governor also serves on: (1) the State Lands Commission, (2) the University of California Regents, and (3) the California State University and College Board of Trustees. Finally, like the vice-president, the lt. governor can be given important assignments by the chief executive. Lt. Governor McCarthy has played a leadership role on economic issues, and he has also offered (though Governor Deukmejian has not taken him up on it) to serve in a mediating role between the governor and Democratic legislative leaders. Hence, the lt. gover-

nor's role in the state's political milieu depends heavily on the willingness of the governor to delegate authority.

Attorney General

Next to the governor, the attorney general is the most important
elected executive in California. As head of the Department of Justice,
the attorney general is theoretically responsible for enforcing all state
and local laws; this extends his jurisdiction to local district attorneys,
sheriffs, and police chiefs. In fact, because of the strong tradition of
home rule in California, the attorney general seldom enters into local
law enforcement matters.

Law and order responsibilities of the attorney general cover a wide
range of activities including both civil and criminal law, investigation,
legal advice, and, in emergencies, authority over local law enforcement.

The attorney general is responsible for representing dozens of state
agencies in court; in short, the attorney general is the state's attorney.
However, on some politically sensitive issues, the attorney general
may not always choose to defend the state. For example, in court cases
involving state-funded abortions, environmental protection regulations, and public employee collective bargaining rights, then Attorney
General Deukmejian either refused to defend the state's policy and in
a few instances, actually joined with the other side in challenging the
state's position. The courts have upheld the authority of the attorney
general's actions in these few cases.

In recent years, the office of attorney general has become a key
stepping stone to the governor's office. Earl Warren (1942), Pat Brown
(1958), and George Deukmejian (1982) went directly from being attorney general to governor. There is considerable speculation that current
Attorney General John Van de Kamp may be a candidate for governor
in 1990.

Controller

The controller is chief fiscal officer of the state. The main duties of
the controller are to pay state bills and keep track of state accounts.
This officer is responsible for four major programs: fiscal control, tax
administration, local government fiscal affairs, and administration. The
controller is also a member of the State Lands Commission, Franchise
Tax Board, and a member of the state Board of Equalization.

However, perhaps because fiscal policy excites little political interest, controllers traditionally have tended to have little political mobility. Only two have been able to move up politically—both to the U.S.

9-2 *Partisan control of executive offices 1923–1986.*

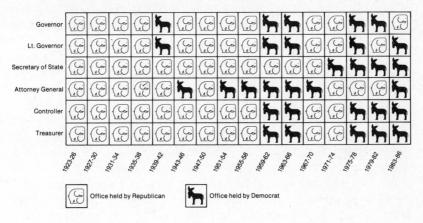

 Office held by Republican   Office held by Democrat

Senate. Current controller, Gray Davis, clearly has loftier political ambitions.

Secretary of State

The secretary of state is guardian of documents and records for California. In addition, the secretary serves as chief elections officer for the state. Until the 1970s, this office aroused little interest. Two incumbents, Frank C. and Frank M. Jordan (father and son), held the office from 1911 to 1970 (except for 3½ years).

When Jerry Brown was elected secretary of state in 1970, he used the office to promote campaign reform (particularly Proposition 9 in 1974) and to generate personal publicity for his gubernatorial race in 1974. Brown was the first secretary to go on to higher office. His successor, March Fong Eu, is the second woman and first Asian elected to statewide office.

Treasurer

The treasurer is state banker and investment counselor. This officer has four major duties—two are important but not very exciting to the average citizen, and two are relatively unimportant.

The treasurer's most important duty is to prepare, sell, and redeem state bonds. These bonds, which are sold to large financial institutions, provide the money required to pay for major state construction projects (such as the California State Water Project) or to support such programs as the California Housing Finance Agency's low- and moderate-income housing projects.

With an annual sale of over $3 billion in various bonds, it is important that the treasurer secure the lowest possible interest. A difference of one half a percentage point is equal to $150 million per year! In addition, by carefully managing the state debt, the treasurer plays an important part in maintaining state credit.

Until recently, the treasurer's second important task has been to invest surplus state funds. However, since 1981, there have been only occasional surpluses to invest.

Since Jess Unruh (recently deceased) was elected treasurer in 1974, the office has taken on new importance. During this time the legislature appointed the treasurer to over thirty commissions dealing with fiscal matters of one kind or another. The treasurer is the commission chair in many cases. Unruh put together and led a coalition nationally of twenty-six separate state employee and union pension funds groups, the Council of Institutional Investors, with combined assets of over $100 billion in an attempt to protect shareholders from the manipulations of Wall Street financiers and corporate takeovers. To succeed Unruh, Gov. Deukmejian has nominated Republican Congressman Brian Lundgren, whose appointment must be confirmed by the state legislature.

Superintendent of Public Instruction

The superintendent is an unusual executive. Elected to office on a nonpartisan ballot, the superintendent is responsible to a ten-person board of education appointed by the governor. As the administrative head of the state Department of Education, the superintendent is expected to implement board policy. Yet this officer is elected and, hence, ultimately responsible to the voters rather than to the board. Further complicating the situation is the fact that most of California's education is delivered at the local level. Most Department of Education policies directly affect the state's local school districts. But the vast bulk of K–12 educational funds (approximately 98 percent) are spent by local districts.

State and local education programs cover a wide range of activities in addition to the three Rs: child-care centers, migrant child care, preschool and early childhood education programs, programs for the disadvantaged, and programs for the physically handicapped, to list a few (see Chapter 12).

An important and often controversial area for the Department of Education is its text adoption authority for school grades kindergarten through eight. Local districts may only use texts on the approved list. Controversies over "God and science," sex education, and "fundamentals or frills" often end up on the superintendent's desk.

With over one-third of the state budget flowing through the Department of Education, the superintendent is clearly a major figure in California government. Since the state supreme court *(Serrano* v. *Priest)* ruled that local property taxes do not provide equal funding opportunities for every child, California state government has been forced to substantially increase its support to local school districts. More recently, voter approval of Proposition 13 in June 1978 cut local school district revenues by about one-third. The state replaced most of the lost funds out of its budget surplus. Increased pressure for more state money as a result of Proposition 13 promises to make the superintendent's position more powerful and more politically sensitive than in the past. In fact, the superintendent is the chief lobbyist for California's some 1,000 school districts.

Historically, this office has not been a springboard to higher office. Incumbent Superintendent Max Rafferty's U.S. Senate effort failed in 1968. Two years later, he was defeated by Wilson Riles. Riles became the first black to hold statewide elective office in California. Twelve years later (1982), Bill Honig defeated Riles in a hotly contested race.

Both the Rafferty-Riles and Riles-Honig contests focused on the quality of public education in California. Honig stressed the steady and worrisome decline in high school students' test scores, public dissatisfaction with school discipline, teacher tenure, and nonacademic curriculum.

After Honig's 1982 victory, he toured the state generating public support for increased public school revenues, and a bipartisan school reform package was introduced in the legislature. While Governor Deukmejian and Superintendent Honig had a relatively harmonious relationship in the governor's first term, it has become much more acrimonious in Deukmejian's second term. Basically, their differences hinge on the financing of public education. Honig argues that while California has made some improvements in educational quality, there is much to be done—and this means more money. Deukmejian argues that money is not the only factor in improving educational quality and that Honig should suggest which programs should be cut or eliminated since funds are limited. Honig notes that California on a per capita basis spends far less on its public schools than most other states. Governor Deukmejian cites the quality of schools in Japan and their very high faculty-student ratio as a factor suggesting that not all education programs can easily be solved by simply pouring more money into the system. This debate is likely to continue for the foreseeable future. The office of the superintendent has become the focal point for the politics of public education in California.

State Board of Equalization

This board has five members—four are elected from approximately equal population districts, and the fifth is the state controller. The board has two major functions: collecting sales taxes and supervising property tax assessments of counties.

The Board of Equalization's most important function is to administer and collect state and local sales and use taxes. It also has the responsibility for several state excise taxes, including those on alcoholic beverages, cigarettes, and gasoline. It collects about half of state tax revenues each year.

The board's other major function is to review each county's tax assessments and procedures. It is responsible for maintaining equal assessment-to-market-value ratios among the counties.

Board members, though elected on a partisan basis, have an exceedingly low political profile. Once elected, members are usually reelected and often face only token opposition. Since 1942, board members have averaged better than three terms (over twelve years) apiece.

Predetermined and Semipredetermined Executives

Membership on several executive boards and commissions is predetermined in some cases. For example, most of the state Lands Commission and Franchise Tax Board members are automatically "appointed" because they hold some other elective office. Some boards, such as the Wildlife Commission Board or the State Board of Control, have some predetermined and some appointed members. To a large extent, these government bodies are independent of direct control by either the voters or some appointive authority.

State Lands Commission.   The state Lands Commission is a little known but important government unit comprised of the lieutenant governor, controller, and director of finance. It has control over the management of all state lands (some 4 million acres). Increasingly important is its authority to administer state land leases, permits, and sales of state oil, gas, and minerals.

Franchise Tax Board.   The Franchise Tax Board is comprised of the controller, chair of the state board of equalization, and the director of finance. It has responsibility for administering three major tax programs: (1) personal income tax, (2) bank and corporate tax, and (3) senior citizens property tax.[2]

California's personal income tax provides the state with its largest

---

[2]Usually, the board simply administers tax policy. Occasionally, though, the board can issue controversial decisions. Thus, in April 1987 the board announced a new policy: members of private clubs that practice discrimination would not be allowed to deduct their membership fees and meal costs as necessary business expenses. In Sacramento this decision profoundly affected the Sutter Club (men only) which comprises a who's who of the powerful in Sacramento lobby ranks. Lobbyist members of the Sutter Club have frequently invited legislators to the elegant facilities to dine and discuss pending legislation. If the new regulations of the board stand, the private dining clubs could lose many members.

source of revenue—over one-third of the total collected. The board supervises income tax withholding, collection, and refunds while processing about twelve million individual returns each year. The Board also collects the bank and corporation tax, a major source of state revenues. Finally, the board supervises payment of property tax relief to about 500,000 of the state's senior citizens each year.

Appointed Executives

Department of Finance. The Department of Finance is the governor's budgeting and fiscal control agency. Its director, appointed by the governor, is normally the second ranking member of the administration. The department is responsible for (1) preparation of the annual fiscal plan (usually called the budget), (2) administration of the plan, (3) analysis of program effectiveness and efficiency, and (4) economic and demographic research. The budget and size of staff of this department is relatively small when compared to other state agencies, but nevertheless, it is the single most important and powerful department in California government. (See Chapter 10.)

The department's second most important task is to analyze state programs. This includes an evaluation of program management and effectiveness in achieving program goals. From this information, the governor will decide on the worth of the program and the priority to be given to it in future budget allocations.

The director, in addition to overall management of the department is also a member of the state Lands Commission, state Public Works Board, and the Franchise Tax Board.

The Super Agencies. Much of California's administrative system is organized into five super agencies—each housing several departments, boards, and commissions (see Illustration 9–3). The governor appoints each agency head, "secretary," and in addition, the governor appoints the department heads and most members of the many boards and commissions. The basic function of the agency secretaries is to provide communication, coordination, and information.

State and Consumer Services Agency. This agency is mainly devoted to serving the state's public employees and consumers.

Business, Transportation, and Housing Agency. This agency contains three distinct types of departments. One type is concerned with transportation—the California Highway Patrol and Department of Motor Vehicles, for example. The second contains departments oriented toward business activities—the Department of Banking and the Department of Corporations. The third type includes the Department of

9-3 *California's administrative structure.*

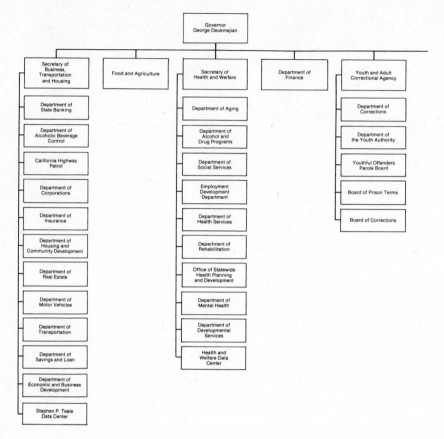

Real Estate and the Department of Housing and Community Development.

Resources Agency. This agency is responsible for the state programs related to management and preservation of water, air, land, natural life, and recreational resources.

Health and Welfare Agency. This agency deals with health, welfare, and corrections programs. Given the rapid increase in the costs of health and welfare, the controversial nature of abortions and drug treatment programs, the middle-class reaction to welfare programs, and the budget squeeze imposed by Proposition 13, the programs and departments in this agency are under intense political pressures.

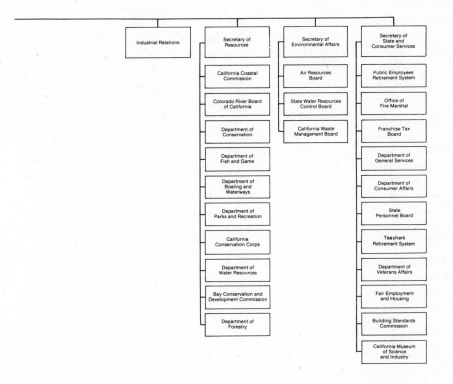

Youth and Adult Correctional Agency.   This agency has two departments and three boards all concerned with prisons, prison terms, youth corrections, and parole.

Independent Departments.   *Department of Food and Agriculture.* This department serves the state's agricultural interests. Its cabinet status reflects the political and economic significance of California's agricultural enterprise.

Environmental Affairs Agency.   This is the smallest of the agencies including the Air Resources Board, state Water Resources Control Board, and California Waste Management Board.

Department of Industrial Relations.   This department is concerned with work and employment conditions in California.

Commissions and Boards.   Commissions and boards differ from agencies and departments in several ways. First, a commission or board is comprised of several people (typically five or seven) each of whom has an equal vote in the making of policy. Responsibility for program control and policy is shared by all members. When members' terms of office extend beyond the governor's, they may find themselves in sharp disagreement with the new governor's appointees (the Agricultural Labor Relations Board, for example). On some boards and commissions, appointments are made by different public officials. On others, such as the Consumer Advisory Council or the Commission on the Status of Women, legislators may be directly involved as members. As one can note, a number of key boards and commissions listed below were launched in the 1970s when this state confronted a variety of complex issues.

Public Utility Commission.   The Public Utility Commission is one of the state's most important regulatory agencies. It has five members, appointed by the governor with state senate confirmation. The commission, established by constitutional amendment in 1911, is theoretically politically independent. The staggered six-year terms of members were designed to make it difficult for a governor to "pack" the commission. In fact, the commission usually reflects the governor's position on utility issues.

The commission is charged with regulating utility rates (natural gas, water, and electricity) and transportation rates within the state. These rates are supposed to provide utilities and common carriers a fair return on their investment.

At the same time, the commission is also supposed to protect the consumer against unreasonable rates by seeing that utilities and common carriers provide adequate facilities and services. In essence, the commission tries to balance demands from consumers with demands from utilities and common carriers. It is both an administrative and quasi-judicial body.

Energy Resources Commission.   Legislative concern over the inability of the Public Utilities Commission to fulfill its responsibilities, its apparent bias in favor of utilities, and the energy crisis led to the establishment of the Energy Resources Conservation and Development Commission. This commission was given authority over locating new power plant sites in the state. It has adopted the development of alternative energy resources including solar and geothermal energy as a top priority.

Agricultural Labor Relations Board.   After years of turmoil, including strikes, violence, and consumer boycotts, the state finally established an agricultural relations board in 1975 an idea championed by the then Governor Jerry Brown. There was hope that the long-simmering conflicts over working conditions, pay, fringe benefits, and collective bargaining could be resolved. In its early years bitterness between growers and farm workers (UFW) and attempts by the Teamsters Union to organize farm workers led to continued conflict. The board was so overloaded with charges of unfair labor practices and challenges to its rules that it exhausted its first year's budget in thirty weeks.

When the ALRB requested additional funds from the legislature, growers' representatives were able to persuade legislative majorities to delay them. In retaliation, the UFW resorted to a ballot initiative (Proposition 14) in November 1976 to protect the board's authority and funding from the legislature. Following a bitter contest, Proposition 14 was rejected by the voters, and farm-labor disputes remained unresolved.

Governor George Deukmejian has significantly modified the ALRB's role and powers in agricultural policy. Long a critic of the board—and a staunch friend of the growers—Deukmejian has placed progrower commissioners on the board and appointed former GOP Assemblyman David Stirling as general counsel (the board's attorney). Stirling immediately clashed with the board over the hiring and firing of personnel, the budget, and procedures.

Public Employee Relations Board.   Created in 1975 to oversee collective bargaining activities involving school employees, the board's powers were enlarged to include collective bargaining of state employees in 1977. (See discussion of collective bargaining below.)

California Coastal Commission.   Created by initiative in 1972, six coastal conservation commissions were merged with the statewide commission in 1981. The commission, charged with regulating land use and development along California's coastline, has been involved in numerous conflicts with coastal cities, counties, and developers.

Fair Political Practices Commission.   Created by initiative in 1974, the commission has control over implementation of the Fair Political Practices Act. (See discussion in Chapters 3 and 5.)

Consumer-Licensing.   Housed in the Department of Consumer Affairs are some forty different boards and commissions charged with regulating and licensing various occupations. Including among others: doctors, dentists, barbers, morticians, cosmetologists, veterinarians, nurses, accountants, architects, and employment agencies. In the 1970s, legislation added several public members to these boards in an effort to keep them from being dominated by those they are supposed to regulate.

Public Education.   Public education—kindergarten through high school (K–12) and higher education—provides a good example of the many boards and commissions involved in delivering a particular service to the people of the state and reflects the diversity of needs involved. Public education (K–12) is essentially a local activity, but it is largely funded by the state (see next chapter on the budget). Higher education is a state function constituting the state's largest single expenditure (it has the largest number of state employees).

State Board of Education.   This board consists of ten people appointed by the governor to staggered four-year terms subject to state senate confirmation. The board sets policy and exercises oversight of the Department of Education; but the department is headed by the independently elected superintendent of public instruction. Theoretically, the board is supposed to set policy and goals for the state's elementary and secondary schools (K–12).

State Department of Education.   An independent department because its head (the superintendent of public instruction) is elected, the department is supposed to oversee a whole host of education programs and distribute funds to local school districts.

Commission for Teacher Preparation and Licensing.   This commission's twenty members (fifteen appointed by the governor) review teacher training programs, give licensing examinations, and enforce teacher standards.

Higher Education.   Higher education has both a local and state component. The state's 106 community colleges are financed and funded, in theory, by some seventy local community college districts with locally elected boards of trustees. Each of the districts covers a county or part of a county. Since Proposition 13, however, these local colleges have become increasingly dependent on the state for funding, and under pressure from the governor in 1983, they imposed tuition fees for the first time in the state's history. These colleges are designed to serve four kinds of students: first, high school graduates whose grades are too low to win admission to a four-year college (some of these students go on to one of the state universities or colleges); second, students who are interested in a two-year associate degree program (often vocational); third, students who are interested in a more casual noncredit course; and fourth, sometimes older students, retired

9-4 *Total Budget $34.5 billion, 1985–86.*

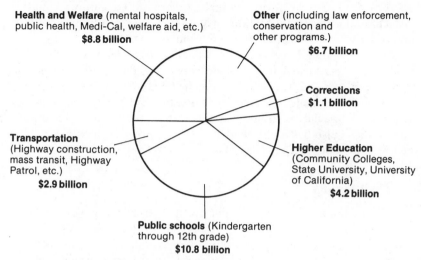

Health and Welfare (mental hospitals, public health, Medi-Cal, welfare aid, etc.)
$8.8 billion

Other (including law enforcement, conservation and other programs.)
$6.7 billion

Corrections
$1.1 billion

Transportation
(Highway construction, mass transit, Highway Patrol, etc.)
$2.9 billion

Higher Education
(Community Colleges, State University, University of California)
$4.2 billion

Public schools (Kindergarten through 12th grade)
$10.8 billion

Source: Legislative Analyst 1985–86 Budget.

or housewifes, who come to the community college campus as a preliminary entry into higher education.

State University and College System. These nineteen campuses offer many different bachelor's and master's degrees. Graduating high school students in the top one-third of their class are eligible for admission based on grades and standardized national tests. These institutions stress instruction rather than research; most of their funding (about 95 percent) comes directly from the state. This gives the governor and legislature great power over the system.

The CSU system is governed by a twenty-three member Board of Trustees, eighteen of whom are nominated by the governor with senate confirmation. They direct a system with more than 340,000 regular students and another 140,000 students in part-time non-state-funded extension, summer session, and external degree programs.

The University of California. Recognized as one of the premier academic institutions in the world, its students are among the top eighth of the state's graduating high school seniors. Of its 130,000 students, 92,000 are undergraduates, 26,000 are graduates, and some 12,000 are in professional programs including law or medicine.

As a major research university, UC relies on the state for about 40 percent of its annual income and the federal government for about 20 percent. The remainder comes from student fees, private sources, and income generated by the university. UC has several facilities devoted

exclusively to research activities, including Scripps Institute of Ocean-
ography, Lick Observatory, Lawrence Livermore Laboratory, and the
Agricultural Experiment Station, in addition to the traditional graduate
and postdoctorate research of a major university.

The UC system is governed by a twenty-six member Board of Regents, which is vested by the state constitution with full powers of
organization and management. Unlike the CSU system, the UC system
has virtually independent authority to hire faculty, develop curriculum,
and pursue special programs. As the state's intellectual-educational
pacesetter, it also has a profound effect on all other segments of public
and private education in California.

Civil Service

State employees are responsible for delivering the goods and services that California government provides. Patrolling freeways, distributing tax forms, checking the accuracy of gas station pumps, helping
campers at state beaches, or collecting and distributing money—all require people. The standards by which state employees are hired, promoted, or fired are important in determining the quality of service provided to California citizens.

In the good old days, California's public employees were hired on
a political patronage basis, there was little or no concern about their
ability to do the job. One of the major reforms of the Hiram Johnson
Progressive administration was to establish a civil service system. In
1934, civil service was extended to virtually all state employees except
for legislative staff.

Civil service means that state employees are hired and promoted
on the basis of job skills, education, and experience. They are not hired
on the basis of politics, because they know someone higher-up, or to
pay off an obligation—in short, there is no patronage. Civil service
regulations protect the state employee from subsequent pressures to
participate in the "correct" political party or to support a particular
candidate for office. Critics argue, however, that civil service has produced mediocrity, cumbersome procedures, and stifled innovation.

While the state's civil service, or "bureaucracy," appears to be
ponderous and rigid, it has changed and is under substantial pressures
for more change. Among the changes recently instituted are: (1) collective bargaining, (2) affirmative action, (3) changes in personnel practices (hiring, firing, and discipline), and (4) some preliminary steps toward contracting for services.

As we can note from Table 9–2 the percentage of the state work
force employed by the state increased steadily in the 1950s and 1960s
but has declined slightly in the 1980s.

TABLE 9-2
State Employees and State Population by Decade

Year	State Population (thousands)	Number of State Employees	Population per Employee
1955–56	13,004	77,676	6.0
1960–61	15,863	115,737	7.3
1965–66	18,464	151,199	8.2
1970–71	20,039	181,151	9.1
1975–76	21,537	206,361	9.6
1980–81	23,780	225,567	9.5
1985–86	26,365	227,209	8.6

Source: Governor's Budget Summary, 1987–88.

Collective Bargaining.   In a major departure from tradition, state employees (both in civil service and higher education) have borrowed from the private sector and entered into collective bargaining elections. Workers in these collective bargaining elections select an organization to represent them in negotiations with their employing governmental agency. These negotiations cover wages/salaries, fringe benefits, and working conditions.

Affirmative Action.   Affirmative action—a program that tries to bring blacks, Hispanics, women, and other historically underrepresented groups into state employment—has posed a serious challenge to the fundamental philosophy of civil service as well as the validity of civil service exams. Although civil service exams, according to critics, have a built-in bias toward white, middle-class males, since the latter half of the 1970s there has been substantial growth in state hiring from historically underrepresented groups and in promoting some of these individuals into key policymaking positions.

Recently, cuts in state employment have threatened the new jobs found by blacks, Hispanics, and women. Under traditional civil service practice, seniority determines layoff practices. Thus, those most recently hired—blacks, Hispanics, and women—were the first to be laid off. However, in 1980, legislation authored by Assemblyman Elihu Harris (Democrat-Berkeley) required that all layoffs be achieved without reducing the proportion of affirmative action jobs. As a result, senior white males found their job security threatened by those with less seniority because of race or gender. Serious questions about reverse discrimination have been raised.

In the 1980s affirmative action efforts have been paralleled by wom-

9-5 *Two state employees looking over some files. The bureaucracy feeds on paper!*

Photo courtesy Sacramento Bee

en's groups promoting "comparable worth" in the private and public sectors. Those supporting "comparable worth" argue that many women historically have been relegated to relatively low-paying jobs as secretaries, clerks, or nurses, but that these professions require substantial technical-academic skills and impose considerable responsibilities. Some males, it is argued, earn far more in jobs demanding substantially less training and fewer responsibilities. Critics of "comparable worth" argue that market place conditions, not some arbitrary authority, should determine salary structure.

Contracting for Services.   Can private business do the same job at less cost than the civil service? Court interpretations of the state constitution restrict the performance of routine jobs to state employees. Such jobs as freeway maintenance, janitorial work, or clerical tasks may not be contracted out to private firms. However, the legislature did approve a law in 1982 authored by Assemblyman Stan Statham (Republican-Chico), which established clear standards by which some state work may be contracted out to private firms.

PROBLEMS AND REFORM

California's plural executive has been the subject of considerable debate. Several reforms have been suggested ranging from abolishing all of the minor offices to elimination of one or two.

As discussed above, the duties of the secretary of state, controller, treasurer, and Board of Equalization are largely administrative. It has been suggested that they should be appointed by the governor. Further, the argument goes, electing executives who have little or no policymaking functions makes the office unnecessarily political. Reducing the number of elected executives would shorten the ballot and make voting less confusing to Californians. The plural executive also obscures responsibility. The average voter does not often know which elected executive is responsible for which policy area.

There are also good reasons why no change should be made. First, making these positions appointive would increase the governor's powers. Many feel that the governor is already too powerful. Second, electing these minor executive officers gives minorities and the politically disadvantaged an opportunity to get into politics at a statewide level. For example, two women, two blacks, and an Asian have recently been elected to some of these offices. Third, and perhaps most telling, is that the *rational-logical arguments* for change miss the *political argument*. California's voters do not want to give up their power to elect minor executives.

Another suggested reform would be to have the lt. governor run on the same ticket as the governor, as in half the states and in presidential/vice-presidential elections. Since the lt. governor is often the acting governor, the argument is that the occupant of that office should be someone who is in general agreement with the governor on the major issues.

Those who argue against change point out that historically, the lt. governor has usually (until recently) come from the same party as the governor. Further, they suggest the lt. governor has more authority acting as an independently elected official. A more modest reform of the lt. governor's office would be to eliminate this official's power to preside over the state senate and cast a tie-breaking vote, but this idea was rejected by voters in 1982.

Finally, the unusual situation of placing an elected nonpartisan superintendent of public instruction under the authority of a board appointed by a partisan governor has also evoked criticism. One suggested reform would be to elect the board, which would then appoint the superintendent.

Conclusion

How responsive to the needs of the public is California's bureaucracy? Being immune from political pressure, is the bureaucracy so independent that it pursues its own goals and ignores the public's? In theory, the constitution and statutes establish two kinds of executives—those who make policy and those who administer it. Those who make policy are either elected by the public or appointed by elected officials to positions *exempt* from civil service. On the other hand, those who administer policy—deliver services—are required to secure their positions by passing tests. Elected officials and exempt appointed officials are subject to election results; civil service personnel are not. In theory and in law, it appears that policymakers are subject to public will. But reality and theory are not always the same.

The some 2,300 part-time executives who serve on the various boards and commissions broaden the base of citizen participation in the administration of government, but at the same time, these citizen executives are sometimes in conflict-of-interest positions. This is particularly true for the professional, occupational, and product promotion bodies.

Until recently, boards and commissions were usually dominated by the very people they were supposed to regulate. Attorneys were appointed to the California Bar, dentists to the Board of Dental Examiners, doctors to the Board of Medical Quality Assurance, real estate brokers to the Real Estate Commission, and termite exterminators to the Structural Pest Control Board. The few public members on these bodies were heavily outnumbered. But under former Governor Jerry Brown, many of these boards and commissions were given a majority of public members, and, it is hoped, more accountability to the public.

SUMMARY

Clearly, in a democracy, there can be conflict between a professional civil service and the public. The pressures for affirmative action and for patronage appointments are good examples of that conflict. The plural executive obscures policy responsibility. And citizen executives are sometimes in conflict-of-interest positions. Yet in comparison to many other states, California has an efficient and responsible executive-administrative-bureaucratic system.

Whether the administrative system needs a major overhaul or just a tune-up is debatable. Nevertheless, the pressures for change will continue.

10

California State Finance: Revenues and Expenditures[1]

In this chapter, we will look at the political process by which the annual budget is put together. We will look at the money the state collects and the money it spends. And we will consider how well the process is working. Is it fair? Does it work for all Californians? Does it make sense?

If we are going to understand how policy is made we need to understand the budget process and what the annual budget fight is all about. First, the budget is *the central policy decision* made each year by government; it is the dollars-and-cents statement of *state policy and priorities*. No other decision is nearly as important! And since 1978, when voters approved Proposition 13's property tax cuts, state budget decisions have become even more important because they directly affect local government, too.

Second, it is important to understand that the state budget is closely linked to both the federal budget and the several thousand local budgets within California. While we will focus on the state budget in this chapter, we will also take into account local and federal budgets (revenues and expenditures) as they affect the state budget. As we will see, the state is quite often a "middleman" who collects and distributes more money than it controls. In fact, the state's direct expenditures are a small part of total government expenditures within California.

Third, budget size and complexity have grown markedly in the last few years. More and more groups of people are becoming involved in the budget process—usually represented by interest group lobbyists,

[1]The authors want to thank Elizabeth Kersten, Jim Pfiffner, and Mark Sektnan for their help in preparing this chapter.

legislative committee staff, local government agencies, or state government agencies.

Fourth, factions and partisanship have become increasingly significant.

Fifth, the state budget situation changes dramatically over relatively short time spans. During the Deukmejian years the state went from budget deficits in 1983–84 to substantial surpluses in 1985–86 to austerity in Governor Deukmejian's 1987–88 budget—triggered to a large extent by Paul Gann's spending limits initiative (Proposition 4, 1979). This initiative was designed to keep governmental taxing and spending in check. However, because of a sluggish economy and high inflation, the spending limits imposed by the initiative had not had to be confronted until the 1987–88 budget was formulated. Some Democratic experts argued that through judicious shifts in the budget the Gann strictures could be averted in 1987, but Governor Deukmejian disagreed, and his viewpoint eventually prevailed.

Sixth, no budget stands alone. Each budget is greatly influenced by those preceding it. Thus, each of the last three governors (Ronald Reagan, Jerry Brown, and George Deukmejian) found the tax and spending policies of previous administrations and legislatures substantially limiting their budget options.

Seventh, budget decisions made by state officials have an enormous impact on California citizens. For example, thousands of Californians suddenly became aware of the importance of the state budget on July 1, 1983. Because the budget had not been passed on time, the state had no spending authority (it could continue to collect taxes, however). Thus, some 130,000 Californians did not receive unemployment and disability insurance checks. After ten days of deadlock, the number of those waiting for state money grew to 400,000. By the end of the deadlock—just before the legislature passed and the governor signed the budget—$21 million in medical insurance payments had been withheld; another $8.9 million in doctor and drug bills were pending; at Napa State Hospital, vendors stopped delivery of gasoline for fire trucks and ambulances; and employees in several state agencies staged a work slowdown. In turn, those who did business with the state or its employees suddenly realized that when the state didn't pay its bills or payroll, they didn't get paid either.

THE BUDGET PROCESS

Administrative

Illustration 10–2 shows the budget process from the time some eighteen months before the start of the fiscal year (which begins each July 1) to the time the governor signs the budget. This is the *budget con-*

10-1 *Total state and local government expenditures 1986–87.*

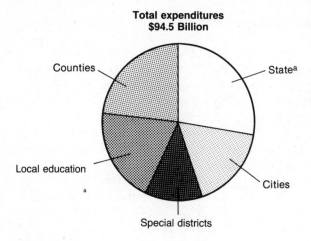

**Total expenditures
$94.5 Billion**

Counties

State[a]

Local education

Cities

Special districts

[a]Net state expenditures

Source: Legislative analyst, 1987–88 Budget.

struction phase, in which the document is prepared, evaluated, modified, and finally enacted. (*Budget implementation* takes place during the fiscal year when the authorized funds are spent.)

Essentially, the first six months are devoted to internal budget preparation by field offices and specific units of the larger departments. How many new file cabinets will the San Bernardino Highway Patrol office need? Does the Oroville office of the Water Resource Agency need a new pickup truck? How many faculty positions are needed in the political science department at San Jose State University? All the various offices of the state's many departments prepare budget requests.

Budget requests are based on three major considerations: first, *previous budget levels;* second, *estimated changes in workload* for the coming budget year; and third, *plans for new programs* and *modification or abandonment of old programs.* If, for example, the political science department expects more students in the budget year under consideration, it must estimate how many more faculty members will be needed to teach the increased number of students. How many more secretaries, how much more ditto paper, and so forth will also have to be estimated.

As the local agency and field office requests move up the bureaucratic ladder, they are combined and modified. By July, each department is working on its total budget—made up of all the "local" requests. By late August, each department submits its budget request to the Department of Finance, which represents the governor (see Chapter 9). In September, the Department of Finance meets with each de-

10-2 *Budget construction process for three fiscal years.*

	State Agencies, Departments, and Offices	Governor and Department of Finance	Legislature	
			Legislative Analyst	Legislators
Fiscal year 1				
January	Field			
February	offices			
March	prepare			
April	budget			
May	requests			
June	Departments work on budgets			
Fiscal year 2				
July				
August	Departments submit budgets to Department of Finance			
September	Department of Finance meets with departments			
October		Department of Finance prepares governor's budget	Budget analyst begins analysis of the budget	
November		Departments may meet with governor to appeal Department of Finance decisions		
December		Prepare final budget draft		
January		Governor submits budget to the legislature		
February			Analyst submits budget analysis to legislature	
March				Hold budget
April				hearings in committees
May				Conference committees
June		Governor vetoes parts of the budget he doesn't like, signs the rest		Pass budget
Fiscal year 3				
July		Budget goes into effect for fiscal year (July 1 to June 30)		Legislature may try for veto over-ride

10-3

Courtesy of Dennis Renault, Sacramento Bee

MATTER OVER MIND

partment's budget officer(s) to review their budget requests. In October, the Department of Finance prepares the governor's budget. And in November, each department head has the opportunity to meet with the governor to appeal Department of Finance decisions. After any final adjustments, the governor submits his budget to the legislature in early January.

In October, three months earlier, the legislature's budget analysis staff (in the legislative analyst's office) starts reviewing Department of Finance budget data. Working from Finance data and its own information, the analyst's office prepares a budget evaluation for the legislature.

After the budget has been introduced by the governor in January, lawmakers hold hearings on it. In reviewing the governor's budget, legislators rely heavily on the analyst's evaluation of the budget. Budget hearings are held by the assembly Ways and Means Committee and the senate Finance Committee in March, April, and early May. These hearings give the public (represented by interest group lobbyists, the state agencies, local governments, and, of course, legislators) an opportunity to support or oppose programs, suggest changes, or defend pet projects.

During this process, each house amends the governor's budget, so that by late May, there are in fact three budget documents: (1) the governor's original budget, (2) the assembly version, and (3) the senate version. These different documents reflect different goals and values and must be compromised in order to have a budget.

The first compromises occur within the legislature. The assembly and senate budget versions are sent to conference committee where one legislative budget is prepared. After the required two-thirds vote by both houses, the budget is sent to the governor. The constitutional deadline for sending the budget to the governor is June 15, which gives the governor fifteen days to act on the document before the start of the fiscal year. (In recent years, the legislature has often failed to meet the deadline.)

After receiving the budget, the governor meets with legislators, staff, and others to decide which sections are acceptable and which are not. California's constitution gives the governor item veto power, which means that the governor can eliminate or reduce budget items he does not like.

After signing the budget, the governor sends it back to the legislature. While the legislature has the constitutional authority to override the governor's vetoes by a two-thirds vote in each house, this seldom happens.

Thus, the governor has both the first and last word on the budget. He prepares it and submits it to the legislature. And, after the legislature sends it back to him, he has the item veto. As a result, the budgets signed into law usually look very much like the budget originally submitted by the governor some six months earlier.

Trailer Bill

At the same time the budget is being heard in the legislature, a trailer bill is prepared which amends state law as needed to accommodate changes required by the budget. Much of state spending policy is set out in statute—perhaps as much as 80 percent of general fund expenditures. Because the budget bill does not have legal authority to change (amend) a law already on the books, a separate bill must be passed by the legislature and signed by the governor to make the needed amendments. The budget today is, in effect, a policy plan for state government, and the trailer bill contains dozens of policy changes. A prime example of the trailer bill's function is in changing cost of living (COLAs) statutes. By law, welfare recipients and state employees are supposed to get annual cost of living adjustments in their benefits and salaries. But the tight budgets of the early 1980s did not meet these statutory requirements. A trailer bill, reducing COLAs to the amounts provided in the budget, was required.

Political

The governor has a broad range of legislative powers. This is particularly true if the governor is fiscally conservative and wants to cut the budget, eliminate regulations, or reduce the number of state employees. The governor, having prepared the budget and having the item veto, is in a very strong position to say no. Moreover, the regular veto gives the governor a weapon over lawmakers' others bills. However, if the governor has a program that requires legislation, he needs at least a majority vote in both houses before the bill can get to his desk for signature. It may be difficult to get those votes, particularly if the governor has vetoed some legislators' pet projects. But the governor has a lot to give: a signature on a bill, an appointment of a legislator's friend to some board or commission, and for lawmakers in the governor's own party, the promise of campaign support.

Legislators are usually no match for the governor in budget fights.[2] Each lawmaker must get a majority of votes in both houses for any legislation he or she may be supporting. To get the budget approved requires a two-thirds majority in both houses, which means some degree of bipartisan support. It also means that a disgruntled minority of one-third can block the budget. It takes a lot of compromise among legislators to get the budget approved. That compromise usually involves giving something to everyone.

In general, the rules and procedures favor a conservative position. There are many points along the legislative road at which a bill may be killed or a budget item reduced or eliminated.

Public Opinion

Another major dimension of budget politics is public opinion. Since the Proposition 13 property tax revolt of 1978, followed by the budget limit initiative of 1979 (Proposition 4), elimination of both gift and inheritance taxes (Proposition 6), indexing of the income tax (Proposition 7) in 1982, and Howard Jarvis's 1986 limit on local government's ability to levy taxes (Proposition 62), legislators and governors have become reluctant to propose new taxes. Public opinion about taxes and expenditures can be a crucial factor in policymaking. Opinion polls indicating

---

[2]The ability of the governor to get his way was highlighted in 1987 when, after months of opposition, Democratic legislative leaders decided to go along with Governor Deukmejian's proposal to eliminate the budget surplus by sending cash rebates to California taxpayers in 1988 (an election year).

10-4 *Governor Deukmejian's proposed 5 percent pay raise was protested by California State Employees Association members.*

Sacramento Bee *photo by Dick Schmidt*

the public's attitude about taxes and government services are closely watched. There is some modest new evidence suggesting that the tax revolt has perhaps reached its crest and is slowly subsiding. In 1987, Superintendent of Instruction Bill Honig was publicly locked in a bitter dispute with Governor Deukmejian over the former's demands for substantial increases in spending for public schools. Surveys suggest that citizens appear to be giving grudging but growing support to providing more money for public schools—even if it means new taxes.

The Governor's Goals and Priorities

Given the central role the governor plays in the budget process, the chief executive's goals and priorities have a substantial impact on the final document. Deukmejian came to office knowing exactly what he wanted to do with the budget. As a legislator (1963–78) and attorney general (1979–82), he had acquired a good grasp of the budget process. With his strong conservative ideology and tenacious political style, Governor Deukmejian has been able to impose his fundamental budget philosophy on the legislature and the state of California.

By refusing to consider any new taxes, the governor effectively set a ceiling on the state's budget. His next priority, has been to cut pro-

TABLE 10-1
1987–88 Expenditure Dollars (in millions)

Function	General Fund Expenditures	Special Fund Expenditures
Education (K–12)	$12,244.3	$ 79.5
Health and Welfare	9,295.0	177.6
Higher Education	4,969.0	4.0
Business, Transportation and Housing	73.8	2,391.4
Tax Relief	863.4	—
Local Government Subventions	0.5	2,940.9
Youth and Adult Correction Agency	1,873.4	26.6
Resources	667.7	402.0
State and Consumer Services	211.8	252.4
Other	1,064.7	391.1
Total	$31,263.6	$6,665.5

Source: Governor's Budget, 1987–88.

grams. Today, the Gann spending limits initiative (Proposition 4 passed in 1979) further strengthens the goveror's hand in promoting fiscal conservatism. Table 10–1 shows the proposed Deukmejian budget for 1987–88.

While Table 10–1 describes Governor Deukmejian's proposed spending for the various state agencies, it does not tell us about his specific priorities. For the most part, Governor Deukmejian has favored trimming spending for welfare and resources and increasing spending on public education and prisons. In 1983, Governor Deukmejian cut funds for the Coastal Commission by 18 percent from the previous year. In his 1987–88 budget Governor Deukmejian proposed increased spending for public education, criminal justice, state highways, toxic cleanup, Medi-Cal local assistance, and promotion of California products overseas. The legislative analyst argued that the Deukmejian budget underestimated the costs of school desegregation, child care, K–12 apportionments, Aid to Families with Dependent Children (AFDC), and child welfare services. Deukmejian critics contended that not enough was being proposed for public education or toxic cleanup, and that programs for gifted and talented children (GATE) should be continued. The battle over the budget by the various political forces is at the center of California politics.

The governor's fiscal strategy can also be influenced by political ambition. Certainly, Jerry Brown's swift conversion to support for fiscal restraint after Proposition 13 was approved was motivated, in part, by his ambition for higher office. No less ambitious, Governor Deukmejian understands the strong national position he will be in with Republicans if he holds the budget line in California. As his former finance director, Michael Franchetti, observed in 1983:

> It is the consensus of the governor's advisers as well as the Republican leadership in the senate and assembly that if the governor were to veto a billion and a half dollars out of this budget to avoid tax increases, he would literally be a national figure in the Republican party . . .[3]

The Legislature's Goals and Priorities

While one can usually identify the governor's goals and priorities, it is much harder to identify the legislature's goals and priorities. Initially, they are the sum of 120 individual legislator's goals and priorities. But each legislator quickly learns to compromise—to trade off with others. Some legislators have more power than others and so get more of what they want—in particular the assembly speaker, senate president pro tem, chair of the assembly Ways and Means Committee, and chair of the senate Finance Committee; minority leaders in the assembly and senate; as well as other legislators who are "close" to the leadership. But one reason individual legislators earn leadership positions is that they know how to work with other legislators.

The speaker is probably the single most powerful person in the legislature. For example, Speaker Brown decided to support Governor Deukmejian's 1983 tax loophole bill. Using parliamentary procedures, he was able to sidestep the usual lengthy committee hearing process. The tax loophole bill quickly passed the assembly. Senate leadership, however, decided to move slowly on the governor's bill, and the speaker could do nothing about it. Neither could the governor. In 1987, Speaker Brown and his Democratic assembly colleagues decided to employ a new tactic in confronting Governor Deukmejian's budget. Instead of the usual Ways and Means subcommittees debating the budget, Brown had the assembly convene on the floor as a "committee of the whole" (all members) to consider some of the more controversial parts of the governor's budget. Republican assemblymembers, for the most part, were unenthusiastic with this new format; Democrats hoped that it would focus public opinion on the budget and spending priorities.

And of course, legislators have pet projects near and dear to the hearts of their constituents or campaign supporters. They are quite willing to argue for these pet projects even while castigating the overall budget.

[3]*Sacramento Bee,* June 14, 1983.

Partisanship

Clearly, partisanship has become stronger in the assembly. On budget issues the combination of a militant Republican minority in the assembly and the constitutionally required two-thirds vote for both the budget and taxes give the Republican minority power to block the budget and any new taxes. If election fortunes should make the Democrats a minority party in the legislature, they too would have the choice to take advantage of the two-thirds rule. As long as the minority party has more than a third of the votes, it can block the budget and stop any taxation measures.

REVENUES

We are often reminded that death and taxes are inevitable. But unlike death, which falls evenly on all of us, some pay more in taxes than others.

The annual budget fight has two components: first, who pays for government services; and second, who gets those services. In this section, we will look at *who pays*. We will also consider the various *kinds of taxes* the state of California collects—the *tax structure*. And we will examine the *tax burden*—does everyone pay a *fair share?* We will also consider some of the *nonrevenue aspects of taxes*—the things that the tax structure does in addition to raising money for government programs.

But, first, what do we mean by the word *tax?* And how do we decide if a tax is *good* or *bad?* In general, a tax is the extraction of resources from citizens by government under law. At one time, people often paid their taxes "in kind" with grain or livestock or by labor on government projects.

Today, in our complex economy, most wealth is not in property or goods; most government jobs demand training and skills far beyond simple day labor; and money is *credit, checks, plastic cards,* and *computerized accounts.*

Thus, California's government revenue structure has become highly complex, involving over fifty different kinds of taxes, fees, and other revenue sources. Each of these serves a purpose, not only to raise money but often to balance inequities in another source, to encourage (or discourage) some particular activity, to compensate for hardship, or to tie in a government service with a fee imposed on those who use that service. Or more broadly, how do we evaluate the complex mix of government revenue sources that add up to the whole *revenue structure?*

There are several ways to do this:

1. Is the revenue source administratively efficient? Are the costs of collection low in comparison to the amounts collected?
2. Is the revenue source economically efficient? Does it cause a minimal interference with the state's economy?
3. Is it certain? Is collection unavoidable?
4. Is it predictable? Do people know how much it will be?
5. Is the tax or fee reasonable?
6. Is it equitable? Does the tax—or mix of taxes—fall evenly on everyone?

The first five tests are relatively easy to apply—efficiency, certainty, predictability, and the association of a fee with a service are not hard to determine and/or measure. The last test—*equality*—is more difficult to measure.

There are two dimensions to tax equality. First, *horizontal equality*—the idea that people in the same circumstances should pay the same amount in taxes. If you and your neighbor own the same type of tract home and receive the same governmental services (police, fire, trash removal, etc.), each should pay the same property tax. In fact, as a result of Proposition 13, if you recently bought your house but your neighbor lived there before 1978, you will pay far more property taxes than will your neighbor (the tax is based on what was paid for the property, not what it is worth).

The other dimension of tax equality is *vertical equality*. Essentially, the idea is that people with high incomes should pay a larger percentage of that income in tax than should people with low incomes. This is often called a *progressive tax*. The reason for it is that taxes should "hurt" everyone about the same. It wouldn't hurt as much to pay an 11 percent tax on a $50,000 income as on a $10,000 income. The idea of tax equality is reasonable but difficult to apply. The complex real life differences between individual taxpayers cannot be easily equated, not even with the most complex tax structures. At best, the notion of tax equality is a goal worth striving for but never achieved.

In addition to trying to make taxes fair while producing revenue for the state, California (like the federal government and other states) tries to use tax laws to promote certain social or economic goals. One can deduct charitable contributions, mortgage interest payments, and sales taxes paid in the year from state income taxes. Each dependent child is "worth" a tax reduction of thirteen dollars. The idea behind these deductions and tax credits is to encourage home buying and contributions to charity, and to recognize the cost of children. The rationale for cigarette and alcohol taxes is that these are "sin" products and making them more expensive for Californians may discourage their use.

California collects many different kinds of revenues to support gov-

10-5 *General fund revenues and transfers, 1987–88.*

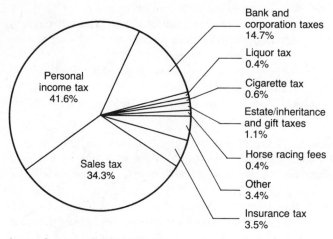

Bank and
corporation taxes
14.7%

Liquor tax
0.4%

Cigarette tax
0.6%

Estate/inheritance
and gift taxes
1.1%

Horse racing fees
0.4%

Other
3.4%

Insurance tax
3.5%

Personal
income tax
41.6%

Sales tax
34.3%

Source: Governor's Budget, 1987–88

ernmental activities. But unlike the federal government, it has not engaged in deficit financing. A constitutional prohibition against deficit spending (Article XVI, Section 1) is supposed to prohibit that. This does not mean that the state may not spend more in a year than it collects. It does mean that it cannot spend more than it has (this year's collections plus last year's surplus). The Governor's successful deficit "roll over" in 1983 indicates how this can be done.

While the state has many kinds of revenue sources, most of its money comes from two taxes: (1) the sales tax, and (2) the personal income tax. The remainder comes from a wide variety of sources (see Illustration 10–5).

Sales Tax

One of California's major revenue sources is the sales tax (6 cents on each dollar of taxable purchases). Some basic necessities, such as food, prescription drugs, and utilities, are not taxed. The major attractiveness of this tax is that it is easy and inexpensive to collect and generates large revenue. But the sales tax is considered *regressive* by many critics because it imposes a heavier burden on the poor who spend more of their income on sales tax items than do the rich.

Personal Income Tax

California's other large revenue source is the personal income tax. The tax rate is *progressive*—the rate increases as personal income increases. But like other states, the tax rates are low—1 to 11 percent (in 1988 with the new tax reform, 1 to 9.3 percent). Income tax rates levied by the federal government are considerably higher (12 to 50 percent). Since 1971, California has utilized payroll withholding to collect income tax. This has increased compliance and produced a steady flow of revenue into the treasury. In 1982, voters approved a constitutional income tax indexing proposal. Now tax brackets move up with inflation.

Bank and Corporate Franchise and Income Taxes

The state also levies taxes on business income and collects a fee for the right to do business in California. For years one of the more controversial taxes California (and a few other states) imposed was the unitary tax. Basically, under the unitary framework companies doing business in California were taxed on the basis of their worldwide profits adjusted for property, payroll and sales in the state. Under the unitary system international corporations (Japanese, German, British, etc., as well as some American) paid higher taxes than local domestic corporations. The unitary tax conflict battle pitted, in particular, Japanese high-tech industries versus domestic Silicon Valley firms. In 1986, through the leadership of Governor Deukmejian, who strongly supports promoting California products internationally, the state substantially modified its unitary tax. Business taxes are the third ranking source of state governmental revenue in California.

Other Taxes

Several other taxes generate significant state general revenues. These include taxes on insurance companies, horse track racing, cigarettes, and alcoholic beverages. None of them alone produce a very large part of total revenue, but together they are important.

Lottery

In 1984 California voters approved a statewide lottery with part of the proceeds to be distributed to the state's schools. In 1986–87 the University of California received $15.1 million; California State University, $27 million; community colleges, $72.4 million; and public K–12 schools, $484.1 million (eighty-eight dollars per pupil). While the lottery generates a half billion dollars a year for public education, ticket buyers tend to be low-income individuals. So the lottery becomes, in effect, a regressive "tax."

Special Fund and Nontax Revenues

In addition to general fund revenues discussed above, the state also collects additional funds which are designated by law for specific purposes.

Federal Funds

Revenues from the federal government included in California's state government budget are important both in the total amount ($15.3 billion in 1986–87) and in the programs they support. For example, one dollar out of every two spent by the state of California on health and welfare comes from the federal government. The federal government also plays a major finance role in transportation, unemployment, health, and education, among many programs. About $3 out of every $10 administered by the state comes from the federal government.

TAX BURDEN

Tax burden means two things: (1) how much does the *average citizen* pay in taxes and fees, and (2) is the burden the same for everyone? By adding all state revenues and dividing by the state's total population, we find that in 1985–86 the average burden was 9.6 percent of personal income.

But is the burden the same for everyone? Obviously not! "Average" ignores the many individual differences: number of children, obligations, whether one owns or rents his or her home, medical expenses, and so forth. In a sense, the tax burden is inescapably different.

One major factor contributing to the average tax burden is the extent to which people actually pay the taxes they owe. A recent study by the Franchise Tax Board found that the state of California lost $1.9 billion in tax revenues in 1981 due to underpayment or nonpayment of taxes. This was more than the state's total budget deficit for 1983–84. Nonfiling seems to be the major cause of lost revenues. Underreported income accounted for the greatest single loss—some $1.3 billion; overstating deductions and credits accounted for another $246 million.

But the major cause of what some believe to be unequal tax burdens is in the tax structure itself—the mixed impact of sales and income tax rates, assessment of property, and levels of taxation on some kinds of commodities and services.

Some types of income are taxed while other types are not. Social security benefits, scholarships, food stamps, and welfare benefits—and a wide range of other programs designed to help the poor—are not considered income for tax purposes. At the other end of the economic ladder, high-income individuals have real estate depreciation, interest deductions, income deferrals, and capital gains to reduce their tax burden.

Overall, it would be fair to state that those with higher incomes pay a larger share of that income in taxes than do those with lower incomes. In terms of burden, however, it would be hard to assert that the wealthy feel as much tax pain as do the middle- and lower-income payers.

In times of tight government budgets, there are two alternatives—either cut spending or increase taxes. Where can or should the state increase taxes? There are two general answers: first, by increasing existing taxes; second, by adding new ones. If large amounts are needed, the state would be well advised to either increase the sales tax one cent (from 6 percent to 7 percent) or raise the income tax brackets by 1 percent. A one-cent increase in the sales tax would produce almost $2 billion more in tax revenues each year; the 1 percent income tax increase would yield about $1.75 billion.

Higher tobacco and alcohol taxes appeal to the general public—perhaps because they view them as fair taxes (the wages of sin)! California's liquor taxes are 40 percent lower than the national average. According to Common Cause, "Just bringing California into line with other states on alcohol taxes would raise an estimated $176.6 million a year." However, alcohol and tobacco taxes are essentially sales taxes paid by the consumer. As such, they contribute to the *regressive* nature of the tax structure.

Another potential source of added revenue would be split-roll property tax and a state lottery. A split-roll proposal by Assemblyman Dave Elder (Long Beach) began circulation in mid-1983, and would create two property tax roles—one for residential property, the other for business property. Residences would continue to be taxed at 1 percent of assessed value, but business property would be taxed at 2.5 percent. Residential property would not be reassessed on resale, while business property would be reassessed every year. Such a proposal would shift much of the property tax burden from residential to business property while raising substantial tax revenues.

EXPENDITURES

General fund expenditures can be classified in two ways: first, the *structure* of expenditures; second, the *function* of expenditures. Illustration 10–6 shows the *structure* of California's budget expenditures. Almost half of the budget, goes to assist local governments, primarily school districts. Another large part goes to aid individuals at the local level. Of the total general fund budget, the state spends only 26.3 percent directly at the state level.

Another way to look at expenditures is by *function* or *policy*. Illus-

10-6 *General fund budget structure, 1987–88.*

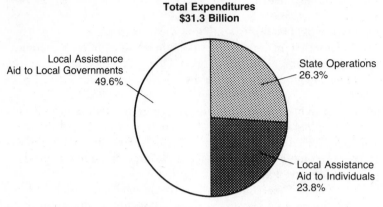

**Total Expenditures
$31.3 Billion**

Local Assistance
Aid to Local Governments
49.6%

State Operations
26.3%

Local Assistance
Aid to Individuals
23.8%

Source: Legislative analyst, 1987–88 Budget.

10-7 *Expenditures 1986–87 fiscal year.*

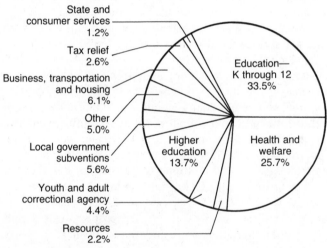

State and
consumer services
1.2%

Tax relief
2.6%

Business, transportation
and housing
6.1%

Other
5.0%

Local government
subventions
5.6%

Youth and adult
correctional agency
4.4%

Resources
2.2%

Education—
K through 12
33.5%

Health and
welfare
25.7%

Higher
education
13.7%

Source: Governor's Budget, 1986–87.

tration 10–7 shows us which programs get the most money and which get the least. Public education (K–12) gets the most, closely followed by health and welfare. It is important to note that both of these programs are almost totally administered at the local level. Higher education is the only "big-ticket" item in the general fund budget on which the state spends directly. In short, most state money is spent at the local level by local government agencies. The state collects the money, but the counties, school districts, special districts, and cities spend it!

Much of this is the result of post-Proposition 13 "bail-out" funding by the state for local government to make up for lost property tax revenues. Much of the budget growth since 1978 has been due to increases in local government assistance!

Tax Expenditures

Tax expenditures are another important piece in the budget jigsaw. *Tax expenditures* are popularly known as *loopholes*—devices by which taxes are avoided or reduced. Once written into law, they tend to remain, and the lost tax revenue tends to be forgotten—until it is needed. The legislative analyst reported that tax expenditures totaled nearly $17 billion in 1986! The largest single expenditure was the deductability of mortgage interest expenses. Few loopholes ever get closed because of powerful interest group pressure, and new loopholes tend to be added each year. Some of these loopholes were removed in the historic new tax reform law of 1987. However, not all tax loopholes were removed and some new ones were added. It is inevitable that various interests will seek tax relief in the next budget go-round and in the years that follow.

BUDGET GROWTH AND CHANGE

A number of factors contribute to budget growth and change. Some are beyond the state's control—population growth, inflation, the nation's economic health, or natural disasters. Other factors—the decision to add or expand programs, or to cut or add taxes—are within political control of the legislature, governor, courts, and voters.

Perhaps, the most important new ingredient influencing budget growth is, as we have noted previously, Proposition 4 of 1979. Briefly, this Gann initiative:

1. Limits the level of tax-funded appropriations which can be made by state and local governments in any year to the limit for the prior year (base year was 1978–79) adjusted for cost of living and population changes.
2. Requires state and local government to return to taxpayers any monies that exceed the amount that can be appropriated.
3. Requires the state to reimburse local governments and school districts for the cost of complying with state mandates.

The 1986–87 fiscal year is the first one in which the state's budget was close to the limit. Governor Deukmejian proposed that the legislature prioritize and choose which programs to fund in order to comply with Proposition 4. The governor also wanted a "rainy day" reserve of approximately $1 billion. The legislative analyst's office proposed that

10-8

Courtesy of Dennis Renault, Sacramento Bee

'I'VE GOT THIS SPLITTING HEADACHE FOR SOME REASON.'

the legislature consider: (1) relying more on voter approved bonds; (2) relying more on user fees, penalties and permits; (3) giving excess revenues to local agencies; and (4) establishing additional tax expenditure programs. Battles over the budget are at the heart of the California political process.

SUMMARY

When state government rescued local government after Proposition 13, local governments lost substantial control over their revenues (see Chapter 12). Yet citizens expect their local governments—city, county, or school district, for example—to make program decision, determine policy, and decide how to spend the money. But local governments often cannot make those decisions because along with state money comes state control. This means that locally elected officials—particularly in counties and school districts—are often unable to respond to local citizen desires. Can the state restore local control? Is local government ready to make the hard decisions which are now made in the state capitol?

In the state legislature, a minority of legislators frequently take advantage of the two-thirds vote requirement for both the budget and new taxes—denying the majority will. Should the state budget be held hostage by a minority? Should the Gann spending initiative be amended to provide for more fiscal flexibility? Is the California tax structure reasonably equitable? Given the state's tight budgets, tax loopholes are under close scrutiny. Will some be closed in the near future? These are some of the questions that decision makers will be wrestling with in the future in reforming and/or changing the budget process system in California.

Perhaps most fundamental of all, will California voters learn the fundamental civics lesson of Proposition 13? You can't make a massive tax cut and expect government services to remain at the same level. It's clear that the voters believed in 1978 that they could cut the property tax by over 50 percent without hurting services. As we will see in Chapter 12, they were wrong. There is no free lunch. If the state had not replaced the revenues lost by local governments in 1978, the voters might have realized that fundamental truth in 1979. Others believe that the government provides too many services and would like to see more cuts. In the long run, tax levels and programs will change as the voters' needs change. Budget policy is never fixed and pressures to reform the process will continue.

11

California's Justice System

For most Californians, the state's justice system is represented by the traffic officer, "bail by mail," or lurid newspaper headlines describing the latest sensational trial. Yet the system is much more than that. And for students of state government, the justice system is very significant because unlike health, welfare, or transportation, the justice system remains one of the few governmental activities still mainly a *state function*.

Nine out of ten cases in the United States are heard before state courts: attorneys are licensed to practice by states; and corrections—jail, prison, parole, and probation—are largely state activities. For most citizens, it is state laws which have the most frequent and immediate impact. It is state courts, as Justice William Brennan once observed, that deal with the day-to-day issues of life, liberty, and property—marriage, divorce, annulment, juveniles, will probate, contracts, consumer protection, and a variety of other subjects. For some the state's justice system is their most frequent contact with government.

Clearly, the justice system is not just the courts. Equally vital are police, district attorneys, public defenders, private attorneys, witnesses, trial and grand juries, jail guards and prison officials, and probation and parole officers. Each plays an important part in adjudicating conflict, allocating rewards, imposing punishment, and attempting to rehabilitate.

These functions can be divided into two categories—criminal and civil. In a criminal case, the state acts as prosecutor against an individual charged with violating some criminal statute. A civil suit, on the other hand, is usually between two private parties; the state is not a party to their dispute.[1]

FUNCTIONS OF THE JUDICIAL SYSTEM
Criminal

Criminal cases fall into three categories: felonies, the most serious; misdemeanors, less serious; and infractions, minor violations. Felonies involve criminal acts such as murder, rape, or armed robbery. Conviction of a felony may carry a penalty of one or more years in state prison, a heavy fine, or both. Misdemeanors involve crimes such as assault, drunk driving, or speeding. If found guilty, the defendant may be imprisoned in county jail, fined, or placed on probation. In felony and serious misdemeanor cases, the defendant must appear before the court and enter a plea (guilty or not guilty).

For less serious misdemeanors—an illegal U-turn, for example— the accused may post bail (often by mail) and, failing to appear, automatically plead guilty and forfeit bail as a fine. The least serious crimes (infractions) are acts such as jaywalking, driving a motor vehicle with a faulty headlight, illegal parking, or a minor animal control law. In an effort to relieve courts of an ever-increasing crush of cases, the legislature has eliminated the right to jury trial in these cases, and the accused is not guaranteed legal counsel. Punishment is limited to fines.

Civil

California state courts hear over 1 million civil cases each year. Essentially, there are two kinds of civil cases. In civil cases at law, *the plaintiff* sues *the defendant* for damages—usually a certain amount of money. Such suits may arise from property damage, personal injury, medical malpractice, or failure to live up to contractual obligation. A civil case *in equity* is brought to prevent harm or irreparable damage (for example, the plaintiff asks the court to issue an *injunction,* a court order prohibiting a defendant from doing something). Equity also involves such things as probate of wills, administration of trusts, or divorce.

[1]On occasion, the state can be a party to a civil suit—for example, if they seek damages in a consumer fraud case.

ESTABLISHING THE SYSTEM

Much of California's justice system is established in Article VI of the state constitution. Included are features such as: the court structure, the Judicial Council, Commission of Judicial Performance, and the state bar. Article I provides for basic citizen rights including grand juries and trial juries, and allows the state to imprison a person for a crime.

The state legislature is another link in the justice system. Thus, the Department of Corrections was established by an act of the legislature. Recently, lawmakers set up three night trial courts on an experimental basis. The legislature has also recently reformed divorce proceedings, and they abolished the state's indeterminate sentencing laws by replacing them with a form of fixed-term penalties.

The California supreme court also plays a key role in the justice system through its interpretation of the state constitution and laws. In 1974, the court held that justice court judges had to be attorneys in cases where the defendant might, if convicted, be sentenced to jail.

Another important source of legal rules is the California Judicial Council. Under the authority and limits of the state constitution and codes, the council has the power to establish court rules of procedure.

Cities and counties play an important role, too. The county board of supervisors appoints the public defender and is responsible for the operating budget of the sheriff, public defender, and district attorney. However, both the district attorney and sheriff are directly elected by the voters. Cities are directly responsible for the selection and quality of their police departments.

COURTS

There are four levels to the California court system (Illustration 11–1): (1) municipal and justice courts—sometimes known as inferior courts, (2) superior courts, (3) district courts of appeal, and (4) the state supreme court. For the most part, municipal, justice, and superior courts are trial courts where cases are first heard. District courts and the supreme court are appeals courts; they hear cases brought to them on appeal from the trial courts. The Judicial Council oversees the entire operation of California's court system.

Inferior Courts

Municipal and justice courts handle the vast majority of court cases in California—about 96 percent of over 18.2 million filings per year. These are the courts with which most of us have come in contact. They process millions of parking citations and traffic violations each year.

11-1 *California court system.*

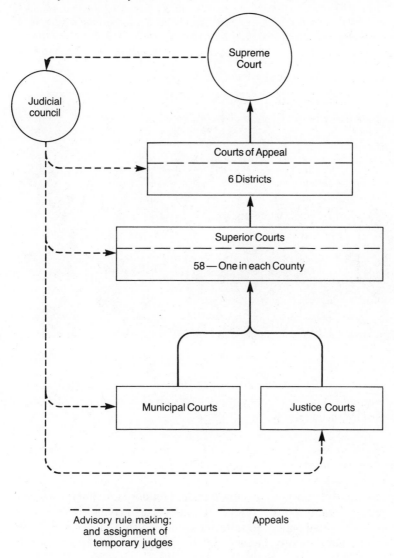

(Nine out of ten parking and traffic cases never go to trial but are settled at the bail clerk's window.)

Jurisdiction. Municipal and justice courts jurisdictions are the
same. They hear civil suits of less than $15,000, small claims ($1,500
or less), minor traffic violations, and some lesser crimes which do not
have penalties of more than one year in jail or a fine of more than
$1,000.

11-2 *California's new State Supreme Court. Standing from left to right are: Justice Edward A. Panelli, Justice David N. Eagleson, Justice John A. Arguelles, and Justice Marcus M. Kaufman. Seated from left to right are Justice Stanley Mosk, Chief Justice Malcolm M. Lucas, and Justice Allen E. Broussard. In 1987 Governor Deukmejian filled three vacancies on the court, created when the voters removed Chief Justice Rose Bird and Justices Cruz Reynoso and Joseph Grodin.*

Courtesy of Administrative Office of the Courts

Justice courts serve rural areas of the state. As California has become more urban, the number of justice courts has declined. Municipal courts serve urban areas.

Small Claims.   Both justice and municipal courts serve as small claims courts in cases involving amounts of $1,500 or less. Unlike other courts, no attorneys are allowed. The parties to disputes over unpaid bills, a defective refrigerator, or a smashed fender argue their own case before the judge (there is no jury). Unlike cases brought before other courts, most small claims go to trial (about two-thirds).

Small claims, is not, however, the "people's court" as it is often said to be. A 1979 study by the state's Department of Consumer Affairs and the state Judicial Council revealed that almost six out of ten cases filed in small claims courts were by corporations, other businesses, or government agencies. These cases most often involved suits over credit or loan transactions.

Superior Court

There are over 630 superior court judges in California. Each county has at least one superior court, and large counties are divided into several departments, with judges specializing in various kinds of law (family, juvenile, probate, or criminal).

Superior courts have original jurisdiction over (1) civil cases where the suit is for at least $15,000, (2) divorce and dissolution of marriage regardless of amounts involved, (3) probate, (4) major crimes that carry a penalty of one year or more in state prison, and (5) cases involving juveniles. Superior courts also act as courts of appeal from the inferior courts.

A small proportion of court cases are heard in superior courts— approximately 730,000 a year (out of 18.2 million). Of these, less than one in twelve is a criminal case. And about one in nine involves juveniles. Most superior court cases involve family law (40 percent), probate and guardianship (17 percent), and civil suits. Most cases are settled either before trial (40 percent) or after an uncontested trial (49 percent).

Probation.   Attached to each county superior court is a probation department. This department is concerned with criminal cases as well as custody of juvenile wards of the court. Probation departments provide background information to the court about criminal defendants critical in determining sentence.

Courts of Appeal

District Courts.   California is divided into six court of appeals districts. About 60 percent of these cases are brought on appeal from a lower court—usually a superior court. Very few cases are appealed further—about one in seventy of those heard in the superior courts.

Cases brought on appeal usually concern an interpretation of law. Arguments are presented in written form to three judges. There is seldom any oral argument, and there is no jury.

While much has been made in recent years of so-called abuses of the appeal process, in fact few criminal defendants exercise their right to appeal. And of those that do appeal, only 5 percent succeed.

Supreme Court

The state supreme court is at the top of California's judicial structure. Very few cases, less than 4,000 a year, reach the court. The court usually has discretionary jurisdiction; it decides if the case is important enough to be heard. Most of the cases heard by the Supreme Court come on appeal, and the court automatically reviews all death penalty cases.

Essentially, the court only considers cases involving a substantial question of public policy. State supreme court written opinions—about

11-3 *Qualifications and terms for California courts.*

Court	Term	Qualifications*
Justice court	6 years	Member of state bar
Municipal court	6 years	Member of state bar for five years or judge of a court of record
Superior court	6 years	Member of state bar for ten years; citizen of United States for five years; resident of county for two years
District court of appeals	12 years	Member of state bar for ten years or judge of a court of record; citizen of United States
State supreme court	12 years	Same as district court

*Judges must also be registered voters in order to run for reelection.

160 per year—are based on interpretations of the California constitution and statutes. The court's decisions are final except for appeal to the U.S. Supreme Court (which rarely happens).

Judicial Council

California, like most other states, has a judicial council which oversees the state court system. The chief justice of the California supreme court chairs the council and appoints fourteen judges to it. The state bar appoints four members, and each house of the legislature appoints one.

The major responsibility of the council is to study the state's court system and make recommendations to the legislature for needed constitutional or statutory changes.

SELECTION AND RECRUITMENT OF JUDGES

All California judges must be members of the state bar when selected. In addition, they must meet separate standards for the different levels of the court system (see Illustration 11–3). The governor nominates judicial candidates to the appellate (supreme and appeals) courts and to the trial courts (superior and municipal). Before designating his judicial choices, the governor is required to consult the Judicial Nominee Evaluation Commission (to be discussed later), comprised of nineteen attorneys elected by the bar association and six public members selected by the governor. The twenty-five member Commission is charged with determining the fitness of prospective candidates and has ninety days to make its assessment. While the governor is not required to follow commission recommendations, a public finding leveled against a governor's judicial prospect would be embarrassing. After the governor nominates judicial candidates for the appellate courts, they must be approved by the Commission on Judicial Appointments (comprised of the chief justice, attorney general, and senior presiding justice on the court of appeals). Normally, the commission goes along with a governor's judicial choices. On only two occasions in its nearly one-half century history has this commission failed to approve a governor's candidate. Finally, at the bottom rung of the judicial ladder, justice court appointments are made by the various county boards of supervisors. Few judges are initially elected to office; most are first appointed to fill a vacancy. Following appointment, the judge must run for election for the balance of the term at the next regularly scheduled election. And in order to serve for another term, a judge must run for reelection.

Appellate court judges have usually served on lower courts, typically a county superior court. Sometimes, however, the governor will nominate someone to a district court of appeals or the state supreme court who has had little or no prior judicial experience. Governors usually justify such "inexperienced" appointments on the basis that the supreme court is a policymaking body and that the appointees' social philosophy and personal values are of greater importance than judicial experience.

Prior to the 1970s, governors' nominees to the supreme court and the appeals court generally were made on the basis of judicial experience and competence. As partisanship has increased over the last several decades, governors increasingly have nominated or appointed judges who share their own values and frequently belong to the same political party. This does not mean that the appointees are not qualified, but rather that politics is an inseparable part of the judicial process.

Electing Judges

Should judges run for election like other political candidates? After all, federal judges, once appointed, remain on the court until they die, resign, or on rare occasions are impeached. They never have to stand for election, and, it is argued, they can be more independent because of this. Judges in California after initial appointment must run for election to hold their position, and they also can be recalled. This probably makes California judges more accountable to the public than their federal counterparts, but this feature also helps politicize our courts.

In an attempt to minimize politics, all judicial elections in the state are nonpartisan. Moreover, appellate court judges do not face actual opponents. Voters are asked "yes or no" whether a particular judge should be elected.

11-4

JUDICIAL	Vote Yes or No for Each Candidate

For Chief Justice of the Supreme Court

Shall ROSE ELIZABETH BIRD be elected to the office for the term prescribed by law?	**YES 69** ➤
	NO 70 ➤

Source: Butte County Clerk's Office, 1986 Ballot.

In trial court elections, an incumbent judge can be challenged by an opponent. In an occasional open judgeship (perhaps the incumbent has died and the governor has not nominated a replacement), there might be a half dozen or so judicial candidates who might file for the office.

Trial Court Judicial Elections

As a general rule, most trial court judges are not challenged for reelection. Usually, about 90 percent of these judges face no opposition and are automatically reelected. In these uncontested races little campaign money is spent; judges can coast to reelection. Many voters have little notion about the merits or demerits of their local judge (unless they have had to spend time in court as defendants, witnesses, or jurors). Even in the 10 percent of judicial races that are contested, incumbents invariably prevail. They are usually better known; can list their profession as, for example, superior court judge; can engage in local community charitable activities, can perform marriages for what may be potential voters, and can usually raise more campaign money than their opponent (usually most judicial race campaign money comes from local attorneys vitally concerned about the election outcome). Defeat usually requires an unusual set of circumstances. Thus, in 1970, a judge of the Los Angeles superior court, Alfred Gitelson, lost reelection after he issued a highly unpopular decision in a school desegregation case. In 1974, a San Francisco Superior court judge lost an election because voters thought he had been too lenient in sentencing a rapist. In 1982 out of some ninety low-profile superior court races in Los Angeles County, only one incumbent was defeated: Kenneth Byung-Cho Chang. Racism clearly contributed to Judge Chang's defeat.

In the late 1970s, as the crime issue became a central concern to citizens, a growing number of superior and municipal court judges (twenty-eight out of several hundred running in 1978) found themselves challenged by opponents—frequently, district attorneys who stressed they would be "tough on law and order." Since 1978 though there has been a steady decline in the number of trial court judges challenged (in 1986 only nine superior court judges faced an opponent, and of these only one incumbent lost). The crime issue seems to have faded and, in addition, former Chief Justice Rose Bird may have served as a convenient lightening rod for court bashing in the 1980s.

Appellate Court Elections

Prior to the 1960s appellate court elections were considered pro forma—the percentage of the public voting yes usually ranged from 90 to 95 percent. The California Supreme Court had a well-deserved national reputation for the quality of its highest court. In the 1960s the public attitude toward the state supreme court began to change. The civil rights struggle, mandatory busing, rights of defendants, and reapportionment were issues that sorely divided Californians, and decisions made by this liberal court were inevitably unpopular with conservatives. Through the late 1960s and early 1970s the percentage of the public voting no on supreme court justices tended to steadily increase.

When Governor Jerry Brown nominated Rose Bird to be chief justice of the supreme court, conservatives were quick to denounce her appointment. Bird's critics argued that she had no previous judicial experience; and that the appointment was designed to appease women's groups. Not unexpectedly, several incumbent justices on the court were upset that they weren't selected for this post. After her selection to the court, Chief Justice Bird became a consistent member of the liberal bloc on the state court at a time when crime was quickly becoming the number 1 state issue. While the public and state legislature were clamoring for tougher penalties, and, in particular, the death penalty, Justice Bird and the liberal majority tended to emphasize defendants' legal rights, police abuse, and illegal search and seizure issues. The liberal majority on the court were also proabortion and supportive of affirmative action which further antagonized conservatives.

In 1978 in her first election confirmation, Rose Bird received the lowest percentage of yes votes (52 percent) ever. Several other liberal judges up for confirmation in 1978 had only 55 to 60 percent approval votes.

After narrowly squeeking through in their confirmation elections, the liberal bloc on the court were immediately confronted with a host of new controversial issues. In December 1978 a charge was leveled at the Chief Justice that she had delayed issuing a decision ("use a gun—go to jail") until after the election because it would have been unpopular, and there was a Commission on Judicial Performance (to be discussed later) investigation of the court. While charges of delay were never proved, the once lofty reputation of the court was badly tarnished. In the early 1980s unhappy Republican legislators and other conservative activists launched a steady stream of initiatives, many of which came under legal challenge and eventually reached the supreme court. When Chief Justice Bird and the liberal judges supported a Democratic position, they were attacked for being partisan. On several occasions conservative activists began recall drives against Rose Bird, though none ever succeeded.

Six of the seven supreme court judges were up for reconfirmation in the 1986 election. Two judges, Malcolm Lucas and Edward Panelli, appointees of Governor Deukmejian, were supported by conservative groups and were never seriously threatened. Judge Stanley Mosk, originally nominated by Governor Pat Brown, was on some conservatives' hit lists, but was viewed as being more politically independent than his other liberal colleagues and was not a prime target of conservatives. Chief Justice Bird and Justices Cruz Reynoso and Joseph Grodin were the focal point of conservative anger. Bird and her liberal colleagues were attacked for various reasons but, clearly, the most damaging issue for the liberal bloc was the failure of the court to order an execution of a prisoner during the tenure of Chief Justice Bird. And public opinion polls in California show a growing public support (by the 1980s about 70 percent) for the imposition of this penalty.[2] Yet from 1978 to 1986 none of the 213 convicts on death row was sent to the gas chamber, and in 52 out of 55 cases (the other three were under federal review) the Supreme Court reversed lower court death rulings on procedural grounds or because of the vagueness of the Briggs Death Penalty Initiative law.

For the first time in state history, the former rubber-stamp Supreme Court confirmation elections were at the center of a California state election. Because of her controversial status and Democratic fears that her coattails might drag other Democrats and the other liberal judges down to defeat in 1986, Democratic officeholders faced a dilemma. Some Democratic leaders publicly urged Justice Bird not to seek reelection; others refused to get involved in the race contending the decision was up to the voters; a few Democratic state legislators announced they were opposed to her; and a handful (including Speaker Willie Brown and Pro Tem David Roberti) urged voters to support her.

The targeted liberal judges and their outspoken opponents (Republican state senator leader H. L. Richardson was their chief spokesman) waged a campaign unparalleled in judicial election history. Supreme court campaigns in 1986 resembled partisan campaigns—complete with

---

[2]Two recent Field Polls attest to voters' pro-death penalty attitudes. In April 1985 voters agreed (67 percent yes, 24 percent no) that "in death penalty cases the court has gone too far in protecting the rights of those convicted of murder." In October 1986 just prior to the Bird confirmation election, when respondents who opposed Bird were asked why they did, they overwhelmingly cited her death penalty position (45 percent).

public relations firms, fund raising, television spots, and negative hit pieces. Millions were raised by the campaign committees working against the liberal judge trio and they, in turn, raised lesser but substantial amounts in their own behalf. Chief Justice Bird noted during and after the election that her efforts to win reelection were complicated by the fact that judicial rules forbade justices from commenting on pending court cases.

In the November 1986 general election, for the first time in state history, three justices on the supreme court (Bird, Reynoso, and Grodin) lost their reelection bids. Only 33.8 percent of California voters voted yes on Bird, and the margins against Reynoso and Grodin, while not as one-sided, were decisive. It is not clear whether future supreme court confirmation elections will be as bitter as those of 1986, but the potential is there.

The defeat of the three liberal judges gave Governor Deukmejian the opportunity to nominate (some might say "pack" the Supreme Court with) three new, conservative judges—Marcus Kaufman, David Eagleson, and John Arguelles. He also appointed a new chief justice from the holdover members, Malcolm Lucas. Clearly, the new court is likely to veer to a more conservative tack in its decision making in the years ahead.

Commission on Judicial Nominee Evaluation

This twenty-five-member commission evaluates all potential judicial nominees before the governor appoints them. A nominee is rated on a four-point scale from "exceptionally well qualified" to "well qualified" to "qualified" to "unqualified." A governor is not required to follow the commission's recommendation.

Commission on Judicial Appointments

The three-member Commission on Judicial Appointments has the authority to approve or reject the governor's appointments to the court of appeals and supreme courts.

Most nominations cause little controversy, but also, most governors try to make nominations that will win the commission's approval. Thus, though seldom fully exercised, the commission's power is potentially important.

Commission on Judicial Performance

The Commission on Judicial Performance reviews the quality and performance of judges after they have been appointed. The commission receives, investigates, and evaluates all complaints against California judges. The commission has nine members: five judges appointed by the supreme court, two lawyers appointed by the state bar, and two laypersons appointed by the governor (subject to senate approval). If the commission finds that a judge has performed in an unprofessional manner, it makes a report to the state supreme court, and the court has the authority to discipline or even remove the judge.

The commission receives about 300 complaints a year, of which some 200 to 230 will concern a judge's ruling or some other legal problem. These complaints are not considered by the commission. But some 70 to 80 complaints about unprofessional or improper conduct are investigated. Between 1961 (when the commission was established) and 1986, nine judges were removed from office, two were involuntarily retired, thirteen were censured, and seventy-three retired or resigned while under investigation.[3] In addition, a number of judges have been privately reprimanded for misconduct.

As discussed previously, in December 1978, the commission was requested by the chief justice to investigate the state supreme court following charges that the court (or some of its members) deliberately delayed highly controversial decisions until after the November 1978 elections.

The commission's hearings—held in public—revealed a court badly split by both ideological and personality conflicts. On November 5, 1979, the commission issued its final report stating it would not bring charges of misconduct against any of the seven supreme court justices. But the year-long investigation, irreparably damaged the reputation of a court once perceived as the leading state court in the nation. *The Wall Street Journal* had said in 1975 that "the California State Supreme Court is to courts what UCLA is to basketball." Unfortunately, the Supreme Court's (and UCLA's basketball team's) fortunes declined in the 1980s.

ATTORNEYS

No one may practice law in California *or act as an attorney* for a client, without being admitted to the state bar. The bar's authority is provided by the state constitution, which gives it the power to set ethical standards, admit to practice, discipline, and expel attorneys. Essentially, admitting to practice means passing an examination administered by the bar.[4]

Attorneys occupy a central position in California's justice system.

[3]The most notable case was the removal ("retirement") of Supreme Court Justice Marshall F. McComb in 1977 for failure to perform his judicial duties.

[4]Concerns have been raised repeatedly in the legislature that the state bar has not done a very good job in disciplining its "bad apples."

Judges must be members of the state bar. The attorney general, prosecuting attorneys for cities and counties, and public defenders must also be members of the bar. And with few exceptions, in major cases heard before a court, both parties to a conflict depend on attorneys to represent them.

Clearly, there is a strong antilawyer sentiment with certain segments of the public. Proposition 51 (Deep Pockets) initiative of June 1986, which was approved by a solid majority of voters, was aimed in part at "excessive" contingency fees paid attorneys in settlement suits. A new initiative was launched in March 1986 which would have prohibited lawyers from holding public office in California. This initiative did not qualify for the ballot. In certain parts of rural California some candidates for the state legislature have been known to boast that they were *not* attorneys in their campaign appeals to voters.

Prosecuting Attorneys

The district attorney is the government's prosecuting attorney at the county level. After an arrest is made, this official decides whether to prosecute, change the charge, or drop the case. Given the statutory time limits, limited staff, and backlog of pending cases before the courts, the prosecuting attorney has to limit the number of cases pursued. In some counties, the prosecuting attorney may drop as many as half of the felony cases and prosecute the rest—very few will actually go to trial.

Usually, the district attorney will reduce the charge in exchange for a guilty plea. This is commonly called plea bargaining or "copping a plea"—about 90 percent of prosecuted felony cases are decided this way. In effect, most criminal "trials" are negotiations between the district attorney and the defendant's attorney. The negotiated plea of guilty to a reduced charge is then formally presented to the judge in court.

Defense Attorneys

The California constitution provides that the accused (in a criminal case) has the right" . . .to appear and defend in person and with counsel."

In fact, prosecution may not begin until the defendant has had an opportunity to secure legal counsel. In a few instances, the court may allow individuals to defend themselves without legal counsel, but there is no absolute right to do so. Those who can afford to will hire a private attorney, but the great majority of criminal defendants have limited financial resources and must depend on the public defender or assigned counsel.

Public Defender

The public defender, like the district attorney, is a county employee, but the job of the defender is to defend the accused in a criminal case when the defendant cannot afford to hire a private attorney—a situation that exists in the majority of criminal cases. Since the district attorney usually prosecutes cases only where there is a good chance of conviction, the public defender, given staff limits, usually tries for reduced charges through plea bargaining. In small counties where there is no public defender, the court uses *assigned counsel,* an attorney in private practice appointed to defend the accused.

Clinic Groups

In the last few years, new types of legal assistance have emerged to assist defendants or plaintiffs who cannot afford private counsel. These new forms include legal insurance ("liticare") and legal service clinics, such as the California Rural Legal Assistance or the Western Center on Law and Poverty. The American Civil Liberties Union has a long history of defending accused in cases involving constitutionally protected liberties. And in some counties, the local bar organization or legal aid society will provide attorneys for defendants.

POLICE

The police officer is also a key figure in the criminal justice system. Besides law enforcement, today's police are civil servants involved in a broad range of social and personal problems—family fights, runaway children, neighborhood disputes, enforcement of racial integration, crowd control at demonstrations and marches, or keeping the peace at an athletic event. But more time is consumed by *automobile-related* activities, including traffic control, parking, and accident investigation, than any other area.

Under the California constitution, law enforcement is a local function. Each of California's fifty-eight counties has an elected sheriff who is responsible for law enforcement within the unincorporated areas. The sheriff also provides crime lab and other technical services to city police within the county and jail facilities for cities without them.

The bulk of police work is done by city departments, since most Californians live in cities. City departments are headed by chiefs who are usually appointed either by the city manager or by the city's police commission. Problems facing city police departments are varied. Large-city police departments, such as Los Angeles, San Diego, Oakland, San Francisco, or San Jose, frequently deal with serious crimes, such as murder, arson, or armed robbery. Smaller cities are more fre-

11-5

Cartoon by Robert Minter

quently concerned with traffic and burglary. In addition, the California Highway Patrol is responsible for traffic on state freeways.

CITIZEN PARTICIPATION

The citizen also plays a role in the state's justice system as a witness and as a member of trial or grand juries. About one out of six Californians has been in a court as a witness; about one out of twelve has served on a trial jury. Very few ever serve on a grand jury.

Trial Juries

This jury form is used only in trial courts—justice, municipal, and superior courts. Most cases do not go to trial but are settled by plea bargaining. Of those cases which do go to trial, only about one in twenty is argued before a jury.

Under California law, every adult citizen is required to serve on a trial jury when called. Previously, many people were excused from jury duty because they were employed in "crucial" occupations—doctors, hospital employees, teachers, and utility workers, for example. They are no longer automatically excused. Only a few—police officers, lawyers (and their wives), ex-felons, felons, aliens, and some governmental employees—are excused from jury duty. Even the governor is required to serve if called—as Jerry Brown discovered in 1981 when he was required to sit on a jury.

Most counties use lists of registered voters to draw names of potential jurors. But increasingly, counties are also using lists of drivers' licenses. This new practice is designed to produce juries that are more representative of all the people living in a community (and, perhaps, not to discourage people from registering to vote).

Grand Juries

Grand juries are different from trial juries. Every county has a grand jury, usually nineteen citizens, selected by the county's superior court judges. Serving one-year terms, grand jurors are the county's "watchdogs." They spend most of their time investigating the conduct and operation of local governmental agencies—only rarely these days do grand juries indict.

Typically, in a year, the grand jury will make several investigative reports on various agencies and departments, call attention to deficiencies, cite needed improvement, and perhaps make recommendations for reform.

Witnesses

All parties to a trial—the accused, the plaintiff, and the defendant—have a constitutional right to present witnesses in their behalf. In fact, the court has the authority to compel people to testify (except against themselves).

RIGHTS OF THE PEOPLE

The Accused

The accused has many rights: proper notification of a suit (subpoena), correct arrest and interrogation in a criminal case, knowledge of the charges, bail (in most cases), advice of legal counsel, a fair trial, trial by jury (in most cases), and the right to appeal an adverse decision (in most cases).

For an individual charged with a crime, first contact with the justice system is usually arrest by a police officer or sheriff's deputy. After booking, the suspect may make at least one phone call to an attorney, friend, relative, or bail bondsman. At the time of arrest, police are required to inform the suspect that *under the constitution* he or she has the right to *(a)* remain silent and *(b)* have an attorney. Suspects also have the right to know the charges under which they were arrested, protected and are against self-incrimination.

Before trial, the suspect is brought before the court—usually a municipal judge—and *arraigned*. At arraignment, the judge formally notifies the suspect of the charge and his or her legal rights, sets a date for a preliminary hearing, and establishes bail.

Juveniles.   Juveniles (anyone under the age of eighteen) are treated differently than adults in our legal system. This difference in treatment comes from the basic idea that juveniles are *not responsible for themselves*. Typically, the juvenile's case is heard in juvenile court. The juvenile criminal becomes a ward of the court, which attempts to isolate him or her from the conditions that contributed to the juvenile's problem. Juveniles are not punished by terms in jail or prison. They may be housed in a detention facility (separate from adult prisoners), placed under probation, or put into some form of counseling program. The essential difference is that in criminal cases involving an adult, the court acts to protect society. In cases involving a juvenile, the court acts to protect the juvenile as well as society.

PENALTIES, CORRECTIONS, REHABILITATION, AND DAMAGES

Courts are involved in both the determination of guilt (in criminal cases) and liability (in civil cases). Following a criminal trial, the court begins what is known as the *penalty phase* of proceedings. In a civil suit, the court determines the dollar amount of the settlement—*damages*. In suits in equity, the court may order performance or issue an injunction.

Corrections, penalties, and damages are vitally important to the justice system. In criminal cases, penalties and corrections are supposed to provide *punishment, deterrence,* and *rehabilitation.* In civil suits, the damages awarded or orders are supposed to *right the wrong.*

Determining Penalty

Criminal.   Following conviction, the court requests that the county probation department recommend a suitable sentence. In addition, the district attorney and defense attorney also make recommendations. In imposing sentence, the judge weighs several factors. First, what are the statutory penalties? How severe was the crime? What are the circumstances surrounding the crime? Does the defendant have a prior record? The defendant's age, mental competency, and community status will also be considered.

Between 1917 and 1977, California law provided for an "indeterminate sentence." The judge would remand the convicted defendant to the California Adult Authority for an indeterminate period of time (for example, one to ten years). The goal of the indeterminate sentence was rehabilitation. Felons were to be incarcerated until, in the judgment of the parole board, they were rehabilitated and ready to rejoin society. However, most legal experts have now concluded that very few criminals are rehabilitated in prison.

California courts now impose sentence under the Uniform Determinate Sentencing Act of 1976. This act provides three specific periods of time which may be imposed by the judge in sentencing for a specific crime. For example, a person convicted of robbery may receive a minimum sentence (three years), a medium sentence (four years), or the maximum sentence (five years). The circumstances of the crime must be considered in adding to the basic sentence imposed. If the robber had a prior conviction, the judge may add three more years to the sentence. If a firearm had been used, two more years may be added. If someone had been injured during the crime, another three years may be added. Thus, a first-time offender under mitigating circumstances might be sentenced to three years. But the same crime committed by someone with a prior record during which a person was injured could lead to a sentence of thirteen years.

Civil.   Following determination of liability in a civil suit, the court (or jury) may award the damages asked by plaintiff. Or the award may be less. The award may simply be the amount needed to pay for repairing an automobile or the doctor's fees. Such an amount is easy to calculate. But if the award is for loss of a leg or an eye or a life, what is the correct amount? How much should be awarded for pain and suffering?

Most civil suits are settled out of court. The attorneys for the plaintiff and for the defendant agree on a settlement, and the judge then records that agreement and orders the liable person to pay.

Imposing Penalty

Probation.   Rather than fill prisons, judges often place the convicted person on probation. This is particularly true for first-time offenders who are less likely to commit another crime. Often an individual will be given a sentence of time to be served in jail, with two-thirds of it on probation. Technically, the convicted person is sentenced to a specific time in jail but is then *placed on probation* and allowed to remain free. A county probation officer is assigned the case, and the convict is required to report at specified intervals. Failure to meet the requirements of probation can lead to a return to jail.

Incarceration. As an agent of the state, each county has a jail which is administered by the county sheriff. The state Department of Corrections also administers twelve penal institutions. County jails have two types of prisoners: first, persons held for trial who have been denied bail, or who cannot make bail, or who do not qualify for release on their own recognizance; and second, persons convicted of lesser crimes.

State institutions hold prisoners convicted of the more serious crimes—homicide, assault, rape, and robbery. Over 60 percent of the prison population has committed one or more violent crimes. Most of these prisoners are male (94 percent), nonwhite (61 percent), under thirty years old (58 percent), and have less than a high school education (76 percent). Today, the state prison population is largely made up of "repeaters." Only 18 percent have never been in a prison or jail before.

As the crime wave continued to rise in California during the late 1970s and early 1980s intense pressure was put on state lawmakers to increase penalties for various felonies committed, this, in turn, has led to severe overcrowding in California jails and prisons. In the early 1980s voters approved several different prison construction bond acts in an attempt to meet this looming crisis. Of course, another issue: where to construct prisons. Many affluent communities are "unenthusiastic" about having a prison in their midst. Conflict over prison siting in 1987 pitted Governor Deukmejian, who wanted a prison constructed in east Los Angeles (a Latino neighborhood), versus Democratic legislative leaders. This issue was finally compromised in the closing days of the 1987 legislative session.

Parole. Since California's lockup facilities have not kept pace with state population growth, judges are able to sentence only the most serious cases to the state prison system.

Under law, after serving two-thirds of a sentence, a prisoner is eligible for parole. Parole for each eligible inmate is considered once a year by the California Adult Authority and is granted on the basis of the inmate's behavior and prior record. A prisoner with a record of "good time" will probably be granted parole, unless there is a prior record to suggest that parole will be violated. Anyone on parole is still under the jurisdiction of the California Adult Authority and may be returned to prison for violation of the terms of parole.

Juveniles. Juveniles detained for a criminal act may not be kept in custody with adults. After a hearing, juveniles may be placed on probation, placed in custody of the county, or sent to the California Youth Authority (CYA). Only the most hardened juveniles, who are found guilty of a very serious offense or repeated acts ("incorrigible"), are sent to the CYA. According to Mark Soler, Director of the San Fran-

11-6

Dennis Renault, Sacramento Bee

"IF THERE ARE SO MANY 'SOFT' JUDGES, GOVERNOR,
WHY ARE THERE SO MANY OF US IN THE PRISONS?"

cisco Youth Law Center, California laws dealing with juvenile defendants are the most progressive in the nation.

Rehabilitation.   California's sixty-year experiment with indeterminate sentencing was based on the hope that criminals could be rehabilitated while in prison. Today, California has abandoned attempts to rehabilitate criminals in prison. Prisons and jails, it is generally believed, do not rehabilitate. In fact, prisons and jails are fine places for the young criminal to learn more about crime.

COURTS AND POLICYMAKING

A simplistic view of the judicial system is that courts are *not supposed to make policy*. Thus, the argument goes, given the American governmental framework, legislatures make policy, executives administer policy, and courts ensure everything is done according to the laws and constitution. It's this last expectation that leads to the court's policymaking.

11-7

Dennis Renault, Sacramento Bee

"IF YOU THINK THE POLITICAL REAPPORTIONMENT MAP IS A HASSLE, WAIT UNTIL WE HAVE TO GET INTO THIS ONE!"

Judicial policy making occurs when judges are *asked to resolve a conflict* between two laws or between a law and a constitutional provision. Policy is also made when courts *interpret* a law or constitutional provision. Frequently, legislators will enact a law in general terms, doing little more than stating their *legislative intent.* The legislature will not spell out the details, definitions, or specific applications of the law. This they leave to administrators and the courts. Thus, the courts find themselves inevitably making policy.

In fact, appellate courts and the state supreme court were established to resolve conflicts between laws and the constitution. A state supreme court has the constitutional authority to significantly interpret or modify U.S. Supreme Court decisions involving their state's activities. For example, the California supreme court in 1975 significantly restricted police searches of suspects. The U.S. Supreme Court had earlier ruled that full-body searches by police of persons arrested for minor offenses did not violate the U.S. Constitution. But, the California state supreme court, citing the California state constitution, substantially restricted police searches *in California.*

Courts may also review the substance of referendums and initiatives. Those who lose in an election may feel that some constitutional rights have been denied or infringed upon and go to the court for an opinion (see Chapter 4).

The courts are also frequently asked to interpret laws. The state's 1973 death penalty law was challenged, and the state supreme court held the law unconstitutional because it was inflexible. The state court relied on an earlier U.S. Supreme Court decision in this case (as contrasted to the police search case).

Finally, it should be noted that the court makes law in some instances. The court ordered the state legislature to equalize public school financing in *Serrano* v. *Priest*. This decision required the addition of $1 billion to the state's budget in 1972 and another $4.3 billion in 1977. And reaching into the heart of the political process in 1973, the court reapportioned the state legislature after the governor and legislators became deadlocked on the issue.

The controversial issues of our society get to the court because those who lose the struggle in other political arenas hope for success in the courts. Those who opposed the 1972 school busing initiative (Proposition 21) lost the election fight but won the court battle. Those who opposed the death penalty won a modified victory in the courts after losing in the legislature. Those who were adversely affected by the traditional method of financing local public education went to the courts and won a victory that could not have been achieved in any other political arena. The authority of courts to resolve conflicts in law is a vital part of our governmental process.

As long as the courts are empowered to resolve conflicts, they will be involved in controversy and the making of public policy.

Politicizing the Courts

Will the defeat in the November 1986 confirmation election of the three liberal state Supreme Court justices (Bird, Reynoso, and Grodin) mark an end to the court-bashing of the last several decades? In a sense, this was the culminating event in a long series of clashes between conservatives and the courts. Clearly, the trend in superior and municipal elections is away from challenges of incumbent judges. And, the crime issue, which provided much of the momentum for the anti-court sentiment, seems to have abated. The Field Institute reported in November 1985 that crime was only the third most critical issue Californians were concerned about—and only 5 percent of the respondents mentioned it. The new judges appointed by Deukmejian who now comprise a substantial majority on the court (five of seven) are unlikely to embark on a course that could bring them into substantial conflict with the governor, legislature, or electorate. For the time being, the court is likely to have a far less visible profile. While peace has been restored, the leadership role the California Supreme Court used to exercise among the state courts on various legal fronts is unlikely to continue with its newly constituted membership.

The dilemma remains, of course: How can we have a politically independent and innovative court (given the highly charged political-legal-social issues they must confront) and yet retain an accountable judiciary? Not surprisingly, there is considerable legislative interest in modifying our supreme court selection process. Should we elect appeals and supreme court judges or should we provide life tenure as is done at the federal level? Should trial court judges be forced to face potential opponents, or should these elections be like appellate elections with a simple yes or no voter option? How should judges campaign for office—as other major political candidates do? Should political parties be allowed to endorse judges? One perennial proposal is to have supreme and appeals court nominees be approved by the senate rather than the Commission on Judicial Appointments as other governor nominees are. But, would this lead to further politicizing of the court by a partisan branch of the legislature? Would the court become a haven for retired state senators who, it might be anticipated, would give speedy approval to nominations of their former colleagues? Court reform issues are clearly on the legislative frontburner.

REFORMING THE SYSTEM

In addition, to reforms in nominating and electing judges there are a host of other legal reform issues. Some see the California justice system as arbitrary; others see it as too soft on criminals; still others see it as too hard on minorities. Almost everyone is concerned about the deterrence of crime, but there is little agreement on how to do it. Almost everyone wants to make the courts more available to people and to speed up the civil calendar, but not everyone wants to spend more money to do it.

Victim's Rights

In June 1982, voters approved Proposition 8, known as the "Victim's Bill of Rights." This initiative proposed substantial changes in California's justice system. The measure enacted the following changes:

Provides restitution for victims of criminal acts.
Acknowledges the right to safe and secure schools.
Forbids exclusion of relevant evidence in criminal proceedings.
Allows prior felony convictions to be used to impeach a witness or
  enhance a sentence.
Abolishes the diminished capacity defense.
Provides longer sentences for habitual offenders.
Prohibits plea bargaining in serious felony cases.

Gives victims or the next of kin the right to appear at sentencing and to state views concerning the crime, the defendant, and restitution.

Generally speaking, Proposition 8 has eliminated a number of criminal trial procedures and rules, but judges, prosecutors, and defense attorneys have continued to use the "old rules" because they are familiar and usually adequate and reasonable. In short, Proposition 8 has had only a modest effect thus far.

Police

Two major police reforms are most frequently suggested: (1) increasing training and standards and (2) establishing civilian review boards. First, quality of police training, recruitment, and training standards varies considerably among the cities and counties in California. At present, less training is required to be a police officer than to be an electrician or barber. Opposition to statewide standards comes from many cities and counties who want to hold down police salaries. Second, most police are bitterly opposed to having any outside civilian review boards review police actions. On the other hand, many citizens feel that the city council, police commission, mayor, and/or city manager do not adequately control the police. Charges of police brutality or unnecessary use of force revive the demand for greater civilian control of the police.

Courts

Other court reform issues include: (1) the role of the press, (2) jury size and selection, (3) civil case backlog, and (4) night courts.

In 1979, the Judicial Council ruled that TV and still cameras should be allowed in criminal court unless they threaten the defendant's rights.

Sometimes the press reveals facts that a judge feels damages the judicial process. Judges have sometimes demanded that reporters reveal their sources. Newspapers traditionally refuse to reveal sources, and reporters at times have been jailed for their refusal to do so. The media argue the public is best served by providing more, not less, information and being forced to reveal sources would dry up the information and deprive the public. In June 1980, California voters approved a "press shield" constitutional amendment supposed to protect confidential sources from judicial inquiry.

Another major problem plaguing courts is the civil case backlog. Delay in hearing civil cases has been steadily increasing. The average wait to have a civil case tried is over three years in some counties. If "justice delayed is justice denied," the civil case backlog is a major problem.

Perhaps no institutional reforms can solve the underlying problem—Californians seem increasingly inclined to settle disputes in court. It may be that the mobile, impersonal, urban lifestyle in California has further eroded the influence of community, family, and church. Lacking the traditional informal methods of settling differences, people turn to the formal methods—civil suits at law.

Prosecution/Defense

Plea bargaining is another critical reform issue. Given the present number of courtrooms, judges, and clerks, plea bargaining is a necessity. If every criminal case went to trial, there would have to be over twice as many new judges, courtrooms, and so on. Few people are willing to support such a costly expansion of the court system. On the other hand, many feel that the accused should be tried for the crime committed and not allowed to plead guilty to a lesser charge.

Juvenile Justice

The juvenile justice system has been under reform pressure from two directions: (1) those who see it as too harsh on juveniles and (2) those who see it as too lenient.

The first group has won a partial victory in eliminating the status offense—detention because of an act which is illegal only for a juvenile (e.g., curfew). In California, juvenile courts have been closed to the public to protect the juvenile's identity. Recent court decisions have held, however, that juveniles are entitled to a public hearing and an attorney.

Treating some juveniles as "responsible adults" is the goal of some reformers who view the juvenile justice system as "soft on juvenile felons." Should a youth of seventeen charged with premeditated homicide be tried as an adult? It would be hard to say without knowing other facts. Should a youth of eight charged with premeditated homicide be tried as an adult? Most people would say no. At what age is an individual responsible?

Trial Jury

Following voter approval in November 1980, the state legislature established an experiment in Los Angeles County's municipal courts, allowing eight-member juries (rather than twelve) in civil suits between July 1, 1982, and July 1, 1985. It is believed that eight jurors are more likely to agree on a verdict than twelve.

Cases disposed of by jury trials represent only about 1 percent of all cases heard by courts.

Trial Procedure

Several major reforms offer a potential for improvement of the justice system. The use of videotaped testimony by witnesses unable to appear in court physically has sometimes been used. A much larger issue is the admissibility of illegally obtained evidence—the exclusionary rule, which is "the right of the people to be secure in their persons, houses, . . . against unreasonable seizures and searches." California courts tend toward strict interpretation of this prohibition.

Capital Punishment

The debate over California's death penalty centers on several key issues. First, there is the basic philosophical question—should the state take a life if, through its own laws, it asserts the high value of life? Second, has the convicted murderer waived his claim to life having taken the life of another? Third, on a more practical level, does the death penalty deter crime? And fourth, there is the nagging worry: what if the state executes an innocent person?

Proponents and opponents of the death penalty have different answers for these and other questions. But one factor stands out: the three new Deukmejian nominated state supreme court members (Arguelles, Eagleson, and Kaufman) sworn in on March 17, 1987, join two previous Deukmejian picks, Chief Justice Malcolm Lucas and Edward Panelli, and provide conservatives a solid five to two majority (the two holdover moderates are Stanley Mosk and Allen Broussard). There are clear indications that the new court will be far more willing to impose this ultimate sanction.

Corrections

The new determinate system is clearly designed to punish. The theory is that punishment will act as a deterrent to crime. The legislature's enactment of a mandatory prison sentence for anyone using a gun to commit a crime is a good example of the punishment-deterrence theory. As yet, no one knows for sure if the theory will work.

Given the high costs of prison—over $50,000 in construction costs per cell and $14,000 a year for each prisoner—the legislature and governor have been considering several prisoner work programs which would help pay for state prison costs.

SUMMARY

In this chapter we have looked at the various parts of the California justice system. Two major features stand out. First, it is not so much a system as a number of governmental agencies functioning in the same area. And second, the system is under heavy pressures for reform due to increased use.

Each year, there are more court cases—more civil suits and more criminal trials. And the largest number of cases comes from our use of the automobile. (What would a highly efficient, inexpensive public transportation system do to the court load?)

Pressures for reform fall into three categories. First, there are the demands for change that will make the justice system fairer. Rules of evidence, bail bond practices, and the method for selecting trial juries are examples of this concern. Second, there are demands for greater accessibility. Night traffic and small claims courts, reduced delay in getting a civil suit to trial, and bail-by-mail are examples.

Third, there is the larger debate over the function of the criminal justice system itself. What should be its goal? Can the wayward juvenile be saved from a life of crime? Should jails and prisons serve as agents of rehabilitation? Or should the criminal system be concerned only with making the streets safe for law-abiding citizens? Much of this debate is rooted in our view of crime and of human nature. The wide-ranging debate over the death penalty is a good example.

Californians place a heavy burden on the state's justice system and have made many demands for reform. Change and reform are difficult to achieve, but it is encouraging to see that some advances have been made.

12

Local Government in California[1]

Local governments provide more services to citizens than any other branch of government. Local government in California and in other states is different from state and national government in two significant ways. *First,* local governments have no inherent constitutional existence but are, rather, agents or creatures of the state. *Second,* individual local governments share jurisdictions with other local governments; their territorial areas often overlap.

There are four basic kinds of local government in California: county, city, school, and special district. California has 58 counties, and in 1985 it had 438 cities, over 1,000 school districts, and more than 5,000 special districts. These local units provide most of the day-to-day services we associate with government—police, fire, education, parks and recreation, streets, sewage disposal, libraries, social welfare, land use regulation (including zoning), water, public transportation, and flood control. In addition, many local governments also provide electricity and gas, harbors and airports, hospitals, cemeteries, and housing.

As discussed in Chapter 10, most governmental expenditures in California are made at the local level by local government. Of the $94.5 billion spent by state and local governments in California in fiscal year 1986–87, $68 billion (70 percent) was spent by the local governments. Thus, it is not surprising that most governmental employees, about

[1]The authors wish to acknowledge the thoughtful comments of Tom Hoeber, publisher of the *California Journal* and Peter Detwiler, consultant to the senate local government committee on this chapter.

seven out of ten, work at the local level. Local government is obviously important.

California has a tradition of home rule. Elements of this tradition may be found in both the state constitution and in the political values of citizens and politicians. In theory, much of our local government could be abolished, consolidated, or sharply reduced by legislative action. In fact, political pressures from citizens, locally elected public officials, and many interest groups would make it difficult for legislators to change dramatically the powers and scope of local government.

Because of the importance of local government and the easy access to local officials, many citizens are more involved in it. Local government tends to be government by local elites and activists.

CONSTITUTIONAL PROVISIONS

The authority of the state to create city and county governments, organize their structures, and define their powers is found in Article XI of the California constitution.

Two other articles in the constitution deal with local government. Article IX provides for local school districts, county schools, basic financial aid to local schools, and the authority to borrow money. It also provides for school boards to govern local schools. Article XIII is concerned with the taxing authority exercised by local governments.

Special districts are not directly established by the California constitution. Most of them are created by counties, some by cities, some by voters, and a very few by the legislature.

Local government authority can be classified in one of two ways: (1) corporate and (2) police. *Corporate power* refers to the authority to provide services (streets, water, sewers, etc.). *Police power* refers to the authority to regulate behavior (traffic and crime, land use, building codes, etc.). Cities and counties have both kinds of powers; other local governments do not have the police power.

COUNTY GOVERNMENT

When California entered the Union, it was divided into twenty-seven counties. As population grew, more counties were created until there were fifty-eight by 1907.[2] Everyone lives in a county (see Illustration 12–1), which is a geographically defined administrative agency established by the state to provide statewide services at the local level. "State" services provided by the county include: welfare, health, courts, elections, probation, jail, records, and tax assessment and col-

---

[2]Including San Francisco, which is both a city and a county. There have been seven abortive attempts to form additional counties.

12-1 *California counties, 1984.*

lection. Services with more local control include: roads, parks, land use planning, development regulations, libraries, and law enforcement (the sheriff).

Thus, county government serves two masters—the state which established it and the local voters who elect county officials. As a result, home rule is a complex problem for counties. This has become most evident in recent years as the state increasingly requires counties to provide various kinds of services but does not always provide the money needed to fund those services.

County Forms

General Law Counties.   General laws, enacted by the state legislature, provide for a statewide pattern of structures and powers for forty-seven counties. Each general law county has the same legal form. Elected officials include five members of the Board of Supervisors, a sheriff, district attorney, coroner, assessor, tax collector, superintendent of schools, and five other minor officials. Many general law counties (particularly smaller ones) combine some of these positions. For example, Alpine County (population 700) elects a combined county clerk-auditor-recorder, and several other counties combine the position of sheriff and coroner.

These counties are divided into five geographic districts of equal population which elect a representative to that county's Board of Supervisors. The board is authorized by the state legislature to enact county ordinances (laws) governing the county. The board is also authorized to prepare an annual budget, to collect the county's property tax, and to receive state and federal funds designated for locally administered programs (welfare and roads, for example).

The supervisors also appoint a number of administrators including: the county's chief administrative officer, the director of social services, head of public health, head of the planning department, chief probation officer, and head of public works (roads, bridges, etc.).

Charter Counties.   Eleven counties have adopted their own individual charters (constitutions). With approval of the local voters, charter counties are able to set up different political structures. This is supposed to give them greater ability to meet local needs. Los Angeles was the first county to adopt a charter (1912). Since then, ten others have joined the list: Alameda, Butte, Fresno, Sacramento, San Bernardino, San Diego, San Francisco, San Mateo, Santa Clara, and Tehama.

Charter counties tend to be urban (excepting Butte and Tehama) with large populations. San Francisco, has a unique charter. It is a mix of both city and county forms. It combines the office of mayor and an enlarged (eleven-member) board of supervisors. San Francisco exercises both the powers of a city and a county. It has over 600,000 people living on only forty-six square miles.

Charter status permits a county more organizational flexibility than for general law counties. For example, charter counties can make some officials appointive rather than elective (sheriff, county clerk, etc.).

They can also elect the Board of Supervisors "at large" rather than by districts.[3]

But, in practice, regardless of the supposed advantages, California's charter counties are not very different from general law counties.

Boards of Supervisors

These elected boards combine legislative and executive functions and govern counties as a collective executive. While in the past most boards were dominated by men with business/law backgrounds, more recently, substantial numbers of women have been elected. Several counties have recently had more women supervisors than men. In a number of counties, expanding cities eager to annex shopping malls and housing tracts have fought bitter battles with the board of supervisors. For cities, expansion means an expanded tax base; for county government, reduced revenue.

County Administrator

The top appointed official in most county governments is the chief administrative officer. In some counties, this official is known as the county executive and in others as the chief administrative officer. Whatever the title, over forty counties have someone who manages the day-to-day administration of county services, oversees county operations, and controls expenditures. Those few counties that do not have such an official are generally small and are relatively uncomplicated.

Major County Programs/Services

In describing county functions or activities, it is useful to distinguish between the core or traditional functions and those that have been added more recently. Core functions include: law enforcement (the sheriff, jails, and courts), record keeping, welfare, road building and maintenance, and tax collecting. In recent years, as counties have become urbanized, they have added such services or functions as: recreation and parks, land use control, trash collection, and public transportation.

Another way of looking at county functions is to distinguish between those provided to all county residents and those that are provided only to those living in unincorporated areas. All county residents

---

[3]Tehama County elects supervisors at large, and San Francisco County alternated several times in the late 1970s and early 80s between district and at-large elections.

receive recordkeeping, court, welfare, and criminal prosecution services, for example, but only those people living in the unincorporated parts of the county receive law enforcement or roads from the county.

Welfare.   Regardless of county size, welfare programs are the largest part of the budget. The various forms of public assistance take about 40 percent of county budgets. Aid to Families with Dependent Children (AFDC) is the largest part of the welfare budget. But other forms of welfare are important too—aid to the blind and infirm, hospital care for the poor, and general relief for those who are needy but do not meet the requirements of other welfare programs.

In recent years, the federal government has provided a major part of the funding for welfare. And since passage of Proposition 13, which put limits on property tax assessments, the state has picked up more of the costs, but counties continue to administer the programs.

Public Safety.   The sheriff, courts, jails, flood control, and fire protection combine to make the second largest part of the typical county's budget (about 27 percent). The sheriff heads the county's police department. This officer is an independently elected public official, frequently well-known and powerful. However, the board of supervisors controls the sheriff's department's annual budget. The county jail and juvenile hall are other major areas of public protection expenditures. Many criminal suspects are kept in the county jail or juvenile hall prior to pretrial hearings. If not released on bail or on their own recognizance, the suspect remains in county custody.

The district attorney, public defender, trial courts, and probation department are also important parts of the public safety program (see Chapter 11).

Environmental Protection.   Environmental management, including pollution control and land use planning (and in unincorporated areas, zoning, subdivision controls, use permits, and development agreements) have become significant county activities. Much of California's population growth has taken place in the suburbs—often in unincorporated areas. The county's zoning and land use plans are crucial in preventing destruction of natural resources, open spaces, and agricultural lands.

Public Health.   Sanitation, drug and alcohol abuse programs, mental health and inspecting restaurants for cleanliness are important county jobs. An often unnoticed but crucial service is "vector control"—keeping the community safe from rats and rabid or other disease-carrying animals. These activities take about 11 percent of the average county budget. In addition, some counties have a hospital (or medical center) which may provide a wide range of care to county residents.

Recreation. Parks and recreation are another county responsibility. This is particularly important in the urban counties where crowded living conditions place a premium on open space.

Roads. Road construction and maintenance are other important county activities. Citizens tend to take "surface transportation" for granted until roadbeds crumble or are flooded out.

Selected Problems. In recent years, California counties have had increasing difficulty in meeting their citizens' needs.

First, many problems that counties face originate outside their boundaries and cannot be solved by the individual counties. For example, pollution, poverty, immigration, and unemployment are subject to little or no county influence.

Second, state-county fiscal relations were fundamentally altered by Proposition 13 in 1978. The average county's revenues were reduced by about 20 percent by Proposition 13–requiring significant program cuts even with increased state aid. Along with that increased state aid came increased state control. Sometimes the state has required (*mandated*) the counties to provide services without providing the money to pay for those services. These mandated programs have become a central issue in county-state fiscal relations (see below).

Third, because there are so many elected public officials (on the average seven or eight per county), responsibility and authority are scattered. Voters seldom know who is in charge.

Fourth, in the larger counties, supervisorial districts have too many citizens to permit meaningful representation. In Los Angeles County, the average district has 1.5 million residents (larger than three congressional districts). In Orange County, the average is 386,000, and in Santa Clara, the average is about 259,000. Statewide, the average supervisorial district has about 81,000 residents.

And, fifth, there is no county executive comparable to a governor or mayor, and no one has a veto. Thus, there are no checks and balances in county government except in San Francisco which does elect a mayor.

CITY GOVERNMENT

Cities, unlike counties, are not created by the state. Any group of residents who decide that county services do not meet their needs can (with a few restrictions) form a *municipal corporation*—a city. And as

12-2 *Los Angeles in 1853—a small pueblo on the fringe of civilization.*

Photo courtesy California State Library

California has grown, so have the number of cities. Today, some 438 cities from Amador City (population 146) to Los Angeles (population 3.2 million) provide a wide range of services to their residents.

California's early cities were established during the Spanish era long before the state was formed. San Diego, the state's first city, was founded in 1769, followed by Monterey (1770), San Francisco (1776), and Los Angeles (1781). After California became a state, these early cities were incorporated under provisions of the new state constitution.

Sometimes cities are formed for unique reasons. The cities of Vernon, Commerce, and Industry in southern California and Emeryville in northern California were formed to provide tax shelter to businesses located there and to protect them from regulations which would have been imposed if neighboring cities had annexed them.

Sometimes cities are formed to provide greater local political control—to protect their residents from being "swallowed up" by larger neighboring cities. And sometimes cities are formed as a matter of local pride and identity. Thus, Hispanic activists have twice tried to form a city in the east Los Angeles area which would be, they believe, more responsive than the county to their social and cultural needs.

Usually, however, municipal incorporation occurs when area residents need additional governmental services. Cities are often formed to provide:

1. More control over land use (perhaps reacting against a county's land use policies).
2. Traffic control.

12-3 *Los Angeles at night in the 80s.*

Courtesy of Tony Quinn, Office of California Economic Development

3. Control over expenditures for services.
4. Better sanitation and/or sewage disposal.
5. Better police and/or fire protection.

Many cities have been formed as a result of suburban migration—people moving from major cities to the suburbs surrounding them. Those who leave the central cities often complain about dirt, noise, and crime rates; many are looking for more room and privacy. In recent years, many Californians have left central cities because of racial tensions or fears. These "white flight," middle-class residents move to unincorporated areas and form new cities over which they hope to have more control.

As noted in Chapter 1, most of California's post-World War II population growth has been in the suburban rings around the state's metropolitan areas. Thus, it's not surprising that most of the state's municipal incorporation has occurred in the same areas. However, this suburban pattern was modified in the late 1970s and early 80s. Increasingly, new cities are springing up in rural and low-density, urban fringe areas. One study of recent incorporations (Sokolow and Matlin 1983) found the average size of these new cities to be about 13,000 population residing in 14 square miles.

In recent years, the pace of incorporations has increased. It may reflect a desire by these new city residents to protect their rural atmosphere, to control local land use planning, or to express dissatisfaction with county services (slow response time by the sheriff or poor road conditions).

Contrary to expectations, Proposition 13 may have accelerated the formation of new cities. Cities have greater tax resources than counties. Residents of a particular area can, by incorporating, gain access to more tax revenues and therefore provide more governmental services for themselves.

City Forms

California cities are organized in one of two basic ways—under the state's general laws or by charter. Unlike counties, which are established by the constitution, a city does not exist until a group of people decide to incorporate. Once incorporated under the state's general laws, each city has a city council, mayor, and administrative structure. It also has authority to provide a wide range of services. Charter cities usually modify the basic mayor-council structure and provide additional services not available under the general law form.

General Law Cities.   Most California cities (some 360) are incorporated under the state's general law provisions. At one time, incorporation was relatively easy. But in response to the haphazard city formation of the late 1940s and 1950s, state law was altered to make municipal incorporation more difficult. Currently, state law requires a minimum of 500 residents to form a city. A proposal to incorporate is usually initiated by voter petition or by a resolution of the board of supervisors. After being approved by the Local Agency Formation Commission (LAFCO) elections are held in the area proposed for incorporation.

In fact, population size has not been important in recent years. The smallest city incorporated since 1968 had 1,700 residents (Adelanto). More important is the intent under state law that the new city be able to provide a "broad spectrum and high level of community services and controls" (Sokolow et al., 1981).

In an election in the area proposed for incorporation, voters are asked if there should be a new city of _____ (yes or no). Voters are also asked to elect five city council members who take office if the incorporation is approved.

The new city council selects one of its members to be mayor, an honorary position, to preside at council meetings. Mayors in general law cities have no more formal power than any other member of the city council. All formal political authority resides in the council which makes policy for the city. Most general law city councils appoint a city manager to administer city policy and take charge of the day-to-day city activities and services.

City managers have specific responsibility for the hiring and firing of city department heads (streets, parks, etc.), policy implementation, preparation and submission to the city council of proposed new laws, and the annual budget. While not elected, the typical city manager exercises considerable authority.

Charter Cities.   California has eighty charter cities. Typically, charter cities are large. Nearly all of the state's major cities and most of those over 100,000 population have charters.

Charter cities are formed in much the same way as general law cities—by petition and election. Charters, like constitutions, can be amended by the city's voters. One of the strongest arguments for a charter is that local citizens voters can make changes in city forms. Prior to 1982, they were also able to raise local revenues. The legislature extended this power to general law cities in 1982.

Charter cities can adopt forms that are different than those available under the general law. For example, Los Angeles has a city council of fifteen members elected by district and a mayor elected at large. Santa Ana, a medium-sized city in Orange County, has a city council of seven members, nominated by districts but elected at large.

While most charter cities retain the council-manager form, some have established a strong mayor form. As a rule, larger cities elect council members by district and their mayors at large. The mayor is not a member of the council. This pattern more closely resembles the pattern of executive-legislative separation of powers found in the national and state governments. These independently elected mayors have substantially more administrative and budget authority than the "ceremonial" mayors of general law cities. Sometimes they become statewide political figures. Los Angeles Mayor Tom Bradley's 1982 and 1986 gubernatorial campaigns, San Diego Mayor Pete Wilson's victory in the 1982 U.S. Senate race, and San Francisco Mayor Dianne Feinstein, a 1984 vice-presidential "potential" are recent examples. (Of course, California's big-city mayors are weak when compared to big-city mayors in the East.)

City Activities

Public Safety.   One out of four city dollars is spent on public safety. This is the largest single budget item in a typical city. Since most Californians live in cities, it is the city that provides most of us with our police and fire services.

Police tasks vary somewhat depending on the kind of city. In general, these duties include: regulation of traffic, investigation of traffic accidents, patrol, crime prevention, investigation of reported crimes, apprehension of suspects, gathering and presenting evidence, detention of suspects, and custody of property.

Traffic control, which includes parking regulation, is the single largest police activity (about 75 percent of a city's police budget) in the typical California city. Rapidly rising crime rates, particularly in urban areas, are also a major police concern. In a 1972 survey of California residents, 45 percent reported that they or some member of their family had been the victim of a crime in the previous year (Field and Scott, 1974). In addition, over half of those interviewed expressed fear of leaving their home.

Until recently, most Californians gave police good marks. In 1972, eight out of ten citizens rated police "somewhat good" to "extremely good" (Field and Scott, 1974). In some large cities there have been demands for some form of civilian police review process. Police departments often appear reluctant to investigate or punish an officer charged with illegal or unprofessional acts commited in the line of duty.

Public support for police has declined somewhat over the last ten years particularly in the minority community. Increased recruitment of minorities to police and fire departments may discourage this trend.

Fire fighting and fire prevention also contribute to public safety costs. In addition to the usual fire problems associated with residential, commercial, and industrial structures, many California cities also have severe problems with brush fires. Insurance rates that cities pay are affected by the quality of their fire services.

Streets.   About one of ten city dollars is spent on street construction, maintenance and repair, parking, lighting, and storm drains. This is the second largest city budget item. In California, where the automobile is a way of life, an adequate street system has high priority.

Parks and Recreation.   A little less than one out of ten city dollars is spent on parks and recreation. Due to California's rapid population growth, large communities of tract homes frequently have few parks or community recreation facilities. Inner-city and ghetto parks are often small and poorly maintained. The accessibility of beaches and mountains has until recently reduced the desire for parks among many of the middle class. But as travel costs increase, more demands will be made for them.

Utilities and Transportation.   Many of the state's cities provide water and electricity to their residents. San Francisco brings water 150 miles from the Sierras via the Hetch Hetchy Aqueduct. Los Angeles gets much of its water from the Owens Valley (170 miles northeast of the city). Los Angeles, San Diego, and many other southern California cities also get their water supply in part or entirely from the Colorado River Aqueduct on the Arizona border.

Most major cities also provide airport facilities. Bus and street cars are often provided either by a city (Santa Monica and San Francisco) or jointly with other cities in regional transportation districts. The seaport cities of San Diego, Long Beach, Los Angeles (San Pedro), San Francisco, and Oakland have substantial harbor facilities.

Land Use and Planning.   One of the major functions of most cities is the control of land use and planning. While not a significant budget item, it is important to the quality of life and economic health of a city. In fact, several cities have incorporated because their residents wanted to control local development and feared county control of the process.

One major feature of land use and planning policy in cities is growth itself. Limiting growth has become a major policy issue in Petaluma, Costa Mesa, Camarillo, and Davis, for example, which have found that growth is a mixed blessing. Growth brings new jobs and a larger tax base, but it also brings increased demands for tax-supported services. Proposition 13's reduction of property tax revenues has made land development more expensive and less useful for many cities. Growth also makes fundamental changes in the quality of life in small towns.

Another set of planning questions involves building and zoning policy. How large should residential lots be? What is the best mix of single-unit dwellings and apartment houses? How wide should streets be, and how should the city control traffic flow? Where should shopping centers and commercial and industrial facilities be located? All of these questions are central to land use planning in new or growing cities.

Another set of land use and planning problems emerge as a city ages and begins to decline. How can a city, with limited financial resources, attract investment capital into the inner core to restore blighted areas? How can the city facilitate construction of affordable housing? Often, these questions are closely related to the problems of job opportunity, new industry, and public transportation.

Cities have considerable power over land use. They zone land areas for type of use—single-unit or multiple-unit housing, commercial, industrial, light, or heavy manufacturing, and so on. Under California law, each city (and county) is required to have a long-range land use plan. Zoning and zoning changes must conform to the plan. But as population patterns change and as the needs of people change, zoning patterns may also have to change. Because of the enormous value these zoning decisions have for developers, contractors, banks and the real estate industry, these interests have extended hefty campaign contributions to local elected officials sympathetic with their development plans.

Selected Problems. Like counties, California's cities seem to be increasingly burdened with problems they cannot solve. Typically, many of these problems originate beyond the city's authority. Smog, transportation, land use, and crime problems are not localized within city boundaries. A whole range of economic problems—inflation, unemployment, housing, and tax resources—are national problems.

Proposition 13 complicated cities' problems and the new Jarvis initiative, Proposition 62 of 1986 designed to close "loopholes" opened through court interpretation of Proposition 13, will further compound these problems. But left largely on their own in the search for revenues (compared to counties and school districts which receive substantial state assistance), most cities have managed to find other funds.

SCHOOL DISTRICTS

Public education in California has historically been a local activity. In 1985, there were 721 elementary school districts, 131 high school districts, 270 unified school districts, and 106 community college districts. Student enrollment in all of these was about 5.2 million, at a cost to taxpayers of $15 billion dollars. Public education is clearly a major part of local governmental activity in the Golden State.

Each public school district is governed by a five-member board of trustees often called the "school board." Trustees are usually elected at large on a nonpartisan basis. Los Angeles Unified School District is an exception—since 1978, it has been governed by a seven-member board elected by district.

School board members, like most city council members, serve part-time. They usually meet once or twice a month on a week night. Board members are usually homemakers, businesspeople, occasionally an attorney or an accountant, sometimes a downtown merchant.

Board members are not professional educators. School boards set policy but do not attempt to be directly involved in the day-to-day management of the district's business. School boards hire a district superintendent who is a professional educator to manage the district. Authority and responsibility for management of the school district rests with the superintendent. This official prepares the annual budget, hires and fires school personnel, and prepares policy proposals.

There are thousands of teachers, administrators, teacher aides, pupil service employees, clerks, secretaries, gardeners, janitors, maintenance personnel, and others employed in California schools. School districts have more employees than any other type of local government in the state.

The course of instruction offered in the state's schools is varied. Each school is required by the state to offer 180 days of instruction (thirty-six weeks) each year. Every child over six and under eighteen years of age is required to attend. However, a certificate of proficiency is available to those who pass an exam. Students who pass that test need not continue school. The certificate is not the same as a high school diploma, however.

California is the only state that prints its own textbooks and provides them free of charge to elementary school districts. High schools purchase their texts directly from the publishers. Some of the curriculum is determined by the local district board of trustees. But the state Board of Education (appointed by the governor) establishes instructional guidelines and requirements for graduation.

California also provides funds for education of the physically handicapped and the gifted (GATE students), but funding for the latter is threatened in Governor Deukmejian's 1987 budget. Additionally, the state provides financial assistance for programs on conservation and requires driver education in the high schools. These are only a few of the many state-mandated and/or funded programs required of local schools.

Selected Problems.   There has been a growing dissatisfaction with the quality of education in California public schools—lack of "fundamentals," poor student discipline, uninspired instructors, and minimal graduation standards. School Superintendent Bill Honig was able to defeat incumbent Wilson Riles in 1982 by championing a more rigorous educational system.

The California educational crisis is clearly part of a national problem. In September 1987 Lynne Cheney, chairman of the National Endowment of the Humanities, presented a particularly biting indictment of public schools. In her report "American Memory: A Report on the Humanities in the Nation's Public Schools," Cheney argues that schools disregard history, now called social studies, in the name of progress, while English has been replaced by language arts. Teacher training, she complains, relies too heavily on methods courses, and the ranks of curriculum specialists and other such staffers have grown five times as fast as classroom teachers. Cheney's findings will undoubtedly help Superintendent Honig in his push for reforming California public schools. Honig notes that courses in subjects such as English, algebra, French, Western Civilization, and U.S. government had been declining in numbers in California, but there had been a substantial increase in classes such as food and cooking, driver education, marriage and adulthood, and health and physical education.

Further attesting to this problem, 30 percent of the state's 1980 high school juniors failed a state-mandated proficiency test. In 1983, 35 percent of the newly graduated teachers failed the state's basic educational skills test. Moreover, those teachers who leave the system ap-.pear to be among the best (Kirst & Guthrie 1983).

Compounding these problems has been a decline in the level of tax support for state schools. In 1982, California ranked fiftieth—at the bottom of the states—in the percentage of its taxpayer wealth devoted to public school finance; in 1973, it ranked ninth. In 1982 the legislature and governor provided an additional $4.2 billion dollars over the next three years in a major effort to improve state education. By 1986 California was only slightly below (about $87 per pupil) the national average.

Another problem facing California's schools is the large number of students who do not speak English very well and the many students who are not interested in being in school. And, as of 1982, over half of the students in kindergarten and first grade were Hispanic, black, or Asian. Hispanics, the state's single largest minority, make up over half of the students in the Los Angeles school system. The state's schools must therefore work with students from many different cultures with different values. Overwhelming approval by voters of Proposition 63 of 1986, which makes English the state's official language, will complicate efforts to use bilingual instruction in the schools.

School desegregation, once the central issue in many school districts, has been replaced by questions about educational quality and school finance. Yet the basic housing patterns that led to segregated schools remain. Whether or not school desegregation will become a major issue again is unclear. At present, Proposition 1 (1979) prohibits mandatory busing as a solution to segregated schools.

School hiring practices have been modified by affirmative action regulations, which require schools to make an extra effort to hire blacks and Hispanics. This is one area of employment, however, where women tend to be overrepresented.

Collective bargaining is now available to teachers in California public schools. School boards increasingly find themselves under pressure from the local teachers union for higher pay and better working conditions. And, teacher salaries have improved recently. In the past three years teacher salary increases have been double the rate of inflation.

In addition, California's supreme court in *Serrano* v. *Priest* (1971) held the property tax to be an unconstitutional base for funding public schools. The court observed that:

> . . . the California public school financing system, with its substantial dependence on local property taxes and resultant wide disparities in school revenue, violates the equal protection clause of the Fourteenth Amendment. (Post and Brandsma, 1973)

The court reasoned that the wide differences in financial support for children in different school districts produced an unacceptable differ-

12-4 *Distribution of state lottery receipts to education 1987–88 estimates.*

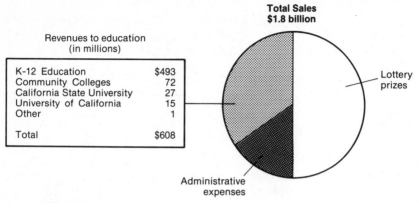

Revenues to education (in millions)

K-12 Education	$493
Community Colleges	72
California State University	27
University of California	15
Other	1
Total	$608

Total Sales
$1.8 billion

Lottery prizes

Administrative expenses

Source: 1987–88 Governor's Budget.

ence in the quality of education they received. Holding that education should not be a function of any particular school district's wealth, the court required the legislature to provide equalization funding.

Some school districts have turned to private sources for additional revenues by setting up independent tax-exempt foundations. These foundations, perhaps as many as sixty to eighty by 1983, sprang up in the state's wealthier school districts after *Serrano* v. *Priest* (1971) and Proposition 13.

Out of some $15 billion spent by local school districts in 1982, 69 percent came from the state, and another 5 percent from federal sources. Local property taxes accounted for only 26 percent of the schools revenues. Clearly, the state is the largest source of school funding. Finally, the state lottery has generated about $600 million annually for public schools (see Illustration 12–4).

Reforming Education

Because school districts needed more money and citizens demanded higher performance levels for both teachers and students, the state legislature and Superintendent of Public Schools Bill Honig drafted a major education reform package in 1983 that included:

Mandated high school courses in English, math, physical science, social science, fine arts, and a foreign language.
Established a minimum teacher's salary of $18,000.
Increased disciplinary authority over disruptive students.

Increased district authority over hiring and firing of teachers.
Increased funding for computer and technical education.

Finally, while tests scores for California students have improved in the 1980s perhaps in part because of these reforms, Governor Deukmejian contends that Superintendent Honig exaggerates the need for increased public school funding in 1987–88. Honig contends we must reduce class size in our schools, but Governor Deukmejian is unconvinced this is a problem. The growing antagonism between governor and superintendent promises to complicate further educational reform for the foreseeable future. In addition, the substantial increase of the state Latino and Asian populations and its corresponding impact on local schools is still to be felt. Will white Anglo voters (who have the highest turnout rates among the races) support school bond issues or other fee raising proposals for public schools whose enrollments are becoming increasingly non-Anglo?

SPECIAL DISTRICTS

Less is known about special district government and functions than any other form of local government, yet these governmental units provide a wide array of vital services to their residents. While they provide many different kinds of services, they are relatively simple in organization. A special district is a local public agency that provides services within a defined boundary.

Most special districts provide one service, are governed by a board of directors, and are located within a single county. A few special districts may encompass territory in two counties, and a handful are regional in scope (see the section on regional government). A few special districts provide more than one service—they are usually called community service districts.

There are over sixty different types of special districts. The greatest number of districts are: (1) county service areas, (2) county maintenance, (3) fire protection, (4) highway lighting, and (5) cemetery. These five types constitute almost half of all the state's special districts. The other half provide a wide range of services, such as parking, library, garbage disposal, citrus pest control, hospitals, irrigation, and mosquito abatement.

Reasons for Forming a Special District

Local residents and landowners form special districts because they want more services than existing local governments provide. They often want only one or two additional services, so forming a specialized agency is cheaper than creating a new city with broader powers and duties. California pioneered the use of special districts by creating irrigation districts in 1887. San Joaquin Valley farmers wanted a publicly owned water supply that would give them economic independence from private water companies and unpredictable water rates. The pattern of forming special districts in response to specific local service demands persists even today.

Because of their rapid proliferation and lobbying pressures from cities and counties, Governor Ronald Reagan appointed a Local Government Reform Task Force in 1974 to examine special districts. After extensive study, the task force reported that special districts were effective forms of local government (Salzman, 1974). However, most experts viewed this report as decidedly one-sided.

District Types

Dependent Districts.   Ross (1987) reports that 36 percent of special districts are governed by county supervisors and 6 percent by city councils.

Such districts are typically established in response to requests from an area's residents for either increased services or new services. Usually the area is not part of a city, and its residents want a specific service—water, road maintenance, or street lighting. The proposed special district must then be approved by the county's Local Agency Commission (LAFCO).

Independent Districts.   About 58 percent of special districts are independent. Their governing boards are wholly (or partially) elected by district residents. A group of residents gets together and decides to form a special district, and defines its service activity and its geographic boundaries. The plan is then submitted to the county's LAFCO and, if approved, is then submitted to the area's residents for a vote.

District Governance

Independent districts hold separate elections to fill some or all seats on the board of directors. These boards usually have five or seven members who are seldom opposed for reelection. In fact, there will often be no candidate for one of the open seats on the board of directors. When a vacancy occurs, the other members of the district's board appoint a successor who serves until the next election. If the district's board does not fill the vacancy, then state law requires the board of supervisors to make the appointment.

Programs and Budgets.   Special districts, unlike other forms of government, usually offer only one service—water, fire protection, parks, or whatever service they were organized to provide. Their annual budgets are based on: property taxes (29.3 percent), state and federal agencies (24.3 percent), charges and fees (17.7 percent), assessments (13.5 percent) use of property (8.4 percent), licenses and permits (2.0 percent), and "other" (4.8 percent). Some districts derive most of their funds from service fees or material charges. Harbor, airport, transportation, water, utility, and hospital districts all collect substantial revenues for services rendered. On the other hand, such activities as pollution control, fire protection, flood control, and parks and recreation do not generate much revenue from users. These districts depend largely on taxes.

Selected Problems.   The growth of special districts, particularly in suburban areas, has raised several criticisms. First, they can reduce the ability of city government to provide a coherent and rational package of services. This can weaken suburban city governments.[4] Second, some dependent special districts are subsidized by county property taxpayers who do not live in them. Third, special districts tend to be politically invisible. The average citizen doesn't know who is on the district's governing board, much less how to contact them. A study of 1981 Orange County special district elections found less than 11 percent of the electorate voted, sixty-one out of ninety-five seats were not contested, and in three races no candidates filed for the vacant positions.

Hybrid Forms

Municipal Advisory Councils.   An interesting new form of local government is the Municipal Advisory Council (MAC). Typically, they are found in some of the more rapidly growing unincorporated suburbs or in isolated unincorporated communities. MACs are formally established by a county Board of Supervisors in response to petitions by area residents. Examples may be found in the suburbs of Los Angeles, Orange, and San Mateo Counties, and in Big Bear, a remote mountain community of San Bernardino County.

MACs have no independent authority or tax base. They are essentially advisory groups that express their area's needs to the board of

---

[4]But, should the various cities in the Helix Water District (San Diego County) pull out to form their own individual water systems, or should Orinda, Moraga, and Lafayette be required to have their own separate fire departments? No way!

Perhaps the problem is the growth of so many new cities.

supervisors. Some MACs have elected boards, and others are appointed by the Board of Supervisors.

Some communities which have MACs hope that they will lead to municipal incorporation. Other MACs are simply advisory, and there is no intention that they be anything else.

Local Agency Formation Commissions.   LAFCOs are a unique form of governing agency. They have both planning and regulatory power. LAFCOs were established by the California legislature in 1963 in response to the explosive growth of cities and special districts following World War II. Their primary purpose is to (1) discourage urban sprawl, (2) encourage the orderly formation and development of local government agencies, and (3) promote the creation of planned, well-ordered, efficient urban development patterns. Each of California's counties has a LAFCO except San Francisco.

LAFCOs hear proposals for (1) new cities, (2) new independent special districts, and (3) all annexations. LAFCOs have authority under state law to accept, modify, or reject these proposals. As a result, they can exercise great power within a county in the development of local government agencies and in the modification of a county's master plan. Most LAFCOs have five members—two from the county Board of Supervisors, two selected by the county's cities, and one public member chosen by the first four. (A few LAFCOs include a special district representative.)

Recently, the legislature gave LAFCOs authority to establish city "spheres of influence."

Those LAFCOs which have fully exercised their powers appear to have been successful in creating order and structure in the growth of established local government.

Regional Governance

Most of California's population is located in its urban counties. It is a highly mobile population with many people living in one city and working in another. In the same way, many of our social and governmental problems cross city and county lines. Smog ignores governmental boundaries, the need for urban area transportation transcends city and county lines, and the metropolitan area's need for water cannot be met by local supplies. In these and similar situations, the ability of a single city or county to meet or solve its problems is sharply limited.

For example, when the city-county of San Francisco was first formed in 1853, it was the dominant economic and political center of the bay area. Today, however, it is only a small fraction of the area's population, economy, and government. In 1987, the San Francisco Bay area includes nine counties, 90 cities, 127 school districts, and 695 special districts—921 governmental units in total. Similarly, the number of governmental units in the Los Angeles-Orange-San Bernardino-Riverside area is staggering. Hundreds of school districts and cities and thousands of special districts are included.

Regional Activity. In an effort to work through some of their common problems, the governmental units of an urban area sometimes form regional districts. But any attempt to form a regional government inevitably means reducing the power or authority of already established local governments. Such proposals trigger automatic opposition. As a result, regional government has been typically limited to three functions.

First, regional governments often serve a research, advisory, or communicative capacity—these are Councils of Governments (COGs). Two prime examples of COGs are the Association of Bay Area Governments (ABAG) and the Southern California Association of Governments (SCAG).

The second function of regional government is to deliver a specific service or material which the individual governments within the region cannot provide. Smog control, water, mass rapid transportation, and coastal conservation are prime examples of such single-service regional governments.

The third function is regulation. Air quality control, for example, is clearly a problem that crosses county and city boundaries. Los Angeles, which has long had a smog problem, could not control the air emissions of industrial plants outside the county limits. Thus, four counties—Los Angeles, Orange, Riverside, and San Bernardino—have formed the South Coast Air Quality Management District (SCAQMD). Similarly, the San Francisco Bay counties have established the Bay Area Air Pollution Control District (BAAPCD).

Los Angeles and much of southern California have to import water a long distance. Local supplies are simply not adequate. The Metropolitan Water District of Southern California (SCMWD), which includes Los Angeles, Orange, and San Diego counties and most of their cities and water districts, is a prime example of regional government meeting a regional need. The district constructed a delivery system from the Colorado River including dams, tunnels, pump stations, artificial lakes, and all the other components of a complex water system in order to deliver water over 200 miles to the region. Another example is the East Bay Municipal Utility District (EBMUD), which delivers water from the Sierras.

Perhaps the most famous of California's regional governments is the Bay Area Rapid Transit district (BART). This rail transit system has helped reduce traffic problems in the three bay area counties it serves.

TABLE 12-1
Comparison of Local and State Politics

Structure and Function	Local	State
Citizen participation	Low	Moderate
Elections	Nonpartisan	Partisan
Legislative elections	Usually at large	By district
Legislative bodies	Unicameral	Two houses
Elected executive	Usually a figurehead and appointed	Powerful
Appointed executives	Usually influential	Sometimes influential

Regional Government.   Regional government in California is usually managed by an appointed board of directors rather than by an elected body. Appointment is usually by constituent units—the cities, counties, or special districts—which are a part of the region served. Each member government gets at least one representative on the board plus additional representatives based on its total assessed property value. Each member casts votes based on its total assessed property values. The BART district was originally governed by an appointed board, but since 1974, it has been governed by an elected nine-member board of directors.

Regional government has not always been very attractive to voters or political leaders. In spite of the "jungle of jurisdictions" in the state's urban areas and what often appears to be a declining capacity to govern at the local level, regional governments have attempted, at times successfully, to grapple with areawide problems in a coherent manner. In fact, given the rapid growth of special districts and the continued increase in the number of cities, it appears that California's citizens prefer smaller rather than larger local government.

LOCAL POLITICS

Local politics are substantially different from state politics in California. The comparison in Table 12–1 lists some of these major differences. From these differences flow a wide range of situations which are important to understand.

Citizen Participation

City elections typically attract few voters; normally about one of three registered voters goes to the polls. Voter participation in school district and special district elections is even lower. Only county elections, which are held at the same time as state and national elections, have substantial turnouts.

One obvious reason for the lack of voter participation in local elections is their timing. City, school board, and special district elections are usually held in odd-numbered years and sometimes in the spring before national and state elections. This effectively separates them from the partisan effects of state and national elections. It also substantially reduces visibility and citizen interest. Thus, only citizens with strong political interests in local government go to the polls. In 1981, only 6.2 percent of Anaheim's voters went to the polls in a city election. A few charter cities recently have received voter support for changing their election date to coincide with November state elections.

Elections

Partisanship. To run for local office one must be at least eighteen years old (several teenage politicians have been elected to office recently) and be a resident of the district for thirty days. All California local elections are nonpartisan. There is no indication on the ballot of the candidate's party affiliation (see Illustration 12–5). Of course, candidates for local office are usually registered Republicans or Democrats. Traditionally, partisan political organizations do not become involved in local elections. But recently, there has been a growing partisan interest in some local elections. Political clubs in San Francisco, Berkeley, San Diego, and parts of Orange and Los Angeles Counties have supported candidates for city council, school board, and board of supervisors.

In California, city council members tend to be more Republican than the community they represent. One study of the many San Francisco Bay area city and county elections revealed that Republicans enjoy about a 15 percent bias. That is, the percentage of Republican-elected officials is about 15 percent greater than the percentage of Republican voters (Scott, 1968).

District or "At Large". Most cities, school districts, and special districts hold their elections "at large." In an at-large election, candidates seek votes within the entire city or district. There are no election districts as in county, state, or national legislative elections. This tends to favor candidates from the local elite—those whose friends and business associates are active in local government and who have access to the local press and civic groups. At-large elections tend to discriminate against those who are black, Hispanic, poorer, or who come from communities where few people are politically active.[5]

---

[5]Nevertheless, the U.S. Supreme Court has upheld the constitutionality of at-large elections in Mobile, Alabama (*City* v. *Bolden*).

12-5 *Typical local nonpartisan ballot.*

For MEMBER of the CITY COUNCIL Para MIEMBRO del CONCILIO de la CIUDAD	Vote for No More Than Two Vote por No Mas De Dos
ROBERT (ROB) D. CROMWELL Community Relations Director (Director de Relaciones de la Comunidad)	
CHARLES ROSEN U.S. Treasury Officer (Oficial de la Tesorería de Los Estados Unidos)	
JACK H. REID Self-Employed (Empleado de Su Parte)	
BARBARA C. ADY Air Traffic Controller (Controlador de Tráfico Aereo)	
JACQUELINE (JACKIE) HARRISON Homemaker (Ama de Casa)	
ERNEST W. (BILL) HARVEY Manufacturing—Wood Products (Manufactura—Productos de Madera)	
HENRY W. WEDAA Incumbent (Incumbento)	

Source: Official sample ballot, City of Yorba Linda.

A few cities elect by district. Los Angeles, Sacramento, and San Jose are examples. Their legislative bodies tend to be more representative of all people in their city. Santa Ana, an Orange County city, has a combination of at-large and district elections. Candidates must live in the district they want to represent, but they are elected by a citywide (at large) vote. In 1977, a black woman candidate for city council won the election in her district but lost to a white male who got more votes from the total city than she did.

While at-large elections are typically biased in favor of the white middle class, they are also biased for any group of people who are organized and politically motivated. Thus, public employees tend to have strong voices in local government. Gays have considerable power in San Francisco; students wield power in some university towns; in 1981 a Socialist was elected mayor of Santa Cruz; and a Libertarian was elected mayor in Bakersfield. In addition, many women have been elected to city councils or elected as mayors (Dianne Feinstein, San Francisco; Janet Gray Hayes, San Jose; Maureen O'Connor, San Diego; or Ann Rudin, Sacramento) in the 70s and 80s—they are no longer "good ole boy" clubs. Many of these women have used the political skills honed locally to run for higher office.

Legislative Bodies

Local government is unicameral in California. There is only one legislative body as compared to two in the state's legislature. Local legislative bodies are also small, typically having five members. And unlike state legislators, most local government legislators are part-time. Few have staff or offices. Local legislators tend to rely upon the bureaucracy, lobbyists, and friends for information and expertise.

Executive

Most city mayors are members of the city council. They serve for one year as presiding officers and are primarily figureheads. Some of the larger California cities (121) have independently elected mayors. They run for the office of mayor and are not part of the city council. They can have considerable political power—more by dint of personality than through charter provision.

There is no independently elected executive in county, school, or special district government. Legislative bodies for these agencies will select a chair to preside over meetings. But executive tasks are typically shared by all legislative members and substantially delegated to a full-time professional employee—the superintendent of schools, district manager, or county administrative officer, for example.

These appointed executives often become quite influential. The city manager, county administrative officer, school superintendent, and special district manager are hired because they are *policy experts* and *proficient managers*. The elected officials they serve—and who hired them—usually cannot devote full attention to the task of governing. For example, the annual budget and policy changes are prepared by the hired executive. If the hired executive is skillful, the elected officials become increasingly dependent on the appointed executive for advice. These hired executives frequently are high turnover positions.

Lobbying

Interest groups operate at the local levels just as they do at the state and national levels. There are some significant differences, however. First, there are fewer interest groups because there are fewer issues on any particular local government's agenda. Second, more of the lobbying is amateur and casual—a few homeowners meeting with a member of the city council to discuss a traffic problem or a delegation from the PTA conferring with the school superintendent about an after-school sports program.

Some interest groups tend to become formal and permanent—public employee and property-owner groups, for example. Civic, community, and business groups such as the Chamber of Commerce, PTA, Rotary, Kiwanis, and Lions are often involved in local issues. Less formal, but very powerful groups, such as real estate brokers, land developers, bankers, and construction unions will be found in growing suburban cities and counties.

Candidates for county supervisor and city council are particularly susceptible to pressure from interest groups. Lacking support from their political party, these candidates must turn elsewhere for campaign workers and campaign money. Groups which have a supply of potential campaign workers—public employees, labor unions, and the PTA—can exercise considerable influence if they are organized. Groups or individuals which can supply funds are also powerful, because campaigns for city council and County Board of Supervisors in the larger cities and counties are becoming expensive. Finally, local newspapers are often politically influential—particularly in larger cities and counties.

LOCAL GOVERNMENT REVENUE

There are three broad generalizations that describe local government revenues. First, there are many revenue sources. Second, local governments have been historically dependent upon other governments (state and federal) for a substantial part of their total revenues and, Proposition 13 of 1978 and Proposition 4 of 1979 have accelerated this trend. Third, the property tax, which at one time was the major source of local government revenues, has been reduced by Proposition 13.

Table 12–2 summarizes local government revenue sources and types before and after passage of Proposition 13. Proposition 13 of 1978, the Jarvis-Gann Initiative, limited property taxes to 1 percent of full cash value. It also restricted assessment increases to no more than 2 percent each year except when property was sold or exchanged. As property tax revenues dropped, local governments have increasingly had to look to state government for help. Twenty-five percent of county revenues came from state government in 1977, but in 1985, 35 percent did. Cities and counties were able to adjust to the post-Proposition 13 era better at first than school districts and special districts because they could more easily raise fees. Approval by voters of the Jarvis sponsored Proposition 62 initiative of 1986, while currently being fought out in the courts (it is unclear whether the measure applies only

TABLE 12-2
Sources of County Revenues* 1976–77 and 1984–85 (Dollars in Millions)

Revenue Sources	1976–77	Percent of Total	1984–85	Percent of Total	Percent Change From 1976–77
Taxes					
General property	$2,604	35.4%	$ 2,980	23.8%	14.4%
Sales and use	161	2.2	258	2.1	60.2
Other	47	0.6	139	1.1	195.7
Intergovernmental aid					
State	1,821	24.7	4,394	35.1	141.3
Federal	1,759	23.9	2,692	21.5	53.0
Other	9	0.1	41	0.3	55.6
Charges for current services	657	8.9	994	7.9	51.3
Use of money and property	115	1.6	492	3.9	327.8
Other revenue	192	2.6	529	4.2	175.5
Totals, current dollars†	$7,366	100.0%	$12,519	100.0%	69.9%
Totals, current dollars‡	$7,366		$ 6,860		−6.9%

*Source: State Controller. Excludes the City and County of San Francisco, and revenues from county-owned enterprises.
†Detail may not add to totals due to rounding.
‡Adjusted by the GNP implicit price deflator for state and local governments.

to general law cities and not to charter cities), may complicate the ability of city and county local governments to levy taxes. Under Proposition 62, creating new taxes would require approval of two-thirds of a local governing board *and* a two-thirds majority of voters.

Shared revenues

Sales Tax. Out of each six cents collected by the state, 1.25 cents is returned to the cities and counties. Cities get about two-thirds of these tax dollars.

Cigarette Tax. The state collects ten cents on each pack of cigarettes purchased. Of this, three cents is returned to the cities and counties.

Fuel Tax. The state collects nine cents per gallon on motor fuel. Of this, four cents is returned to local government. County governments get a little more than half these funds—about 54 percent—while cities get the rest.

Federal Funds

The federal government provides local governments with funding for specific programs—usually called grants. In addition, under the block grant program, it provides funds which cities and counties may use as they wish. Federal funding has been a significant source for counties, cities, and some special districts. Flood control, highway construction, municipal airports, and harbors are examples of such funding. And, much of welfare is also funded by the federal government.

Other Sources

A large number of other revenue sources provide substantial funds for cities, counties, and special districts. Cities have the richest source of such funds, with about 62 cents out of every revenue dollar coming from permits, fines, licenses, service charges, and miscellaneous taxes. Special districts receive about 21 cents out of every revenue dollar from service charges, fees, standby charges, return from investments, and a few minor taxes. Counties get slightly less—about 11 cents—of every revenue dollar from similar sources.

Public Employment

Since most public employment is at the local level, the problems and issues of public employment are usually local government problems. These include "contracting out," public employee collective bargaining, and various forms of "agency shop" public employment contracts.

Contracting out—the use of private firms to provide services which have traditionally been supplied by public employees—has been repeatedly suggested but seldom utilized. It has been vigorously and successfully opposed by public employee groups throughout the state.

Public employee groups have been successful in securing the right to engage in collective bargaining and agency shop contracts, and, in effect, the right to strike. Public employees have on a few occasions refused to work without contracts, sometimes calling that approach "job actions." Sometimes charges of reverse discrimination (whites losing jobs to blacks) or demands for comparable worth pay scales (in reaction to women in female-dominated professions, such as elementary school teaching, secretarial jobs or nursing, getting paid less than men in blue-collar occupations that require very modest educational skills) lead to strikes by public employees.

Finally, in a 1982 legislative victory, public employee organizations won the right to collect mandatory dues from government employees

Dennis Renault, Sacramento Bee

'*THAT* WAS JUST TO GET THE RANGE!'

they represent in contract negotiations whether or not the employee is a member of the organization. Usually called "agency shop," the new law was a major victory for public employee groups.

SUMMARY

California government is largely urban government. Over 90 percent of the state's population lives in an urban area. The many governments in California's urban areas—about 6,500—provide most of the services we associate with government. Moreover, the money California's local and state governments spend is largely generated from urban areas. The major problems of our society—education, welfare, housing, crime, pollution, transportation, racial and ethnic equality—are largely urban problems.

However, there is no rational urban governmental structure to attack these complex and difficult social and economic problems. There is, instead, a jungle of jurisdictions with overlapping authority, complex boundary lines, divided responsibilities, and conflicting powers.

The average urban resident may pay taxes to several local governments, such as the (1) county, (2) city, (3) unified school district, and (4) community college district. In some areas there may be both an elementary and high school district—rather than a unified school district. And, in addition, the taxpayer may have to support one or more special districts (water, park, or mosquito abatement).

Those who are responsible for the management of these various governments are elected by the voters residing within the district, city, or county, but most voters are not able to follow the workings of all of them.

It is not surprising that many citizens are confused. Faced with a problem, where does the citizen go? The problem may overlap from one jurisdiction (i.e., city) to others (i.e., county, planning commission). Because there is no single urban government, local governments can only work with the citizens' problems on a piecemeal basis.

The record suggests that local governments will somehow muddle through—they have adapted. Local governments have continued to provide high levels of quality service to citizens even though whiplashed by Proposition 13. And, now tax revolt fever seems to be subsiding. Voters seem increasingly concerned and willing to pay for services. In 1986, voters approved bond issues for local parks and jails, tort reform (which local governments strongly supported), and guaranteed local revenues.

References

___

Chapter 1

"Battle over Gay Rights." (1977, June 6) *Newsweek,* pp. 16–26.

Bell, Charles G. (1984). *"California."* In Alan Rosenthal and Maureen Moakley (Eds.), *The Political Life of the American States.* New York: Praeger Publishers.

Bottoroff, Dana. "Californians in Washington." (1986, August). *California Journal* 17, pp. 378–82.

Bowman, Ann O'M. and **Kearney, Richard.** (1986). *The Resurgence of the States.* Englewood Cliffs, N.J.: Prentice-Hall.

Bradshaw, Ted K. (1976, August). "New Issues for California, The World's Most Advanced Industrial Society." *Public Affairs Report* 17, pp. 1–6.

Burns, John. (1971). *The Sometime Governments.* New York: Bantam.

"California's Top 500 Companies." (1983, May). *California Business* 18, pp. 81–112.

"California 2000: The Next Frontier." (1982, Summer). *California Tomorrow* 17, pp. 1–80.

Crotty, William J. (1977). *Political Reform and the American Experiment.* New York: Thomas Y. Crowell.

Field Institute. (1982, April). "Economic Well-Being." *The California Poll.* San Francisco.

———. (1985, November). "Living in California." *California Opinion Index.* San Francisco.

———. (1985, November). "Living in California." *The California Poll.* San Francisco.

Gray, Virginia. (1973, December). "Innovations in the States: A Diffusion Study." *American Political Science Review* 67, pp. 1174–85.

Hill, Gladwin. (1968). *The Dancing Bear.* New York: G. P. Putnam's Sons.

Lamott, Kenneth. (1971). *Anti-California: Report from Our First Parafascist State.* Boston: Little, Brown.

La Porte, Todd, and **C. J. Abrams.** (1976). "Alternative Patterns of Post Industria: The California Experience." In Leon Lindberg (Ed.), *Politics and the Future of Industrial Society.* New York: McKay.

Leary, Mary Ellen. (1983, February 13). "Is California Just Another State?" *Los Angeles Times,* part V, p. 1.

Leonard, George. (1962). "California: A Promised Land for Millions of Migrating Americans." *Look* 26, no. 20, p. 27.

McWilliams, Carey. (1949). *California: The Great Exception.* New York: A. A. Wyn.

Naisbitt, John. (1982). *Megatrends.* New York: Warner Books.

Peirce, Neil. (1972). *The Megastates of America.* New York: W. W. Norton.

Royko, Mike. (1979, April 23). "Should America Fence Off California?" *Los Angeles Times,* II, p. 5.

Salzman, Ed. (1977, May). "Does the Golden State Deserve Its Tarnished Reputation?" *California Journal* 8, pp. 148–51.

Shuit, Douglas. (1983, February 13). "California: No Longer Out Front?" *Los Angeles Times,* part V, p. 1.

Walker, Jack L. (1969, September). "The Diffusion of Innovations among the American States." *American Political Science Review* 63, pp. 880–89.

Walters, Dan. (1986). *The New California.* Sacramento: *California Journal.*

Chapter 2

Bell, Charles G. (1981, October). "California: The Start of a New Era." *The Social Science Journal,* pp. 15–30.

Delmatier, Royce D.; Clarence F. McIntosh; and **Earl G. Waters.** (1970). *The Rumble of California Politics.* New York: John Wiley & Sons.

Freedberg, Louis. (1987, January). "On the Edge of Power." *California Journal* 18, pp. 12–18.

Mowry, George E. (1951). *The California Progressives.* Los Angeles: University of California Press.

Older, Fremont. (1926). *My Own Story.* New York: Macmillan.

Sample, Herbert A. (1987). "Black Political Power." *California Journal* 18, pp. 232–39.

Scammon, Richard, and **Ben Wattenberg.** (1971). *The Real Majority.* New York: Capricorn.

Tachibana, Judy. (1986, November). "California's Asians." *California Journal* 17, pp. 535–43.

Walters, Dan. (See Chapter 1 reference).

Chapter 3

Anagnoson, J. Theodore. "Campaign Finance." *California Journal* 17, pp. 557–59.

Endicott, William. (1986, December). "Twas the Season To Be Nasty." *California Journal* 17, pp. 583–85.

Field Institute. (1982, March). "Ethnicity and the Political Process." *California Opinion Index.* San Francisco.

———. (1982, June). "A Survey of June Primary Election Voters." *California Opinion Index.* San Francisco.

———. (1983, November). "Electoral Process and the Party System." *California Opinion Index.* San Francisco.

———. (1984, October). "Largest Ever Absentee Vote Expected in November Election." *The California Poll.* San Francisco.

———. (1985, October). "Big Gains in GOP Identification. Democrats No Longer Have Edge." *The California Poll.* San Francisco.

———. (1987, February). "Will Independents Vote in Partisan Primaries?" *California Journal* 18, pp. 101–4.

Gregg, James. (1966). *Newspaper Endorsements and Local Elections in California.* Davis, Calif.: University of California, Institute of Governmental Affairs.

"The New Gold Rush: Financing California's Legislative Campaigns." (1985). Center for Responsive Government, Los Angeles, California.

Putt, Allen D., and **J. Fred Springer.** (1977). "Impacts of Campaign Disclosure and Lobbying Provisions of the Political Reform Act of 1974." Sacramento: Evaluation Research Consultants.

Quinn, Tony. (1978, February). "Why The State Hasn't Bought Public Financing of Elections." *California Journal* 9, pp. 60–62.

———. (1981, March). "The Comatose State of Political Reform." *California Journal* 12, pp. 113–15.

Stemmler, Hal. (1983, August). "Absentee Ballots, A New Frontier in California Electoral Politics." *California Journal* 14, pp. 296–98.

Wolfinger, R. E., and **F. I. Greenstein.** (1969, March). "Comparing Political Regions: The Case of California." *American Political Science Review* 63.

Chapter 4

Berg, Larry. (1978). "The Initiative Process and Public Policy-Making in the States: 1904–1976." Paper prepared for the annual meeting of the American Political Science Association.

Brestoff, Nick. (1975, February 5). "California Initiative Process Needs Reform." *Los Angeles Times,* II, p. 7.

Field Institute. (1983, November). "Initiative Process." *California Opinion Index.* San Francisco.

———. (1986, October 15). Among Those Aware of Prop 64 (AIDS Initiative), Sentiment Running Strongly against It." *California Opinion Index.* San Francisco.

———. (1986, October 16) "Prop. 65 Getting Increased Voter Attention with Supporters Having Big Edge." *California Opinion Index.* San Francisco.

———. (1986, October 17). "The Initiative Which Would Declare English as the Official Language Has Very Large Support." *California Opinion Index.* San Francisco.

Lee, Eugene. (1978). "California." In David Butler and A. Ranney (Eds.), *Referendums: A Comparative Study of Practice and Theory.* Washington, D.C.: American Enterprise Institute for Public Policy Research.

Lowenstein, Daniel H. (1982, June). "Campaign Spending Ballot Propositions: Recent Experience, Public Choice Theory and the First Amendment." *UCLA Law Review* 29, pp. 505–641.

———. (1983, June). "California Initiatives and the Single-Subject Rule." *UCLA Law Review* 30, pp. 936–75.

Magleby, David B. (1984). *Direct Legislation: Voting on Ballot Propositions in the United States.* Baltimore: The Johns Hopkins University Press.

Mueller, John E. (1969, December), "Voting on the Propositions: Ballot Patterns and Historical Trends in California." *American Political Science Review* 63, pp. 1197–1212.

Owens, John R. and **Larry L. Wade.** (1985). "Campaign Spending on California Ballot Propositions, 1924–1984: Trends and Voting Effects." Paper presented at the Conference on Political Reform, University of California, Davis.

Price, Charles M. (1975, June). "The Initiative: A Comparative State Analysis of a Western Phenomenon." *Western Political Quarterly* 28, pp. 243–62.

————. (1981, October). "The Mercenaries Who Gather Signatures for Ballot Measures." *California Journal* 12, pp. 357–58.

————. (1983, April). "Recalls at the Local Level: Dimensions and Implications." *National Civic Review* 72, pp. 199–206.

————. (1985, July). "Experts Explain the Business of Buying Signatures." *California Journal* 16, pp. 283–86.

Quinn, Tony. (1978, May). "How the Establishment Destroys Initiatives Like Jarvis." *California Journal* 9, pp. 53–54.

————. (1979, November). "Recall Fever." *California Journal* 10, pp. 400–401.

Samish, Arthur H., and **B. Thomas.** (1971). *The Secret Boss of California.* New York: Crown Publishers.

Wolfinger, Raymond E., and **F. I. Greenstein.** (1968, September). "The Repeal of Fair Housing in California: An Analysis of Referendum Voting." *American Political Science Review* 62, pp. 753–69.

Chapter 5

Berg, Larry L., et al. (1976). *Corruption in the American Political System.* Morristown, N.J.: General Learning Press.

Berthelsen, John. (1983, August). "The Power Brokers." *California Business* 18, pp. 58–62.

Briscoe, Jerry, and **Charles G. Bell.** (1985). "Lobbyist-Committee Consultant Communication Patterns." Paper presented at the Western Political Science Association Meeting, Las Vegas, Nevada.

Kerr, Jennifer. (1986, February). "Government Spends Tax Dollars to Lobby—Government." *California Journal* 17, pp. 99–102.

Price, Charles M. (1983, January). "A Special Class of Lobbyists." *California Journal* 14, pp. 33–35.

Price, Charles M., and **Catherine Melquist.** (1983, October). "Women Lobbyists." *California Journal* 14, pp. 371–72.

Samish, Arthur H., and **B. Thomas** (See Chapter 4 reference.)

"Twenty Who Gave $10 Million." 1981 California Common Cause Report.

Velie, Lester. (1949, August 13 and 20). "The Secret Boss of California." *Collier's* 124.

Wiggins, Charles W.; Keith Hamm; and **Charles G. Bell.** (1984). "Interest Groups and Other Influence Agents in the State Legislative Process: A Comparative Analysis." Paper presented at the American Political Science Association Meeting, Washington, D.C.

Zeiger, Richard. (1986, February). "The Persuaders." *California Journal* 17, pp. 71–73.

Ziegler, Harmon, and **Michael Baer.** (1969). *Lobbying: Interaction and Influence in American State Legislatures.* Belmont, Calif: Wadsworth.

Ziegler, Harmon, and **Hendrik von Dalen.** (An). "Interest Groups in the States." *Politics in the American States.* Ed. Herbert Jacob and Kenneth N. Vines. Boston: Little, Brown.

Chapter 6

Buhler, Lois. (1976, July). "County Central Committees: The Elected Officials Nobody Knows (or Needs to)." *California Journal* 7, pp. 237–38.

Jacobs, John. (1976, August). "The Coalition Politics of Dellums' East Bay Machine." *California Journal* 7, pp. 258–60.

Jewell, Malcolm E., and **S. C. Patterson.** (1966). *The Legislative Process in the United States.* New York: Random House.

Keefe, William J., and **M. S. Ogul.** (1977). *The American Legislative Process.* Englewood Cliffs, N.J.: Prentice-Hall.

Lawson, Kay. (1980). "California: The Uncertainties of Reform." In Gerald Pomper, (Ed.), *Party Renewal in America.* New York: Praeger Publishers.

Le Blanc, Hugh L. (1969, February). "Voting in State Senates: Party and Constituency Influences." *Midwest Journal of Political Science* 13, pp. 33–57.

Lee, Eugene C. (1960). *The Politics of Nonpartisanship: A Study of California City Elections.* Berkeley: University of California Press.

Lee, Eugene and **W. D. Hawley,** (Eds.). (1970). *The Challenge of California.* Boston: Little, Brown.

Littwin, Susan. (1977, December). "Power Brokers in L.A." *California Journal* 8, pp. 405–7.

Older, Fremont. (See Chapter 2 reference.)

Price, Charles M.; Charles G. Bell; and **Vic Pollard.** (1984, December). "The Party Renewal Movement" 15, pp. 472–74.

Smith, Martin. (1983, March). "David Roberti's New Weapon: The Organized ROAR of Animal Lovers." *California Journal* 14, pp. 97–99.

Trounstine, Phillip J. (1987, April). "After Reagan." *California Journal* 18, pp. 171–173.

Willens, Michele. (1981, December). "The Real '82 Opponents: Garth, Haglund and Rietz." *California Journal* 12, pp. 413–15.

Zeiger, Richard. (1987, March). "Future Uncertain for State's Democrats." *California Journal* 18, pp. 120–23.

Chapter 7

Bell, Charles G., and **C. M. Price.** (1969, May). "Pre-Legislative Sources of Representational Roles." *Midwest Journal of Political Science* 13, pp. 254–70.

———. (1975). *The First Term: A Study of Legislative Socialization.* Beverly Hills, Calif.: Sage Publications.

———. (1987, January). "20 Years of a Full-Time Legislature." *California Journal* 18, pp. 36–40.

BeVier, Michael J. (1979). *Politics Backstage, Inside the California Legislature.* Philadelphia: Temple University.

Burns, John. (1971). *The Sometimes Governments.* New York: Bantam.

Driscoll, James. (1980). *California's Legislature.* Sacramento: State of California.

Jeffe, Sherry Bebitch. (1987, January). "For Legislative Staff, Policy Takes a Backseat to Politics." *California Journal* 18, pp. 42–45.

———. (1987, May). "Can a Speaker Make Policy and Still Hold Power?" *California Journal* 18, pp. 243–46.

Keefe, William J., and **M. S. Ogul.** (See Chapter 6 reference.)

Malan, Rian. (1982, April). "Willie Brown." *California* 7, pp. 94–99.

Muir, William K. (1983) *Legislature: California's School for Politics.* Chicago: University of Chicago Press.

Patterson, Samuel. (1978). In Susan Welch and J. G. Peters (Eds.), *Legislative Reform and Public Policy.* New York: Praeger Publishers.

Price, Charles M., and **C. G. Bell.** (1970, March). "Socializing California Freshmen Assemblymen: The Role of Individuals and Legislative Sub-Groups." *Western Political Quarterly* 23, pp. 166–79.

———. (1970, November). "The Rules of the Game: Political Fact or Academic Fancy?" *Journal of Politics* 32, pp. 839–55.

Rosenthal, Alan. (1981). *Legislative Life.* New York: Harper & Row.

Chapter 8

Harvey, Richard. (1969). *Earl Warren: Governor of California.* New York: Exposition Press.

Lockard, Duane. (1963). *Politics of State and Local Government.* New York: Macmillan.

Melendy, H. Brett, and Benjamin F. Gilbert. (1965). *The Governors of California.* Georgetown, Calif.: Talisman Press.

Sabato, Larry. (1983). *Goodby to Good-time Charlie: The American Governorship Transformed.* Washington, D.C.: Congressional Quarterly.

Salzman, Ed. (1982, June). "Judging Jerry" [an evaluation of the Jerry Brown Administration]. *California Journal* 13, pp. 189–94.

Zeiger, Richard. (1986, December). "Duke's Landslide." *California Journal* 17, pp. 579–81.

Chapter 9

Bell, James R., and Thomas J. Ashley. (1967). *Executives in California Government.* Belmont, Calif: Dickenson.

Fairbanks, Robert. (1983, February). "New Power for an 'Old Statesman': Unruh's $3 Billion Lending Machine." *California Journal* 14, pp. 48–52.

Gunnison, Robert. (1987, February). "Exiled from the Capitol, Gray Davis Takes Control(ler)." *California Journal* 18, pp. 91–93.

Taylor, Bob. (1981, September). "Collective Bargaining." *California Journal* 12, pp. 331–32.

Willett, Cynthia. (1979, September). "The Confrontation Politics of Rival State-Employee Unions." *California Journal* 10, pp. 325–27.

For more information about any specific agency, department, division, board, or commission see the following: "California Roster [annual]" or the annual "Analysis of the Budget Bill" by the legislative analyst.

Chapter 10

Fairbanks, Robert. (1983, February). "Deukmejian's Budget Surprise." *California Journal* 14, pp. 45–47.

Governor's Office Annual. *Economic Report of the Governor.* Sacramento, Calif.

Kirlin, John J. (1982). *The Political Economy of Fiscal Limits.* Lexington, Mass.: Lexington Books.

Kirlin, John J., and Donald R. Winkler, (Eds.) (1986.) *California Policy Choices Annual.* Sacramento Public Affairs Center, School of Public Administration, University of Southern California.

Legislative Analyst Annual. *Analysis of the Budget Bill.* Sacramento, Calif.

———. *The . . . [Annual] . . . Budget: Perspectives and Issues.* Sacramento, Calif.

Shuit, Douglas. (1983, April 3). "Will Tax Breaks Break the State?" *Los Angeles Times,* p. 3.

Schmidt, Robert. (1987, March). "Is the Gann Limit Unbearable?" *California Journal* 18, pp. 154–57.

State Controller Annual. *Annual Report.* Sacramento, Calif.

Walters, Dan. (1983, July). "Closing Tax Loopholes." *California Journal* 14, pp. 255–56.

Chapter 11

Bell, Charles G., and **Charles M. Price.** (1983, June). "Running for Judge in California . . ." *California Data Brief.* Berkeley: University of California, Institute of Governmental Studies.

Cochran, Dena. (1980, September). "Why So Many Judges Are Going down to Defeat." *California Journal* 11, pp. 359–60.

———. (1981, June). "Paying for Judicial Races." *California Journal* 12, pp. 219–20.

Cuno, Alice. (1983, June). "The Expanding Role of the Judicial Performance Commission." *California Journal* 14, pp. 237–39.

Fairbanks, Robert. (1987, May 10). "Why Did the State Let Lawrence Singleton Out of Prison?" *Sacramento Bee.* Forum Section, p. 3.

Judicial Council of California Annual. *Annual Report.* Sacramento, Calif.

Medsger, Betty. (1983). *Framed.* New York: Pilgrim Press.

Price, Charles M., and **Charles G. Bell.** (1986, September). "Anti-Bird Fervor Has Little Effect on Lower Court Races." *California Journal* 17, pp. 447–49.

Roach, Ron. (1987, September). "On the Defense." *California Journal* 18, pp. 211–15.

Salzman, Ed. (1980, August). "California's Unseen [Appellate] Courts." *California Journal* 11, pp. 216–21.

Stolz, Preble. (1981). *Judging Judges.* New York: Free Press.

Zeiger, Richard. (1986, September). "Rose Bird Faces the Ultimate Jury." *California Journal* 17, pp. 423–27.

Chapter 12

Borenstein, Daniel. (1986, June). "The Brown Act." *California Journal* 17, pp. 316–17.

Cheney, Lynne. (1987). "American Memory: A Report on the Humanities in the Nation's Public Schools." A Report of the National

Endowment for the Humanities. U.S. Government: Washington, D.C.

Cochran, Dena. (1981, August). "Sheriff Power." *California Journal* 12, pp. 277–78.

Field Institute. (1983, June). "Proposition 13 Five Years Later." *California Opinion Index.*

———. (1983, July). "California's Public Schools." *California Opinion Index.*

———. (1985, April). "The State Judiciary." *California Opinion Index.* San Francisco.

———. (1986, October). "By a Five to Three Margin, Voters Still Opposed to Bid." *California Opinion Index.* San Francisco.

Field, Mervin, and **Stanley Scott.** (1974). *Public Opinion of Criminal Justice in California.* Berkeley: University of California Institute of Governmental Studies. "54 Percent of Complaints on Police Held Valid." 1974 *Los Angeles Times* (March 3).

Hawkins, Robert B., Jr. (1976). *Self Government by District.* Stanford, Calif.: Hoover Institution Press.

Hawley, Willis D. (1971, June). "The Partisan Consequences of Nonpartisan Elections." *Public Affairs Report.* Berkeley: University of California, Institute of Governmental Studies.

Kirst, Michael W., and **James W. Guthrie.** (1983, April). "Declining Teacher Quality: Public Schools' Toughest Problem." *California Journal* 14, pp. 141–44.

LeGates, Richard. (1970). *California Local Agency Formation Commission.* Berkeley: University of California Institute of Governmental Studies.

Lee, Eugene. (1960). *The Politics of Nonpartisanship.* Berkeley: University of California Press.

Post, A. Alan, and **Richard Brandsma.** (1973). "The Legislature's Response to Serrano v. Priest." *Pacific Law Journal* 4, 28–46.

Prewitt, Kenneth. (1970). *The Recruitment of Political Leaders: A Study of Citizen-Politicians.* Indianapolis, Ind.: Bobbs-Merrill.

Ross, Robert (Ed.). (1987). *Perspective on Local Government in California.* Belmont, Calif.: Star Publishing.

Salzman, Ed. (1974, January). "Reagan Task-Force Surprise: Special District Is the Most Efficient Form of Local Government." *California Journal* 5, pp. 28–31.

Scott, Stanley. (1968). *Governing a Metropolitan Region.* Berkeley: University of California, Institute of Governmental Studies.

———. (1975). *Governing California's Coast.* Berkeley: University of California, Institute of Governmental Studies.

Shores, Randall. (1973, January). "Regional Government." *California Journal* 4, pp. 15–21.

Sokolow, Alvin, and Linda Martin. (1983, May). "The Rush to Incorporate." *California Journal* 14, pp. 193–94.

Sokolow, Alvin D.; Priscilla Hanford; Joan Hogan; and Linda Martin. (1981). *Choices for the Unincorporated Community: A Guide to Local Government Alternatives in California.* Davis, Calif.: University Institute of Governmental Affairs.

State Controller Annual. *Annual Transactions of California's Cities.* Sacramento, Calif.

———. *Annual Transactions in California's Counties.* Sacramento, Calif.

———. *Annual Transactions of California's School Districts.* Sacramento, Calif.

———. *Annual Transactions of California's Special Districts.* Sacramento, Calif.

Taub, J. S. (1986, November). "COGS." *California Journal* 17, pp. 551–54.

Index

A NOTE ON THE TYPE

The text of this book was set in 10/12 Times Roman, a film version of the face designed by Stanley Morison, which was first used by *The Times* (of London) in 1932. Part of Morison's special intent for Times Roman was to create a face that was editorially neutral. It is an especially compact, attractive, and legible typeface, which has come to be seen as the "most important type design of the twentieth century."

Composed by Compset, Inc., Beverly, Massachusetts.

Printed and bound by Malloy Lithographing, Inc. Ann Arbor, Michigan.

ABOUT THE AUTHORS

Charles G. Bell and **Charles M. Price** first became acquainted when they were graduate students at the University of Southern California, Los Angeles, in the early 1960s. After completing their doctorates, Professor Bell taught at California State University, Fullerton, and Professor Price, at California State University, Chico.

Over the last 25 years, the two "Chucks" have worked jointly on a number of research projects. In 1973 they coauthored *The California Legislative Process* (American Political Science Association), under a state legislative fellowship. In 1975 Professors Bell and Price also authored *The First Term* (Sage Publications), a text on the legislative socialization of California freshmen assembly members. In addition, the two have coauthored dozens of articles on state politics which have appeared in publications such as: *Western Political Quarterly, American Journal of Political Science, Journal of Politics, California Data Briefs,* and the *California Journal*. The authors' long amicable association means each is able to read the other's work and recommend editing changes or stylistic improvements yet still remain friends—no easy feat. Since 1970 they have also both served on the California Assembly Fellowship Board.

Professor Bell is now retired from California State University, Fullerton. He teaches part-time at the University of California, Davis and is also director of the Capital Campus internship program of private universities and colleges in cooperation with University of California, Davis. Professor Bell has authored many articles on state legislatures and the lobby process; he is the author of the California chapter in the 1984 Rosenthal and Moakley's, *The Political Life of the American States* (Praeger). Professor Price serves as coeditor of the *California Journal Annual*; he has written extensively on direct democracy and lobbying, and teaches at California State University, Chico.